D1547701

Buddha Shakyamuni

The Padmakara Translation Group gratefully acknowledges the generous support of the Tsadra Foundation in sponsoring the translation and preparation of this book.

The Adornment
of the
MIDDLE WAY

༄༅། །ཁྲིམས་རྒྱུན་གྱི་རྩ་བ་དང་འགྲེལ་པ་འཛམ་

དབྱངས་བླམ་དགྱེས་པའི་ཞལ་ལུང་

བཞུགས། །

པཎ་ཀུ་པའི་སྒྲ་བསྒྱུར་མ་ཕྱུན་ཚོགས་ནས་

སྒྲ་བསྒྱུར་ཞུས།།

THE ADORNMENT

OF THE

MIDDLE WAY

Shantarakshita's
Madhyamakalankara

with commentary by
Jamgön Mipham

TRANSLATED BY THE
PADMAKARA TRANSLATION GROUP

SHAMBHALA
BOSTON & LONDON
2005

Shambhala Publications, Inc.
Horticultural Hall
300 Massachusetts Avenue
Boston, Massachusetts 02115
www.shambhala.com

9 8 7 6 5 4 3 2 1

First Edition
Printed in the United States of America

⊛ This edition is printed on acid-free paper that meets
the American National Standards Institute Z39.48 Standard.

Distributed in the United States by Random House, Inc.,
and in Canada by Random House of Canada Ltd

Library of Congress Cataloging-in-Publication Data
Śāntarakṣita, 705–762.
[Madhyamakālaṅkāra. English & Tibetan]
The adornment of the middle way: Shantarakshita's Madhyamakalankara
with commentary by Jamgön Mipham/translated by the Padmakara
Translation Group.—1st ed.
p. cm.
Includes bibliographical references and index.
ISBN 1-59030-241-9 (alk. paper)
1. Śāntarakṣita, 705–762. Madhyamakālaṅkāra. I. Mi-pham-rgya-mtsho,
'Jam-mgon 'Ju, 1846–1912. Dbu ma rgyan gyi rnam bśad 'Jam dbyaṅs bla ma dgyes
pa'i źal luṅ źes bya ba bźugs so. II. Padmakara Translation Group. III. Title.
BQ3182.E5S26 2005
294.3'85—dc22
2004023929

Contents

Foreword

THE *MADHYAMAKALANKARA* was probably the first Madhyamaka text to be rendered into Tibetan, and it was translated under the auspices and with the guidance of its author. Shantarakshita was famous for the way he presented the conventional truth according to the wisdom of the Mind Only school, which provides the best and most subtle way of understanding the functioning of phenomenal existence. This he combined with the profound view of Madhyamaka as a means of entering the ultimate truth. The *Madhyamakalankara* is therefore an extraordinary text, for it brings the Mind Only and the Madhyamaka schools together into a single system, thereby unifying the two great traditions of the Mahayana, the Buddhism of the great vehicle. The *Madhyamakalankara,* the Adornment of the Middle Way, is moreover an ornament for the whole of the Madhyamaka teachings. Not only does it set forth the position of the Svatantrikas, by making a distinction between the two kinds of ultimate truth, but also, when explaining the actual ultimate in itself, it does so in a way that is no different from that of the Prasangikas.

In studying this text, we are reminded of Shantarakshita's immense wisdom and kindness. He was a scholar of encyclopedic learning and his great work the *Tattvasamgraha* is still studied today as one of the most extensive records of the philosophical schools and traditions of medieval India. It is amazing that, despite his advanced age and the length and difficulty of the journey, Shantarakshita was willing to travel to Tibet where, at the invitation of King Trisongdetsen, he played a crucial role in the establishment of the Dharma. He ordained the first monks and transmitted the entire range of sutra teachings: the vinaya discipline, the Mahayana teachings on bodhichitta, both relative and ultimate and, within that context, the doctrine of the Middle Way. He was also an accomplished master of the Secret Mantra and it was he who advised the king to invite Guru Padmasambhava to come to Tibet. As we know, Guru Rinpoche filled the country with the teachings of the sutras and the tantras, and created an environment in which the full extent of the Buddhadharma could be preserved and practiced for over twelve hundred years. All this happened thanks to the great compassion of Shantarakshita, Guru Padmasambhava, and the Dharma king Trisongdetsen.

We are very happy and grateful to be able to make this text available in English—not only the stanzas of Shantarakshita himself, but also the great commentary of Mipham Rinpoche whom our teachers Kyabje Kangyur Rinpoche and Kyabje Dilgo Khyentse Rinpoche met in person and whom they considered to be one of their main teachers. It is certainly thanks to the blessings of these great beings that it has been possible for us to study these texts, the genuine expressions of the Buddha's teaching composed by truly authentic masters and, on the basis of the explanations that we have been fortunate to receive, to make a humble attempt at translating them.

JIGME KHYENTSE
Dordogne, 2004

Translators' Introduction

THIS TRANSLATION of Shantarakshita's *Madhyamakalankara* and of the commentary on it composed by Jamgön Mipham Rinpoche was made following the detailed explanations given by Khenchen Pema Sherab of Namdröling Monastery, Mysore, India, during four summer study sessions at Chanteloube in Dordogne, France. When first requested to expound these texts, he remarked smilingly on their difficulty—much greater than in the case of the *Madhyamakavatara* of Chandrakirti, which, despite its profundity, is comparatively straightforward. One of the main challenges for the nonspecialist reader of Shantarakshita's text—and even more so that of Mipham—is that they presuppose a considerable knowledge of the teachings on pramana, the system of logic and epistemology associated with the Indian masters Dignaga and Dharmakirti. Khen Rinpoche went on to say, however, that one should not allow oneself to be discouraged by such difficulties. For in bringing together the traditions of Madhyamaka and Chittamatra, respectively associated with Nagarjuna and Asanga, the *Madhyamakalankara* is a key text—a valuable tool that facilitates the acquisition of a full and balanced understanding of Mahayana Buddhism. In addition, Mipham's commentary on it is widely recognized to be one of his masterpieces. It is a penetrating and wide-ranging analysis, which, in Khen Rinpoche's estimation, ranks as one of the most profound commentaries on Madhyamaka ever written. This is all the more amazing when one considers that Mipham composed the work at the age of thirty-one, spent no more than a few hours on it each day, and completed the task in three weeks!

Given the difficult and intricate questions discussed in Mipham's commentary and the appeal that it is likely to have for students who are already familiar with Madhyamaka ideas, it is unnecessary in the present introduction to discuss basic principles, presentations of which are readily available elsewhere.[1] Instead, in order to place the present work in context, we wish only (and with all due diffidence) to draw the reader's attention to certain important issues that may help to explain the reason for Mipham's composition as well as its remarkably fresh and invigorating approach to what is indeed a profound and interesting subject. In addition to supplying a brief biographical note on Shantarakshita, therefore, we have attempted to review briefly three questions: the Svatantrika-Prasangika distinction, which Mipham himself discusses at some length; the role played by the Yogachara or Chittamatra doctrine in Shantarakshita's synthesis; and certain logical and epistemological issues that will perhaps be unfamiliar to the nonspecialist.

Shantarakshita and Mipham's Commentary

Although we have very few details of the life of Shantarakshita, the fact remains that, thanks to his importance in the history of Tibetan Buddhism, more information is recorded about him than most other Indian masters. The brief biographical notes supplied by Mipham in the general introduction to his commentary bring together the scant, more or less hagiographical details culled from various traditional sources: Butön, Taranatha, *The Blue Annals*, and so on. From these we may gather that Shantarakshita was the son of the king of Zahor, that he became the abbot of the great monastic university of Nalanda, that he was a faultless upholder of the monastic discipline, and that he was a formidable expert in the art of philosophical disputation, universally admired for his intelligence and learning. His reputation as a unique authority spread beyond the borders of his native land, and when the king of Tibet, who, Mipham tells us, "knew nothing about India," wished to propagate the Buddhist teachings in his country, it was to Shantarakshita that he naturally appealed.

With regard to the role Shantarakshita played in the establishment of Buddhism in Tibet in the eighth century, the few facts that we have speak for themselves. It was he who, at the behest of King Trisongdetsen, established the first important Buddhist institutions in the country. He began the construction of the first monastery at Samye, ordained the first monks, had texts brought from India, and inaugurated the great work of translation. In addition, and perhaps most crucial for the Tibetan tradition, it was Shantarakshita who advised the king to invite Guru Padmasambhava to Tibet in order to quell the occult forces that were hindering their work, and to create a propitious environment for the propagation and practice of the Buddhist tantras. Finally, it seems to have been Shantarakshita who, foreseeing the difficulties to come, provided for the visit to Tibet of his disciple Kamalashila, who, according to tradition, successfully contended with the representative of a Chinese tradition of "sudden enlightenment" and established as normative the gradual methods of Indian Buddhism.

Shantarakshita's writings, lost for the most part in Sanskrit but preserved in Tibetan translation, give evidence of the encyclopedic range of his learning, which embraced all the religious and philosophical currents of his time, Hindu and Buddhist alike. The traditions of scholarship (teaching, composition, debate, and so on), for which Shantarakshita was famous, were favored by the cultural environment, which was stable and prosperous. Taranatha informs us that Shantarakshita's life coincided with the reigns of the first two kings of the Pala dynasty, whose rule, extending over the northeast of India, marked a period of confident expansion for Buddhist institutions. The great monastic complex of Vikramashila, for example, was founded during the reign of the second king, Dharmapala.[2]

The previous political dispensation, that is, the empires of the Gupta dynasty and of Harsha, although not hostile to Buddhism, had been favorably inclined to the development of Hinduism, and a spirit of religious and philosophical tolerance encouraged the growth of intellectual and scholarly activity. Hinduism, which in a still earlier age had been overshadowed by the dominant Buddhist culture inaugurated by Ashoka, revived. And stimulated in the long run by the penetrating critique implicit in the Buddhist teachings, it had evolved a powerful and sophisticated response. This resulted in intense intellectual exchange, in the refinement and reformulation of positions, and in an increase in subtlety on all sides. Within Buddhism itself, there was a proliferation of different schools, and as far as modern scholarship is able to determine, most known tenet systems of Indian Buddhism (including those associated with the early period) still existed in the eighth century—a spectrum of Hinayana and Mahayana views that were still living issues in Shantarakshita's time.[3]

Shantarakshita's importance in the scholarly field stems from the fact that he effected a synthesis that was to mark the last great development of Buddhist philosophy in India. To this synthesis—according to which the ultimate truth is presented in terms of Madhyamaka, while the conventional is understood in terms of the Chittamatra or Mind Only school—was added another crucial component: the logico-epistemological tradition of Dignaga and Dharmakirti. This all-inclusive presentation of the Mahayana is the hallmark of Shantarakshita's teaching. Moreover, the significance of the fact that this final synthesis was disseminated in Tibet not in the form of translated texts propagated by scholars, but through the direct intervention of its author, was not lost on the Tibetans, for whom it counts for much that Shantarakshita went to Tibet himself and delivered his message in person. Throughout the early period of Buddhism in Tibet (that is, approximately the first four centuries), it was Shantarakshita's synthesis that, on the level of the sutra teachings, dominated the religious and intellectual scene.

With the passage of time and for reasons that we will discuss presently, the tradition of Shantarakshita fell into shadow, superseded by a quite different systematization and presentation of the Madhyamaka teaching. There is therefore an element of controversy in the modern-day composition of such an extensive and lively commentary on the *Madhyamakalankara*, the principal statement of Shantarakshita's view. For in Mipham's opinion, this view had been marginalized by an interpretation of Madhyamaka that, however influential and well established, was nevertheless severely flawed.

It is important to situate Mipham's intellectual and scholarly activities in the context of the Rimé (*ris med*) or nonsectarian movement inaugurated in the nineteenth century by such masters as Jamyang Khyentse Wangpo, Jamgön Kongtrul Lodrö Thayé, Patrul Rinpoche, and Loter Wangpo. In a bid to combat widespread intellectual narrowness, the bitter fruit of sectarian animosity, the aim of this great endeavor was to recover as much as possible the open-minded and eclectic spirit that had characterized Tibetan Buddhism in an earlier age but had vanished largely as a result of the political and religious conflicts that had troubled Tibet since the fifteenth century.[4] Although the Rimé movement is sometimes described as "ecumenical," its aim was not to effect a union, still less a uniformity, between different traditions or religious obediences. Instead it was to collect and preserve the many teachings and practices of the entire spectrum of Tibetan Buddhism—especially those that were in danger of being lost—in an all-embracing initiative that recognized the value of all traditions and was tolerant of differences.

The Rimé movement exerted a powerfully revitalizing influence on the Sakya, Kagyu, and Nyingma traditions, which had previously felt themselves overwhelmed, if not actually supplanted, by the institutional and intellectual hegemony of the Gelug school. Reviving interest, supported by the financial sponsorship of the secular authorities at Derge in Kham, led to the founding of new centers of learning that encouraged the study of the different scholarly traditions, contributing to a general enrichment of spiritual and intellectual life and providing respectable and viable alternatives to the dominant approach of Gelugpa scholasticism.[5]

In this new wave of activity, Mipham played an important role. As recorded in the biography composed by his disciple Kunzang Palden,[6] he was commissioned by his teacher Jamyang Khyentse Wangpo to compose commentaries on all the great Mahayana shastras, presenting the characteristic approach of the Old Translation school in a form suitable for use in the Nyingma commentarial colleges.

In the final stanza of the introductory verses to his commentary on the *Madhyamakalankara*, Mipham remarked that the tradition contained therein had "dwindled now to embers." He was referring to the extraordinary fact that, despite the almost mythical status that Shantarakshita occupied and continues to occupy in the religious history of Tibet, by the nineteenth century, his writings had been forgotten and were practically unknown. Composed in 1877, Mipham's commentary was the first to be written on the *Madhyamakalankara* in four hundred years. In keeping with the principles of the Rimé movement, however, Mipham's work was not intended merely as a piece of philosophical archaeology. It is clear that he meant to revive what he believed to be the specificity of the Nyingma understanding of Madhyamaka, reaching back through such figures as Longchen Rabjam and Rongdzom Pandita to the teachings and view of Shantarakshita himself. Even more striking is Mipham's presentation of Shantarakshita as the very equal of Nagarjuna and Asanga. He was the "third charioteer," whose *Madhyamakalankara* united the traditions of his illustrious predecessors, integrating in a profound synthesis the two great streams of Mahayana Buddhism. Mipham's commentary embodied, as we shall see, a powerful reassessment of Madhyamaka and was in effect a challenge to the establishment. Shantarakshita's teachings had almost disappeared. "But if they be revived," Mipham's prefatory verses conclude, "and burn like forest fires, let those who chatter carelessly beware!"

Mipham and the Svatantrika-Prasangika Distinction

For the first four centuries after the introduction of Buddhism to Tibet, the Madhyamaka teachings were upheld principally according to the tradition of Shantarakshita. Bhavaviveka's commentary on Nagarjuna, together with its extensive subcommentary by Avalokitavrata,[7] were also translated in the early period, and this gave rise, in the early doxographical literature, to the perception of two Madhyamaka traditions, differentiated according to the way they discuss conventional phenomena in terms of other, non-Madhyamaka, tenet systems. In his *lta ba'i khyad par*, therefore, Shantarakshita's disciple Yeshe De describes the view of Bhavaviveka (Bhavya for short) as Sautrantika-Madhyamaka (*mdo sde spyod pa'i dbu ma pa*) and refers to that of Shantarakshita and Kamalashila as Yogachara-Madhyamaka (*rnal 'byor spyod pa'i dbu ma pa*). The principal difference between these two views concerns the acceptance or rejection of extramental phenomena on the conventional level.[8] Considering that, on the conventional level, phenomena are material and outside the mind, Bhavya explains them in terms of the Sautrantika tenet. Finding such a view to be philosophically untenable, Shantarakshita and his followers adopted the Yogachara position and denied the extramental status of phenomena appearing within the sphere of conventional truth. For them, conventional phenomena are the display of the mind and have no existence apart from the consciousness that observes them.

The general popularity of Shantarakshita's view no doubt owed something to the original impetus given to it by its founder—as well as to its acknowledged sophistication and the fact that it was more closely in line with the view expounded in the tantras. In any case, by the turn of the twelfth century, the Yogachara-Madhyamaka tradition was well established and counted among its adherents such important figures as the translator Ngok Loden Sherab (1059–1109) and the great logician Chapa Chökyi Senge (1109–1169).[9] This situation began to change in the first half of the twelfth century when important works by Chandrakirti were for the first time translated into Tibetan by Patsap Nyima Drak (1055–1145).

When studying the history of Madhyamaka, it is important to resist the impression of timelessness created by the generally ahistorical character of the doxographical literature. For example, one often reads about the "disagreement" between Chandrakirti and Bhavya, and one might almost imagine that these two masters contended face to face. Similarly, the fact that Bhavya and Shantarakshita are commonly referred to as Svatantrikas could give the impression that both these masters were the object of Chandrakirti's critique. It is easy to overlook the fact that, for the most part, the main protagonists in the history of Indian Madhyamaka were separated by long periods of time. Although Buddhapalita and Bhavya were historically quite close (both lived in the sixth century), there is no evidence that they ever met. The fact that Buddhapalita returned no answer to Bhavya's criticism gave rise to the legend that he was intimidated by the latter's princely rank. But there are reasons for thinking that by the time Bhavya composed his critique, Buddhapalita was no longer alive. Chandrakirti (seventh century), for his part, wrote his defense of Buddhapalita and critique of Bhavya at a distance of over a hundred years, and he himself was dead at least a century before Shantarakshita composed his works. The historical perspective is obviously crucial for an accurate understanding of the quite complex way in which the Madhyamaka tradition developed. It is important to be aware of the order in which the great Madhyamaka texts were composed in India and also of the quite different order in which they were translated in Tibet. For it is only by knowing what texts were available to the Tibetans, and when, that we can have some idea of the manner in which their understanding of Madhyamaka evolved.

Before the twelfth century, the Tibetan scholars who studied Bhavya's *Prajnapradipa* and its subcommentary would have been well aware of the fact that he had criticized an otherwise little-known master by the name of Buddhapalita,[10] whose own commentary had also been translated in the early period. The reading of these works would have revealed that Bhavya had—no doubt as a means of underlining the correctness of his own approach—attacked Buddhapalita for what he considered to be the latter's unsatisfactory method of expounding Nagarjuna's text. It is worth considering this matter in some detail, since an awareness of what Bhavya was doing (and what he thought he was doing) is helpful in gaining a balanced understanding of the Svatantrika-Prasangika distinction.[11]

It will be remembered that in the *Mulamadhyamaka-karika (Root Stanzas on the Middle Way)*, Nagarjuna had subjected other Buddhist tenet systems to a searching critique. His aim was to show that despite their efforts to systematize the Buddha's teachings and facilitate their implementation, they had fallen short in their understanding of the nature of phenomena. In making their assertions and negations in terms of phenomenal existence, they had failed to penetrate the heart of the Buddha's insight that ultimate truth lies beyond the expression of thought and word and is known only when the mind has transcended every conceptual extreme, whether of existence, nonexistence, both, or neither (this is the famous tetralemma). In pointing out this truth, it was obviously impossible for Nagarjuna to define, by any kind of positive statement, what he himself believed to be ineffable. When subjecting the imperfect view to critical analysis, therefore, Nagarjuna abstained from making any kind of positive assertion that could itself be taken as a description of the ultimate. Instead, his favorite method was not to contradict a defective position outright but to press it to its logical conclusions in accordance with principles acceptable to the opponent, thereby revealing its implicit absurdity by drawing out unwanted consequences that the opponent could not deny. By such a technique, theories are refuted not by being overwhelmed by some other, more cogent formulation but by being subjected to such a strain that they collapse under their own weight. When every possible position is thus annihilated, it is as if the mind is rendered speechless. For the implication is irresistible that the nature of phenomena—which, regardless of any theory, undeniably appear—lies beyond the range of the discursive intellect.

Bhavya was fully aware of Nagarjuna's intentions in adopting such a strategy. The use of consequential arguments had served Nagarjuna well. One could even say that given his evident objective—namely, to indicate the inexpressible nature of the ultimate truth—such a debate procedure was indispensable. Bhavya certainly had nothing to say against it. He nevertheless objected strenuously to the fact that, in his own commentary, Buddhapalita had done no more than follow Nagarjuna's example and confined himself likewise to the exclusive use of prasanga, or consequential arguments. Bhavya severely castigated Buddhapalita for what he had accepted in Nagarjuna without demur. What could be the reason for such a flagrant double standard? Bhavya has been accused of unfairness, but further reflection suggests that his criticism of Buddhapalita was consistent with what he apparently considered to be the role of commentary.

We have seen that the very nature of Nagarjuna's intentions had necessitated the use of consequential arguments, the purpose of which was not simply to demolish the imperfect position but to suggest an insight that, by definition, remained unstated. Bhavya, on the other hand, seems to have thought that a technique that was both appropriate and inevitable in the original text was quite out of place at the commentarial level. Commentary is after all a form of mediation. Its role is not to repeat verbatim the message of the original author but to elucidate it and to render its meaning accessible to a remote and uncomprehending audience. Now, the success of the kind of consequential argument just described depends not only on the cogency of the reasoning advanced but also on the ability of the interlocutor to understand the (unstated) point that is being made. As a result, there remains an inescapable element of doubt, which the exclusive use of consequentialist arguments necessarily leaves unresolved. For this reason, in Bhavya's view, the use of consequences—quite admissible in the original text—is undesirable in commentary because consequences leave the kind of uncertainty that it is precisely the role of commentary to remove. The task of the commentator, as mediator and teacher, is to assist the reader and to ensure, by the use of positive statements, that he or she understands what Nagarjuna means.[12]

In other words, it seems that Bhavya believed that Buddhapalita was failing in his duties. As commentator, it was his responsibility to explain Nagarjuna's procedure, not merely to duplicate it. Nagarjuna had intended, by the indirect method of consequential arguments, to bring the mind to the limits of rational discourse and to point out the ultimate nature that lies beyond. By contrast, the commentator's role is not to repeat Nagarjuna's already superlative performance but to discuss it and to present it skillfully. The task at hand is to resolve the element of doubt intrinsic to the consequentialist method, to deal with possible objections, and generally to facilitate the intellectual comprehension of those who require explanation and who cannot as yet penetrate, directly and unaided, the profound message of the original author. To that extent, it is both necessary and fitting to make positive, explanatory statements. These do not of course perform the same function as Nagarjuna's arguments, which is to indicate the ineffable truth, but they at least have the merit of explaining what Nagarjuna is actually doing. Commentary therefore has an essentially secondary and ancillary role. It is a pedagogical tool, its modest purpose being to unpack the meaning, and remove the obscurities, of the original text.

Throughout his own commentary, therefore, Bhavya makes extensive use of formal logic, which, in the wake of Dignaga's important and still recent work, was very much in vogue at Bhavya's time. He devotes much energy to recasting, or rather "reversing," Nagarjuna's consequentialist arguments (*thal ldog*) in the form of independent inferential statements, in other words, syllogisms or probative arguments consisting of (1) a subject, (2) a probandum, (3) an evidential sign endowed with forward and reverse pervasion or concomitance, and (4) an example. Following this enthusiastic lead, logic came to be closely associated with the kind of commentarial exposition of Nagarjuna's teaching of which Bhavya himself could be regarded as a pioneer. It is important to notice that at no time does Bhavya give the slightest suggestion that he is in any way questioning Nagarjuna's essential message about the ineffability of the ultimate truth. Nagarjuna himself had severely restricted the use of logic to the conventional level. Insight into the state beyond conceptual extremes obviously cannot be the conclusion of reasoned argument but arises only when the mind enters a state of silence that is free from all discursive activity. Similarly, although Bhavya, for his part, was greatly interested in logic as a means of producing intellectual certainty, he too seems to have been well aware of the provisional nature of its role in the Madhyamaka context. This becomes evident when one considers how the use of logic obliged Bhavya to make certain important adjustments in his presentation of the two truths.

Nagarjuna had emphasized that the two truths coincide and are perfectly united in phenomena. The ultimate truth of phenomena is their emptiness of intrinsic existence; their relative truth is the fact that they ineluctably appear through the play of interdependence. Bhavya does not deny this. Nevertheless, he made a provisional division between the two truths in a move that reflected his essentially pedagogical concerns. The aim of this division was to create a basis for debate between Madhyamikas and non-Madhyamikas on the subject of the nature of phenomena.

Meaningful communication demands at least a modicum of shared premises. The participants in any debate must agree on what it is they are talking about. Let us take the stock example. Buddhists and Hindus disagree about the nature of sound. The former believe that sound is impermanent, the latter that it is permanent. They both accept, however, that what they are proposing to talk about is sound: the phenomenon that everyone experiences regardless of whatever properties they may ascribe to it. On the basis of this agreement, the debate can proceed, and both Buddhists and Hindus can go on to propound their own theories and respective arguments. By contrast, in matters where there is no shared ground, no meaningful exchange can take place. If, for instance, a Hindu were to approach a Buddhist wishing to discuss the various aspects attributed in the Vedas to "permanent sound," no debate is possible. Since the Buddhist considers that there is no such thing as permanent sound, he or she has nothing to say about its supposed properties.

Turning to the question of the inherent existence of phenomena, it would seem that, since Madhyamikas deny this and non-Madhyamikas assert it, there is no shared ground. The two positions are at loggerheads and there is no room for discussion. From the Madhyamaka point of view, on the other hand, compassion demands that some effort be made to communicate the truth about the nature of phenomena (in other words, the view of the Buddha and of Nagarjuna). For it is only by the realization of this truth that the sufferings of samsara can be brought to an end. A bridge has to be created between the two sides; it is necessary to find a premise that they both share. Once this is done, the whole apparatus of reasoning can be brought into play and the non-Madhyamika can be induced, through logical argument, to see the error of believing in substantial existence. It is undoubtedly in this spirit that Bhavya adopts his important strategy. He divides the two truths on a temporary basis and accepts, for the sake of argument with his opponent, that phenomena exist "according to their characteristics." As a result, discussion between the Madhyamika and the non-Madhyamika can get under way. They are talking about phenomena, the characteristics of which they both perceive. They can now debate about whether or not such phenomena exist inherently in the way that they appear.

This division between the two truths and the implied necessity of defining them in relation to each other makes necessary a further distinction, this time in relation to the ultimate truth. In the *Tarkajvala*,[13] Bhavya considered the important objection that since the ultimate truth transcends the discursive intellect, it follows that no verbal formulation can possibly express it. How therefore is it possible even to talk about the two truths, distinguishing ultimate truth in opposition to the relative? If the ultimate cannot be talked about, how can it be distinguished from anything at all? In response, Bhavya draws a distinction between two kinds of ultimate truth. On the one hand, he says, there is the ultimate that is "world-transcending" (*'jig rten las 'das pa*). This is the ultimate truth in itself, the completely ineffable state beyond conceptual elaboration, which can only be experienced but never expressed. On the other hand, there is an ultimate that Bhavya describes as "pure worldly wisdom" (*dag pa 'jig rten pa'i ye shes*), which, in the context of the division of the two truths, is the counterpart of the relative and is the object of thought and word. It is "the ultimate that can be talked about." These expressions run parallel to another, better-known distinction, which first appears in another text also attributed to Bhavya,[14] between the "ultimate truth in itself" (*rnam grangs ma yin pa'i don dam*) and the "approximate ultimate" (*rnam grangs pa'i don dam*) or "concordant ultimate" (*mthun pa'i don dam*).

All these points serve to demonstrate the close association, established quite early between Madhyamaka and the use of logic within a commentarial tradition inaugurated by Bhavya, that in all probability constituted the mainstream presentation of Madhyamaka in India up to the time of Shantarakshita and beyond. As the inheritors of this tradition, the Tibetan Madhyamikas between the eighth and twelfth centuries would have been perfectly conversant with the expository methods and terminological distinctions just described. In other words, the logico-epistemological tradition of Dignaga and Dharmakirti was primarily and intimately linked with the kind of Madhyamaka that was dominant in both India and Tibet until the twelfth century—that is to say, the view that, after Patsap's translations of Chandrakirti's works, would be referred to as Svatantrika.

One is tempted to wonder how much the Tibetans before Patsap were aware of the importance of Chandrakirti. It seems inconceivable that Shantarakshita could have been ignorant of his illustrious predecessor, a confrere indeed of the same monastic center. But to what extent he enlarged upon Chandrakirti's view to his Tibetan disciples is something we shall never know. What we do know, however, is that a text by Chandrakirti—his commentary on Nagarjuna's *Yuktishashtika*—was translated in the early period by Jinamitra, Danashila, Shilendrabodhi, and Shantarakshita's disciple Yeshe De. Thus, although Chandrakirti was known in Tibet as early as the eighth century, this was specifically in connection with the logical tradition. Approximately four hundred years were to pass before he was identified as a great master of Madhyamaka. It is worth noting too that even in India, and despite the excellence of his writings, Chandrakirti seems to have attracted almost no following and made no impact on the development of the Madhyamaka tradition there. The first known commentary on the *Madhyamakavatara*, for example, was composed by Jayananda, no earlier than the eleventh century, over three hundred years after Chandrakirti's death.

One can well imagine therefore that the translation of Chandrakirti's works, especially the *Prasannapada* (his detailed commentary on Nagarjuna's *Mulamadhyamaka-karika*) must have caused a sensation in Tibet. For the first time, Tibetan scholars were confronted with a new and important fact, namely, that the hitherto obscure victim of Bhavya's critique had been powerfully vindicated, and that Bhavya had himself been subjected to withering criticism, by a commentator who was evidently of the highest capacity. Chandrakirti refuted Bhavya's criticism of Buddhapalita point by point, vindicated the use of consequential arguments as the best means of establishing the view, and rejected Bhavya's use of independent arguments as being wholly out of place in the Madhyamaka context. "Bhavaviveka," he says in the *Prasannapada*, "wishes only to parade his knowledge of the logical treatises. He adduces independent arguments, despite the fact that he claims to be a Madhyamika. The Madhyamaka system, to be sure, creates lots of difficulties for such a would-be logician. He makes one mistake after another."[15] Chandrakirti's criticism of Bhavya's use of autonomous inferences was part of a wider rejection of the logico-epistemological tradition of Dignaga, which he regarded as a misguided attempt to find "philosophical completeness" and a sense of intellectual security that is antithetical to the fundamental insight of Madhyamaka.[16] For Chandrakirti, Bhavya's division between the two truths was neither necessary nor desirable and was in any case a thorough misrepresentation of Nagarjuna's approach. This is not to say that Chandrakirti rejected the use of reasoning, but for him its purpose, as with Nagarjuna and Buddhapalita, was to mark the limits of the discursive inquiry. It is perfectly true that in debate about the true existence of phenomena, there is no shared ground between the Madhyamika and the substantialist. Therefore, in Chandrakirti's view, consequences (*prasanga*) are the only kind of argument appropriate for Madhyamikas, for it is only by such means that they can indicate the ultimate without making statements that of necessity compromise, or at any rate obscure, their own position. The use of autonomous arguments, for the very reason that they imply the acceptance (however provisional) of entities, is ruled out. In reply to Bhavya's thesis that such arguments are demanded by the very nature of commentary, Chandrakirti could and did point out that in the autocommentary on the *Vigrahavyavartani* (his defense of Madhyamaka method), Nagarjuna himself had abstained from using independent probative arguments.[17] For Chandrakirti, it serves no purpose to divide the two truths or to explain the relative in philosophical terms. For such explanations do violence to the relative truth, in the sense that they produce theories that are more or less far-fetched in relation to the phenomena that are actually experienced. On the contrary, Chandrakirti says, the relative truth consists simply of phenomena as we observe them, the unanalyzed constituents of the common consensus.

Following the work of Patsap, a new doxographical distinction came into being. It was now possible to differentiate Madhyamikas not, as previously, by the way they discussed conventionalities but according to the type of arguments they used to establish the ultimate truth. On one side are the Prasangikas, who in debate make no assertion of their own but seek to demolish the opponent's position by the adduction of unwanted consequences. On the other side, there are the Svatantrikas, who, not content with mere refutation, make their own positive assertions, independently of the views of their opponents. On the basis, therefore, of the critique laid out in the *Prasannapada*, it became customary to describe Buddhapalita and Chandrakirti as Prasangikas and Bhavya as Svatantrika. And given the fact that Shantarakshita and Kamalashila also made use of autonomous inferences, they too are classified in the doxographical literature as belonging, despite important philosophical differences, to the same group as Bhavya. Henceforth, an unwieldy terminological difference came into being between Sautrantika-Svatantrika-Madhyamaka and Yogachara-Svatantrika-Madhyamaka.

Once again it is important to emphasize the close connection between the Svatantrika school and logico-epistemological tradition (that is, the teachings on pramana) to which Shantarakshita himself made important contributions and in which the followers of his tradition, namely, the early Tibetan Madhyamikas, showed a keen interest. This was especially true of the school of Sangpu, founded by Ngok Loden Sherab and continued by Chapa Chökyi Senge. The latter composed the first Tibetan summary of Dharmakirti's thought and played a crucial role in the founding of Tibetan scholasticism.[18] This is in contrast with the radical Prasangika distrust of "philosophy" (at least as far as Chandrakirti was concerned) and in particular of logic and epistemology as being relevant to the establishment of the view. Given the degree to which the earlier tradition of Madhyamaka was entrenched in Tibet and also the intellectual tools and debating skills already at their disposal, it is not surprising that, despite the intrinsic quality of Chandrakirti's texts, the introduction of Prasangika to Tibet met with a powerful resistance. Chapa, for example, who was reputedly formidable in debate, is said to have brilliantly defended the Svatantrika view against Prasangika innovation and to have composed several refutations of Chandrakirti. In the interesting story of the encounter between him and the Indian master Jayananda, it was perhaps to be expected that the victory should go to the Svatantrika master of logic and not to his Prasangika opponent.[19]

Despite such opposition, the Prasangika approach gained in popularity and received powerful support from Tsongkhapa (1357–1419), the founder of the Gelugpa school, who greatly emphasized its superiority. For him, the two subschools of Madhyamaka are divided by a significant difference of view. The misguided use of autonomous inferences by Bhavya, Shantarakshita, Kamalashila, and others indicated important, if residual, ontological commitments that resulted in an imperfect understanding of emptiness. The Svatantrika view is hence considered a lower tenet. It presents a path that of itself is unable to lead to liberation, something that only the Prasangika approach can achieve. For Tsongkhapa, one of the criteria for having a correct understanding of Madhyamaka is precisely the ability to distinguish correctly between the Prasangika and Svatantrika views and to understand that they do not have the same object of negation. It is said therefore that the Prasangikas refute the reality of phenomena on both the ultimate and conventional levels but that the Svatantrikas, in claiming that phenomena exist conventionally according to their characteristics, only manage to do so on the ultimate level. Since the Svatantrika view retains a certain clinging to substantiality, it is to be classified as the highest of the lower views, ranked beneath Prasangika, the supremacy of which Tsongkhapa threw into even sharper relief by the formulation of eight special features: his so-called eight difficult points.

The brilliance of Tsongkhapa's teaching, his qualities as a leader, his emphasis on monastic discipline, and the purity of his example attracted an immense following. Admiration, however, was not unanimous, and his presentation of Madhyamaka in particular provoked a fierce backlash, mainly from the Sakya school, to which Tsongkhapa and his early disciples originally belonged. These critics included Tsongkhapa's contemporaries Rongtön Shakya Gyaltsen (1367–1449) and Taktsang Lotsawa (1405–?), followed in the next two generations by Gorampa Sonam Senge (1429–1487), Serdog Panchen Shakya Chokden (1428–1509), and the eighth Karmapa, Mikyö Dorje (1505–1557). All of them rejected Tsongkhapa's interpretation as inadequate, newfangled, and unsupported by tradition. Although they recognized certain differences between the Prasangika and Svatantrika approaches,[20] they considered that Tsongkhapa had greatly exaggerated the divergence of view. They believed that the difference between the two subschools was largely a question of methodology and did not amount to a disagreement on ontological matters.

Not surprisingly, these objections provoked a counterattack, and they were vigorously refuted by Tsongkhapa's disciples. In due course, however, the most effective means of silencing such criticisms came with the ideological proscriptions imposed at the beginning of the seventeenth century. These followed the military intervention of Gusri Khan, who put an end to the civil war in central Tibet, placed temporal authority in the hands of the Fifth Dalai Lama, and ensured the rise to political power of the Gelugpa school. Subsequently, the writings of all the most strident of Tsongkhapa's critics ceased to be available and were almost lost. It was, for example, only at the beginning of the twentieth century that Gorampa's works could be fully reassembled, whereas Shakya Chokden's works, long thought to be irretrievably lost, were discovered only recently in Bhutan and published as late as 1975.[21]

The only reason for alluding to these unfortunate events is to make the simple point that by the time Mipham came to write his commentary on Shantarakshita, the general understanding of Madhyamaka in Tibet was defined by the Gelugpa interpretation to the point where no other assessment could be seriously entertained. The hierarchy of views, which exalted the Prasangika approach and relegated the Svatantrika to an inferior rank, was so well entrenched as to appear practically self-evident. Placed indiscriminately in the same category, Bhavaviveka and Shantarakshita were dwarfed by the towering figure of Chandrakirti, and their works had long since ceased to be the object of serious study. Their views were reduced to a few salient points preserved in the doxographical literature—little more than philosophical museum pieces—to be cursorily reviewed and refuted with stock arguments by students on their way to understanding and establishing the Prasangika view as the pinnacle of all tenets.

In view of these generally held assumptions, it is obvious that, in representing Shantarakshita's *Madhyamakalankara*, Mipham could not proceed without first redefining the notions of Svatantrika and Prasangika. To advocate Shantarakshita's view without justification would have been automatically self-defeating. For in the intellectual climate that then predominated, it would have meant adopting a view that was universally held to be inferior. As one modern scholar has remarked, it would have been as bizarre and unintelligible as propounding the supremacy of Newtonian physics in the present century.[22] No one who held such a view could hope to be taken seriously. Mipham therefore prefaces his commentary with a long and important introduction in which he presents in fine detail an alternative and extremely refined interpretation of the Svatantrika-Prasangika distinction. He integrates them into a workable synthesis. He reformulates them, shows how they relate to each other, and affirms the necessity of both.

When discussing the two Madhyamaka approaches, Mipham of course uses the terms "Svatantrika" and "Prasangika." In his day, it would have been confusing and counterproductive to do otherwise. On the other hand, the question of dialectical preferences (the use of consequences as opposed to autonomous inferences) to which these terms allude is for him of only secondary importance.[23] For Mipham, the key to understanding the difference between Prasangika and Svatantrika lies in the distinction between the two kinds of ultimate truth: the actual ultimate truth in itself (*rnam grangs ma yin pa'i don dam*) and the approximate or concordant ultimate (*rnam grangs pa'i don dam* or *mthun pa'i don dam*). The first to make this distinction was, as we have seen, Bhavya; it was part of his general pedagogical strategy of dividing the two truths. Given the importance of this distinction for Mipham, it is worth considering it a little further.

Chandrakirti says in the *Prasannapada* that the aim of the consequentialist dialectic is to bring the mind to a state of silence. This silence is not of course a state of mental paralysis. It is the silence of the wise, the silence of nonconceptual wisdom. For Chandrakirti, the purpose of the exclusive use of consequential arguments is to introduce the mind to the direct knowledge of emptiness, not to an intellectual understanding of it, however subtle. But here there is an obvious practical problem.

If the ultimate truth is ineffable, how can it be communicated to those who are without realization? How is one to avoid misunderstanding? What is to prevent one from taking Nagarjuna's message at face value and assuming that the ultimate is a mere negation, a kind of nihilism that undermines moral action? We know of course that Chandrakirti, like any other Buddhist teacher, must have expounded the doctrine and guided beings on the path, from the four noble truths onward. And, by milking the painting of a cow, he might have given his disciples a little help in calling into question their deeply held conviction of the solid reality of phenomena.[24] But when establishing the view, he makes no assertion and gives no description. From the very beginning, he presents the two truths as undivided: Phenomena appear yet are empty; they are empty and yet they appear. And either we are able to understand this and immediately perceive the unreal, dreamlike quality of phenomenal appearance—grasping at once that "form is emptiness, emptiness is form"—or we are not. It is clear that the Prasangika approach makes no concessions to the spiritually unprepared. Its success depends not only on the skill of the teacher but also on the aptitude and merit of the disciple.

In contrast with this, the Svatantrika approach, while not denying that the ultimate is completely mind-transcending, seems devised to meet the needs of beings of more ordinary capacity. This being so, it is not surprising that for so many centuries it should have remained the dominant tradition. It accepts, on a provisional basis, that the phenomenal world is to all intents and purposes real—real according to the characteristics that appear in the common consensus of unenlightened beings, who have an ingrained tendency to apprehend as truly existent whatever appears to their senses. *On the ultimate level*, however, these phenomena do not exist, for ultimately phenomena are empty. For the purposes of explanation therefore, the two truths are separated, and the ultimate truth, understood in terms of this division, is, as we have said, the *approximate ultimate*. It is the negation of the real existence of phenomena and is not to be mistaken for the *actual ultimate in itself*, which refers to an insight that transcends not only the existence but also the nonexistence of phenomena.

For Mipham, it is in relation to the distinction between the approximate and actual ultimates that the difference between the Prasangika and Svatantrika approaches is most clearly seen. "It should be understood," he says, "that the authentic Svatantrika is the approach that emphasizes the approximate ultimate, while the Prasangika approach emphasizes the ultimate in itself, beyond all assertions." Chandrakirti's Prasangika method aims to place the mind immediately and directly in the state of freedom from conceptual elaboration (as experienced in the meditation of those who have attained the path of seeing and beyond). To this end, consequential reasoning is used only in order to abolish the attempts of reason to account for the true status of things. By contrast, the Svatantrika method is gradual. It begins with the phenomena of which the world seems to be composed and which impinge upon our senses. These phenomena—which ineluctably appear to us whether we think them real or not—are provisionally accorded a certain existence. This creates the space for debate and the reasoned demonstration that phenomena cannot possibly exist in the way that they appear. By this means, the (approximate) ultimate truth is posited, in contrast with the conventional truth of appearance. "Finally," Mipham says, "the ultimate truth in itself, which is completely free from all assertion, is reached." The ultimate truth that the Svatantrikas expound and demonstrate by rational means is but a distant if concordant image, "no more than a conceptual reflection" of the ultimate truth in itself. And with regard to the latter—which is what noble beings on the Bodhisattva grounds "see with the utterly stainless primordial wisdom of meditative equipoise"—the Svatantrikas, like the Prasangikas, make no assertion. The final goal of the Svatantrika and Prasangika approaches is therefore the same. The difference lies only in the pedagogical methods adopted. Obviously, these reflect the needs of the disciples, not the level of realization of the teacher. Consequently, it is inappropriate to classify the great masters of Madhyamaka as higher or lower on the scale of views. If a hierarchical distinction does exist between the Prasangika and Svatantrika methods, it can only be in terms of the qualities and aptitudes of the disciples for whose sake they are expounded. "The two approaches, Svatantrika and Prasangika, belong respectively to those who follow the gradual path and those whose realization is not gradual (*rim skyed*) but immediate (*cig car*)."[25] Both approaches are therefore to be prized—especially the Prasangika, for "this profound view resembles the manner in which primordial purity is established in the texts of the Great Perfection."[26] Finally, whereas the *Madhyamakalankara* embodies for the most part the Svatantrika method, brief but perfectly clear passages indicate that, on his own account, Shantarakshita "indeed possesses the ultimate and essential view of the Prasangikas." Consequently, Mipham roundly declares, his view "is in perfect agreement with the view of the glorious Chandrakirti."[27]

Mipham's point therefore is that, in addition to bringing together both the Middle Way and Mind Only teachings, the *Madhyamakalankara* also embodies a synthesis of the Prasangika and Svatantrika approaches. It is consequently an ornament for the entire Madhyamaka and not just for one subschool. By elaborating such a synthesis, Mipham's aim is to recover the work of Shantarakshita and the Svatantrikas generally as objects of respectable study. And he shows at some length that the neglect of their teachings, encouraged by imperfect and superficial doxographical classifications, leads to a distorted understanding of the entire tradition and constitutes an important hindrance to the realization of the Madhyamaka view.

A Rival Interpretation

The form and content of commentary, given its essentially mediatory function, is dictated not only by the insights of the commentator into the meaning of the commented text but also by the needs and expectations of the targeted readership. In his presentation of Shantarashita, Mipham was obliged to deal with what he considered to be mistaken interpretations of Madhyamaka, and many of the topics referred to (sometimes quite indirectly) in his commentary, particularly in the field of pramana, were controversial, given that competing positions had crystallized along sectarian lines. These points of view were well known, and in refuting a given idea, it was often unnecessary for Mipham to specify its provenance. Generally speaking, however, in his various works on Madhyamaka, Mipham could not avoid calling into question the dominant Gelugpa view and answering the attacks of Gelugpa critics. He does this, as we have said, in the spirit of the Rimé movement. Although his writings show that he was certainly no stranger to the art of disputation, Mipham's purpose in writing was not polemic. The principal objective, as he himself declared, was to enrich, at the request of his teacher, the scholarly and religious field. Unlike the more controversial scholars of the preceding centuries, Mipham is invariably and sincerely respectful of Tsongkhapa, and his attitude toward the Gelugpa school, though occasionally stern, is generally irenic and accommodating. But even if he does not express himself with the same stridency as Tsongkhapa's earlier critics, it is clear that, on all important philosophical issues, he shares their opinions. In the case of the eight difficult points, for instance, a reading of Mipham's works shows that even if the tone is rather low-key and sometimes even humorous,[28] he rarely misses an opportunity to refute them.

Since, as we have said, most of Mipham's critique is directed at the Gelugpa presentation of Madhyamaka and its attendant issues, it would perhaps be useful to review, albeit tentatively, the basic position of this school and to highlight the specific points that Mipham, along with the majority of non-Gelugpa critics, found so objectionable.

We have seen that, following Bhavya, a close connection was established between the pramana tradition and the kind of Madhyamaka that was later to be designated as Svatantrika. Chandrakirti disapproved of logic and epistemology[29] but had little influence on his contemporaries (as also, in this respect, on subsequent generations). The association between Madhyamaka and pramana continued in Tibet, notably, as we have also seen, in the Sangpu tradition and the key figure of Chapa. These facts are of relevance to an understanding of Tsongkhapa's Madhyamaka interpretation. Rejecting the Svatantrika view defended by Chapa in favor of the Prasangika view of Chandrakirti (and Patsap), Tsongkhapa nevertheless embraced with enthusiasm the pramana teachings of Dignaga and Dharmakirti, and this according to Chapa's interpretation. This was a highly paradoxical move. For he adopted the logical method but rejected the view with which it was traditionally associated, and proceeded to apply this same method to a view that had traditionally rejected it. Pramana plays an important role in Tsongkhapa's unique presentation of the Prasangika view,[30] which was on this account censured with great severity by his Sakyapa critics. Taktsang attacked Tsongkhapa in terms that are strangely reminiscent of Chandrakirti's criticism of Bhavya quoted earlier.

> The cause for such a burden of contradictions [in Tsongkhapa's writings] is that, despite [Chandrakirti's and others'] statements again and again [that phenomena exist] only for the world without analysis, [Tsongkhapa] applied reasoning and proved [their valid conventional existence] due to the force of his habituation to logic.[31]

For Tsongkhapa, the principles of logical discourse apply not only to the investigation of the nature of phenomena but also to the actual findings of such an investigation. Not only the relative truth but also the ultimate truth of emptiness must remain intelligible in logical terms. It seems, in other words, that, for Tsongkhapa, the ultimate truth is not completely ineffable and in a sense still remains the object of the discursive mind. For him, the purpose of the fourfold refutation familiar from Nagarjuna and Chandrakirti is not (as it is for Mipham and other non-Gelugpa Madhyamikas) to put an end to intellectual activity in the ordinary sense of the word. Instead of being an introduction to a state beyond conceptual activity, the tetralemmic refutation is understood figuratively, as applying not to phenomena themselves but to a separate object of negation referred to as "true existence" or "intrinsic existence." And it is upon this object of negation, and not phenomena themselves, that the Madhyamaka reasoning is brought to bear. As the stock expression goes, "The pot is not empty of pot; it is empty of true existence." For Mipham, by contrast, the purpose of the Madhyamaka critique is to mark the limit beyond which rational discourse has no place. Once the state beyond conception has been brought into view, the next step is not more thought, certainly not more talk, but the settling of the mind in meditative equipoise. When the Madhyamaka arguments have done their work, there is nowhere for the ordinary intellect to go. The next step can only be the cultivation of the direct experience of that to which the words "ultimate truth" only approximately refer.

Tsongkhapa took a quite different view. It would seem that for him, the above strategy is far too vague, far too open to delusion and self-deception. For him, ultimate reality is "understood through conceptual schemes that follow the classical canons of rationality."[32] Meditation on emptiness "is not a matter of withdrawing from conceptuality."[33] At the risk of caricature, we could perhaps say that Tsongkhapa was defending discursive reason from the deconstructive onslaught that results from a particularly, let us say, "apophatic" interpretation of Nagarjuna and Chandrakirti. For him, even after the tetralemmic refutation, philosophy is still possible.

Given the distinction, in Tsongkhapa's presentation of Madhyamaka, between phenomena and their true existence, there is a crucial step in the understanding of emptiness that consists in the so-called "identification of the object of negation." It is necessary to refute only the true existence of phenomena and not phenomena themselves, and this presupposes the ability to recognize, within the phenomena of conventional existence, the putative "true existence" that the mind deludedly reifies and ascribes to them.

> Thus Madhyamaka deconstruction does not concern existence proper. Things do not exist ultimately, as Nagarjuna's deconstructive reasonings demonstrate, but they do exist conventionally (and therefore can be said to exist). Madhyamaka reasonings do not affect the existence of phenomena, including emptiness, that can be understood according to the canons of rationality presupposed by a moderate realist interpretation of Buddhist epistemology. Essencelessness can then be integrated within a global account in which reality can be described coherently, without any conflict between the two truths. This account also strengthens the validity of the conventional realm, which gains a kind of existence (albeit only conventional).[34]

One of the most surprising aspects of Tsongkhapa's interpretation (to which, however, Mipham does not refer in the present commentary) is the fact that although he said that the correct realization of emptiness is impossible without the recognition of the object of negation just described (true existence as distinct from conventional existence), he also said that the ability to distinguish these two factors is possessed only by those who have already realized emptiness. His presentation, in other words, seems to involve an insuperable contradiction. Tsongkhapa's followers are well aware of this conundrum, and, in practice, it is accepted that before emptiness is realized, the distinction between phenomena and the true existence falsely attributed to them can never be more than theoretical. It is something that ordinary beings cannot perceive but must accept in a "correct assumption," the result of mental analysis (*yid dpyod*). In terms of the realist epistemology accepted by the Gelugpa school, it is only after emptiness is realized that the object of negation is identified by valid cognition. Once again, the Gelugpas are aware of the further problems that this solution raises. "At the very least, it constitutes a sleight of hand that hides the radical difference between the two truths."[35] In point of fact, Gelugpa thinkers recommend various solutions as means to overcome these difficulties.[36]

Anyone who has read Mipham's commentary on the *Madhyamakavatara* will know that this account of "true existence," as something separate from phenomena, is for him extremely problematic and dangerous. He attacked it repeatedly and at great length. The Gelugpa interpretation of Prasangika has often been described by its critics as a form of Svatantrika in disguise, since its presentation of "conventional," as distinct from "true," existence seems very close to the "existence according to characteristics" that Bhavya had ascribed to phenomena on the relative level. It is in reference to this that Mipham remarks ironically that it must have been owing to some causal interdependence (*rten 'brel*) set in motion by the fact that Madhyamaka first appeared in Tibet in the form advocated by Shantarakshita that Tibetan Madhyamikas always seem destined to revert to the Svatantrika position! Contrary to what one might expect, however, this is not a recommendation. The separation of a putative object of negation from phenomena themselves is regarded as a piece of sophistry with unfortunate results. The use of probative arguments to establish emptiness, and the acceptance of phenomenal "existence according to characteristics" that these same arguments imply, constituted, in the hands of the Indian Svatantrikas, a provisional strategy. As we have seen, within the context of the separation of the two truths that this strategy implies, the ultimate truth is regarded as no more than an approximate, concordant mental image. This, however, is a temporary device. Its purpose is to elicit an understanding of emptiness on the intellectual level. As a mental image, it enables the mind to draw close to a reality (the actual ultimate) that it does not directly express but only resembles. For Bhavya, this is as much as the discursive intellect can do. The correct understanding thus achieved must then be supplemented by meditation, as a result of which the mind may blossom into a direct experience of the ultimate truth in itself, which is free from all conceptual elaborations. At no point in the Svatantrika approach is any attempt made to bridge the gap between the two truths in intellectual, rational terms. On the contrary, the reason for distinguishing the two kinds of ultimate is precisely because the construction of such a bridge is impossible.

This, however, is what Tsongkhapa seems to do. He insists that the emptiness is intelligible in terms of logic and epistemology. Reason can still lay hold of it, and it remains the object of the discursive mind. For if emptiness is not an object of valid cognition, he says, it is a mere nothingness. In Mipham's view, this is a serious mistake. He says that the ordinary mind of worldly beings, the object of which is phenomenal appearance on the relative level, is not a valid means of knowledge in relation to the ultimate truth. For the latter transcends all conventionalities. Ordinary consciousness is produced in dependence on a support, and this is precisely why it is unable to grasp the dharmadhatu. For the latter "is not based on anything and is the field of primal, world-transcending wisdom."[37] To claim therefore that intellectual cognition can attain to the ultimate truth is as foolish, Mipham says, as thinking that a newborn baby can look directly at the sun. Instead of entertaining a misplaced confidence in the powers of reason and the processes of logic, it is essential to make a clear distinction between the lack of true existence as apprehended as a mental object (namely, the approximate ultimate) and the authentic ultimate in itself, which is beyond all assertions and concepts. Of course, even when such a distinction is rejected, it is still possible to speak of a union of the two truths, but within the parameters of such a view, this amounts, in Mipham's opinion, not to a union but to a mere juxtaposition. The negation of an extrinsic real existence, which leaves phenomena untouched, results, so to speak, in the placing of the two truths side by side (like a black thread and white thread twisted together). They remain distinct and are not unified.

On the other hand, when it is applied to its proper object, intellectual understanding plays a vital and liberative role. For its function is to orient the mind correctly and thus provide a sound basis for meditative training.

> By thus acquiring a certain conviction in that which surpasses in-
> tellectual knowledge, *and by training in it*, one will eventually actual-
> ize it. . . . And we should not only abandon the fond hope that
> strenuous mental effort in the ordinary sense of the word can achieve
> profound emptiness, but we should also avoid any kind of depressed
> discouragement, thinking that it is unattainable. . .
> Emptiness entails appearance; appearance entails emptiness. The
> two can never be separate. If you gain a conviction that this is indeed
> the way things are—a conviction that is irreversible though a thou-
> sand Buddhas should deny it—you have, by learning and study, pen-
> etrated to the deepest point of the Madhyamaka scriptures. You can
> then pursue in earnest the paths of the sutras and the tantras, for you
> have found their vital root.[38]

Consequently, while being appropriate for different needs and tempera-
ments, the approaches of the Prasangika and Svatantrikas converge. The
latter is ancillary to the former. With regard to the ultimate truth in itself—the object of primordial wisdom experienced by the Aryas in meditative equipoise—Prasangikas and Svatantrikas are alike in making no
assertions. But when in the postmeditation period distinctions are made, it
is easier to divide the ultimate truth into two categories as the Svatantrikas
do. Summing up his assessment of the practical value of the Svatantrika
approach, particularly as this is enshrined in Shantarakshita's teaching,
Mipham declares:

> The intelligent should ask themselves sincerely whether they
> would be able to realize the profound view of the glorious Chan-
> drakirti (the Middle Way of primordial wisdom in meditative
> equipoise) without relying on the path set forth according to the
> present approach.[39]

Chittamatra

The four tenet systems familiar from the doxographical literature are arranged in a hierarchy of views according to the way in which they define the ultimate nature of phenomena, an ascending scale that culminates in Madhyamaka, which shows that the ultimate status of phenomena is beyond the reach of conceptual and verbal formulation.

According to the usual description, the Chittamatra, or Mind Only, school defines as the relative truth the field of phenomena that appears to the deluded mind as divided between perceived objects and the perceiving mind. In reality, however, phenomena are not separate from the consciousness that observes them. Furthermore, the mind that underlies the impression of subject and object but transcends them, being "empty" of both (*gnyis stong gi shes pa*), constitutes for the Chittamatra the ultimate ground or truth. Because the Chittamatra view establishes this ultimate as a specific entity, namely, the mind itself, it is refuted by Madhyamaka and is assigned a position lower down the doxographical scale.

The adequacy of this description of Chittamatra has been questioned. In the opinion of some modern scholars,[40] the Madhyamaka refutation is directed only against what was in effect a later distortion of the original teachings. This negative development had come about through the mistaken interpretation of certain passages, found in the writings of Asanga and Vasubandhu (400–480) to the effect that "All is consciousness." Instead of understanding such expressions in the sense in which they were intended, namely, as descriptions of meditative experiences, some later philosophers, notably Dharmapala (530–561), had interpreted them literally in an ontological sense. This led to the mistaken impression that Asanga and Vasubandhu had propounded a philosophically idealist position that "All is mind." The term "Chittamatra" has therefore been called into question as an appropriate name for the teachings of Asanga and Vasubandhu, preference being given to "Yogachara," a name that more obviously evokes the meditative context in which these teachings were first formulated.

Attractive as this thesis may be, the fact remains that no distinction is to be found in the doxographical literature between an original doctrine of Yogachara as opposed to a later idealist philosophy of Chittamatra. And in his commentary, Mipham has no qualms in using the term "Chittamatra" (*sems tsam*) on all occasions and in a manner that is evidently synonymous with the term "Yogachara" occurring in the well-established expression "Yogachara-Madhyamaka." This is not to say, however, that the distinction just mentioned is imaginary. On the contrary, it appears to be corroborated by oral tradition, which recognizes a similar, if not identical, division between (1) the scriptural Chittamatra, that is, the Mind Only teachings found in the sutras (*bka'i sems tsam*), and (2) the Chittamatra regarded as a tenet system (*grub mtha'i sems tsam*). The point of difference between these two forms of Mind Only doctrine is precisely the matter of whether the mind is considered to be a truly existent, ultimate reality. Only Chittamatra as a tenet system affirms this, and consequently it is only the tenet system that is the proper object of Madhyamaka refutation. By contrast, as recorded in the *Lankavatara-sutra* and the other scriptures that expound the Mind Only doctrine, the Buddha himself never said that the mind is truly and ultimately existent.

Without going into the question of how Chittamatra as a tenet system could have evolved from the Buddha's actual teachings and whether it constitutes a deformation of the original doctrine, the important point to bear in mind in the present instance is that, in Shantarakshita's synthesis, the adoption of the Madhyamaka view on the ultimate level necessarily implies a rejection of the fundamental position of the Chittamatra system, namely, that the mind is ultimately real. When therefore it is said that Shantarakshita accepts the Chittamatra on the conventional level, the view in question is identified as the scriptural Chittamatra (*bka'i sems tsam*) and not Chittamatra as a tenet system. It diverges from the doctrine expounded, for example, by Dharmapala, but it is nevertheless in perfect harmony with the statements of the Mind Only sutras, and this is specifically identified by Mipham as the authentic tradition of Asanga and Vasubandhu. The point is made furthermore that only the Chittamatra as a tenet system asserts the ultimate existence of the mind, and therefore it is only the tenet system that figures in the doxographical hierarchy of views, being assigned a subordinate position beneath Madhyamaka. By implication, the scriptural Chittamatra, insofar as it does not make such an assertion, escapes such a classification and need not be considered inferior to, or at variance with, the Madhyamaka view. This placing of Madhyamaka and Chittamatra (understood as *bka'i sems tsam*) on a comparable level is typical of the Nyingma approach, which resists the tendency to distinguish hierarchically the scriptures of the second and third turnings of the wheel of Dharma (placing the second above the third, or vice versa). Instead, the teachings of the two turnings are accepted as complementary. The tradition of vast activities deriving from Maitreya and Asanga and the tradition of the profound view of Manjushri and Nagarjuna are regarded as equally important. Neither should it be thought that Shantarakshita's association of the Chittamatra with the relative, and the Madhyamaka with the ultimate, truth is meant to suggest that the latter is more important than the former. For the relative and ultimate coincide in phenomena and are of equal significance. All this is a reminder that there are limits to the usefulness of doxographical classifications. The latter are summary, simplified accounts of a reality that must have been far more complex and interesting.

It is important to recall that each of the four tenet systems presents its own version of the two truths. When defining the ultimate truth of phenomena (as the partless particle, the nondual, self-knowing mind, or the emptiness of intrinsic existence), each system is in effect formulating an ontology, informing us of what phenomena actually are. When, on the other hand, these systems go on to consider the relative or conventional truth, that is, the things appearing to the senses and with which we interact (defined as, for example, gross extended phenomena, or in terms of the duality of subject and object), the point of interest is not so much what phenomena are but how they are perceived and known. Ontology gives way to epistemology. In the context of Svatantrika-Madhyamaka, this parallel association between ontology and ultimate truth, and epistemology and conventional truth, is of particular importance. In both Svatantrika subschools, the ontological question of the ultimate nature of phenomena is settled in terms of Madhyamaka. This necessarily implies that the ontological component specific to each of the non-Madhyamaka tenet systems adopted with a view to explaining the conventional truth is annulled. The Sautrantika and Chittamatra tenets are refuted on the point of their ontology but retained for what is essentially their epistemological usefulness. Bhavya, for example, does not believe in the ultimate existence of the partless particle, but finding the theory of an extramental world to be plausible on the relative level, he uses the atomic theory of the Sautrantikas as a convenient means to undermine the belief in the reality of gross extended phenomena, and as a stepping-stone to an understanding of the Madhyamaka view. Likewise, Shantarakshita does not believe in the ultimate existence of the mind, but being well aware of the philosophical difficulties involved in claiming that we can have knowledge of an objective and extramental world, he opts to present the conventional according to the much more subtle model of Mind Only. This will become clearer when we consider the role of the pramana tradition in Shantarakshita's synthesis. For the moment, it is important to keep in mind the essentially epistemological thrust of the Svatantrikas' respective explanations of the conventional truth, because it brings into focus the fact that in Svatantrika-Madhyamaka, non-Madhyamaka tenet systems are never adopted in toto on the conventional level. This would be an obvious absurdity. A "relatively true ontology" is a contradiction in terms.

What are the advantages of using the Mind Only teaching as a means to understanding phenomenal experience? Perhaps the most important effect of the Mind Only approach is to remove the enormous gulf that appears to separate the subjective observer from the "objective fact." This facilitates an understanding of the doctrine of karma, since it is understood that perceptions and experiences—even when they appear to impinge upon us from outside—are a matter of our own creation. And once one understands that experience, good or bad, happy or miserable, is the result of former action, one acquires the key to the creation of happy and wholesome states and the removal of misery. This knowledge is, for Buddhists, a source of meaning and freedom, the complete antithesis of a hopeless Heideggerian "thrownness" according to which the objective situations of life—the fact that, for instance, one is American or Iraqi, strong or weak, affluent or destitute, talented, cruel, good-natured, or whatever—are as unintelligible and uncontrollable as the chance throwing of a dice.

The Chittamatra approach emphasizes the fact that no matter how real and solid external objects may seem, all experience of them—including our knowledge about them and their apparently objective constitution—occurs wholly within the sphere of consciousness. This carries the important implication that even if one accepts the objective existence of phenomena separate from the mind, their extramental mode of existence, if such there is, is by definition unknowable. To reach beyond the mind and to experience phenomena exclusively from their side, in a complete self-contained objectivity, is as impossible as it is for us to climb out of our own skin. Indeed, the very suppositions that there is a "mind" and that there is a "world," and that there is a separation between the two, are themselves mental events.

Philosophically, Chittamatra provides us with an interesting and perhaps more cogent explanation of shared experience than realist theories do. The latter can only explain the apparently parallel perceptions of several observers by an appeal to extramental objectivity, the knowledge of which, as we have just suggested, is problematic. Let us imagine that several people are looking at the same thing, a tree, for example. Their common experience is possible, the realist says, because there *really* is a tree endowed with objective existence, separate from the people observing it. It is assumed that the tree has a specific location, size, shape, color, texture, and so on. But what grounds have we for believing this commonsense assumption? A closer inspection reveals that so-called shared experiences are, at best, only approximate and never identical. There is no certainty that coexistent observers see exactly the same things. All knowledge about the tree, for example, even the understanding that there is a tree at all, must derive from perception. And perception generally depends on the kind and constitution of the sense powers available. We may assume, for instance, that humans and mosquitoes inhabit the same world, but given the very different organization of their respective sensory apparatus, it is unlikely that what they perceive is the same or even remotely similar. "Yes, of course," the realist will object. "Perceptions differ, but there must be an objective basis that gives rise to perception." This is the general assumption. But who is to say which set of perceptions—ours or the mosquito's—correspond more closely with the "real world." Even among humans, the physical considerations of location and perspective dictate that the simultaneous observation of a single thing must result in different sensory perceptions, none of which can claim to represent the object as it actually is. Because they must observe it from several locations, when different people see the "same tree," they cannot actually have the same visual experience. They see different shapes and colors according to the tree's remoteness or proximity, the angle from which it is seen, the way the light falls, and so on. Analogous sets of variables can be found for all the sense powers, and it is clear that the kind and quality of our perceptions of a given thing are imposed by factors that have nothing to do with the thing itself. Any perception of a thing is partial and inexact, and no perception corresponds to what we suppose the thing actually is. In other words, the belief that there really is an extramental object involves an assumption that goes beyond the data that are actually available to the observing mind. On a more general psychological level too, experience of a thing by different individuals varies according to their levels of interest and sensitivity. For these dictate the strength with which different aspects of things emerge. Certain characteristics of a tree, for instance, will be immediately apparent to a botanist but may completely escape the attention of the artist painting it, the civil engineer wishing to remove it, or the hurrying commuter who does not even notice it.

All such paradoxes, which emerge from a realist account of perception, are avoided by the Chittamatra view, which denies that observed objects exist in separation from the consciousness observing them. According to the Chittamatrins, the sort of world that we perceive and the phenomena that we encounter within that world are entirely a matter of the fructification of karmic seeds and tendencies lodged within the mind. Our perceptions of the world and its contents coincide (but not exactly) with the similar perceptions of other beings to the extent that the ripening of their karmic seeds resembles our own. The experience of beings is increasingly similar in proportion as their "karmic constitution" converges. It is unnecessary to go into further details at this point, but it is worth emphasizing that, from the point of view of spiritual training, the Chittamatra account of experience has, as we have already suggested, a practical application of obvious importance. Insofar as the experience of beings is explained entirely in terms of the mind, it follows that this same experience can be manipulated and transformed to the extent that the mind is understood and brought under control. The adoption of a Mind Only account in this sense consequently forms a useful basis for ethics, as also for meditative training, since it prepares the way for the tantric view of phenomena as the display of the mind. On the other hand, as Mipham mentions, the contrasting view set forth in the lower tenet systems is highly problematic. The view that there is an extramental world consisting of extended objects that may be broken down into real indivisible particles is difficult to reconcile with fundamental Buddhist ideas such as karma. If the indivisible particles that make up the universe exist separate from the mind, how are they to be accounted for? They cannot be the product of karma because, as Chandrakirti observes, karma is mind-dependent. If therefore the particles exist, they must either arise uncaused or be the product of a creator, whether purusha or some divine entity. Neither view is acceptable. By contrast, to say that the world has arisen through the power of the mind "is none other than the teaching of the entire Mahayana."[41]

This brief outline of the Chittamatra view emphasizes its psychological and pragmatic aspects. It is found to give a more satisfactory account of perception than realist theories and has a practical appeal in the sense that it focuses attention on the role of the mind in the understanding and transformation of experience.

As we have said, the Yogachara-Madhyamaka synthesis does not incorporate the Mind Only view as a complete philosophical system. Shantarakshita makes no claim that the phenomenal world *is* the mind alone, and it would be incorrect, in fact absurd, to describe Shantarakshita as a philosophical idealist on the conventional level. For according to Madhyamaka, the true status of phenomena lies beyond conceptual and verbal qualification. Nevertheless, on the conventional level, Mind Only is an epistemological account—in fact the best and most profitable account—of phenomenal appearance. Viewed in this way, as Mipham points out, Shantarakshita's understanding of Mind Only is not different from the view expressed by Chandrakirti in the *Madhyamakavatara*.[42]

The Madhyamakalankara and the Pramana Tradition

One of the features of the *Madhyamakalankara* most likely to cause trouble for the nonspecialist reader is the frequent reference to the logico-epistemological tradition of Dignaga (fifth century) and Dharmakirti (530–600)[43]—a tradition to which Shantarakshita himself made important contributions.[44] Undoubtedly the full appreciation of Mipham's commentary would require an extensive knowledge of this difficult and complex subject. This is certainly not the place to attempt even a summary exposition of these theories, but the following reflections may help the general reader to gain an overall impression of the tradition's salient features and its relevance to the *Madhyamakalankara*.

Doxographically, Dignaga and Dharmakirti are usually referred to as "Sautrantikas following reasoning" (*rigs pa rjes 'brang gi mdo sde pa*). This classification identifies them as philosophical realists (who accept the existence of an extramental world) but distinguishes them from the position of the Vaibhashikas and the "Sautrantikas following scripture" (*lung gi rjes 'brang gi mdo sde pa*), owing to, among other things, their complex and sophisticated theory of perception. Dharmakirti, whose view for present purposes will be identified with that of Dignaga, refutes the naïvely commonsense approach of the Vaibhashika system, according to which nonmental objects are known directly by the sense organs. Taking as axiomatic the essential difference between mind and matter, the Sautrantikas following reasoning explain the process of perception by positing the existence of mental aspects. These are understood to bridge the gap between the inner consciousness and the outer world. Being of a radically different nature from matter, the mind cannot enter into direct contact with physical entities but detects them indirectly via the aspects, or mental images, that these same entities are said to cast upon it, in the same way that things cause their reflections to appear in a mirror. The aspect, which is considered to be an accurate representation of the nonmental object that causes it, does not constitute a discrete entity within the mind but is best understood as a configuration of consciousness whereby consciousness itself assumes the form of the external thing. Being consciousness, this configuration is said to be automatically self-cognizant and does not require additional conscious activity for knowledge of the object (or more directly the aspect) to take place.[45] The impression that we have of being directly in touch with an external world is therefore an illusion. The mind is in direct contact only with the mental aspect, which is therefore said both to reveal and to veil phenomena. Mipham concludes his general presentation of this view with the remark that for those who posit the existence of an external world, no epistemology is "more coherent than this, and more tenable."

Attractive as it seems, the theory of aspects, or sakaravada (which resembles the representationalist theories of certain Western philosophers), turns out to be problematic when subjected to close scrutiny. And the insuperable problems that emerge oblige Dharmakirti to adopt a procedure that is of great interest, especially in relation to Shantarakshita's Yogachara-Madhyamaka synthesis. As a means of explaining perception, the mental aspect had been posited as a connecting link between material things and the nonmaterial mind. This solution, however, is only apparent; the problem is not removed but only displaced. The aspect seems to throw a bridge across the mind-matter divide. But since the aspect is itself a feature of consciousness, a new and unexplained gulf now opens between the external object, which is material, and the aspect itself, which is mental. This difficulty is the inevitable result of positing two radically different entities and then trying to connect them in terms of only one of these entities. The aspect theory tries to explain the link between consciousness and matter, but it does so exclusively in terms of consciousness. The difficulties of explaining perception within the parameters of the Sautrantika tenet system are thus insuperable. Only two solutions are possible, and both involve a rejection of Sautrantika presuppositions. Either one must posit a third principle, which is neither mind nor matter but somehow encompasses both, or one must decide that the separation between mind and matter is itself unreal. Dharmakirti adopts the second solution. When confronted by the ultimately unworkable nature of the aspect theory, he does not attempt to devise a solution in terms of Sautrantika but instead shifts his position to a Yogachara framework. This enables him to evade the difficulty rather than answer it. According to Yogachara, the aspects are produced not by external objects but by latent tendencies in the mind. Since there are no objects outside consciousness, the problem of the relation between aspects and external objects does not arise.[46]

This willingness to retreat to a more idealistic position is an important feature of Dharmakirti's system. It is also disquieting, since Dharmakirti appears to be contradicting himself on fundamental issues. His procedure, however, was essentially pragmatic and closely linked to the general strategy of defending Buddhism against its Hindu opponents, who for their part were strong believers in the reality of the external world. For his defense to be viable, Dharmakirti was obliged to present his view in terms that, at least to begin with, were acceptable to his mainly Nyaya opponents. Within the context of the philosophical confrontation, it would have served no purpose to advocate an idealist position from the outset, for this would have been rejected by the Hindus out of hand. Therefore, since his opponents were realists, Dharmakirti began by adopting the realist stance of the Sautrantika tenet system, thus creating a commonly acceptable basis for discussion. And the fact that he expresses himself in Sautrantika terms throughout most of his work does not alter the essentially provisional nature of this move. The Sautrantika position thus adopted did not, however, reflect Dharmakirti's own view. His references to Yogachara, although comparatively rare, are enough to show that he believed that it provided a more accurate and profound insight into the nature of reality. "It is well known," Mipham observes, "that Dharmakirti said, 'When I investigate outer phenomena, I take the Sautrantika as my starting point.'"[47] But in the long run, it is clear that Dharmakirti himself found this view to be inadequate, and he therefore adopted what has been called a strategy of an ascending scale of analysis, according to which "commonsensical views are subsumed by more critical but more counterintuitive views."[48] A Sautrantika approach is adopted as a point of departure, but when, in the course of investigation, problems emerge that are unanswerable in Sautrantika terms, the conclusion is inevitable that answers can be found only by adopting a more elevated, less realist view. The purpose here is not merely apologetic. For Dharmakirti, reasoning demonstrates that it is impossible to formulate a coherent theory of perception in terms of a belief in the existence of external, nonmental objects. Some form of idealism is logically inevitable. The entire thrust of his exposition therefore is to prove to his Hindu opponents that philosophical consistency demands that they abandon their belief in the real existence of entities and adopt the Buddhist position.

This logically induced progression of ideas is paralleled in the historical development of the Svatantrika-Madhyamaka tradition. Coming after Dignaga but before Dharmakirti, Bhavya had adopted the Sautrantika tenet in his presentation of the conventional truth. But as Dharmakirti shows, epistemology, if it is to be consistent, is forced to retreat from a comparatively unsophisticated acceptance of external phenomena into a more idealist position. Set against this background, Shantarakshita's acceptance of Mind Only on the conventional level, which is, as Mipham remarks, "in agreement with the view of the glorious Dharmakirti," is both natural and inevitable. Based on the principles of logic and epistemology, Shantarakshita's Yogachara-Madhyamaka synthesis is therefore shown to be superior to the Sautrantika-Madhyamaka solution of Bhavya.

Universals and Exclusions

In addition to the theory of mental aspects and the complex discussions provoked thereby, the reader of Mipham's commentary will have to contend with the question of universals. This is a large and difficult field. Basically, and once again in terms of the Sautrantika tenet as he interpreted it, Dharmakirti made a radical distinction between two kinds of phenomena. On the one hand, there are the causally efficient entities that we encounter through sense perception. These are described as *specifically characterized* (*rang mtshan*), meaning that they are things (*dngos po*) located in a given time and place and endowed with specific properties. They are impermanent, are produced by causes, and are themselves causally effective (*don byed nus pa*). These are the things that populate the "real," as distinct from the imaginary, world. Contrasted with such entities are abstract thoughts, such as the general ideas that enable us to identify and classify things, and the illusory (from the Buddhist point of view) notions of whole and separate thingness that we impute to collections of elements. These phenomena are described as *generally characterized* (*spyi mtshan*); they are nonthings (*dngos med*) and cannot be specifically pinpointed in space and time. They are static, causally ineffective, conceptually constructed entities. Above all, they are unreal.

This distinction led Dharmakirti to a wholesale rejection of philosophical realism, especially in the extreme form advocated by the Hindu Nyaya.

For the Nyaya, language is regarded as an accurate reflection of reality. When, for instance, I say, "This is a house," two things are being referred to: "this," meaning the object in front of me, and "house," meaning a general "something" that all individual houses share and that is separate from them. In saying, "This is a house," I am saying that "This is an instance of house(ness)." So far, this account of universals is familiar from Western philosophy, but for the Nyaya, universals include not only the referents of general terms (such as houseness) but the wholeness and discreteness that are normally detected in individual extended objects and are usually felt to be distinct from their parts. A cloth, for instance, is not just reducible to its threads but is an added extra that comes into being when the threads are woven together.

As a Buddhist, Dharmakirti rejects this theory. For him, wholes and general ideas are no more than unreal mental constructs, imputed onto collections of real individual elements. From the epistemological point of view, however, the rejection of universals is problematic, since without them it is difficult to elaborate a theory of knowledge. How do I know that the flat-bottomed, bulbous, water-holding object I am holding is a vase if I do not have an idea of what "vaseness" is? And if there is no such thing as "vaseness," how am I to explain my ability to identify a variety of loosely similar objects with different shapes and sizes as vases, that is, as belonging to the class of vase?

In order to deal with this matter, the earlier philosopher Dignaga, who of course recognized the necessity of general ideas, devised a way in which the arising of these ideas could be explained without an appeal to a theory of real universals as propounded by the Nyaya. He elaborated a theory to explain how general ideas are possible even though there are no general entities to which they refer. This is the doctrine of apoha, elimination or exclusion (*sel ba*), according to which, on the basis of former experiences in which the similarities between concrete objects have been observed, the mind identifies objects, not by evoking a general entity that they are supposed to instantiate but by isolating them through an exclusion of everything that they are not. When I say, "This is a house," the only real object referred to in this statement is the actual physical thing in front of me, which is indicated by the word *this*. And I am able to identify "this" as a house, not because of some real, independent "houseness" but because I can identify features that isolate it from all other things that are not houses. I identify "house" by eliminating "nonhouse."

This is of course an elementary exposition of a highly technical and complicated matter. Suffice it to say that the doctrine of apoha was vigorously attacked by the Nyaya philosophers. It was defended and consolidated by Dharmakirti and is an essential feature of Buddhist epistemological theory.

In Mipham's commentary, the references to this subject, as to other aspects of the pramana tradition, are complicated by the fact that he is obliged to deal with conflicting interpretations of Dharmakirti's thought deriving from two different traditions of logic that existed in Tibet: the so-called earlier tradition of Chapa, upheld by the Gelugpas, and the later tradition of Sakya Pandita (Sapan for short), which contested it.

In the face of Dharmakirti's uncompromising rejection of real universals, and the perceived epistemological difficulties arising therefrom, there already existed, even in India, a minority Buddhist interpretation that had tried to attenuate Dignaga and Dharmakirti's thought in the direction of a moderate realism, thus granting a certain existence to universals. Owing to what may have been no more than a historical accident, it was this interpretation that Chapa encountered and adopted.[49] Subsequently inherited by Tsongkhapa, it molded the general philosophical outlook of the Gelugpa school, fitting well with Tsongkhapa's interpretation of Madhyamaka and his strong assertion of the reality of conventional phenomena (as distinct from truly existent phenomena).

Chapa's interpretation of Dharmakirti was attacked by Sapan, who, in his celebrated masterpiece the *Tshad ma rigs gter,* strongly reffirmed Dharmakirti's antirealism. Sapan's approach, powerfully sustained (with minor differences) by Gorampa and Shakya Chokden, was accepted as normative by Sakyapas and the other non-Gelugpa traditions. On several occasions in Mipham's commentary, the reader will be able to detect the underlying tension between these rival interpretations of Dharmakirti's thought, and Mipham's preference for the antirealist interpretation of Sapan.

Before leaving this topic, it is worth pointing out that while the pramana tradition exerted an enormous influence in Tibet, its acceptance was not universal, and there has always been a current of distrust in its regard. It will be remembered that Chandrakirti had been critical of the use of Buddhist logic and epistemology in the Madhyamaka context. But although in Tibet the Prasangika interpretation of Chandrakirti came to be regarded as the supreme view, Tibetans in general have not shared his distrust of pramana. This is even more remarkable given that Atisha (982–1054) also discounted

logic and epistemology as being in any way necessary for a genuine understanding and practice of the Dharma. A Prasangika *avant la lettre* in the
sense that although he advocated this view, he had been dead more than a
century before Patsap translated Chandrakirti, Atisha had refused to teach
logic and epistemology, saying that the doctrines of Dignaga and Dharmakirti were elaborated in order to defend Buddhism against its Hindu opponents. In India, they had been relevant and (in his view) successful, but
there was little purpose in expounding them in Tibet.[50] Although, for reasons that we have already seen, this dismissive attitude toward pramana
may seem natural on the part of avowed Prasangikas (pace the paradoxical
trajectory of Tsongkhapa), the same cannot be said of the Svatantrikas.
The philosophical expositions of Bhavya and Shantarakshita are perfectly in
line with their provisional presentation of the ultimate truth, as well as with
their pedagogical concerns in regard to the conventional. The intense
interest in pramana evinced by Chapa, for example, harmonized well with
his Svatantrika leanings.

Mipham in his turn valued the study of logic and epistemology. This
was certainly not because he attached particular value to the practice of debate per se, or to the endless, hair-splitting refinement of scholastic categories, about which, if anything, he appears to have been rather skeptical.
Nevertheless, he had no doubt that certainty of understanding is of vital
importance in the establishment of the view. It is not enough to accept authoritative statements of the teaching merely on faith. The practice of the
Dharma must be grounded in an absolute conviction, and this can only
come through the exercise of reasoning, which finds its proper place in the
examination of phenomena on the conventional level. Whereas Mipham
clearly disapproves of what he considers the inappropriate use of reasoning
evinced perhaps by his Gelugpa contemporaries, he is equally trenchant in
his criticism of a tendency (more visible in his own Nyingma tradition) to
reject the use of reasoning even on the occasions when it is appropriate and
necessary.

> The Buddha's doctrine, from the exposition of the two truths on-
> ward, unerroneously sets forth the mode of being of things as it is.
> And the followers of the Buddha must establish this accordingly,
> through the use of reasoning. Such is the unerring tradition of
> Shakyamuni. On the other hand, to claim that analytical investiga-
> tion in general and the inner science of pramana, or logic, in partic-

ular are unnecessary is a terrible and evil spell, the aim of which is to prevent the perfect assimilation, through valid reasoning, of the Buddha's words.[51]

The Argument of Neither One nor Many

The *Madhyamakalankara* invokes the argument of "neither one nor many" more intensively (throughout sixty-two of its ninety-seven stanzas) than any other text in Buddhist literature. This argument is one of a series of proofs used to demonstrate that phenomena are without real existence. Different authorities give slightly varying lists of these arguments, but on the whole, their accounts coincide. Khenpo Yönten Gyamtso enumerates them as follows.[52] (1) The "diamond splinters" argument (*rdo rje gzegs ma'i gtan tshigs*), which is an investigation of causes; (2) the refutation of production of existent and nonexistent effects (*yod med skye 'gog gi gtan tshigs*); (3) the refutation of production related to four possible alternatives (*mu bzhi skye ba'i gtan tshigs*), which is an investigation of the causal process; (4) the argument of dependent arising (*rten 'brel gyi gtan tshigs*); and (5) the argument of neither one nor many (*gcig du 'bral ba'i gtan tshigs*).[53]

There were of course precedents for Shantarakshita's use of the neither one nor many argument, perhaps most notably in stanza 334 of Aryadeva's *Four Hundred*, which is repeated almost verbatim in stanza 61 of the *Madhyamakalankara*.[54] Interestingly enough, the argument was not unknown in Western philosophy, and a striking example of it can be found in the refutation of existence by the Greek skeptic Gorgias.[55]

Mipham mentions that the argument of neither one nor many is "easy to understand," and it is true that the oral transmission explains it in quite uncomplicated terms. Western scholarship, on the other hand, has discovered some rather troublesome complexities in the argument, which it is important to mention here since they have a bearing on our translation of the first stanza of the root text and of all subsequent references to the argument in both Shantarakshita and Mipham.

Essential to the force of the argument is the fact that it is based upon a dichotomy. A dichotomy consists of two mutually exclusive terms that between them are understood to cover all possible cases. There is nothing that is not one or other of these terms, and there is nothing that is both of them. For example, I may contrast an apple with an orange. The two fruits are mutually exclusive in the sense that whatever is an apple is not an orange and vice versa, and there is nothing that is both an apple and an orange. They do not, however, constitute a dichotomy, since apples and oranges do not exhaust the range of phenomenal possibilities. The world contains other things that are neither apples nor oranges. By contrast, a pairing between "apple" and "nonapple" *is* a dichotomy, since the world is certainly divided between apples on the one hand and everything that is not an apple on the other. All phenomena are contained in such a distinction. And if I am able to prove that something is neither an apple nor a nonapple, I shall have succeeded in proving that it does not exist.

Within the terms of the present argument, the pairing of "one" and "many"—or, as we shall see, "singular" and "plural"—is understood to form a dichotomy of mutually exclusive terms (*phan tshun spang ba*). The phenomena asserted "by our and other schools" are shown to fall into neither category. Therefore they do not exist.

The peculiarity of the argument stems from the fact that there is an ambivalence in the terms "one" and "many," and this has given rise to a difference of opinion as to what the pairing "one and many" actually means. Speaking numerically, when something is said to be "one," it is understood to be singular. Contrasted with this, "many" means plural. For example, we might say that there is one tree in the garden but that there are many trees in the park. When we come to grips with the notion of oneness, however, it becomes clear that "one" indicates, perhaps more fundamentally, the notion of individual and indivisible wholeness. In that sense, when we say, "The tree is one," we mean that it is, or is considered to be, a single entity. Now, it is evident that this notion of "single entity" is a prerequisite for an understanding of "one" in the numerical sense, since if things are to be accounted singular or plural, it is evident that they must first be regarded, at least provisionally, as integral, indivisible units. Of course, we all know that things are made up of parts, but the necessities of life demand that we deal with what we consider, on a more or less provisional basis, to be entire wholes. Consequently, because we accept that the tree is one, we can go on to say that there is one tree or that there are many trees in the garden.

Turning now to the word "many," we find the situation is complicated by the constraints of language. "Many" can be contrasted with "one" in a straightforwardly numerical sense, as when we say that there is one person on the bus or that there are many people. And here the contrast between singularity and plurality is well indicated (in English) by grammatical number. If, on the other hand, "many" is contrasted with "one" in the sense of integral wholeness, a different linguistic structure is required. We say "This is one," meaning that it is a "whole thing." But if we say "This is many," the use of the singular verb indicates that the thing referred to is to be understood as a manifold composed of several elements. The point to notice is that whereas "one" in the sense of integral whole is intrinsic to a numerical use of the word, the notion of composition is not relevant to the idea of simple plurality. If I say that there is one person on the bus, I must first accept that the person is a single entity. On the other hand, if I say that there are many people on the bus, I am not implying that they are composite entities but that they constitute a group of individuals.

To bring this complicated discussion to a close, the point we wish to make is that the notion of "one and many," as used in the famous argument, is to be understood in the *numerical* sense. The argument means that things are unreal because they are neither singular nor plural (meaning truly existent singular and truly existent plural).[56] It does not mean that things are nonexistent because they have neither a single nor a plural nature—if the resulting dichotomy is understood in terms of uncompoundedness (one) and compoundedness (many).[57]

The mistake just referred to becomes evident when one reflects on the nature of the dichotomy itself. The use of a dichotomy to prove the nonexistence of something requires a demonstration that the thing in question is not found within the two poles of the dichotomy. If the dichotomy is constructed in terms of uncompoundedness (one) or compoundedness (many), arguments must be adduced to show (1) that the assumption that the thing is uncompounded is false and (2) that the assumption that it is compounded is also false. The first stage of the demonstration (that there are no single uncompounded entities) is comparatively straightforward. When it comes to the demonstration that things are not compounded, however, the situation is less clear.

When things are said to be unreal because they are neither uncompounded nor compounded, it is assumed that their compounded nature is disproved by the fact that, since no individual entities can be found, the constituents of the supposedly compounded entity are themselves compounded. They themselves do not exist because they too can be broken down indefinitely into smaller and smaller parts. Composite entities do not exist, therefore, because their parts do not exist. It is concluded that the second part of the argument (that there are no compounded entities) is shown by the fact that there are no uncompounded entities to serve as their parts. This, however, is irrelevant to the kind of demonstration demanded by the dichotomy. For the task at hand is not to prove the *nonexistence* of compounded entities but to prove that entities are *not compounded*. Instead of doing this, however, the demonstration just described shows not that entities are not compounded but that they are compounded to an infinite degree.

In the *Commentary on Difficult Points*, whereas Kamalashila defines "one" in terms of partlessness (*cha med*),[58] he does not conclude that "many" means "part possessing" (*cha bcas*). He says simply that "many means diversity."[59] At no time during the oral exposition of the *Madhyamakalankara*, on which this translation was based, was the argument of neither one nor many explained in terms of a contrast between uncompoundedness and compoundedness. Moreover, on the several occasions that we consulted our Tibetan teachers on this question, they invariably insisted that the uncompounded-compounded dichotomy was a needless complication. It could perhaps be understood as an application of the argument of neither one nor many, but this is not the latter's primary meaning. On the contrary, they said, the argument simply means that phenomena have no real existence because it can be shown that there is not one truly existent thing and there are not many truly existent things. Truly existent phenomena are neither singular nor plural. The dichotomy is a linguistic one—a matter of grammatical number. Everything must be either singular or plural; there is nothing that can be neither. This is perhaps a surprising conclusion, but it is worth noting that, in contrast with Western logic, which from the time of the Greeks was constructed on a mathematical model, Indian logic was profoundly influenced by the study of grammar, which in ancient India was highly advanced.[60] The disquieting feature of this interpretation (it must be admitted) is that although the concepts of singularity and plurality do seem to form a dichotomy, it is a dichotomy of a special sort in which the law of the excluded middle does not operate. Normally speaking, the disproving of one side of a dichotomy automatically proves the other. In demonstrating that the object in front of me is not an apple, I am proving that it is a nonapple. This is not so with the argument of neither one nor many, for in this case both sides of the dichotomy are proved or disproved together at a single stroke, and it is difficult to see how it could be otherwise. The demonstration that there is no "one" is the proof also that there is no "many."[61] Having spent sixty stanzas showing that there are no single entities, Shantarakshita dispenses with the problem of plural entities in two. Since nothing is truly singular, nothing is truly plural.

The Translation

The character of translation varies according to need, ranging from free and literary interpretation to word-for-word keys for those who require help in reading a text in its original language. In the present case, our primary task has been to convey as accurately as we could the meaning of the original for those who are unable to read the text in Tibetan, and in this we have endeavored to produce a version that, while being of use to serious students, will not be totally opaque to the nonspecialist. The structure of the Tibetan language, particularly in its learned literature, is quite different from English and when translating it, it is very rare that a slavish adherence to the original wording and sequence of ideas produces anything other than an awkward and turgid result. Although it is the duty of translators to keep as close to the original as the character of their target language allows, translation from Tibetan, if it is to be readily intelligible, frequently calls for a good deal of what might be called "judicious paraphrasing." In trying to produce what we hope will be a serviceable tool for English-speaking students, we have provided as much supplementary information as possible, whether in the form of endnotes or by interpolations in the text itself, enclosed in square brackets in the case of extraneous information coming from the translators, or else in parentheses or without punctuation where the material is deemed indispensable to an understanding of the text itself. In making these contributions, we have been scrupulous in following the extremely erudite explanations of an acknowledged authority and holder of the textual transmission and interpretative tradition deriving from the original authors. This being said, it must be admitted that the production of a perfect rendering of Mipham's masterpiece would be a staggering feat and we ask the indulgence of the reader in respect of a task that lies well beyond our powers.

The Textual Outline

The textual outline, or sabche (*sa bcad*), is an important feature of Tibetan commentary. It is the traditional means of showing the structure of an original text, marking out its divisions and subdivisions according to the perceptions and analytical skills of the commentator. Once created, it acts as a kind of interpretive lens through which one can identify, in light of the commentator's insights, the different parts of the text, appreciating the way in which they relate to each other. It is no exaggeration to say that the textual outline of a commentary constitutes the commentary itself in its most essentialized form. It is for this reason that, as a means to assimilating the content of a text, students in the Tibetan commentarial colleges often commit its entire sabche to memory. Memorization of course plays a vital role in such a setting, where the texts studied are completely without footnotes, endnotes, tables of contents, indexes, and bibliographies—the comparatively modern inventions of Western scholarship. It is usual for a Tibetan khenpo to begin each teaching session with a recitation of the part of the sabche for the text already covered. This has the effect of reminding the students of the commentary already explained and preparing them for the sequel.

Although the sabche is traditionally embedded in the text itself, it seems desirable, when making a translation into a Western language, to extract and present it separately in as clear and convenient a form as possible, the aim being to show the way the text is organized. The sabche can also be used as a revision tool, since it facilitates the task of recalling both the structure and contents of the text and fixing them in the memory without too much difficulty.

The task of laying out a sabche in a user-friendly format that might fit easily on a standard book page is not an easy matter, the main obstacle being what may be called the "textual levels" of the commentary. To give an idea of what is meant by this term it may be useful to consider how a sabche actually appears within the fabric of a Tibetan composition.

In composing a commentary a Tibetan author might begin as follows: "This text is divided into three: the preamble, the text itself, and the conclusion. The first (i.e., the preamble) is divided into five." The author will then list the titles or subject matter of the five subsections and then resume, "The first (that is, the first of the five subsections) is divided into two." These subsections will then be listed, and the author will continue, "Now the first . . ." meaning first of the two subsections. Let us imagine that this first subsection has no further divisions. The commentator will then begin an explanation of the point just reached. When this is complete, he or she will continue, "As to the second . . ." and move on to an explanation of the second of the two subsections.

So far, we have what may be regarded as three textual levels: (1) the tripartite division of the entire book, (2) the five divisions of the preamble and (3) the two points pertaining to the first of the preamble's five subsections. This same procedure will be repeated for the text itself, the explanation of which may involve many more textual levels and any number of sections and subsections. When this is complete, the conclusion follows, itself equipped with whatever divisions the commentator deems fit.

Given this method of organizing a text, it should in principle be possible to create an outline in diagrammatic form showing—perhaps by means of symbols and indentations—the different levels of text and their various divisions, thus making it possible to thread one's way through the labyrinth without too much difficulty. Unfortunately, this kind of solution is made difficult if not impossible by physical considerations of page size. An elaborate commentary may have so many levels as to confound even the most ingenious of page designers. In the present instance, for example, Mipham's commentary has no fewer than twenty-two levels. In the face of such complexity, other solutions have been tried, notably a numerical system intended to record both the level and number of textual subdivisions (1, 2, 3; 1.1, 1.2; 1.1.1, 1.1.2; and so on). But with a text of any degree of complexity, one is rapidly confronted with a string of figures so long as to be completely useless. For it is certain that the unhappy reader will have long since given up trying to keep track of the level and subdivision reached.

As an alternative solution to this problem, we suggest the following scheme. In the outline, the headings of the commentary are listed as they appear in the book. The figure at the beginning of each heading shows the textual level to which it belongs. Consequently 1. *The exposition of the root verses* (page 70) and 1. *The necessity for the explanation of the root verses* (page 77) are headings of the first level and constitute the primary division of the text. The rest of the headings follow, showing the divisions and subdivisions principally of the first of these two sections. When consulting the outline, it is important to remember that the headings of any given level are directly subordinated to the most recently occurring heading of the preceding level. For example, the headings 4. *The two truths identified* (page 70), 4. *Answers to the objections made to this distinction* (page 75), and 4. *The benefits of understanding the two truths correctly* (page 76) are all subdivisions of 3. *An examination and establishment of the two truths* (page 70). By contrast, 4. *An outline of the tradition in which the Chittamatra and Madhyamaka approaches are combined* (page 76) and 4. *In praise of this path* (page 77) are divisions of 3. *The conclusion: a eulogy of this approach to the two truths* (page 76). The latter, together with the level 3 heading already mentioned are themselves divisions of 2. *The text itself* (page 70).

Technical Note

Over the last half century, there has been some disagreement in Western scholarship on the use of the terms *Madhyamaka* and *Madhyamika*. The adoption of the latter term on all occasions is supported by eminent Sanskritists such as T. R. V. Murti, a member of the Sanskrit Commission set up by the Indian government in 1959. The prevalent custom nowadays, however, which is also justified by learned authority and which we have decided to adopt in the present translation, is to use *Madhyamaka* for the system and *Madhyamika* for its advocates. This has the advantage of bringing the name of the system into line with the form invariably used in the titles of the great Indian texts: *Mulamadhyamaka-karika*, *Madhyamakavatara*, *Madhyamakalankara*, and so on.

In order to facilitate pronunciation for nonspecialist readers, the names of Indian scholars, texts and philosophical systems have been spelled phonetically and not according to the system of Sanskrit transliteration with diacritical marks (thus, Shantarakshita, Chandrakirti, Yogachara, *Yuktishashtika*, and so on).

Phonetic spelling has also been used for Tibetan names, although the transliteration according to the system devised by Turrell Wylie has been added in the endnotes. When Tibetan expressions are cited in the body of the text, only the Turrell Wylie transliteration has been used.

Acknowledgments

This translation of Shantarakshita's root text and Mipham Rinpoche's commentary was made possible by the detailed and immensely learned exposition of Khenchen Pema Sherab of Namdröling, the exiled foundation of Peyul monastery in Bylakuppe, India. To him we owe our deepest gratitude for his precious oral transmission and untiring patience in answering our innumerable questions. In addition, we would like to thank Khenpo Nyima Döndrub of the same monastery for his invaluable clarifications of difficult points and his generous, good-humored encouragement. The teachings themselves, as well as the translation project, were made possible through the great kindness and enthusiastic support of Jigme Khyentse Rinpoche, to whom we owe an ongoing debt of gratitude.

The text was translated by Helena Blankleder and Wulstan Fletcher of the Padmakara Translation Group. We would like to thank Dominique Messent for kindly sharing the fruits of her research and allowing us to read her unpublished doctoral thesis. We would also like to thank Jennifer Kane for her help in providing reference material. It goes without saying of course that all inaccuracies, misunderstandings, and clumsiness of expression are our responsibility alone.

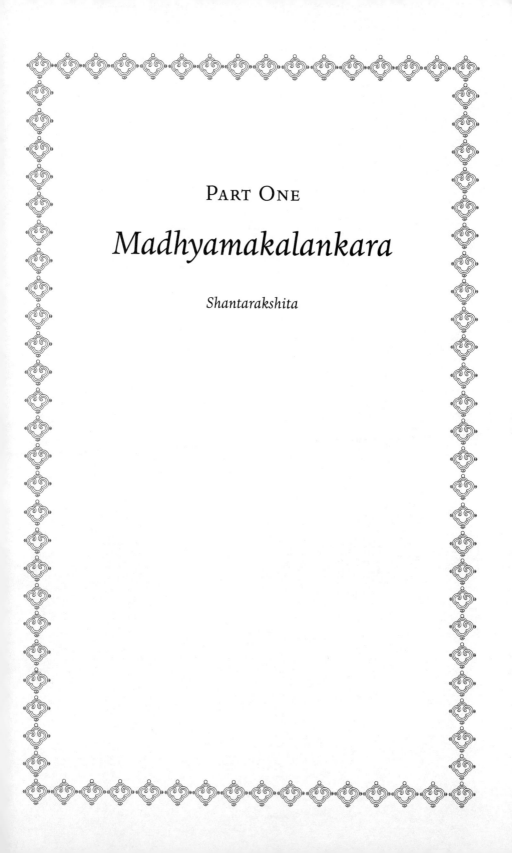

PART ONE

Madhyamakalankara

Shantarakshita

1
The entities that our and other schools affirm,
Since they exist inherently in neither singular nor plural,
In ultimate reality are without intrinsic being;
They are like reflections.

2
Producing their effects sequentially,
Eternal entities cannot be "one."
If each of their effects is different from the others,
These entities can have no permanence.

3
And also in the schools that say the uncompounded
Is cognized by wisdom that results from meditation,
This selfsame object is not one,
For it is linked with knowing instants that arise in
    sequence.

4
If, already known to earlier consciousness,
It continues to be present to a later consciousness,
The earlier consciousness becomes the later;
The later too becomes the earlier.

5
And if the uncompounded is not present
In conscious moments earlier and later,
This very uncompounded, you should know,
Is momentary, like consciousness itself.

6
Should it arise by force of moments
That occur in sequence one by one,
It is not uncompounded.
It is like the mind and mental factors.

7
If you consider that in all these moments
The uncompounded, wholly on its own, occurs,
It must forever be or never be,
For there is no dependence upon something else.

8
What purpose does it serve to pin your fond beliefs
On what is destitute of causal potency?
What use for lustful girls to estimate
The charms or defects of a neutered male?

9
The person is not able to be pointed out
As other than existing momentarily;
It should be clearly noted
That it has no true existence in the singular or plural.

10
How can a pervasive thing be one?
For it is linked with things in different places.
Things extended, likewise, are not one;
For instance, they can be both hidden and revealed.

11
Joining or surrounding,
Or disposed without interstices—
The particle that has a central place
Is turned exclusively toward a single particle.

12
If you insist that this is truly so
(Though it must also face the other particles),

How is it then that earth and water
And all other things extend—or maybe they do not?

13

If you say the sides that face
The different particles are different,
How comes it that the finest particle is one:
A single entity devoid of parts?

14

The particle, it's proved, does not exist inherently.
And therefore it is clear that eyes or substance and the rest,
The many things proposed by our and other schools,
Have no intrinsic being.

15

The former are their nature, or they constitute them.
The latter are the properties of particles, themselves the
    agents of all action.
Universals and instantiated things
Are only their agglomeration.

16

Consciousness arises as the contrary
Of matter, gross, inanimate.
By nature, mind is immaterial
And it is self-aware.

17

A mind that is by nature one and without parts
Cannot possess a threefold character;
Self-awareness thus does not entail
An object and an agent as real entities.

18

Because this is its very nature,
Consciousness is apt for self-cognition.
But how can consciousness cognize
Those things of nature foreign to itself?

19
The nature of the mind is absent from nonmental
    things.
How then could self-cognizing consciousness
Know other things? For you have said
That known and knower are two different entities.

20
According to the theory of the mental aspect,
Mind and object are in fact distinct.
But since the aspect is akin to a reflection,
It's by such means that things may be experienced.

21
For those who disallow that consciousness
Is modified by aspects of nonmental things—
There can be no perception
Of external objects.

22
Since they are not different from the consciousness
    considered to be one,
The aspects in themselves cannot be manifold.
And therefore it cannot be said
That it is through their power that things are known.

23
But since it is not separate from a manifold of aspects,
Consciousness itself cannot be one.
If this is not the case, you must explain
What you intend in saying that these two are one.

24
The color white, you say, and other features
Consciousness cognizes step by step,
But owing to the speed with which this happens,
Foolish people think that they are known at once.

25
But when cognitions such as those of words
        like *lata*
Are produced at extreme speed,
And therefore seem to be perceived at once,
How is it that such words do not correctly manifest?

26
In the mind that is exclusively conceptual,
There is no sequence of cognition either.
Since none of them remains for very long,
Cognitions are alike by virtue of their swift arising.

27
Accordingly, there are no objects
That are grasped sequentially.
But like their different aspects, it is thus
That objects are perceived—grasped all at once.

28
Since it is the firebrand itself
(Mistaken, in the instant, as a wheel of fire)
That clearly is perceived by visual consciousness,
It's not the latter that connects the separate instants.

29
Thus the joining of these moments
Is the work of memory.
The visual sense does not accomplish it,
For sight does not perceive the object that
        has passed.

30
All that is the object of our memory
Is dead and gone; it is not manifest.
Thus what is now appearing as a wheel of flame
Should not indeed be clearly seen.

31
And if the claim is made
That when a painting is beheld,
The many mental states that apprehend its
    aspects
Arise together, all at once,

32
In that case, even the cognition
Of a single aspect such as "white"
Becomes a manifold array,
With up and down and middle parts distinct!

33
The finest particle of something white
That's one by nature and devoid of parts,
Appearing as it is, to consciousness—
That's something I have surely never seen!

34
The five sense consciousnesses have observing
    aspects.
These regard compounded things.
And it is called the sixth that has
The mind and mental factors for its object.

35
And also in the texts of those outside the Doctrine,
Consciousness does not appear as one,
For it is said to observe entities
That are endowed with sundry properties.

36
Some say the aggregate of things is like
The multicolored onyx stone.
The mind that grasps it must be just the same,
And as a single entity it cannot manifest.

37
And also in the doctrine of the ones who say
That objects and the senses that detect them
Are but gatherings of earth and other elements,
There are no single things nor consciousnesses that
    accord with them.

38
For those who say that sound and other things
Are by their nature *sattva* and the rest,
Consciousness cannot appear as one,
For it perceives an object with a threefold nature.

39
The thing is threefold, they will say,
But consciousness is one. Now, does this mean
Perception is discordant with its object?
But how, if so, can consciousness be said to grasp it?

40
External things do not exist; it is the mind,
    they say,
Appearing variously while yet being permanent.
But whether it arises all at once or in succession,
It's very hard to say that consciousness is one.

41
Of space and suchlike,
Names are all that mind experiences.
Because these names consist of many sounds,
'Tis clear that they're perceived as manifold.

42
Even if it is allowed that there are some cognitions
That appear without diversity of object,
Ultimately it is wrong to posit them.
For thus defined, we see that they're disproved.

43

Therefore, consciousness appearing variously
At all times in accordance with the aspects of its
        object—
This is inadmissible
As something that is truly one.

44

Within the mental stream without beginning,
Through maturation of habitual tendencies,
Things manifest, yet these appearances
Are miragelike and due to the delusion of the mind.

45

This view indeed is excellent. But is this mind of theirs
An ultimate existent?
Or do they say that it is only satisfactory
When left unanalyzed? This we shall consider.

46

If consciousness is ultimately real,
It must be manifold, or else its aspects are all one.
Failing this, the mind and object are at variance
And there's no doubt that they diverge.

47

If the aspects are not different,
Moving and unmoving parts and so forth—
        all are one.
All must be in motion or at rest!
It's hard to give an answer to this consequence.

48

And even in the case of outer things,
Since these are not devoid of aspects,
All such features are contained in one:
A consequence that no one can gainsay.

49
If you say cognitions are as many
As the mental aspects,
They can be examined like the partless
     particle,
And it is hard to circumvent such scrutiny.

50
If various aspects form a single entity,
Is not this the teaching of the sky-clad yogis?
Variety is not a truly single entity
But is like various gems and other things.

51
If various items form one thing inherently existent,
How do they appear to us as various?
For some are hidden, some are not.
Now how can they be so distinct?

52
Since, they say, in consciousness itself
There are no mental aspects,
The mind, which in reality is aspectless,
Appears with aspects only through delusion.

53
But if these aspects are without existence,
How do we experience them so clearly?
Indeed there is no consciousness
That from the aspects stands apart.

54
Therefore, where there's nothing present,
Absent also is cognizing consciousness.
Likewise misery cannot be known as bliss,
Nor white cognized as something that's
     not white.

55
Unmediated knowledge of the aspects
Is untenable.
Because they are themselves not consciousness,
These aspects are like blossoms in the sky and all the
    rest.

56
What does not exist is without potency,
Unfit for aspects, like a horse's horns.
Nonexistents thus can have no power
To cause cognitions that resemble them.

57
But since these aspects are, and are indeed experienced,
How do they relate with consciousness?
Nonexistent aspects cannot share the latter's nature,
Nor indeed can they arise from it.

58
And if they are without a cause,
How is it that they can arise sporadically?
But if instead they have a cause,
Why are they not "dependent nature"?

59
And if they don't exist, then consciousness
Itself will be devoid of aspect
Like a sphere of purest crystal.
Such consciousness is surely undetectable.

60
It may be said that it is through delusion that they are
    cognized.
But whether they depend upon delusion
Or arise by reason of delusion's power,
Such aspects are indeed dependent nature.

61

No matter what we may investigate,
A single entity cannot be found.
And since there is no "one,"
Indeed there is no "many" either.

62

A thing cannot exist unless it be in singular or
    plural—
Aside from this, no other mode of being can it have.
For singular and plural
Are mutually excluding contraries.

63

Therefore, all these things possess
Defining features only in the relative.
And if I thought that in their essence they existed
    truly,
What would be the point of all my labors?

64

Only satisfactory when left unscrutinized,
Subject both to birth and to destruction,
Possessing causal potency:
Thus we understand the all-concealing relative.

65

Satisfactory if not examined,
Based upon foregoing causes,
Things arise as though they were
The causes' subsequent effects.

66

Thus it's incorrect to say that in the absence of
A (true existing) cause, the relative could not appear.
And if the latter's cause is ultimately true,
This you should indeed declare!

67

By following the path of reasoning
That's based upon the nature of phenomena,
All other doctrines are dispelled.
No room is left for false positions.

68

"It is," "It is not," "It is both"—
If from all such statements one abstains,
One cannot be the object of attack
Despite the fervor of one's adversaries.

69

Therefore, there is no such thing
That ultimately can be proved to be.
And thus the Tathagatas all have taught
That all phenomena are unproduced.

70

Since with the ultimate this is attuned,
It is referred to as the ultimate.
And yet the actual ultimate is free
From constructs and elaborations.

71

Production and the rest have no reality,
Thus nonproduction and the rest are
        equally impossible.
In and of themselves, both are disproved,
And therefore names cannot express them.

72

Where there are no objects,
There can be no arguments refuting them.
Even "nonproduction," entertained
        conceptually,
Is relative and is not ultimate.

73

Because things are perceived,
Their nature also should appear to us directly.
Then why do simple, uninstructed folk
Not see the nature of phenomena likewise?

74

Their mental stream, beginningless,
Is governed by their false belief that things are real.
All living beings therefore fail
To see the nature of phenomena.

75

Those who sound the nature of phenomena with rea-
    soning
That cuts through misconception and brings under-
    standing
Know this nature. It is known by powerful yogis also,
Through their clear, direct experience.

76

Leave aside the subjects specially defined
In philosophic texts.
For it is to the things known commonly to all—
From scholars down to women and their children—

77

That all these predicates and reasons
Are perfectly applied.
How could we counter otherwise
Such charges as "The subject is unreal"?

78

Things as they appear
I do not negate.
And therefore, unconfused,
I may set forth both predicate and evidence.

79
It should be inferred therefore
That seeds that by their kind accord with what appears,
And likewise with all thoughts of things and of non-
    things,
Are lodged within the mind from time without
    beginning.

80
And these do not occur by power of outer things,
For outer things do not exist.
Indeed the inherent existence of such things
Has been extensively refuted.

81
They appear successively and therefore are not random;
And not occurring all the time, they are not permanent.
Therefore, in the manner of habituation,
    consciousness's first arising
Issues from a moment of concordant kind.

82
Thus the views of permanence and nothingness
Are far from the teaching of this text.
When causes cease, effects will follow,
As plants derive from shoots and shoots from seeds.

83
The wise who know that in phenomena there is no self
Become accustomed to this absence of intrinsic nature.
And thus they effortlessly spurn
Defilement that arises from mistaken thought.

84
Since entities of cause and fruit
Within the relative are not denied,
All the principles of both samsara and nirvana
Are posited without confusion.

85

Since phenomena of cause and fruit
Are in this manner posited,
The pure accumulations also
Are acceptable within this scriptural tradition.

86

When a cause is pure,
Pure is the result that comes from it.
And modes of discipline are pure
That issue from a proper view.

87

Likewise from an impure cause
Impure results will also spring—
Just as it is that from false views
Sexual misdemeanors and the rest arise.

88

Since real existence is disproved by valid reasoning,
To think that things exist in truth
Is to have false understanding—
As when one trusts to things seen in a mirage.

89

And therefore on account of this,
All practice of transcendent virtues—
Like every action that arises from belief
In "I" and "mine"—will have but little strength.

90

But from the view that things have no such real existence
Great results proliferate.
For they arise from fertile causes,
Like the shoots that spring from healthy seeds.

91

All causes and effects
Are consciousness alone.

And all that this establishes
Abides in consciousness.

92
On the basis of the Mind Alone,
We should know that outer things do not exist.
On the basis of the method set forth here,
We should know that mind is utterly devoid of self.

93
Those who ride the chariot of the two approaches,
Who grasp the reins of reasoned thought,
Will thus be adepts of the Mahayana
According to the sense and meaning of the word.

94
Vishnu, Ishvara, and others do not taste
The cause of the abiding in the measureless.
And also those who are the crowns of all the world
Are thoroughly without a taste of it.

95
This perfect state, this pure ambrosia,
Alone enjoyed by Buddhas, those Thus Gone,
Who are themselves results of pure compassion,
None but they can taste of it.

96
Those who have the mind to follow this tradition
Will strongly feel intense compassion
For those who have the mind to trust
To tenets of mistaken teachings.

97
Those rich in wisdom, who perceive
To what extent all other doctrines lack essential pith,
To that extent will feel intense devotion
For the Buddha, who is their Protector.

PART TWO

A Teaching to Delight
My Master Manjughosha

A COMMENTARY ON THE
MADHYAMAKALANKARA

Jamgön Mipham Rinpoche

A Textual Outline
of the Commentary

The title headings of the commentary are listed in the order in which they appear in the book. Each entry is followed by a page number and, where appropriate, by a stanza reference. The figures at the beginning of the lines are markers of textual level. All headings of the same level are indicated by the same figure, and each heading is subordinated to the heading of the earlier level that most closely precedes it. In the present outline, the General Introduction and the Commentary are to be regarded as separate units.

PREAMBLE

To you, O peerless one, who spoke supremely well
Discoursing on the wondrous path: dependent coarising,
Which looses all the strings and fetters of samsara,
To you, Lord, Lion of the Shakyas, I bow down.

And you, remembrance of whose name destroys our foe,
The heart's long sleep in darkness of existence unoriginate,
O Youthful Sun of Eloquence, who from my loving teacher
Are inseparable, I pray you, be my guardian!

I pray to you, whom Manjughosha with his sword
    empowered
And said, "Cut off the tongues of evil speech
That flicker like the jags of lightning in the gloom of false
    belief—
With reason's blade more keen than weapons of the gods!"

The Bön and tirthika of India and Tibet's cool land,
Who hide like antelopes in vales and gorges of the thousand
    aspects
Of the views of self, are frightened merely at the sounding
    of your name;
O fearless Lion of Eloquence, to you the victory!

Your teaching most profound, adornment of the Middle
   Way,
Is like an ocean nourished by a hundred thousand
   streams of reasoning,
A place where learned masters like the naga lords
   disport and play—
'Tis here that I, a man of little worth, will enter with
   delight.

This doctrine honed by those of supreme intellect
Is understood at cost of great travail;
But through the kindness of my teacher I shall broach
This textual lineage of the learned, perfect and
   unspoiled.

The blazing fire of reasoning of him who opened thus
   this way,
In course of time has dwindled now to embers.
But if they be revived and burn like forest fires,
Let those who chatter carelessly beware!

Our Teacher, the perfect, fully enlightened Buddha, first generated the
supreme bodhichitta. He then purified his mind stream by means of the
twofold accumulation, vast like the ocean, and finally attained omniscience. The lion's roar of the Tathagata has terrified and put to flight the
entire herd of elephants and wild beasts, namely, the tirthikas who are
outside the Buddhadharma. In other words, he turned the Dharma wheel
and set forth the doctrine of emptiness free from error. The meaning of
his immaculate, unmistaken words is elicited by the path of reasoning, by
means of which one gains the eye of supreme, unshakable wisdom. One
recognizes therewith that phenomena—which, as long as they are not examined or analyzed as to their phenomenal characteristics, seem acceptable—are, ultimately, like reflections, entirely without inherent existence.
On this basis, one can rid oneself of all obscurations, both emotional and
cognitive, and can thus acquire perfect riches, the qualities that benefit
oneself and others. For those who wish to accomplish all this, the unsurpassable doctrine of the *Adornment of the Middle Way* is like a point of ac-

cess. Wherefore, in order to familiarize myself with this text and with the aim of encouraging others similar to me, I will, ever so slightly, expatiate upon its meaning.

My text has two sections, the general introduction and the commentary itself.

GENERAL INTRODUCTION

FOLLOWING IN the footsteps of the learned masters of old, I shall briefly review the *Adornment of the Middle Way* according to the system of five topics.

1. *Authorship*. The composer of this text was Shantarakshita, a great master who in both India and Tibet was renowned like the sun and moon themselves. For in his life, he attained the summit of learning and the perfection of discipline, and unquestionably reached the pinnacle of all accomplishment.

2. *Those for whom the text is intended*. This book was written for those who strive for a profound and vast wisdom that is utterly indefeasible—a certainty acquired by means of perfect reasoning, the objects of which are all the scriptural traditions of the Mahayana.

3. *Orientation*. This text is oriented toward the general teachings of the Mahayana and toward the profound sutras like the *Chandrapradipa*.

4. *General summary*. This text establishes the correct understanding of the two truths, and this by combining the Chittamatra approach for the relative truth and the Madhyamaka approach for the ultimate truth.

5. *Need or purpose*. The purpose of this text is to help people gain conviction easily in the meaning of the entire Mahayana, and thereby to attain supreme enlightenment.[62]

We will now briefly consider the above points.

1. The author of the text

When, in the *Manjushrimulatantra*, a prophecy is given of the benefactors, monks, and practitioners of the Buddhadharma, it speaks of the monks in the following terms: "In the period when the teachings of the

Buddha are declining in the world, certain monks will appear who will be kings of monastic discipline. Let there be no doubt about this." Having spoken in general terms of the fact that several leading monks or "kings" of monastic discipline would appear, the tantra specifies that out of a multitude of holy beings thus foretold, there would be a "celebrated monk whose name begins with B"—thereby giving a clear indication of the first syllable of Shantarakshita's name (namely, Bodhisattva).[63] Finally, the text predicts that they would all gain accomplishment of the Secret Mantra and attain enlightenment.

It was written in the *Lankavatara-sutra* that in later times, with the appearance of the false views of the tirthikas, a remedy would appear in the form of a guide by the name of Mati. "He will have great courage," the text declares, "and will be a teacher of the five objects of knowledge."[64] Earlier authorities have said that Mati was one of Shantarakshita's abbatial names and that he received the name Shantarakshita when first ordained. In any case, he was known by many names, and it was prophesied that he would establish the five objects of knowledge by reasoning, synthesizing into a single view all the teachings of the Mahayana. In the same way, the *Samadhiraja-sutra* declares, "In a period of degeneration[65] and endless suffering, the courageous being with enlightened mind will guard the supreme Dharma set forth by the Sugata. Thus my son in later times will preserve the teachings; and a thousand million Buddhas will turn their minds to him." This again is a clear reference to Shantarakshita. For the abbot's complete name is Bodhisattva Rakshita, if read according to the Sanskrit. Also if one reads the previous quotation, "In a period of degeneration . . ." and replaces the expression "courageous being with enlightened mind" with "Bodhisattva," it is easy to understand that it refers to Shantarakshita. *Rakshita* in Sanskrit denotes preserving or protecting. Thus this expression is a reference to his name. The fact that the quotations from the scriptures can be interpreted both literally and figuratively is a particular feature of Buddhist teachings. The master Shantarakshita used spotless reasoning to draw out the view of these two sutras, and thus opened the pathway of the union of the two approaches. This is why his coming is foretold in both these scriptures.

This great charioteer is repeatedly foretold in both the sutras and the tantras. Regarding his qualities, it is said in the colophon to the root text that "the *Madhyamakalankara-karika* was composed by the master Shantarakshita, who journeyed to the far shore of the ocean of both Buddhist and non-Buddhist tenets and placed upon his head the immaculate lotus feet of the noble Lord of Speech." The following account of Shantarakshita's extraordinary qualities has been culled from earlier sources and histories.

He was born the son of the king of the eastern territory of Zahor and took his first ordination vows from Jnanagarbha, the Sarvastivadin abbot of Nalanda, receiving the name Bodhisattva Shantarakshita. He became an expert in every branch of learning, and ascending to the rank of abbot of Nalanda, he settled every doctrinal dispute so that his reputation for erudition filled the earth like a lion's roar.

At that time there lived in the south of the country a learned brahmin. He was skilled in all the doctrines of the Hindu Vedas and had worsted in disputation every opponent, both Buddhist and non-Buddhist. No one was able to contend with him. Now, it happened that he framed within his mind the following plan. "If I went to Nalanda," he thought, "and were victorious over Shantarakshita, I should be famous throughout the land for being unassailable in debate." So he made the journey to Shantarakshita's dwelling place. When he entered, however, he saw not Shantarakshita but Manjushri, shining with the color of refined gold. He left the room and asked the bystanders where the abbot might be. "The abbot is in his chamber," they replied. So back he went, and instead of what he had seen before, there was the abbot himself. It was then that he realized that no one would be able to prevail in debate against someone who had so completely accomplished the supreme deity. Filled with faith, he abandoned all thought of disputation. With great devotion he placed Shantarakshita's foot upon the crown of his head and thus entered the door of the Doctrine. This is an example of how Shantarakshita was, throughout his life, without a rival.

When he went to Tibet, he said to the king Trisongdetsen: "If anyone, Buddhist or otherwise, wishes to contend with us, if the contest is to be one of magical prowess, there is none in the world greater than Padmasambhava. Let them strive with him. But if it is a matter of reasoned disputation, let them debate with me. For at the moment, in all the world, there is no one more learned than myself. Having reduced all opposition, we will establish the Buddha's Doctrine, and the king's intention will be fulfilled."

This great master founded the tradition of the Yogachara-Madhyamaka, and of all panditas of this tradition he was like the crest jewel on the banner of victory: clear, sublime, and noble. His life and activities may be summarized under four topics: his scholarship, his monastic discipline, his spiritual attainment, and his excellent qualities generally.

With regard to Shantarakshita's scholarship, those in the noble land of India who upheld the tradition of this great charioteer were the masters Haribhadra, Kamalashila, Dharmamitra, and in fact the majority of scholars. Jnanapada, Vimuktasena, Haribhadra, Abhayakara, and so on also established the view of Prajnaparamita in accordance with this tradition. Previous to Shantarakshita, there had been a few masters (Vimuktasena being one of them) who already advocated a Yogachara-Madhyamaka approach. Nevertheless, it was the master Shantarakshita who clearly propounded, as a full-fledged philosophical system, the tradition of Madhyamaka in harmony with the Chittamatra view, which denies the reality of extramental objects. This the most learned scholars have proclaimed with one voice, as can be rationally demonstrated and understood by consulting the Sanskrit texts.

The great proponents of Madhyamaka were as follows. The founding texts of the tradition were composed by Nagarjuna and his heart son Aryadeva. Then there was Chandrakirti, who established the Prasangika approach; Bhavaviveka, who advocated the view of Sautrantika-Madhyamaka; and Shantarakshita who established the view of Yogachara-Madhyamaka. In the early period in Tibet, the latter tradition was upheld by the majority of great masters. In particular, the great Ngok Lotsawa, Chapa Chökyi Senge, Rongtön Chöje, and so on upheld it completely. Indeed, it was extensively explained and studied right up to the time of Je Tsongkhapa and his spiritual heirs. And he too, together with the holders of his lineage, cherished this view greatly and made commentarial notes upon it. Furthermore, all the proponents of Madhyamaka, such as Sakya Pandita, Lord of Dharma, took closely to heart the writings of Shantarakshita and his spiritual son Kamalashila. In short, if those who possess the eyes of Dharma taste of the feast of the profound crucial points of Shantarakshita's reasoning, their minds will be helplessly ravished and they will be like bees, busy in a garden of lotuses.

These days, however, it is hardly necessary to mention the exposition and study of these tenets; it is a rare thing to find anyone who is even slightly interested in this text. This being so, intelligent people should feel a certain responsibility for the propagation of it, as far and as long as possible. To put the matter briefly, those who uphold without partiality the two approaches of the Mahayana, and especially those Madhyamikas who are keenly interested in pramana,[66] will experience a natural delight in entering the tradition of Shantarakshita, the great charioteer.

As for his monastic discipline, it may be said that among the great up-holders of the vinaya in India, themselves like the range of golden mountains, Shantarakshita was, in his immaculate observance of the monastic precepts, like the supreme Mount Meru. He was the king of monks, renowned for the extreme purity of his discipline.

Concerning Shantarakshita's spiritual attainments, we should remember that even though, in principle, the actualization of the noble grounds of realization may be inferred from the qualities of elimination and realization, in practice, it is impossible for ordinary people to assess this. It is said, nevertheless, that a Bodhisattva who will no more return to the samsaric state can be recognized by his words and deeds. And we are to consider that this great abbot was able to subdue the whole world and in particular the dark, barbarous region of Tibet.

The two charioteers Nagarjuna and Asanga perfectly revealed the meaning of the Buddha's teaching of the Mahayana, and Shantarakshita took birth knowingly in order to create a third system, namely, the synthesis of their two doctrines. It is said moreover that he lived for nine hundred years, having blessed his body to remain until the proper time came, as foretold in prophecy,[67] when the Tibetan king Trisongdetsen would be born and when he (Shantarakshita) could propagate the teaching of the Buddha in Tibet. In other words, he obtained power over his life span. When Shantarakshita was performing the ceremony of consecration at Samye, the king actually perceived him as Manjughosha. All the images in the temple changed into wisdom deities, and a limitless miraculous display occurred that was perceived by everyone. In other words, Shantarakshita had gained power over the outer elements. Most especially in Tibet, a region that had been beyond the power of anyone to subdue, he caused the Buddhadharma to rise and shine like the sun. All these are authentic signs of accomplishments wherein he was superior to other Bodhisattvas.

Finally, Shantarakshita's excellent qualities generally were manifest in the way he benefited the doctrine and beings. The great abbot refined to perfection his practice of bodhichitta, so that the name Bodhisattva fitted him perfectly. He was as famous as the lights of heaven. Oral tradition records that, inseparable from Manjughosha, this great monk lived for many centuries and nurtured and protected the Buddhadharma in Nalanda, in the east of India, in China, and elsewhere. In particular, he inaugurated the immaculate tradition wherein the two tenet systems of the Mahayana are conjoined. All those who advocated wrong views he confuted by reasoning based on the evidence of phenomena.[68] He took as his disciples those of good karma and fostered the threefold practice of exposition, disputation, and composition. In addition, he preserved the purity of monastic discipline so that, as monk and scholar, he was unrivaled and filled the earth with excellent and fitting activities.

Most especially, by the power of his past aspirations and the bodhichitta of the Buddhas and their Bodhisattva heirs, he came to this Land of Snow, then a place of darkness that no one had been able to tame. There he encountered the king Trisongdetsen. He remembered the previous lives of both of them and how they had made prayers of aspiration together. From the manner in which the king was dressed, Shantarakshita foresaw how the king's descendants would be preserved or destroyed, and prophesied accordingly. He set forth the ten virtues, the eighteen *dhatus*, and the twelve-fold chain of dependent arising. And he uttered the prophetic instruction to the effect that the king should invite the master Padmasambhava to come and subjugate the evil spirits that could not be subdued by peaceful means. The abbot and the master together examined the ground of Samye and consecrated the images and temples that had been created. Shantarakshita then ordained the "seven who were tried" and so established in Tibet the vinaya tradition, the root of the Doctrine. He trained the translators and instructed them in their work, setting forth both the outer and inner teachings of the Dharma. By his exposition, he transmitted not only the Buddha's teaching but also all the shastras that comment on their meaning. In this way, he filled Tibet with the light of the Dharma. He overwhelmed with reasoning the hosts of Bönpos who were outside the Doctrine so that now they have only a nominal existence. This resulted in a purification of religious practice.

Before his passing, he declared that the way in which the monastic order would flourish in Tibet was linked with the manner in which his relics were disposed of. He also foresaw times of strife with regard to the view, and gave the instruction that the pandita Kamalashila should be invited to establish the teaching in all its purity, and he sent him a message to that effect. It was thus that Shantarakshita possessed an unclouded vision of the three times, whereby his loving concern for Tibet increased even more. Indeed his kindness was past imagining. The master Kamalashila was a disciple of the abbot and composed commentaries on his works concerning both Madhyamaka and pramana.

In short, therefore, so far as concerns Tibet, the abbot Shantarakshita first implanted the Dharma and then fostered its propagation. Finally, in order to protect this same doctrine, he sent, and continues to send, emanation after emanation in an uninterrupted stream, and he will do so for as long as the teaching remains. Atisha himself declared that Shantarakshita, who established the Doctrine in Tibet, and all the abbots of his lineage, together with all his emanations in the generations to come, would be of the same nature as himself.

Thus there is no doubt that both the establishment and the preservation of the Doctrine in Tibet is due solely to the power of Shantarakshita's bodhichitta and aspirations. Nevertheless, some people consider that this is thanks only to the work of their own lama or their own monastery. Such ignorance is like that of people who are unaware that even the fact that one can shave one's head or dye the robes is a manifestation of the Buddha's activity.[69]

The fame of the qualities of this great charioteer and his excellent activities pervaded the whole land and were renowned as the sun and moon. This was not at all the kind of brash, superficial fame so common in the Tibet of our day. In India, there were many panditas, both Buddhist and non-Buddhist. They would act like goldsmiths examining and testing gold (by smelting, cutting, and rubbing) and would take only the undisputed best as their teacher. India at that time was filled with innumerable panditas and accomplished siddhas. However, the Dharma king Trisongdetsen and the translators and panditas (all of whom were emanations) invited from India, a land of which they were completely ignorant, an abbot Bodhisattva whose fame had reached even them and whose reputation was beyond doubt. This was due to the fact that the extraordinary celebrity of this great master was shining unobscured like the moon amid a host of stars, the light of which fills the heavens.

Generally speaking, those who worked the most for the Doctrine of the Buddha were the eight close sons and the sixteen Arhats. These themselves returned as the six ornaments[70] and a multitude of holy beings. Of these, the great charioteer Shantarakshita was the emanation of Vajrapani, Lord of Secrets, who compiled all the teachings of the great secret of the vajra mind of all the Buddhas. Therefore, his life and qualities cannot be gauged even by those dwelling on the Bodhisattva grounds—no need to speak of ordinary people. Still, in common perception, Shantarakshita did indeed accomplish many wonderful feats both in India and Tibet. These have not been recorded in detail, however. In the present context, I have merely touched on them, basing myself on certain ancient documents, the purpose being simply to recall the kindness of the abbot Bodhisattva. On the other hand, if those who are intellectually capable assess him on the evidence of his marvelous treatises and unlimited kindness, they will consider him a Buddha in truth.

In brief, it should be understood that this treatise was composed by the magnificent master Shantarakshita, whose fame was unquestionably acknowledged in both India and Tibet.

> The good, well-spoken teachings of the Buddha our
>   Protector
> Asanga has explained in perfect texts, according to the
>   mode of vast activities,
> And Nagarjuna has presented them according to the
>   view profound.
> These two great masters thus are famous as the sun and
>   moon.
>
> The learned who came after them, in keeping with their
>   methods,
> Set forth this stream of eloquence according to one side
>   or to the other.
> They thus have failed, till now, to taste and savor to the
>   full
> The banquet of the Buddha's supreme vehicle.
>
> But now this twofold teaching, ocean of instruction,
> You have imbibed in one great draft of reason and
>   analysis;
> Wherefore the vast expanses of the firmament you now
>   adorn
> With clouds of all the doctrines of the Mahayana.
>
> Through having gained the ultimate, the heart of sky-
>   like peace,
> The glorious Moon in beauty sails above the triple
>   world.

Through seeing the conventional, like rainbow hues
   unmixed,
The Dharma's Fame resounds throughout the earth.[71]

And yet the supreme scholars who explained their
   words,
Relying for their transport on a splendid palanquin of
   texts,
Were wanting strength to fathom in a single, easy stroke
The broad range of the two unsullied sources of
   cognition.

But you, in three great strides, have taken in
This great expanse of reasoning concerned with the two
   truths,
And thus you have adorned the all-supporting earth
In various ways with many kinds of argument.

The twofold chariot path of the tradition
Together with the third, which binds these two in one,
These three are gateways to the Buddha's Mahayana;
Aside from them no other may be found.

And as you once compiled the words of all the
   Buddhas,[72]
So in this text you unify the teachings of the supreme
   vehicle.
The sunlight of this text, which is the essence of
   profound and crucial points,
Has scattered the obscurity that weighed upon
   the earth.

The vital teachings of the supreme vehicle, unbounded,
   inconceivable,
Are gathered here with brief, compendious argument.
This perfect text, which sets forth all with ease—
I prize it as the diamond vidya-mantra.

1. Those for whom the text was composed

At this point, three questions should be asked: What is the Mahayana? What are its scriptural traditions? What is the nature of the wisdom elicited by the reasoned examination of scripture?

First, adopting the attitude of bodhichitta, which is the cause, one develops to the full, on the path of the ten paramitas, the three qualities of perfection, maturing activity, and purification.[73] By this means, the fruit is gained, the union of the two kayas, namely, buddhahood. This defines the Mahayana path.

As for the Mahayana scriptures, there are the writings of both the Chittamatra[74] and the Madhayamaka. These excellent traditions are beyond the scope of non-Buddhist philosophers, as also of the Shravakas and Pratyekabuddhas. They are utterly true and unsurpassed in profundity.

Concerning the nature of the wisdom to be elicited by the reasoned examination of the Mahayana scriptures, it is not sufficient merely to have interest and faith in these true and profound teachings. One must generate unshakable certainty, and this comes through the path of perfect reasoning alone. The immaculate wisdom that arises therefrom is both profound and vast. On the side of profundity, all the teachings of the Mahayana have the same honeylike taste—they establish the great Madhyamaka, free from all ontological extremes. As for the vast aspect, this is so called because, without the need of discarding even one letter of the Mahayana pitakas, which were spoken by the Buddha and belong to the Madhyamaka and Chittamatra traditions,[75] this wisdom unites them into one essential statement, in which both are perfectly present. The effect of this wisdom is that once one has gained confidence in such learning, the resulting conviction is utterly unshakable. This is what is meant by "gaining faith through knowledge." It is thus that one enters the authentic path. This text is therefore intended for people who know that the possession of the correct view is the beginning and the very eye of the path and who, on this basis, strive to acquire such certain wisdom for themselves.

1. The general orientation of the text

This treatise investigates "five objects of knowledge" and defines their nature. And since these are an epitome of the whole of the great vehicle, as will be explained later, this text is a commentary on the entire doctrine of the Mahayana. In particular, this text shows the spotless teaching of the *Lankavatara-sutra* and of profound sutras such as the *Samadhiraja-sutra Re-*

quested by Chandrapradipa. On the conventional level, the Chittamatra approach is clearly and repeatedly exhibited by words such as those taken from the *Lankavatara-sutra:*

> *There is no outer form,*
> *For such is but projection of the mind itself.*
> *Because they have not understood the mind,*
> *The simple think that objects are compounded.*

Regarding the two truths, as this scripture says:

> *All things exist within the relative,*
> *While, in the ultimate, they have no real existence.*
> *And that which lacks existence but is misperceived,*
> *That very thing is relatively true.*

The position in which the two approaches (of Chittamatra for the relative and Madhyamaka for the ultimate) are synthesized is also alluded to in this sutra:

> *If you think that there is only mind,*
> *You will not grant existence to the outer world.*
> *And dwelling in the perfect observation of the ultimate,*
> *You will indeed transcend the mind itself.*
>
> *Now, when this mind you thus transcend,*
> *You go beyond the absence of perception.*
> *Yogis who abide within such nonappearance*[76]
> *Behold indeed the Mahayana.*
>
> *Spontaneous are their actions then, and they find peace.*
> *And through their aspirations they see everything as pure.*
> *For them there is the highest wisdom; where the self is not*
>   *observed,*
> *They do not see a blank vacuity.*[77]

The lack of intrinsic existence on the ultimate level is explained in the *Lankaravatara-sutra* and also, specifically, in the *Samadhiraja-sutra:*

> If the nature of the mind is understood,
> Even in the outer world, primordial wisdom will arise.[78]

And:

> Compounded things and uncompounded things
> The wise perceive. And when these dual perceptions melt
>   away,
> The wise abide within a state devoid of every feature,
> In perfect knowledge that phenomena are empty.

And again:

> "Is" and "is not"—both are extreme views.
> "Clean" and "unclean" likewise are extremes.
> Yet when the wise transcend them both,
> Even in the "middle" they forbear to dwell.

And again:

> Devoid of sound and word, it is unspeakable,
> And spacelike is the nature of phenomena.
> If this supreme reality is understood,
> Unending power of wisdom will be gained.

It is by means of these and other scriptures that the character of the approximate ultimate and the actual ultimate is clarified. As Shantarakshita said in his autocommentary, the *Madhyamakalankara-vritti*:

> For thus I have composed this text, adorned with jewels
> Of reasoning and the texts of scripture.[79]
> Let Bodhisattvas grasp this with their subtle minds,
> And armed with all the wealth of their intelligence,
> Let them dauntlessly reflect upon the Chandrapradipa
> And other sutras equally profound.

As Shantarakshita says, we should grasp the crucial points on which this great tradition is based. For the perfect reasoning of this tradition (invulnerable to all contrary views)[80] establishes the true meaning of the Buddha's stainless words.

1. General summary

This text inquires into the correct meaning of the two truths and the two philosophical approaches [Chittamatra for the conventional and Madhyamaka for the ultimate]. The two truths that are to be understood[81] are ascertained by these two approaches. When objects of knowledge are divided into mistaken and unmistaken, all are accommodated within the two truths.[82] The manner in which these two truths are evaluated by the mind, be it completely wrong, partially correct, or perfectly unmistaken, accounts for the existence of a variety of tenet systems, whether Buddhist or non-Buddhist.

The first to be discussed is the non-Buddhist Samkhya school founded by Kapila. This tradition speaks of purusha and prakriti, the latter being the three gunas in equilibrium. Both purusha and prakriti are considered absolute realities. The modulations occurring in prakriti are considered to be relative, deceptive phenomena. When, through the practice of the path, the eyes of samadhi are attained, these same modulations are recognized as having the nature of prakriti, and they merge with it. When this happens, purusha, which is the conscious entity, is freed from the objects that bind and deceive it. Henceforth, it abides separate and alone, and this is what the Samkhya considers to be *moksha,* or liberation.

The Vedanta posits a single supreme self, which has the nature of pure consciousness. This alone exists and is all-pervading like space. It is the absolute. Although this self manifests in the multiplicity of phenomena, the latter are unreal; for they are one and the same with the self, which is pure consciousness. Therefore, phenomena, the world and its contents, which appear to have an individual existence separate from this self, are considered relative. Through meditating correctly on this supreme self, and freeing themselves from ignorance, whether innate or contrived, the Vedanta practitioners achieve union with this great self, as when a vessel is broken and the space that the vessel contained and the great space outside it become indistinguishable. This for them is liberation.

In the different Vedic schools, certain gods like Brahma, Vishnu, and Shiva are adopted as divinities. These are believed to be eternal, absolute realities, whereas the phenomena produced by their creative activity are considered ephemeral and deceptive. Eternal deliverance is said to be attained when the level of these deities is achieved. In order to obtain this, the adepts practice austerities and yoga; they make offerings and engage in meditative absorption, pranayoga, and so forth.

There are a great many other tenet systems, differentiated by name and theory, such as the one that says that the self and space are permanent, existing in and of themselves from all eternity. If summarized, however, they all affirm the existence of a permanent entity that is the cause of either bondage in samsara or liberation from it. These eternalist traditions affirm the reality of liberation, but since they believe in permanent being or entity, they advocate wrong-headed austerities whereby they claim to accomplish the path. In our text, all the theories propounding a permanent entity will be dealt with in due course and will be refuted one by one.

The Charvakas, or materialists, say that the whole of existence is accounted for in the four elements that appear to perception. Since all conscious experience (object, sense organ, and consciousness) is caused by the power of these elements, these same elements embody the absolute. Everything that arises from these elements, and later subsides, is naturally ephemeral and deceptive. Therefore, there is no such thing as a path to be practiced, no such thing as the karmic law of cause and effect related to past and future lives. The present consciousness manifests abruptly in the embryo thanks to the admixture of the elements in the womb. It is like the power to intoxicate that occurs newly when certain ingredients ferment and produce beer. It arises newly and abruptly; it does not derive from a preceding moment of consciousness. For as long as one remains in the world, one has mind and breath; but when death occurs, the body disappears into atoms, like a lamp going out, while the mind itself just evaporates into space. No new existence follows and therefore no karmic retribution, no spiritual progress, and no liberation. The various experiences of pleasure and of pain, the roundness of peas, the sharpness of thorns, the Charvakas say, are simply what they are. They arise by themselves. There are no underlying causes of things, no agent that brings them into existence. Consequently, for as long as life persists and the body and mental consciousness remain together, the sole object of the Charvakas' concern is themselves.

Regarding the refutation of this view, the idea that the four elements exist can be dismantled using the reasoning that disproves the theory of the indivisible particle, while the belief that there are no prior or subsequent existences can be disposed of using the reasoning that refutes the notion of uncaused origination. All this will be understood from the reasoning given in this text during the exposition of the relative truth.

It is thus that non-Buddhist doctrines all presuppose the existence of phenomena. The eternalists regard the self or creator as real and everlasting, and even the nihilists have a gross clinging to the material reality of the objects of perception experienced in this present existence. When this is terminated and destroyed, there is nothing to act as a link between future and past existences.

Thus, however various may be the false and deceptive teachings posited by these schools, in the last analysis they all come down to one thing, the assertion of a truly existent entity. Because all these worldly paths are posited from the point of view of the ordinary mind (which sees only partially and is concomitant with beginningless, coemergent ignorance), it follows that, even though there is an infinite variety of beliefs, none of them ever gets beyond the assumption of true existence. It is like a person suffering from jaundice. He or she can perceive a variety of different objects (a conch, the moon, silver, and so on), but all of them appear yellow. None of those who entertain such wrong beliefs can withstand the great lion's roar of the view of No-Self. They have different ideas about what is relative and what is ultimate, and may even entertain a superficial view of emptiness, but they leave untouched the root of clinging to reality. Such people are mistaken in their understanding of the two truths.

The Buddhist schools, which are of course superior to the worldly paths, are arranged in a hierarchy according to their understanding of the two truths, whether partial or perfect. The two substantialist schools, Vaibhashika and Sautrantika, make many different assertions, but they both affirm that if an extended object is susceptible to destruction (whether physically or by mental analysis—to the point where the object is no longer identifiable), it constitutes a relative truth. By contrast, indivisible instants of consciousness and indivisible particles of matter are irreducible and are therefore ultimately true. For if they did not exist, there would be no basis for the extension of gross objects, whether material or mental, and thus no phenomena could appear—just as there can be no cloth without threads. The five aggregates, which are themselves made up of many particles of matter and instants of consciousness, are produced and disintegrate constantly at every moment. Focusing on them, one thinks "I," but in fact no self is to be found, only the aggregates. Since these aggregates have no characteristics conforming to a self (in the sense

understood by ordinary people), they are not identical with it. For this reason, the self that is grasped as permanent, single, independent, and so
forth, has no existence. Sautrantikas and Vaibhashikas believe, however,
that indivisible, infinitesimal particles and moments of consciousness
(which are empty of this self) do exist. They are however instantaneous
and momentary. With respect to the path, the Sautrantikas and Vaibhashikas meditate on the personal no-self, with the result that, after ex-
hausting the emotions of samsara, the root of which is the view of the
"transitory composite" [the sense of "I"], they gain complete liberation
from the three worlds of samsara. They are reborn no more and attain, so
they believe, a nirvana beyond suffering.

When the Buddhist substantialists comment on such passages in the sutras as "Phenomena do not exist," they explain them away saying that they
are expressions of disdain or else examples of poetic exaggeration. They say
that because things are "contemptible," in the sense that they are, in the
present moment, unstable and impermanent, the Buddha said that they do
not exist. They also say that since things that do not exist (namely, those that
have passed into nonexistence or are yet to arise) are far more numerous
than those that actually do exist, the latter were spoken of as nonexistent.[83]

The adherents of the Chittamatra school regard the nonexistent and
merely "imputed" dualistic appearances of subject and object as relative.
The basis of these appearances is the mind of "dependent nature," which,
in its ultimate condition, is pure consciousness, self-knowing and self-illuminating. This mind, empty of the dualism of perceived extramental object
and perceiving subject, is considered by them to be "the completely existent
nature," the ultimate. They think that if there is no consciousness to act as
the basis for the phenomenal appearances of samsara and nirvana, the latter would be as nonexistent as sky-lotuses. They therefore regard the pure,
self-knowing mind alone as an ultimate reality.

The Chittamatrins therefore reject the notion of matter as something
existing outside the mind, using arguments such as the refutation of indivisible particles. The extramental world cannot be logically accounted for.
In order to explain the appearance of objects such as mountains, fences,
and houses, which are undeceiving and undeniable, they say that such
things, which do not have extramental, material reality, appear in the manner of hallucinations and are like dream visions. The cause of such appearances is the pure consciousness alone, which is knowing and clear like an
immaculate jewel but is governed by the coloring of various habitual ten-

dencies, pure and impure. This consciousness takes the appearing aspect of these tendencies to be outer objects and is known as the mind of dependent nature—a notion not unlike the (Madhyamaka) idea of interdependence. As with our inveterate desires and fears[84] and the yogic visualizations of unattractiveness, it is through the effect of habitual tendencies ingrained in us from beginningless time that we experience the appearances of bodies, possessions, places, and so forth. But ordinary people naïvely fail to recognize these things as manifestations of their own minds. They consider that the mind is here and the object over there, and they imagine that there is a gulf separating the perceiver from the perceived object, which they assume to be real. But this is just as if they thought that an elephant seen in a dream is an extramental reality and not the mind's projection. It is not how things are. The reality of extramental objects is no more than an imputation or imagination; these same things, in other words, are illusory. The ultimate nature of the consciousness of dependent nature, which appears as the duality of subject and object, is nothing but the self-aware, self-illuminating mind. This, from the point of view of its being empty of the two kinds of self,[85] is "completely existent reality." The Chittamatrins believe this to be the profoundest mode of being of phenomena.

To explain at greater length how the mind displays itself in various manifestations would require a discussion of the eight consciousnesses. All this may be found in the writings of the noble Asanga, where it is discussed in fine detail. One will, however, get caught in hopeless confusion if one fails to recognize the vital point that in certain texts, the dependent nature is presented from the ultimate point of view, whereas in others it is discussed in terms of the relative. If the dependent nature is considered from the point of view of its final status, that is, its actual way of being, it is ultimate. If, however, it is considered from the side of its appearing mode, it is proper to include it in the relative. It is crucial to understand this.

Now, whereas adventitious stains, which are not of the nature of the mind, are abandoned, the pure consciousness, the nature of which is luminosity, is not terminated even in the state of buddhahood. It is, so the Chittamatrins say, the basis of the manifestation of the kayas and the buddhafields.

The Chittamatrins believe that through following their system of thought, the nonexistence of the two kinds of self is perfectly realized. They claim that to assert that the imputed reality is empty by its nature, and that the dependent reality is ultimately unoriginated, amounts to the affirmation of the nonexistence of the phenomenal self. When this is investigated by the Madhyamikas, however, the fact that the Chittamatrins say that the ground of appearance is a *really existing* consciousness means that their understanding of the nonexistence of phenomena is defective and of a lesser kind.

The Chittamatrins say that the fruit of striving on the path and completing the two accumulations is buddhahood, which is essentially the transmutation of dualistic consciousness into the five wisdoms. On the level of relative truth, Bodhisattvas don the great armor of their resolve to place all living beings in the state of enlightenment. They practice for many measureless kalpas in order to gather the two boundless accumulations, and finally they attain the fruit of omniscient wisdom. Thus they are able to fulfill the hopes of beings. Over many lifetimes, the specific qualities of their minds become ever more noble, and finally they cannot but have mastery of all wisdoms and perfect qualities. Thus the path of the tradition of vast activities is both worthy and beautiful. This same path of vast activities we must therefore enter, having laid the foundation for it by adopting the Chittamatra way of positing the conventional level. The noble Asanga is celebrated as the founder of this tradition, which should be recognized as being vitally important for all followers of the Mahayana. The approach of the Chittamatrins regarding the conventional relative truth is of enormous value. The only tenet of this school to be rejected is that the self-knowing, luminous consciousness is truly existent.

The assertions of each of the Buddhist and non-Buddhist tenet systems will be briefly explained in the body of the text. For the moment we have given only the essential points with regard to their way of explaining the two truths.

> What goal is served by mind's confused rambling?
> The mind should search the naked, deeper points of
>   tenets
> That are like life itself, on which all faculties are based.
> It should be like a swan that strains the milk from water.

Within these Buddhist schools, emptiness is understood in proportion to the sharpness of mental acumen. The more the understanding of these schools approximates the mode of being of the two truths, the higher and more refined they are. However, since they are all equally incapable of transcending the notion of a truly existing basis for appearance, it is said that their presentation of emptiness is superficial and of a lesser order. In the text that we are considering, however, not even the slightest degree of a real, inherent existence is ascribed to any object of knowledge. As it is said in the *Chandrapradipa:*

> All phenomena are always empty by their nature.
> When the Bodhisattvas analyze phenomena,
> They see that all is void primordially.
> The emptiness of those who cling to some extreme is of a
> lesser kind.

Such quotations establish the Madhyamaka tradition. Now, within this tradition, some do not analyze conventional phenomena. They affirm them simply as they appear empirically in the common consensus. Others examine phenomena and assert them in the manner of the Sautrantikas and other substantialists. But in the *Madhyamakalankara,* conventional phenomena are posited in accordance with the Chittamatra view, and thus this text inaugurates, for the first time, the tradition of Yogachara-Madhyamaka.

When examined with conventional reasoning, this way of positing the relative truth is found to correspond to what, in the final analysis, is the case on the conventional level;[86] it is, moreover, in agreement with the view of the glorious Dharmakirti. In this context, it must be realized that the two kinds of valid reasoning, conventional and ultimate, have different spheres of application. Now, the best way of positing the conventional is that of the Chittamatrins, which as a method is extremely felicitous.[87] Moreover, there are many other good reasons for adopting this procedure, as will be explained in due course.

When we consider the conventional in this way, we are not asking whether phenomena exist as mental projections on the ultimate level. We are instead using conventional valid reasoning to assess phenomena that merely, and incontrovertibly, appear. It is like when someone is asked whether the appearances experienced in dreams are the mind or whether they exist separate from the mind. A sensible investigator will conclude that they are simply the mind experiencing itself and that they cannot exist outside the mind. We speak in a similar vein. However, some people muddle the two kinds of reasoning.[88] They think that to affirm a tenet that investigates conventional phenomena is incompatible with the Prasangika stance, which is to accept phenomena as they are, without analysis, according to the general consensus. It must be said, however, that in the context of pramana, or valid cognition, applied on the relative level, it is quite acceptable to say that phenomena exist according to their characteristics or that they are established by valid cognition and so forth. The important thing, however, is to distinguish (that is, not to confuse) the kind of valid cognition used in the assessment. For if conventional phenomena were assessed from the standpoint of ultimate valid cognition, they would not be even slightly established thereby. They would be just like darkness that disappears in a bright light. On the other hand, if the assessment is made from the point of view of conventional valid cognition, phenomena are, on this level, established ineluctably and undeniably. Therefore, however much conventional reasoning may be used to examine phenomena in accordance with their mode of appearance, this investigation will never become an examination on the ultimate level. We see this, for instance, in the investigations figuring in the texts on pramana, which prove the reality of earlier or later existences. In brief, no Madhyamika (whether Prasangika or Svatantrika) refutes things as they are commonly perceived. On the other hand, no Madhyamika asserts an entity that is truly and intrinsically existent. As a matter of emphasis and according to the degree of realization of the way the two truths are united, there are different ways of establishing the ultimate. But it is inappropriate to assign a high or low position to a tenet system simply on the basis of how it explains the relative. Even though one does not accompany statements like "The pot has no inherent existence" and "The pot is empty" with the specification that they refer to the ultimate level, those who are expert in tenets and in their vocabulary will understand from the context that the statement is in fact being made on the level of ultimate investigation. Likewise, they will understand that statements like "The pot is established by valid cognition" or "The pot exists according to its characteristics" are referring to the conventional level. Such people will not be confused. Others, however, are misled by words. They are full of doubt and quibble over irrelevant details. They are constantly hidebound by their own level of understanding and cling doggedly to words and formulas. Ordinary language, however, can have various meanings, and if one does not take the trouble to establish what it signifies in a given context, the meaning is not automatically conveyed with certainty. For example, the expression "true existence" is usually understood to refer to what resists ultimate analysis. This is how it is generally interpreted. On the other hand, "true" can be understood in the sense of either ultimate or relative truth. Similarly, if we consider the word "existence" in itself, there is no reason it should not be understood also as referring to the conventional level. Therefore, although some people pointedly specify that true existence is refuted only on the ultimate level, there is nevertheless room for considerable misunderstanding. In the great Indian texts, the meaning of terms is easily discerned from context, and the way in which they are formulated is excellently clear. But if, for the sake of precision, one adds certain specifications,[89] there is no harm in doing so. For speech after all serves no other purpose than to express one's thoughts.

The Prasangika texts refute "true existence" (*bden grub*) and "existence according to characteristics" (*rang mtshan nyid kyis grub pa*) indiscriminately.[90] But when one makes a distinction between these expressions—as the Svatantrikas do (refuting true existence on the ultimate level and asserting existence according to characteristics on the relative level)—one must distinguish, if one is not to confuse the issue, the two kinds of reasoning and their respective spheres. If this is not done, and if one tries to comment on a tenet simply on the strength of verbal formulations, one will achieve no more than one's own fatigue.

Therefore, in the postmeditative state, when the two truths are differentiated, one must establish clearly and without confusion the two types of reasoning that assess these same truths. If one fails to distinguish reasoning concerned with the relative from reasoning concerned with the ultimate, and if one thinks that investigation confined to the relative level is on a par with investigation on the ultimate level, the consequence is that any reference to a person entering the Mahayana and attaining enlightenment is tantamount to the claim that he or she exists ultimately.[91] By the same token, the status of so-called relative truth is placed in doubt and would in fact be negated. It would be difficult, indeed impossible, to speak about the path and the accomplishment of its result. Our opponents may object that to say that someone gains enlightenment is a statement made only on the relative level. If they do, they are adopting the language of the tradition that distinguishes the two truths (i.e., Svatantrika). And they should be aware that this same tradition also says that it is on the relative level only that phenomena either exist according to their characteristics or else are the mind only.[92] Once again, our opponents might object that statements about beings attaining enlightenment are made only in relation to the affirmations of others, but that the Prasangikas, for their part, do not assert any position of their own. This, however, contradicts the simple fact that, like everyone else, the Prasangikas, in postmeditation, also expound the grounds and paths[93] and make the assertion that phenomena are merely dependent arisings.

It should be understood that in the [Svatantrika] tradition, which affirms validly cognized conventionalities, a distinction is made between the two truths. But when this distinction is not made, it does not follow that simple conventional reasoning automatically becomes an investigation of the ultimate level.

In short, from the ultimate standpoint, the indivisibility of the two truths (as realized in meditative equipoise by primordial wisdom beyond thought and word), there is no need to make any distinction between the two truths. Phenomena are primordially beyond any thesis that affirms or negates their existence, nonexistence, both, or neither. This is similar to the way in which the Buddha answered certain questions by his silence. Since the ultimate level is beyond all conventionalities, expressions, formulations, and conceptual constructs, and since it is the very equality of all things, it is beyond all assertion. But in postmeditation, according to the appearing mode of phenomena, which is an object of words and thoughts, one reflects on the phenomena of the ground, path, and fruit. Moreover, if there is a need to explain them also to others, one cannot but engage in the refutation or establishment of things, by correctly distinguishing and using the two types of valid reasoning. It should not be thought therefore that the Svatantrika approach differs greatly from that of the Prasangikas. Svatantrikas are different in the way they talk about conventionalities, but they also establish through reasoning the ultimate view of both Nagarjuna and Asanga as being indivisible.

If one understands the matter thus, all the different disputes of Tibetan scholarship,[94] on whether conventional phenomena are established by valid cognition or not, resolve themselves quite naturally. The criticism made by certain people to the effect that the scholars of the earlier period mistook the genuine Prasangika view, and that they failed to understand correctly the view of Nagarjuna and his son, is likewise naturally dissipated.

On the other hand, when establishing the two truths, it may be thought that if the so-called relative is defined as what obscures or covers the utterly pure nature of things, this refers to impure phenomena only. By contrast, this reflection continues, pure phenomena, namely, the Buddha's kayas and wisdoms, which are untouched by ignorance, are not the relative and therefore not empty.[95] In reply to this we follow the words of the *Abhisamaya-lankara:* "One should not have even the slightest clinging to buddhahood." One should eliminate all apprehension of, and clinging to, the true reality of phenomena. As it was said, "Even if there were something superior to the supreme phenomenon of nirvana, that too should be seen as a dream and an illusion." We should be convinced of this.

There are two ways of positing the two truths. These are found both in the Buddha's own teachings and in the shastras. First, according to the reasoning that examines the ultimate mode of things, emptiness is posited as the ultimate, and appearance is posited as the relative. Second, according to conventional valid reasoning, which examines the appearing mode of phenomena, when there is an undeniable agreement between the mode of being and the mode of appearance, in both the subject and the object, this defines the ultimate. When they are in disagreement, this constitutes the relative.[96] The nature of the ultimate just mentioned, according to this second way of positing the two truths, is also emptiness. In the *Madhyamakalankara,* the definition of the two truths is in accordance with the first way.

In this regard, when objects of knowledge are divided into mistaken and unmistaken,[97] the relative truth is posited as "mistaken." By contrast, "unmistaken" refers to the mode of being of phenomena and designates their emptiness, their lack of inherent existence. Thus the so-called relative (or "all-concealing") must be understood as the appearing mode (of production, dwelling, and cessation), which, as it were, conceals and veils emptiness from the sight of ordinary beings. The relative should not, however, be understood as something deceptive and false in all its aspects, something that veils emptiness under all circumstances. This is because, for the Aryas, emptiness and dependent arising reveal each other. Therefore, mere appearance does not veil emptiness. It is due to ignorance, namely, the apprehension that apparent phenomena are truly existent, that one misperceives the nature of the object. In order to dispel the misconceptions of beings, therefore, the Buddha, skilled in means and endowed with great compassion, and in accordance with the capacity of his disciples, referred to appearances as the relative or all-concealing. He said this so that his followers might understand the ultimate truth. Appearance and the relative are indeed the same. One must understand that "appearance" refers to something that appears but does not truly exist in the way that it appears. The statement that appearances lack true existence does not necessarily call them into question. One must understand that it is the emptiness of what appears that is being referred to when one speaks of the lack of true existence. If something exists as it appears and is true *as it appears,* it cannot be called "relative." For in that case it would not be empty. And reasoning perfectly establishes that a thing that is not empty cannot be known. Among objects of knowledge, it is impossible to have a phenomenon that is either appearance alone or emptiness alone. Since this does not exist in the nature of things, no one who reasons correctly can assert it. In brief, the word "relative" indicates that what appears is empty—and this is its only meaning. Otherwise, if, when thinking about the word "relative," one understands this as a defect and something bad, and regards it as of less importance than emptiness, it will be difficult to gain the correct view of the profound Middle Way. Therefore, one refers to untrue appearances as "relative" and to their emptiness, that is, their lack of inherent existence, as "ultimate." If, in respect of all phenomena, from form up to omniscience, one understands that these two truths[98] are evenly united, without prominence being given to one at the expense of the other, this is doubtless the most important thing to understand. By the same token, one should understand that if the appearances of primordial wisdom, indivisible from the ultimate expanse, were not empty, they would be different from this expanse. Being on a par with the ultimate expanse, they have the utterly pure nature—the indivisibility of appearance and emptiness. It is only on the path of the Madhyamaka [Prasangika and Svatantrika] that the ultimate nature of the two truths is correctly realized.

We have just given a brief exposition of the two truths, together with a few reflections on them. It is now time to inquire how practitioners of the Mahayana should understand and internalize these two truths. This is done by following the stainless Mahayana traditions of Nagarjuna and Asanga. And even though the Mahayana is profound and vast, in brief it is as the *Lankavatara* says:

> Within five dharmas and three natures,
> And in consciousness in its eight kinds,
> And in the no-self of both person and phenomena,
> The whole of Mahayana is contained.

In other words, the Mahayana is gathered within the five objects of knowledge (name, sign, thought, perfectly authentic primordial wisdom, and suchness), the three natures (imputed, dependent, and completely existent), the eight consciousnesses (visual and so forth), and the absence of personal and phenomenal selves. The way the three natures and ensuing items are included in the five objects of knowledge should be understood according to the *Lankavatara-sutra*. In this context, the word "sign" refers to what appears as the characteristics of shape, solidity, and so forth (as in the case of an object like a vase). When the name "vase" is attached to the characteristics of a vase, the characteristics of all other things are implicitly excluded, and the label is identified with the vase itself. This is what is meant by a name. By giving a name to something, one gives a clear indication of what the characteristics (i.e., the sign) of that thing are.[99] These two items (sign and name) constitute imputed nature (*kun btags*) because they are the domain of words and thoughts in being the dualistic appearance of subject and object, which, when investigated, are found to be false or deceptive. All the phenomena of the mind and mental factors that apprehend the perceived object are called thoughts. They can be categorized as the eight kinds of consciousness. This refers to the dependent nature (*gzhan dbang*) and is the ground for all manifest appearance merely on the relative level. The two no-selves[100] refer to the dharmadhatu, or suchness. The subject that engages in this suchness is self-cognizing awareness (*so sor rang rig pa*) free from dualistic thought, and this is what is called the perfectly authentic primordial wisdom. The latter two items ("suchness" as the object and "perfectly authentic primordial wisdom" as the subject) are referred to as the completely existent nature (*yongs grub*).[101] This nature is not *truly* existent in itself; it is, however, the unmistaken nature of things—whence its name.

Since reasoning proves that in these five objects of knowledge, the traditions of both the Chittamatrins and the Madhyamikas are included, one should understand that they constitute the entire Mahayana. All the different outer appearances included within the sign and name do not exist truly as extramental objects. These appearances occur through the ripening of manifold habitual tendencies imprinted in the universal ground consciousness. To recognize them as dream visions belongs to the Chittamatra tradition, according to which conventional phenomena are none other than the mind. Of the five objects of knowledge, name, sign, and thought belong to the relative truth and are treated from the point of view of this tradition.

Now, although on the conventional level phenomena in all their variety are but the appearances of the mind, the mind itself does not exist truly. To understand thus that *all* phenomena, from form to omniscience, are untrue and unproduced refers to the ultimate truth. This is the path of the Madhyamaka and covers the last two items in the list of five objects of knowledge. Thus these two approaches are not contradictory. The *Sandhinirmochana-sutra* says:

> The compounded and the ultimate have been defined
> As being neither same nor different.
> Whoever understands them to be either same or different
> Has entered, and is caught, in falsity.

As it is said, the path in which the conventional and the ultimate truths are united, without any assertion of their being either identical or different, constitutes the great vehicle. An individual who adopts this approach can be properly called a practitioner of the Mahayana, and in such a case the name is being used correctly.

As a first step, at the stage of study and reflection, the two truths are combined in a manner whereby production on the conventional level and nonproduction on the ultimate level are the objects of words and concepts. In terms of this pairing, the ultimate level is called the approximate ultimate (*rnam grangs pa'i don dam*) because, on the one hand, it is contrasted with existence on the relative level and because, on the other hand, it belongs to the ultimate side of things and is counted as the ultimate. Within the context of the two truths, it is the counterpart of the relative and is simply an avenue of approach that is in harmony with the actual ultimate in itself. For if one meditates on it, it has the power to destroy one's powerful clinging to the reality of things, which has been built up by force of habit from time without beginning. It should be understood, moreover, that it is only in terms of the approximate ultimate that statements like "There is no production" are made. And the philosophical investigations implied by such statements, however perfect and far-reaching they may be, are only a means of bringing certainty in the postmeditation period. As far as concerns the authentic ultimate mode of things, however, "nonproduction" (formulated in contrast to "production") is no more than a conceptual reflection (*rnam rtog gi gzugs brnyan*) constructed through the mental exclusion of "production." For the actual ultimate in itself is beyond all conceptual constructs such as existence or nonexistence, production or nonproduction, and so on. It is not the domain of thought and language; it is what the Aryas see with the utterly stainless primordial wisdom of meditative equipoise. This is the unsurpassable ultimate. From this standpoint, the Svatantrikas make no assertion either. Now, since the approximate ultimate comes close to the actual ultimate and is in harmony with it, it is counted as "ultimate," being also referred to as the concordant ultimate (*mthun pa'i don dam*).

Those who, through practice associated with the view of the concordant ultimate, thus attain the experience of the ultimate truth in itself may be called either Prasangikas or Svatantrikas depending on the way they make or do not make assertions in the postmeditation period. But one should know that in terms of their realization there is no difference between them. They are both in possession of the wisdom of the Aryas. This is very important and will be explained further when the purpose of this text is expounded.

What is the cause of the wisdom experienced by the Aryas in meditative equipoise? It is the complete assimilation of the correct understanding of the two truths. There is absolutely no alternative to this. Only two sticks together can be used to make a fire; one stick by itself is useless. In the same way, if these two approaches[102] are not evenly united, the certainty of the state free from the conceptual constructs of the four ontological extremes can never be achieved. One may *talk* about something being beyond words and concepts, but this would be just like speaking about the *atman* even though it is supposed to be ineffable. Self-cognizing primordial wisdom (*so sor rang rig pa'i ye shes*) can never, in such a manner, attain to the depth of the ultimate nature. Therefore, having accomplished the eye of learning and reflection through perfect reasoning, and having achieved certain knowledge, one must steep oneself in it through meditation and bring it into experience. If this certain knowledge is not achieved, however, people may sit staring with wide-open eyes and say that theirs is the inexpressible freedom from conceptual extremes, but this is just pretension, mere words. And if this is sufficient to attack the root of samsara, then even the path of the Vedanta and so forth (which says that multiplicity has the same taste) can bring liberation![103]

Therefore, according to the tradition of the great charioteer Shantarakshita, the wisdom fire that comes from uniting the two spotless ways of valid reasoning, which investigate the relative and ultimate, can burn up all the tinder wood of dualistically appearing knowledge-objects, leaving nothing behind. As a result, one will remain in the evenness of the dharmadhatu beyond all conceptual extremes. When two sticks of wood are rubbed together and fire is kindled, the sticks themselves are also consumed. In the same way, the wisdom fire kindled when the two truths are truly united also consumes the apprehension of, and clinging to, the two truths as being two separate things, so that one remains in the perfect freedom from all ontological extremes: the dharmadhatu in which appearance and emptiness are indivisible.

As it is said in the *Condensed Prajnaparamita:*[104]

> *When uncompounded and compounded things, the positive*
>   *and negative,*
> *Are scrutinized by wisdom; when a single atom is no longer*
>   *found,*
> *And when the world is cleansed—then wisdom gains the other*
>   *shore*
> *And is like space without the slightest resting place.*

And:

> *Bodhisattvas, acting thus with bright intelligence,*
> *Will cut away their grasping,*
> *And they will progress though free from all desire for progress,*
> *Like brightly shining suns undimmed by the devouring*
>   *Rahu,*[105]
> *Like fires that burn, consuming forest, tree, and root.*
> *When all is cleansed through knowledge that there's no*
>   *intrinsic being,*
> *Bodhisattvas have the view of wisdom that has gone*
>   *beyond.*
> *They have no thought of agent or of things;*
> *Indeed, this is the supreme practice of transcendent wisdom.*

As we have said, this is a state inexpressible in words and concepts. It is exclusively the field of self-cognizing primordial wisdom, free from the four conceptual extremes.

As the *Avatamsaka* says:

> *The bird's path through the intermediate air*
> *Is hard to indicate and cannot be revealed.*

> *Just so, the grounds of realization of the Buddha's children*
> *Cannot be cognized as objects of the mind.*

The Aryas' clear perception of the dharmadhatu intensifies as they progress from ground to ground. Finally, the dharmadhatu, free from every trace of the twofold veil, appears directly. As the Buddha says in the *Lalitavishtara-sutra:*

> *Deep and peaceful, thought-free, luminous, unmade,*
> *The nectar-truth,*[106] *this now I have discovered.*
> *Were I to teach it, none would understand,*
> *And so I will remain, not speaking, in the forest.*

In brief, the source of all the Buddhas and Bodhisattvas of the three times is the great mother, the Perfection of Wisdom. It should be understood that when ordinary beings train in it, all false conceptions added or tacked on to what is truly the case are to be discarded through study and reflection. Then, when one has achieved the extraordinary certainty that comes through reasoning, one should settle in it in a state of even meditation. This is the only way.

The way of describing the two truths outlined previously is not the preserve of only one tradition. It is a great path of the Mahayana in general. For while all phenomena are empty of intrinsic existence, their mere appearance on the conventional level is said to have no cause other than the mind alone. The *Lankavatara-sutra* says:

> *From time without beginning mental imprints in the mind ap-*
> *pear as objects.*
> *These are like reflections in a looking glass.*
> *But if one sees them as they are, in all their purity,*
> *One finds that there are no external things.*

This shows that there are no extramental objects. All such things are but the mind.

> *The personal continuum and the aggregates,*
> *Causation and the atoms likewise,*
> *Prakriti, the creator God:*
> *All are fancies that the mind alone constructs.*

The second quotation shows that there is no creator outside the mind. This beginningless existence, composed of various phenomena, has not arisen by itself, uncaused. Neither is it brought about by extraneous causes, the passage of time, or the combination of infinitesimal particles, through God, purusha, and so forth. It has arisen through the power of one's own mind, and to speak in this way is none other than the teaching of the entire Mahayana. The venerable Chandrakirti has likewise said:

> *The vast array of sentient life,*
> *The varied universe containing it, is formed by mind.*
> *The Buddha said that wandering beings are from karma born.*
> *Dispense with mind and karma is no more.*[107]

To say that the world of appearances does not arise from the mind necessarily implies the belief that it is caused by something else. And since this involves the assertion that beings are bound in samsara or delivered from it through causes other than their own minds, it will doubtless cause one to fall into non-Buddhist tenet systems. It is therefore established step by step that if there is no external creator and no external world, extramental objects are but the mind's self-experience. Thus this assertion that conventionalities are "mind only" exists in all the Mahayana schools.

Why is it then that glorious Chandrakirti and others do not posit the conventional level in this way? As was explained above, when he establishes the ultimate in itself, which accords with the field of wisdom of Aryas while they are in meditative equipoise, it is sufficient for him to refer to, as objects of assessment, the phenomena of samsara and nirvana as they appear and are experienced on the empirical level, without analyzing or examining them. Since from the beginning these phenomena are beyond the four conceptual extremes, it is not necessary for him to enter into a close philosophical investigation of the way phenomena appear on the conventional level. When one assesses appearances with words and concepts, one may for instance say that phenomena exist or do not exist, that phenomena are or are not the mind. But however one may assert them, they do not exist in that way on the ultimate level. Therefore, with the consequences of the Prasangika reasoning, which investigates the ultimate, Chandrakirti is merely refuting the incorrect ideas of the opponents. And given that Chandrakirti's own stance is free from all conceptual references, how could he assert a theory of his own? He does not. In this way, he can refute, without needing to separate the two truths, whatever assertions are made concerning existence and nonexistence. In the present Svatantrika context, since the two truths are assessed with the reasoning specific to each of them, nothing can be refuted or established without distinguishing these same two truths. But in Chandrakirti's tradition, assessment is made using the valid reasoning that investigates the ultimate nature of the two truths united—the actual ultimate in itself (*rnam grangs ma yin pa'i don dam*). As Chandrakirti quotes from a scripture in his autocommentary to the *Madhyamakavatara:* "On the ultimate level, O monks, there are no two truths. This ultimate truth is one."

Thus the honorable Chandrakirti emphasizes and establishes the ultimate in itself from the very beginning. He does not refute mere appearances, for these are the very basis for investigation into the ultimate; they are the means and gateway to it. He therefore accepts them as a basis for debate and establishes them as being beyond all conceptual extremes. Then, in the postmeditation period, he establishes his own position and refutes those of his opponents concerning the path and result in accordance with the way they are assessed by the two kinds of reasoning. And thus even the Prasangikas make assertions on the conventional level, and these cannot be invalidated. They assert conventional phenomena as mere appearances or simply as dependent arisings. If, with regard to these mere appearances, an investigation is made using conventional reasoning, the Prasangikas do not deny the manner in which samsara and nirvana are produced through the forward and backward progression of the twelve interdependent links of existence. They show that phenomena arise dependently through the power of the pure or impure mind. And in this way they clearly express the doctrine of Mind Only.

In the present text by the great abbot Shantarakshita, emphasis is placed on the approximate ultimate. The two truths are, to begin with, distinguished, and each is established as having assertions proper to it by being examined with the appropriate kind of valid cognition. Finally, the actual ultimate truth in itself, which is completely free from all assertion, is reached. These two approaches, Svatantrika and Prasangika, belong respectively to those who follow the gradual path (*rim skyed*) and those whose realization is not gradual but immediate (*cig car*). If this is understood, it will be clear that Shantarakshita indeed possesses the ultimate and essential view of the Prasangikas. The entire passage from stanzas 67 to 72, from the words "By following the path of reasoning" to the words

"Even 'nonproduction,' entertained conceptually, is relative and is not ultimate," is in perfect agreement with the view of the glorious Chandrakirti.

Therefore, in the case of any given phenomenon, as long as the two truths are taken separately and in isolation, the validly established conventional thing on the one hand and its lack of true existence on the other are irreducible and of equal strength. But when the actual object, in which the two truths are thought of as separate, is refuted by reasoning, and when not even a subtle clinging with regard to it occurs, both the validly established thing and its lack of true existence stand simultaneously refuted and one passes beyond conceptual construction.

Thus even though the two truths are distinguished for the time being and from the point of view of the ordinary mind, the ultimate truth is established as the absence of all conceptual constructs in which the two truths are indivisible. Consequently, it is important to appreciate the difference between meditative equipoise, where the field of nonconceptual primordial wisdom is established, and postmeditation, where the field of discerning wisdom is established. One must distinguish the time when assertions are made from the time when they are not made. The ways in which we are bound in samsara and released into nirvana have no reality from the point of view of the primordial wisdom arising in meditative equipoise. They exist, however, for the wisdom operative in the postmeditation period. It is thus that the honorable Chandrakirti also explains the way in which one trains on the path and gains the fruit of buddhahood. He never said that he was restricting himself only to what appears to the perceptions of ordinary people.

Indeed, with regard to the way in which the Prasangikas assert that the experience of ordinary people constitutes the relative, some think that, of those who are interested in tenets and those who are not, the term "ordinary people" refers to the latter group. But this is a very odd thing to say. For in this context, "worldly folk" must be understood to include both those who enter the path and those who do not. For as Shantideva says,[108] there are ordinary mundane people and mundane people who are meditators. Those who have entered the path and those who have not done so both perceive, through the force of pure and impure dependent arising, various appearances that are accepted in their respective fields of experience. These same phenomena are what the Prasangikas establish as being beyond all conceptual extremes. It is not necessary for the Prasangikas to engage in a detailed philosophical analysis of conventional phenomena. They accept them as they appear to the common consensus, without further investigation. It is important to make the kind of distinction that we have just mentioned.[109] Otherwise, when a yogi discusses the path and fruit, he would have to adjust his position according to the views of ordinary worldly people, and this would be very strange.

Thus there is only one way to establish the ultimate.[110] But in general, it should be understood that the views of the two great traditions—those of Nagarjuna and Asanga, which refer to meditative equipoise and postmeditation respectively—have the same essential meaning. This is a profound question, and even those beings who have perfect wisdom, both innate and cultivated, find it hard to grasp. If someone like myself, a mere logic-chopper, were to reflect on it for a hundred years it would be hard even to puncture the shell of this profound, crucial point. But although I can do nothing on my own strength, by relying on the tradition of the vidyadhara lineage of the textual explanation of the glorious Rongdzom and Longchenpa, the king of Dharma, and others, I have gained an inkling of the truth and on this basis I have spoken. Those who meditate on ultimate reality and those who have perfected their learning in the profound and vast teachings will be quite convinced of the truth of what I have said.

> Many are the ones who talk and teach at length,
> But few are those who in their knowledge taste of this
>   deep view.
> If you have highest eloquence through your
>   unfathomed knowledge,
> The supreme flavor of the deepest meaning you should
>   now experience!

With regard to Shantarakshita's way of expounding the Mind Only view, certain later commentators on the *Madhyamakalankara*[111] consider that the great abbot did not assert a "ground-of-all consciousness" (*alayavijnana*) different from the six consciousnesses. They say that in general the word *alaya* is used to indicate a certain subtle aspect of the mental consciousness and that some great Madhyamikas and many tantrikas make the same affirmation. Since in this text the word *alaya* does not clearly appear, commentators have been able to make whatever assertions suit their purpose. On the other hand, in a view that regards phenomena as being the mind, it certainly would not make sense to deny the alaya as the receptacle in which habitual tendencies are stored. If an authentic Chittamatra doctrine is propounded (as it is done in the *Lankavatara-sutra,* the *Sandhinirmochana-sutra,* and other texts), it is certain that the alaya must be asserted. Indeed the alaya is the very heart, so to speak, of the Chittamatra tenet. And if the alaya is established, the existence of the defiled emotional consciousness is also affirmed and not contradicted—with the result that eight consciousnesses in all are necessarily asserted. In the autocommentary, Shantarakshita says: "I will briefly teach a system (vehicle) that unifies the two traditions." It seems to me, therefore, that in accordance with the quotation from the *Lankavatara-sutra* about the five objects of knowledge, the three natures, and so forth, Shantarakshita *does* affirm the alaya as asserted in the general Chittamatra.

Furthermore, a question must be asked about the subtle mental consciousness mentioned in the tantras, which (according to certain later commentators) corresponds to the alaya. But what is this consciousness? It is alleged to be "different from the six consciousnesses," but what exactly is it? If this mental consciousness, whether subtle or gross, is able to support or contain habitual tendencies like a vessel holding its contents, then it is the alaya by definition. If the subtle mental consciousness is defined in this way, then, subtle or gross, it can only be the alaya. The difference is therefore purely verbal, a matter of nomenclature. On the other hand, if the definition of the alaya does not apply to the subtle consciousness, there is no need to refer to it as such. For in that case, it would be just an empty name, like arbitrarily giving the name "horse" to an ox. In any case, if it is said that the alaya is different from the six consciousnesses, the difference must either be one of nature or else it is just a matter of a distinguishing aspect or isolate (*ldog pa*) on the conceptual level. As for the first of these alternatives, are we speaking of a different stream of consciousness, or is the difference merely one of function and the rest? If the alaya is defined as a conscious continuum different from the six consciousnesses, no one—no Chittamatrin, let alone a Madhyamika—would accept it. For if the consciousnesses do not form one continuum within the actual nature of the mind, it would follow that a single person would be host to two mind streams. If, on the other hand, there is no difference in function [between the six consciousnesses and the alaya], why use the term *alaya* at all? There is no need for it.

Again if one were to think that their difference is just a question of nomenclature, a matter of conceptual distinguishers, it would be permissible to say that there is no alaya. But since the alaya is not excluded by the expression "different from the six consciousnesses," one cannot and should not say that it does not exist. If the alaya is not posited as different from the six consciousnesses even in terms of its conceptual distinguisher, what is the word *alaya* referring to? For even on the level of terminology used to refer to the alaya and the six consciousnesses, there would be no difference between them. All this is merely an introduction to the proper examination; the subject needs to be honestly investigated.

In my opinion, the abbot Shantarakshita did affirm the eight consciousnesses, and I think that nothing but brute force can prevail against this fact—certainly not reasoning! Given that he necessarily asserts that the eight consciousnesses transmute into the five wisdoms, his tradition is a faultless teaching of the general Mahayana. On the merely relative level, to assert the existence of the defiled emotional consciousness, and also the existence of a mind that is but clarity and knowing, which pertains to no particular consciousness and is the "holder" of all the tendencies accumulated from beginningless time, does not go against the general Mahayana. Moreover, reasoning demonstrates that these two consciousnesses must exist. However, this dependent reality, which is the basis of imputed reality, is without true existence. It should be clearly understood that this has been demonstrated by Chandrakirti and others. All Chandrakirti's arguments that disprove the reflexive self-awareness[112] and the alaya apply to the Chittamatra assertion of a *truly existent* reflexive awareness. It should be clearly realized that they do not at all apply to Shantarakshita's tradition, wherein the alaya and reflexive self-awareness are asserted only on the relative level. In the same way, the reasoning that refutes, for example, the true existence of the aggregates, dhatus, ayatanas, paths, and fruit does not at all invalidate the assertions made by Madhyamikas about the same aggregates, dhatus, and so forth, on the merely relative level. On the other hand, it should be understood that something like the self—a permanent and real entity as affirmed by non-Buddhists—cannot exist even on the relative level.

In brief, if something is established as existent from the point of view of conventionally valid reasoning, it is irrefutable on that same level. Conversely, if something is invalidated by conventional valid reasoning, no one can establish it as existent on that level. Finally, if something is refuted as nonexistent by ultimate reasoning, once again, no one can establish it as existent on that level. This is simply the nature of things. To make such distinctions is extremely important in the general Mahayana of the sutras and the tantras. Thus not only in the sutras but also in the tantras, appearances are established as the mind's projection or self-experience;[113] and the nature of the mind is established as great bliss. In brief, the present text expounds a crucial doctrine that is the foundation of the views of all the sutras and tantras of the Mahayana. The Buddha said in the *Lankavatara* that all the teachings of the Mahayana are gathered in the five objects of knowledge, the three natures, and so on. This is accepted by all followers of the Mahayana. However, it was only the master Shantarakshita who established a tradition that actually shows how all this is to be taken into experience on the path. The present text therefore is of the highest importance.

Since he maintains a tradition that upholds the conventional existence of things, in which positive assertions are made using "autonomous" arguments and where emphasis is given to the approximate ultimate, Shantarakshita is regarded as a Svatantrika teacher. Nevertheless, we are not to consider that his view is inferior to that of the Prasangikas. For having inaugurated the tradition that unifies the approaches of Chittamatra and Madhyamaka, and thus englobes the entire Mahayana, he is in full accord with the ultimate union of the two truths: the ultimate expanse that dwells in neither extreme. In this respect, there is no difference whatsoever between the views of Chandrakirti and Shantarakshita.

Now, according to the view of Chandrakirti, appearances are directly purified as they stand. All false, illusory configurations of conventional phenomena dissolve into the ultimate expanse. This profound view resembles the manner in which primordial purity is established in the texts of the Great Perfection. For this reason, in our tradition of the vidyadhara lineage, this view is considered ultimate. This is something to which a lowly being like myself can only aspire. The present text, however, encompasses the whole of the Mahayana, combining the views of both Nagarjuna and Asanga in a single stream. In particular, it brings a unity to the entire ocean of reasoning, that is, the ultimate reasoning of glorious Nagarjuna and the conventional reasoning of Dharmakirti.

Ultimately, this text leads to the great Madhyamaka beyond the four conceptual extremes. It contains all the crucial points of the Buddha's teaching as contained in the Mahayana sutras and in the manner they were explained by the great charioteers and the other four of the six ornaments of India. There is nothing in the whole world to rival this excellent text. Even those who adopt an exclusive stance (whether Prasangika or Chittamatra) should honor it upon the crown of their heads and should by every means try to adopt it. It is a great and ultimate conclusion of the

Buddha's view: the ocean in which are gathered all the traditions of the great charioteers. Therefore, there is no need to ask whether—in even one meditation session—one experiences this view in harmony with the dharmadhatu; the point is that if, when hearing and reflecting on this teaching, one fails to grasp its extremely subtle and decisive points of reasoning, and proudly announces that one is Prasangika, no great benefit will come of it!

One should therefore be skillful in using this text so as to learn how to capture the crucial points of the Madhyamaka. If one masters it thoroughly, one will be like a two-headed lion, as the Tibetan saying goes. One will have the head of Madhyamaka as well as that of valid reasoning. This excellent, incomparable text, wherein the reasonings of the two truths mutually assist each other, bestows supreme erudition. It was unique even in the noble land of India. For it is only in this text and nowhere else that one encounters the supreme and sacred essence of reasoning, which unifies the distinct traditions of Nagarjuna and Asanga.

This then is a summary of the whole range of the present text. It clearly explains the two approaches of Chittamatra and Madhyamaka. One may wonder whether these two approaches occurred to Nagarjuna also. The answer is yes. In his *Yuktishashtika*, we find this stanza:

> When the elements and so forth are explained,
> All is perfectly included in the mind,
> And when one understands this mind, then all will
>   disappear—
> Does this not show them as false imputations?

When commenting on the first two lines of this stanza, he declared their meaning to be that the Buddha explained the four elements and the rest (that is, all that is formed from the elements) on the understanding that there are no objects apart from consciousness. He understood them to be consciousness itself appearing in the aspect of phenomena. He thus included phenomena within consciousness. The latter two lines of the stanza he interpreted as meaning that if one considers the elements to exist, whether as mental projections or extramental realities, it follows that when the nature of that same mind is recognized, the elements cease, for they do not appear to perfectly authentic primal wisdom; they are no more than false imputations. This is the teaching of Nagarjuna himself.

Those who properly apply themselves
To the tradition that unifies the twofold way
Will gain the Dharma kingdom of the Mahayana's
    sublime path.
Now, if I had agreed with those who question this,
They would indeed be very pleased with me.
But I have told the simple truth,
And so be patient, you who are disposed to contradict!

1. The need or purpose of this text

At this point, three questions may be asked. First, how does this text give certainty in the meaning of the whole range of the Mahayana? Second, what is meant when it is said that the approach of this text is easy? Third, how is one to gain buddhahood through the approach thus propounded?

2. How does this text give certainty in the meaning of the whole range of the Mahayana?

Broadly speaking, the term *yana*, or vehicle, refers to that which conveys us to the three kinds of enlightenment. The traditions of the Chittamatra and the Madhyamaka surpass the lesser vehicle by virtue of seven particular features.[114] In Shantarakshita's tradition, the views of these two systems of thought are not left as separate streams; they are synthesized. In order to gain certainty in this, it is important to consider the following points.

In general, the wisdom that results from meditation and experience is what brings us to the ultimate goal. If one does not get used to this unified view and fails to gain experience in it, this wisdom will not dawn. The wisdom of meditation is, in turn, the result of the wisdom deriving from reflection. For it is by reflecting correctly on the teachings that certainty is gained. And the prerequisite for this is listening to and studying the teaching of this excellent text.

Nevertheless, the mere reception of these teachings and a mere interest in them will not ensure progress on the grounds and paths. One must gain certainty in the unmistaken view, meditation, and practice, and abandon the false processes of dualistic thought. If one engages in this path, which establishes through valid reasoning the meaning of the Buddha's words— pure in terms of the three knowledge sources[115]—one will gain an extraordinary conviction in the unmistaken view, meditation, and practice. One will gain an understanding for oneself, and no one will be able to divert one from it. Seeing the great path of the Buddhas of the three times, bathed in the brilliant light of wisdom, it will be impossible not to enter it. Moreover, this conviction will come not through an external inspiration or advocacy. It will be gained not through reliance on others or the effect of some outside influence, but through the strength of one's own reasoning. This is what is meant when it is said that one will have no need of anyone else; one will be convinced on one's own account. Faith will be gained through knowledge, and thanks to this, no adversary or negative force will be able to divert one from the path.

Those who possess the eyes of such wisdom gain certainty in the unmistaken path. They have a sublime certainty that prevails over wrong views, distinguishing true from false, like well-sighted people able to distinguish forms simply by looking at them. As it was said by the Lord Maitreya:

> *The wise who sound with reasoning this perfect Dharma*
> *Are ever guarded from the demons' hindrances;*
> *They have a special confidence; all other views they*
> *   vanquish—*
> *Such are their perfect, ripened qualities that none can take*
> *   away.*

It is therefore important to realize that it is possible to train on the unmistaken path only after one has gained understanding and certainty in it. And if certainty is not gained by one's own efforts, it should be understood that even if one meditates, one is not on the unmistaken path leading to the goal.

The *Madhyamakalankara*, in which both kinds of valid reasoning are found, contains the essence of all reasoning. Through upholding just this text alone, an understanding of the profound and vast teachings of the Buddha—the entire range of the Mahayana—will be effortlessly achieved. Faith will thus be gained and wisdom will spread out on all sides, just as a fire starting from a little spark will consume an entire forest. Just as reasoning can show that this text is superior to all others, the same fact is supported by quotations from the sutras. The *Lankavatara-sutra* first expounds the meaning of the five objects of knowledge, previously explained, and then declares:

> *Those who study this approach with reasoning*
> *Will gain faith, strive in yoga, and transcend all thought.*

> *And those who thus rely on what does not abide*[116]
> *Will find a doctrine that is like pure gold.*

As it is said, the synthesis of the two approaches established by reasoning is found only in the *Madhyamakalankara* and nowhere else. It stands to reason that this text is deserving of high praise—as will become clear if one ponders well the immaculate view of the Mahayana sutras (*Lankavatara-sutra, Ghanavyuha-sutra, Sandhinirmochana-sutra, Pitaputrasamagama-sutra, Samadhiraja-sutra Requested by Chandrapradipa, Hastikakshya-sutra, Akshaya-mati-sutra, Dharmasangiti-sutra, Sagaranagaraja-paripriccha, Ratnamegha-sutra, Prajnaparamita-sutra,* and so on).

Now, in particular, the present text can be used to give sure knowledge of the five propositions specifically associated with Shantarakshita's tradition, which are eminently superior to other understandings of Madhyamaka. (1) This text posits causally efficient things (*don byed nus kyi dngos po*) as the only authentic objects of valid cognition (*gzhal bya*).[117] (2) It has a unique way of asserting reflexive awareness,[118] self-knowing and self-illuminating. (3) Given that the different phenomena of the extramental world appear by the power of the mind, it posits them as mind only (*sems tsam*). (4) It makes a distinction between the approximate ultimate truth and the ultimate in itself. (5) When establishing the approximate ultimate truth, this text regards as noncontradictory the findings of the two kinds of valid reasoning.[119] Each of these five positions serves a particular purpose.

3. The causally efficient thing is the only authentic object of valid cognition

The authentic object of valid cognition is a conventional phenomenon that is causally efficient, in the sense that it is able to perform a function.[120] By contrast, nonthings are unable to appear through their own power.[121] On the basis of real things, they are imputed or constructed by the mind through a process of elimination of all that is other than they.[122] This understanding agrees with ordinary perception and establishes that all objects of knowledge, appearing as objects of ordinary consciousness, are impermanent. Consequently, space and other compounded things are only imagined to be permanent.[123] In fact, nonthings (space, cessation, and so forth) have no positive, causally efficient reality at all; they are just imputations. For whatever is a thing must possess causal efficiency; that is, it must be able to perform a function. And if it functions, its existence is momentary. Thus it is easily established that all efficient things are impermanent. If one understands how one engages in substantial and imputed phenomena, in terms of appearance and in terms of elimination respectively,[124] one will gain a deep understanding of this first point—which is like the heart and eyes of the texts on pramana.

The theory that divides the conventional into unmistaken (*yang dag*) and mistaken (*yang dag min*) and takes the causally efficient as the ultimate truth accords with the Sautrantika view. It is also well known that Dharmakirti said: "When I investigate outer phenomena, I take the Sautrantika as my starting point." In the *Madhyamakalankara*, although it is considered that outer objects are not concealed[125] but arise through the power of the mind, the conventional assessment of their appearing mode must be performed in the way we have just mentioned [in other words, only the causally efficient thing is the proper object of assessment].

3. The self-knowing mind or reflexive awareness

The self-knowing mind (*rang rig*) exists only on the conventional level. Now, although by its nature consciousness cannot be divided into something that knows and something that is known,[126] this text shows that it is quite acceptable to give the name "reflexive awareness" to what simply has the character of experience, of clarity and knowing, and which is, in other words, the reverse of inanimate matter. It is thus that, without falling into the contradictory notion of an agent acting upon itself,[127] self-awareness is established undeniably on the conventional level. It is thanks to reflexive awareness that, conventionally, phenomenal appearances are established as the mind, and the mind is in turn undeniably established as the object-experiencer. If reflexive awareness is not accepted, the mind would be disconnected from its own experience of phenomena and the experience of "outer objects" would be impossible. This would mean the collapse of ordinary perception. Consequently, the self-knowing consciousness is the sine qua non of valid cognition on the conventional level.

3. Mind only

If one accepts that phenomena are the projection or manifestation of the mind, a true understanding of the actual mode of being of the conventional is achieved[128]—together with a confident grasp of how beings enter the samsaric process or turn away from it. According to the *ultimate* mode of being, which is beyond all conceptual extremes, referents, and characteristics, it is true that phenomena are *not* found to be the mind,[129] for this ultimate mode of being transcends the conventional. If, however, one confines oneself to the appearing mode of the *conventional* truth, the existence of extramental phenomena is invalidated by reasoning, and these same phenomena are likewise shown to be the mind only.[130] And as this assertion of phenomena does not contradict empirical experience, there is no better account of the conventional. If one examines phenomena, which are the deposit of mental habituation,[131] they are found not to exist. However, they appear incontrovertibly within the forum of our experience. This cannot be denied. Reasoning based on phenomenal evidence proves that they are merely mental appearances. They are, in other words, the mind's projections—which is to say the mind's self-experience. Beyond this is the ultimate level, which transcends the conventional. One should understand that it is impossible to posit the conventional in any way superior to this. This is also the essence of Dharmakirti's elucidation of the true status of the conventional, as perceived by the Lord Buddha with his wisdom eye. The combination of conventional valid cognition and ultimate reasoning is the particular message of this text.

The recognition that phenomenal appearance is but the play of the mind itself is a means of discovering how beings fall into samsara and how they can be liberated from it. Due to the fact that various misguided habitual tendencies have been deposited upon the mind, the unbroken continuum of samsara occurs as different kinds of dreamlike appearance. And because there is no cause for this other than the mind itself, the fact that the mind falls under the power of defiled emotion and enters into the realms of existence is not something that can be prevented even by the hand of the Tathagata. On the other hand, if one gains control over one's own mind, this very fact alone will bring everything into one's power. Indeed, it is not necessary to rely on other causes, such as making offerings to the gods or trying only to escape from the bad and seek the good. It is by mastering one's own mind that one reaches "acceptance" on the path of joining.[132] One will thus be preserved from falling once again into the lower realms, and all the qualities of the path and fruit will manifest. On the other hand, if all this were due not to one's mind but to some external force, all manner of things both good and evil would uninterruptedly appear. Someone on the path would thus be powerless to avoid suffering, for this would be the product of external forces. Consequently, the knowledge that phenomena are the mind's projection gives rise to a firm and certain understanding of how the samsaric process is set in motion and how liberation from it is to be achieved.

To establish all things as being the mind is the supreme and distinctive feature of the tenets of all the Buddhas. This indeed is the true understanding of the appearing mode of phenomena. It is the supreme crucial point of the pith instructions for meditation. It destroys the whole mechanism of existence with the sure touch of a butcher who knows exactly how to kill an animal, and like a carpenter who understands how to work his wood. And if this point is associated with extraordinary methods, it becomes the very essence of the pith instructions of the Vajrayana.

Nowadays, those who fail to find the root of the Dharma[133] in their experience and who content themselves only with putting words in their mouths depreciate the practice of examining the mind [in meditation] and exalt that of reasoning. They think that it is by logical arguments and extensive explanations that they will accomplish the path. But while it is indeed necessary to have a general understanding of the teachings through hearing and reflecting on them, it is necessary to bring them all into one essential point through the practice. In the eyes of the holy ones who take the Dharma into their hands, such people, as the *Prajnaparamita-sutra* says, "throw away the root but seek the branches. They have found the supreme food, and yet they look for scraps. They have found the elephant but still try to track it down. They fail to ask the Lord who is rich and generous in his gifts, and instead they go a-begging to a mere servant who gives them poor and meager fare." It is thus, as the scripture says with these and other examples, that arrogant intellectuals, who throw away the root of Dharma and taste only the chaff of words, despise those who have grasped the crucial point. They have a completely inverted estimation of what is important in the Dharma and what is of lesser account. By contrast, those who strive on the path of both the sutras and the tantras must have a sure confidence in the understanding that all phenomena are but the self-experience or projection of the mind. There is nothing more important than this. During the night, when one is caught up in one's dreams, if one tries to deal with them using other methods, there is no end. But if one understands that they all arise from the mind itself, all are pacified at a single stroke. We should understand that the appearances of existence, which are endless in time and unlimited in extent, are similar to the visions of our dreams.

3. A clear distinction is made between the approximate ultimate truth and the actual ultimate truth

This excellent tradition is indeed supreme. If it is not pointed out right at the beginning that phenomena have no true existence, there is no means of dispelling our mistaken clinging to reality. For we have grown accustomed to it from unoriginated time. Nevertheless, if this alone is taught as the ultimate truth, certain persons of weak understanding might think that "nonexistence" (that is, the negation of the object of refutation, namely, existence) is the ultimate reality. And clinging to such "emptiness," such people become incurable. This manner of clinging can be of two kinds. One can cling to emptiness as a positive value, a thing (*dngos po*), and one can cling to it as a nonthing, a mere absence (*dngos med*). One may say here that it is improper to cling to any conceptual extreme. But if definite knowledge, which is elicited by rational investigation and is the nectar-spring of profound emptiness (the cure indeed for all the ills of existence), is spurned in the belief that there should be no mental activity of any kind, one falls into a thick and murky state devoid of thought. This renders it very difficult to perceive this profound reality, to realize it, and to bring it into experience. As the *Mulamadhyamaka-shastra* says:

> *Those whose grasp of emptiness is poor*
> *Are brought low by the weakness of their wisdom.*
> *This is like catching snakes unskillfully*
> *And practicing the vidya-mantra without competence.*

> *Knowing therefore that 'tis hard for those of feeble mind*
> *To understand this teaching's depth,*
> *The Buddha utterly refrained*
> *From setting forth this teaching.*

Consequently, it is simply through the approximate ultimate that clinging to reality is, as a first step, destroyed. Later, by means of the teaching on the actual ultimate, clinging to nonreality is also halted. In short, there is no need to add "true existence" and so on to the four extremes (of existence, nonexistence, both, and neither). All such conceptual targets collapse and the great freedom from conceptual constructs, the profound reality to be realized by self-cognizing awareness, is easily recognized. This demonstrates the need for the approximate ultimate. On this point, it should be noted that Shantideva also says:

> *Through training in this aptitude for emptiness,*
> *The habit to perceive real things will fade.*
> *Through training in the view that all lacks "thinghood,"*
> *This view itself will also disappear.*

> "There is nothing"—when this is asserted,
> No "thing" is there to be examined.
> For how can absence, lacking all support,
> Remain before the mind as something present?
>
> When "thing" and "nonthing" both indeed
> Are absent from before the mind,
> Nothing else remains for mind to do
> But rest in perfect peace, from concepts free. [134]

It might be objected that, since it is impossible for there to be an object of reference that is not included in the four ontological extremes, if the four extremes are refuted, how is this different from the absence of all mental activity that typifies the tradition of Hashang? In fact, it is not at all the same as the position of Hashang and others, wherein perception of phenomena is blocked so that no characteristics are seen and there is no mental activity whatsoever. On the contrary, the mere arresting of mental movement—far from being the dispelling of all conceptual extremes—is not even a cause of the dispelling of the ontological extreme of existence. Freedom from discursive thoughts is not like that at all. As it is said in the *Dharmadharmatavibhanga*:

> 'Tis not an absence of mentation nor yet a pure
>   transcendence.
> It is not a pure subsiding nor the insentience of matter.
> It is not a willed fixation—but its character indeed
> Is freedom from these five conditions. [135]

Therefore, following what has been described, freedom from conceptual constructs should be understood as the state that is not adulterated with five conditions, such as an absence of mental activity, as these occur in the experience of worldly beings. Once one has used reasoning to examine phenomena and has found them to be nonexistent, if one meditates while still holding on to this "nonexistence," then, although this acts as an antidote to clinging to existence, it does not get rid of the *idea* that things are unreal. How therefore can this qualify as the freedom from conceptual constructs and as genuine primordial wisdom realizing emptiness? On the other hand, some people say that to affirm a nonimplicative negative, which negates true existence, is the view of nihilism. But the nihilist view is to deny the principle of karmic causality while assuming the true existence of things. How therefore could what has just been said be the nihilist view? Since this focusing (*'dzin stangs*) on nonexistence (which acts as the antidote to clinging to the true reality of things) is in agreement with what is actually the case, it should indeed be meditated on by beginners, just like impermanence and the unpleasant aspects of the body. But if this were taken as the actual view of the great Madhyamaka, which is free from all assertions and has the nature of nonconceptual wisdom, the latter would only amount to an inferior, conceptual view of nonexistence.

Accordingly, in the case of a beginner, it is possible for mere nonexistence (*med rkyang tsam*), the negation of truly existent phenomena, to arise as a mental object. But a person whose Madhyamaka investigation has hit the mark will perfectly distinguish the difference between the lack of inherent existence and mere nonexistence; and will be quite certain that a phenomenon's lack of inherent existence is inseparable from its dependent arising. Such an extraordinary mode of apprehension indeed acts as an antidote to the precipitous extremes of both substantialism and nihilism. For as long as, according to one's mode of apprehension, one is either refuting things or establishing them, one is not actually in the nature beyond all conceptual extremes. When, with reasoned analysis, one arrives at the certainty that phenomena do not dwell in any of the four extremes, and when one settles evenly in the dharmadhatu, by way of the self-cognizing primordial wisdom, this will have the power to dispel all conceptual constructs. Thus one will gain confidence in ultimate reality, in which there are no misconceptions to dispel and no progress to make. One will have confidence in the genuine meaning of "freedom from mental activity" as explained in the *Prajnaparamita-sutra*.

Since ultimate reality, the domain of meditative equipoise, is beyond the referential framework of the four extremes and is not the object of thought and word, it is indeed beyond any assertion. However, if one simply refrains from making assertions, while at the same time entertaining conceptual fixations (i.e., a referential framework), one's view is certainly deceptive. These two kinds of "absence of assertion" have only their name in common. In fact, one is a true absence of assertions while the other is a mere pretense. The first case is like an innocent man saying that he did not steal, and the second is like a thief saying that he did not steal (when he did).

As a means to introducing ineffable suchness, the domain of meditative equipoise, a verbal indication is given by one who possesses the certainty of the postmeditation period. When he establishes ineffable suchness by using expressions like "unborn nature," "lack of inherent existence," "emptiness," "absence of conceptual constructs," "the unobservable," "beyond extremes," and so forth, these terms express only their own particular meaning.[136] And by excluding their contraries, they do indeed appear to be making a (one-sided) assertion—which the conceptual mind grasps accordingly. In point of fact, however, such terms are given precisely in order to dispel assertions and references. For instance, statements like "I make no assertion" and "The primordial wisdom of the Buddha is not the object of thought or word" were made simply in order to deny that assertions were made and that the Buddha's wisdom is the object of thought and words. If, however, one behaves like someone who, instead of looking at the moon, looks at the finger pointing at it, and if one keeps to a stupid literalism and considers that the absence of assertions is in fact an assertion, that the inconceivable is a concept, and that the inexpressible is an expression, one's understanding of the scripture has gone completely awry. One is like the Charvakas, who claim that inference is not a valid source of cognition.[137] This is a great mistake and completely incorrect.

It is extremely important to realize that the words that point to the meaning beyond all assertions are not at variance with this meaning itself. They have the same crucial import. Expressions like "the unborn" do indeed refer to the fact that all objects of reference are empty. There can be no clinging to what is empty,[138] and thus this expression simply means that phenomena are beyond reference. The expression "absence of true existence" refers to the fact that when phenomena are analyzed, they are found to be without inherent existence. "True existence," however, is not an object of refutation separate from the thing itself, and of which the thing is empty. It is phenomena *themselves* that do not exist truly. Since one needs to avert all clinging to them, through an understanding that they do not exist truly, it is necessary to eliminate all the various modes whereby things are apprehended. If, however, there remains an apprehension and clinging to the term "lack of true existence," this is not yet the authentic view. The reasoning that shows that phenomena are without true existence is obviously able to disprove also the conceived object, namely, the "lack of inherent existence" as conceptually apprehended. The pot that lacks inherent nature has no true existence, but if the apprehension of and clinging to "the pot that does not truly exist" does not collapse, it is impossible to avert clinging to things.[139] In this case, the reasoning that aims to arrive at the ultimate status of things simply refutes the so-called true existence of things; it does not refute even one phenomenon. However, if all the apprehensions of the knowing subject are not averted, the dualistic constructs of subject and object cannot be negated as being empty. Furthermore, one will encounter three undesirable consequences, such as the one whereby the meditative equipoise of the Aryas will bring about the destruction of phenomena.[140] For if something remains unrefuted or uneliminated by the reasoning directed at the ultimate, that very thing becomes truly existent. Consequently (and in conclusion), expressions like "unborn nature" are to be used as a means of *introducing* the state of the complete absence of all conceptual constructs.

How could the profound Prajnaparamita, which is beyond all reference, possibly resemble the view of Hashang? The freedom from all four conceptual extremes belongs neither to the side of existence nor to that of nonexistence. It is the field of the self-cognizing primordial wisdom, but words and concepts are unable to express it as it is. All the same, this is verbally referred to as the inseparability of appearance and emptiness, or the Middle Way of the union of the two truths.

[One sometimes hears in this connection that] apprehension is always associated with its apprehended object. For if it were not so associated, the ultimate truth could not be seen. This would mean, however, that the wisdom of meditative equipoise (which beholds the very nature of things) is unable to perceive ultimate reality in a manner in which all perception of a separate subject and object vanishes. This kind of thing should never be said by anyone who has a profound respect for the Buddha's teaching. Although it is a profound teaching difficult to understand, this point is of the greatest importance. It is said that however one may try to explain it, it is like shooting an arrow into open space: The ordinary mind finds no point of entry. What, therefore, is the use of much talk? One should develop certainty on the path of reasoning in the union of the two truths. This is how to reach the heart of the matter without making mistakes. First, one establishes that all appearances are empty. Then one gains conviction that emptiness manifests as dependently arising phenomena. Thus emptiness and dependently arising phenomena occur in union. Though empty, phenomena appear; though they appear, they are nonetheless empty. It is thus that one "tastes without tasting" the great equality of all things: the absence of all conceptual constructs.

In order to eliminate clinging to existence, *outer emptiness* and so on was taught.[141] In order to eliminate clinging to the absence of things (i.e., their nonexistence), the *emptiness of emptiness* and so forth was taught. By these means, the freedom from all ontological extremes is reached. This is the actual ultimate truth. In that respect, the Svatantrikas do at first experience a certain clinging to the notion of the approximate ultimate. Thinking that the apprehension of the reality of phenomena deceives us and leads us into samsara, and that the object of such an apprehension is mistaken because, on the ultimate level, it has no reality whatsoever, they attach great importance to the apprehending of emptiness in the manner of a nonimplicative negative. Although the Svatantrikas refute the four extremes, they do so with provisos such as "in an ultimate sense" or "as inherently existing" or "as truly existing." And after differentiating the two truths, they go on to distinguish the way of refuting the extreme of existence from the way of refuting the extreme of nonexistence, and so on. As a result, believing that phenomena do not exist on the ultimate level, they cling to their nonexistence. And believing that, on the relative level, phenomena exist according to their characteristics (because if one were to regard them as not existing in this way, one would be denying conventional appearances), they cling to existence.

In this connection, given that the absence of production (that is, the approximate ultimate) is simply the reverse of production, one might object that, in respect of their common ground [namely, a phenomenon], production and absence of production are mutually exclusive. The answer to this is that even though a shoot is produced from a seed, there is no truly existent production. And even though, on the conventional level, this production exists according to its characteristics, it does not exist truly. The relative mode of appearance does not militate against the ultimate mode of being; there is no contradiction between production and lack of production. On the contrary, it is highly acceptable, for it is clearly demonstrated by the sheer nature of things. The two truths do not negate each other. However much one or another of these two levels of reality is investigated with the valid reasoning specific to that level, one will never establish its contrary. Thus the arguments establishing each level can be posited in an autonomous way. This is perfectly acceptable.

The Svatantrikas regard the two truths as separate and make assertions concerning each level. They therefore state their position in an autonomous manner. They say that phenomena do not exist ultimately but that they do exist conventionally. The fact that they consider the two truths to be separate is a specific object of refutation for the Prasangikas.[142] It should be understood that if the Svatantrikas were free from this point of contention (namely, considering the two truths as separate), the Prasangika view would not surpass them in the slightest way. For it is difficult to show that, in addition to the concept of freedom from the four ontological extremes beyond all assertion, the Prasangikas have anything else to eliminate.

Consequently, for as long as some kind of clinging remains and the two truths are not blended into one taste, we remain in the domain of conceptual mind, with the result that we are unable to attain to nonconceptual wisdom, the authentic Prajnaparamita, free from the thirty-two misconceptions. The Prasangikas, from the very first, establish the freedom from all conceptual constructs in which appearance and emptiness are united. In this respect, when reasoning refutes the assumption that although phenomena are without true existence, they nevertheless exist, relatively, according to their characteristics, the assumption of, and clinging to, the two truths as distinct entities (as if each of them were situated on its respective level) is destroyed and the two truths blend into one taste. All modalities of apprehension, focusing on either existence or nonexistence, vanish. Thus, in the Prasangika tradition, it is unnecessary to specify the four conceptual extremes in terms of each of the two truths, using expressions like "truly existent" or "in the ultimate." Once the conceived objects of the four extremes are refuted, the Prasangikas gain unshakable conviction in the great emptiness beyond all mental references and beyond all assertion. They gain conviction in ultimate reality, which is in accordance with the primordial wisdom of meditative equipoise experienced by the Aryas. In postmeditation, however, they posit, without invalidation, the phenomena of the paths and results, according to how these are assessed by valid reasonings concerning the two truths. This is perfectly acceptable and coherent. This concurs with the particular position of Longchenpa, who does not consider the Prasangikas as making assertions or otherwise (tout court) but who distinguishes different aspects according to whether in postmeditation they are establishing the view or expounding the path. Conviction may be gained in this if one makes a detailed examination of, for instance, the "reversal of the consequences" in the refutation of production from other.[143]

In this present text, abbot Shantarakshita first establishes the two truths using the stainless wisdom that assesses them separately; and subsequently he establishes the great ultimate truth in itself by eliminating the assumption of, and clinging to, the two truths as being separate. He establishes the ultimate that is beyond all assertions and is in harmony with the nonconceptual wisdom of meditative equipoise. The Prasangika and Svatantrika positions cannot be distinguished therefore on the level of their ultimate view. For this is the same for both.

One may object that, in that case, the Prasangika tradition (as a separate position) serves no purpose. But this is not true. For in this tradition, emptiness, which is beyond all assertion, is established by means of numerous and more detailed reasonings. Therefore, it should be understood that the authentic Svatantrika is the approach that emphasizes the approximate ultimate, while the Prasangika approach emphasizes the ultimate in itself, beyond all assertions. The distinction between Svatantrikas and Prasangikas following the assertion or denial of existence according to characteristics on the relative level, or according to their manner of constructing arguments, and so on, is only a secondary categorization and is already implied in the definition given earlier. For the questions whether assertions are made, whether existence according to characteristics on the relative level is affirmed, or whether the object of refutation (true existence) is predicated only on the ultimate level, and the manner in which the Svatantrikas and Prasangikas present their arguments concerning the absence of inherent existence—all these issues depend on whether the approximate ultimate or the ultimate in itself is emphasized, as we have just explained.

Therefore, inasmuch as certain "Prasangikas" remain on the level of the approximate ultimate truth, making assertions about the distinction of the two truths, there is no distinguishing them from Svatantrikas. All the same arguments, with which they refute phenomena as existing according to their characteristics even on the conventional level, apply also to conventional, validly established phenomena.[144] Both are similar in that neither can resist ultimate analysis. When the existence of phenomena according to their characteristics is refuted even on the conventional level, nothing is gained—apart from making it more difficult to talk about empirical experience! In any case, the Svatantrikas do not themselves say that phenomena exist according to their characteristics in a manner that resists investigation into their ultimate status. Therefore, what grounds have their contestants for claiming that *their* method of realizing the ultimate is superior?

Since, therefore, the great abbot Shantarakshita actually unifies the Prasangika and Svatantrika approaches, his text is indeed the ornament of the entire Madhyamaka tradition. Why then are the terms "Prasangika" and "Svatantrika" used? The Svatantrikas, or Autonomists, are so called because when they evaluate the two truths, they do so with reasoning appropriate to each level, and make assertions accordingly. In so doing, they destroy the position of their opponents by means of arguments that are established through valid reasoning and are mainly autonomous in character. By contrast, the Prasangikas, or Consequentialists, remain in the absence of the four conceptual extremes and do not make assertions. They refute false opinions by pointing out the unwanted consequences of their opponent's position, using, to that end, the same arguments that these same opponents use. The master Nagarjuna has said:

> Others have a point of view
> That may be proved or else refuted
> By perception and the rest;
> But I have no such thing, and thus I cannot be reproached.

He also said:

> If there are things not empty,
> Voidness may exist.
> And if everything is empty,
> How can emptiness exist?[145]

With regard to things, as they merely appear, the Prasangikas say that there are no phenomena existing according to their characteristics—that production and so forth have no reality even conventionally. When they see how phenomena abide in a manner that is primordially free from inherent existence, without establishing or refuting to the slightest degree, they thoroughly assimilate the absence of all conceptual extremes. They thus attain the union of the two truths, which is free from all assertion and from every mode of apprehension and abides in no extreme. This is the immaculate teaching revealed in the texts of Chandrakirti. As he himself says in his *Madhyamakavataraprajna:*

> Assertion and denial must both be left aside,
> For things transcend assertion and denial.

Generally speaking, in whatever is primordially unproduced, there is no flaw to be removed and no quality to be added. But it is difficult to perceive the naked, unvarnished meaning of the words of the Buddha's extremely profound teaching. One has to get used to it over a long period. The true nature of the Prasangika view may be grasped in the verses of Nagarjuna and Chandrakirti just cited. They are referring to primordial emptiness, the great freedom from conceptual construction. This is what we should strive to understand! In their respective teachings, the Prasangikas emphasize the primordial wisdom of the union, or single taste, of the two truths in meditative equipoise, while the Svatantrikas emphasize the wisdom that distinguishes the two truths in the postmeditation period. It is thus that this question should be understood.

There are many important reasons for this twofold distinction of the ultimate truth, by means of which the teachings of the Svatantrikas and the Prasangikas merge into a single stream, and one of them is that, on the basis of a reasoned investigation whereby the two truths are distinguished in the postmeditation period, it is possible in meditative equipoise to penetrate primordial wisdom wherein there is no conception of any ontological extreme.

As it has been said, if one grasps the essential point of either one of these perfect tenet systems, so that its meaning is as clear as a myrobalan fruit lying in the palm of one's hand, one will sound its depth and will have no further doubt. It is very difficult to do so otherwise. And since, in Tibet, even the explanation of the Prasangika view reverts to that of the Svatantrikas,[146] I wonder whether this is in fact due to some former causal link (*rten 'brel*).[147]

> This essential teaching of decisive reasoning
> Is like the thunderous laughter of Manjushri's mirth.
> Those who come across it will be instantly aroused
> From the dreamy sleep of philosophical confusion.

3. When the approximate ultimate is being established, the two kinds of valid reasoning are upheld without entailing any contradiction

It is important not to confuse the kind of assertions made on the level of each of the two truths. The primordial wisdom of meditative equipoise is ineffable, inconceivable, beyond any indication. For this reason, it cannot be the object of thought or language. Therefore, until perfect understanding resulting from valid reasonings related to the two truths occurs, there is no way to penetrate this primordial wisdom. And even though the Aryas do penetrate it, they remain, during their postmeditation period, within the scope of thought and word, assertion or denial. It is thus that they can teach and instruct others, and that they can explain and debate with opposing views, saying things like "It is like this" and "It is not like that." All things they examine and enunciate without confusion or error, demonstrating them with the wisdom that distinguishes phenomena perfectly. It is thus that, by ratifying or refuting through the use of reason all manner of statements about karma or the path and fruit, they are able to posit conventional reality authentically and irrefutably. Having gained the eye of all-discerning wisdom, which is able to distinguish all aspects of knowledge-objects, they are free from all conceptual elaboration and directly see the perfect equality of phenomena. They thus gain possession of the knowledge of primordial wisdom.

According to the argument of neither one nor many—which brings us to an understanding of the union of appearance and emptiness, the perfect equality of phenomena, namely, the absence of the four conceptual constructs (the ultimate truth in itself)—even the assumption of, and clinging to, the two truths as separate is just a concept. This is so because, thanks to such reasoning, the conventional existence of relative phenomena according to their characteristics also stands refuted. By contrast, when one remains in the approximate ultimate truth, that is, in mere nonexistence, conventional valid reasoning is totally unable to negate its own finding, namely, relative phenomena existing according to their characteristics. And if one were to refute relative phenomena and meditate on their mere nonexistence, the two truths would fall into two extremes and all appearances would be denied. One would be like the materialist followers of Brihaspati who, in accordance with the text *bsam gtan dad pa bdun*, meditate on the fact that there is no such thing as relative phenomena.[148] Thinking about this, Longchenpa said in *A Treasure of Wish-Fulfilling Jewels*:

> Not knowing how the two truths are united, they come to
>   blank vacuity.
> They say that from both "is" and "is not" they are free,
> But of the ground of such a freedom they are ignorant,
> And have a view that takes them to the zenith of existence.
> Such teaching is not Buddhadharma.
> They say they have a spacelike mind.
> But let them rather daub themselves with ashes.[149]

Freedom from the four conceptual extremes arises in a person's mind in the following manner. In the case of a beginner who penetrates it step by step, perfect and stainless reasoning first eliminates the "conceived object," that is, the misconception that all compounded or uncompounded phenomena really exist. Reasoning then refutes the conceived objects of the three remaining extremes: that things do not exist, that they both exist and do not exist, and that they neither exist nor do not exist. Subsequently, thanks to meditating in accordance with the extraordinary certainty wherein the conceived objects of the extreme ontological positions have no place, the point will come where all conceptual extremes will stand refuted in a single stroke, and the practitioner will behold the dharmadhatu clearly.[150] It is as the great and omniscient Gorampa Sonam Senge has said: "The intellect of ordinary people, which investigates ultimate reality, cannot refute in a single stroke all four conceptual extremes. But by refuting these four extremes one after the other and by meditating properly, one reaches the path of seeing. This is called the view that sees the dharmadhatu."

The learned and accomplished masters of the Old Translation school take as their stainless view the freedom from all conceptual constructs of the four extremes, the ultimate reality of the two truths inseparably united. In addition, they possess the profound pith instructions of the Vajrayana. They actualize the ultimate nature by developing certainty in it through the path of perfect reasoning—the arguments of the four realizations.[151] And then by their meditation, they achieve unshakable confidence in the inseparability of the two truths—the indivisibility of primordial purity (*ka dag*) and spontaneous accomplishment (*lhun grub*). This is how they have gained and continue to gain accomplishment. Hundreds of thousands of treasures of Dharma burst forth in their minds, and many have reached the realization of the all-penetrating rainbow body. Such is the result of their perfect view, which guides them on the path.

One might think such a view is confined to the Nyingmapas alone, but this is not so. The absence of the four conceptual constructs was repeatedly taught by the Buddha in the profound sutras and tantras. Scholars (for example, the six ornaments of India) have elucidated this teaching both directly and indirectly and it has been the inner practice of all the great accomplished vidyadharas. It is the sole path to omniscience and is the very heart of the views of both the Sarmapa and Nyingmapa. As a slight illustration of this, it is as Marpa the Translator has said:

This particular and final view,
The union that dwells in no extreme,
Is wisdom of the Buddhas of the triple time.
Those who sunder means from wisdom
Fall to extreme views. So this should be avoided.

And Milarepa, the king of all Tibetans who have gained accomplishment, has said:

Appearance and emptiness—when these two are not separate,
The view is fully realized.

And:

Existence, the appearing of phenomena,
Their emptiness or nonexistence,
By nature are not separate; they're of a single taste.
There is no self-cognizing and no other-cognizing.

The great lama of Sakya, Dragpa Gyaltsen, received a pith instruction from Manjushri known as *Separating from the Four Clingings*. This contains the statement: "If there is clinging, there is no view." Sakya Pandita, the mighty scholar of the Land of Snow, has said: "If you ask me what is acceptable as a definition of the two truths, the easiest way for anyone to understand it is to see the appearance aspect as the relative, the emptiness aspect as the ultimate, and their union as their nondifferentiation." Similarly, the *Panchakrama* declares:

When voidness and appearance both
Are seen as each the aspect of the other,
They blend together perfectly
And thus are said to be united.

To understand these three aspects is to establish the view. Then, by unifying means and wisdom, one must meditate on them and bring them into experience. This constitutes the path. With this understanding, one traverses the grounds and paths and finally attains the three kayas. This is the fruit. This approach in no way contradicts scripture and reasoning. It is the view of the pitaka of the teachings of ultimate meaning.

Je Tsongkhapa also says that beginners who do not possess the certainty deriving from rational investigation and who merely talk about the absence of conceptual extremes cannot dislodge their clinging to inherent existence. They therefore deviate from the authentic path. This being so, and in order to protect them with his compassionate hand, he said that, for the time being, it is very important to continue apprehending or focusing on the absence of inherent existence as this is revealed by reasoned inquiry. Nevertheless, his final teaching was as follows:

> *Phenomena that, in dependence, inescapably arise,*
> *And the understanding of voidness free from all*
>   *assertion—*
> *As long as these appear as different,*
> *The teaching of the Buddha is not understood.*
>
> *But when phenomena, arising in dependence,*
> *Are seen at once together with their emptiness,*
> *And when there is no further apprehension that the two are*
>   *separate,*
> *Then your view has been perfected.*

And the glorious Karmapa Rangjung Dorje said:

> *It does not exist; the Conquerors themselves have not*
>   *perceived it.*
> *It is not nonexistent, for it is the ground of both samsara and*
>   *nirvana.*
> *There is no contradiction; all has been united in the Middle Way.*
> *May we know the nature of the mind beyond extremes!*

And Dolpopa, the king of realization, has also said that in postmeditation, the undeceiving ultimate truth, considered in terms of the investigation of conventional reasoning, is described as indestructible reality, the unchanging, stable, peaceful sugatagarbha, expressed as the kayas and wisdoms. By contrast, when one settles in meditative equipoise, one meditates on the absence of all conceptual extremes. The meaning of this is very profound.

The master Sangdak Drolwa'i Gonpo (Taranatha) also said:

'Tis thus that foolish worldly folk impute:
Either there is nothing, like a rabbit's horns,
Or else there are phenomena, existing truly.
And so they fall to views of permanence or nihilism.

"Nothing" by dependence, "permanence" by voidness are refuted.
Because things are dependent, they are empty;
Because of voidness, everything arises.
Therefore, emptiness and phenomena are not two different
    things.

As these and other texts show, all the holy beings, the Buddha and all realized masters, speak with one voice.

All the texts that emphasize either the side of nonexistence or the side of existence, as the case may be,[152] are wise and skillful means for the destruction of suffering and defiled emotion—and for the achievement of perfect purity (that is, nirvana). But they do not establish the ultimate nature as it is. For example, it is a beginner's task to generate fear at the sufferings of samsara and joy at the peace of nirvana. When the great Bodhisattvas see the equality of samsara and nirvana, they necessarily abandon (in their own regard) fear of samsara and desire for nirvana respectively. When the ultimate nature of things is examined, those who possess the four reliances[153] establish the absence of the four conceptual extremes and refute all that contradicts it. But there are among them some who, while being certain of the absence of the four extremes, emphasize—in response to specific need— either existence on the one hand or nonexistence on the other.

By contrast, there are others who are destitute of the four reliances and who claim that their own one-sided path[154] attains to the ultimate nature. Such people, who in meditation do not rest in suchness even slightly, give credence to mere verbal, conceptual refutations and proofs. They are very much mistaken, as the sutras explain. In particular, they commit the great and calamitous downfall of abandoning the Dharma and criticizing supreme beings of both their own and other traditions. Of course, one may think, they criticize others, but how can they be criticizing the supreme beings of their own tradition? The fact is that even though such sectarian people greatly praise the teachers of their own tradition, in fact they are denigrating them. Why? It is just as when non-Buddhists praise Shiva and Vishnu (whom they regard as their teachers) for their sexual prowess, or for their wrath in annihilating their foes, or again for their ways of deceiving others. But the learned see that this is all due to negative emotion and cannot but be a depreciation.[155] In the same way, such sectarian people are actually saying that the accomplished beings of their own (Buddhist) tradition are unable to understand the absence of conceptual extremes, which is undeniably established by the reasoning investigating the ultimate status of things and which is expounded again and again in the profound sutras and tantras by the Buddha. All such wrong paths, whether those of the past or any that might arise in the future, should be abandoned. As Longchenpa said in *A Treasure of Wish-Fulfilling Jewels*:

> Supreme and nonconceptual primal wisdom all the texts
>   propound.[156]
> They teach that we must meditate upon the deep and peaceful
>   unelaborated nature.
> All evil paths at variance with this, which nowadays abound,
> Should be denied by all who wish for freedom.

2. What is meant when it is said that the approach of this text is easy?

What, in the present context, is meant by the word "easy"? It means that the *Madhyamakalankara* will be able to lead us swiftly to a state of certainty and that we shall definitely gain great understanding without much difficulty. This text is concise but clear. It is profound but vast, and though very short (given its vast meaning), it contains sharp and powerful arguments that are able to consume all the shortcomings of tenets imputed by other schools, whether non-Buddhist or Buddhist (up to that of the Chittamatra)—just as inflammable material can be set ablaze by a single spark. The *Madhyamakalankara* furthermore brings together all the essential points of texts such as *Mulamadhyamaka-karika* and *Pramanavarttika*. Its reasoning is most subtle and its ultimate meaning extremely profound. Nevertheless, its arguments and expressions are crystal clear, with the result that they are not hard to grasp. This is why the word "easy" is used. In the autocommentary to this text, Shantarakshita says: "The clear quotations and reasonings expressed in this text are like a great torch that throws light upon the scriptures of the Buddha."

Generally speaking, there are four or five arguments well known to the Madhyamaka treatises. Of these, the most important is the argument of dependent arising, which is like the king of reasoning.[157] All the other arguments are contained within it. And yet of all the other arguments, the reasoning of neither one nor many is like the point of a spear or the blade of a sword. It is easy to understand, simple in analysis, and highly effective, on account of which it is considered special and superior to the others. Shantarakshita himself said that the employment of this argument alone to establish that all phenomena are empty of true existence is like successfully administering medicine to a sick person or using a weapon to strike a vital organ. It completely achieves its purpose (namely, the refutation of truly existent entities). In the eighteenth chapter of the *Mulamadhyamaka-karika*, which is like the heart of the practice of all the twenty-six sections of the text, Nagarjuna explains the argument of neither one nor many. Even in the *Madhyamakavataraprajna* by Chandrakirti, which condenses all the crucial points of Madhyamaka and other texts, the fact that phenomena are without true existence is established just by the argument of neither one nor many—as it is in the present text. Of all the other different kinds of reasoning, this argument is like a sharp blade.

Owing to the crucial fact that all phenomena arise in dependence, there is neither one truly existent entity nor are there many. This being so, phenomena are devoid of independent existence. Produced by conditions, they appear as illusions. They are produced in interdependence. If they did exist by themselves—that is, if they were not produced by virtue of dependence—they would necessarily be either truly singular or truly plural. Since that which exists truly either as singular or plural cannot be dependently produced, all the other reasonings may in fact be condensed in this very argument. In brief, Nagarjuna said:

> To him who taught that voidness and dependence
> Are but one reality within the Middle Way,
> To him who said this supreme, matchless word,
> The mighty Sage, to him I now prostrate.

Accordingly, it is absolutely essential for all Madhyamikas to understand that all the arguments that establish emptiness find their crucial point in the single argument of interdependence. Interdependence subsumes them all. In the autocommentary to this text, Shantarakshita says:

> To all the Conquerors who teach
> That when we understand dependent coproduction,

> *We are set free from endless webs of thought,*
> *I bow down constantly to all who teach this truth.*

Since this text is a shastra wherein all the essential points of the two kinds of valid reasoning are condensed, it is a digest of all the world-adorning treatises of the six ornaments and their followers. The knowledge of this text alone will spontaneously unravel thousands of difficult points of the Madhyamaka tradition. It will bring Manjushri, Lion of Speech, to our thoughts and words and will raise the power of wisdom to its full pitch. Those who are intelligent will be convinced directly of its power, which is like the power of a medicine or of a vidya-mantra. What need is there for much talk? In his autocommentary, Shantarakshita says:

> *Those firm in their compassion teach this text*
> *And set it forth for learned ones.*
> *This supreme reasoning applies to Buddhist and non-*
> *   Buddhist schools,*
> *And it delights our hearts with perfect joy.*

> *From the claims of all conceptual views*
> *This text will set us free,*
> *And all the certainty of perfect knowledge*
> *It raises to its highest pitch.*
> *This text sets forth reality in all its purity,*
> *And everywhere the fame and greatness of the mighty Sage*
> *It spreads and heralds to infinity.*

As it is said, having found conviction in the perfect path [of the two kinds of reasoning], one is able to instruct fortunate beings and banish all adversity. And with powerful certainty, victorious over every bias, one can propagate and spread the teachings of the Buddha.

2. How great enlightenment is achieved through the approach thus propounded

It is by riding upon the excellent vehicle of the perfect and complete path of the Mahayana that, by the irreversible power of cause and effect, one will reach the fruit of enlightenment. When one recognizes the Three Jewels for what they are, one experiences faith; and by understanding that phenomena are without inherent existence, one overcomes both fear of samsara and joy in the peace of nirvana. With compassion focusing on illusionlike beings and with bodhichitta as vast as the sky (these are the main causes), one strives on the path of the stainless accumulations [of merit and wisdom], thus becoming the sovereign of the realm of the Dharma of the Conqueror, rich with the qualities of the twofold goal. Such an ultimate fruit is causally connected with the wisdom that arises gradually through hearing, reflecting, and meditating upon the teachings. Listening to the stainless path of reasoning of this present text, one must gain certainty in it by unmistakenly proving it for oneself. If, having reflected upon it repeatedly, one meditates on the meaning ascertained and becomes habituated in it, one will gradually obtain the three kinds of acceptance[158]—just as they are described in the *Chandrapradipa-sutra*. These different objectives, as explained directly or indirectly in the text, will be understood as the text is explained.

The five topics (the author, those for whom the text is intended, the orientation of the text, its overall conspectus, and its necessity) are not always directly and completely explained in a treatise or shastra. In the present case, the first topic, the author of the treatise, is directly revealed in the colophon of the text, whereas those who are able to uphold this profound and vast teaching are indicated indirectly in stanza 93: "Those who ride the chariot of the two approaches . . . ." The other three topics concern the body of the text. These five topics explain, in a manner that is both clear and profound, a host of other subjects such as the overall meaning of the text, and supply answers to objections. It is thanks to them that one may acquire a slight understanding of the greatness of this work.

> Despite degeneration of both place and time,
> I have explained with clarity the stainless view of this
>   great teaching.
> Not distorting it through my desires and leanings,
> I have unerringly declared its deep and subtle words.
>
> People now are lacking in both wit and erudition;
> Their envy, pride, and bigotry are great.
> It's hard therefore to bring them benefit.
> I wrote this that my mind might grow accustomed to
>   this teaching.

To Sublime and Noble Ones, who value gold as much as
  filth,
What does it serve to offer all the wealth of the four
  continents?
But if we hold the Dharma, to their hearts most dear,
'Tis said that then their minds are moved with perfect
  joy.

Wherefore, protector, only eye of this, the Snowy Land,
You make as if to slumber in nirvana's peace,
And yet from beings plagued by various ills
Your loving eyes are never turned.

Therefore, in whichever sublime place you are,
Whose eyes of peace are lovely like the petals of a lotus,
Look graciously on us.
And with the music of this commentary, my offering, be
  pleased!

THE COMMENTARY

THIS COMMENTARY comprises the exposition of the root verses and a reflection on the necessity of such an exposition.

1. The exposition of the root verses

We have structured this commentary on the *Adornment of the Middle Way,* which in itself is an elucidation of the two truths, in four sections: The meaning of the title, the homage of the translator, the text itself, and the conclusion.

2. The meaning of the title

In Sanskrit, the title of the root text is *Madhyamakalankara-karika.* This has been translated into Tibetan as *dbu ma rgyan gyi tshig le'ur byas pa,* which means *"The Adornment of the Middle Way* set down in stanzas." *Madhyamaka* means "the Middle Way," *alankara* means "adornment," and *karika* means "stanzas," or "metrical divisions."

The term "Middle Way" denotes that which rests in no extreme. It has a twofold application. First, it refers to the ultimate middle way, and, second, to the verbally elaborated middle way (or system) whereby the ultimate is expressed. And whereas the ultimate may be further divided into the Ground, Path, and Fruit,[159] the verbal expression of the middle way is found in the *Prajnaparamita-sutras* and other teachings of the Buddha, as well as in the shastras that comment on their meaning, such as the *Mula-madhyamaka-karika* of Nagarjuna. This "verbal Madhyamaka" is also known as the scriptural Madhyamaka.

An adornment[160] is something that adorns and that attracts the eye. But how may this text be said to adorn the Madhyamaka? If we compare the ultimate Madhyamaka to a beautiful human form, the textual Madhyamaka may be likened to the jewels that are used to embellish it. And since (to continue the same image) Shantarakshita's text sheds light on the ultimate Madhyamaka, it can be compared to a jewel that shines and renders conspicuous—like a mirror that reflects both the body and the gems that decorate it. Moreover, it is in itself a thing of radiant beauty and is an ornament for the whole Madhyamaka, not just for one viewpoint or school.

Does this mean then that the *Adornment of the Middle Way* is also an ornament for the Prasangika Madhyamaka tradition? If it is, one would surely have to say that it is a Prasangika text. On the other hand, if it is not, it cannot be regarded as an ornament for the entire Madhyamaka. The Prasangika view is, after all, the farthest reach of the Madhyamaka position, and if this text does not adorn it, it would be hard to maintain that it authentically adorns the whole tradition.

But whereas this work is indeed an ornament for the Prasangika system as well, it does not follow that it is a Prasangika text. This is so because it deals principally with the postmeditation period, together with the assertions associated with this, namely, the logical demonstration of the approximate ultimate truth. If in postmeditation the nature of each of the two truths is clearly grasped, the union of the two truths—the middle way, free from all assertion—may be established without difficulty. Thus, since this text also indicates, albeit briefly, the ultimate truth in itself, it evinces the same view as the Prasangika tradition. I have already touched upon these important matters when describing the overall meaning of the work, and indeed this is a subject that appears to call for a great deal of discussion. However, since intelligent readers require no more than an elucidation of the essential points, I propose, in the present commentary, to give only a brief explanation of the root verses.

In sum, a careful distinction between the Svatantrikas and Prasangikas according to the manner in which they emphasize either the state of postmeditation (in which the two truths appear as separate) or that of meditative equipoise (in which the two truths are of the same taste) is extremely important and profitable. It is certain that the ultimate Madhyamaka, the primordial wisdom of meditative equipoise, conforms to the view of the Prasangikas. The postmeditation, however, wherein the two truths are validly cognized,[161] corresponds to the tradition of the Svatantrikas. In the sutras also, some texts point out the ultimate truth in itself, which is beyond any assertion of existence, nonexistence, and so forth, and cannot be spoken of, conceived, or taught. Other texts, by saying things like "There is no form" or "There is no consciousness," indicate the approximate ultimate truth, which is simply a nonimplicative negation (*med dgag*).

In accordance with such scriptures, the master Nagarjuna, having first established that phenomena (causes and conditions, and the effects deriving therefrom) are without true existence, went on to demonstrate through reasoning that, in the last analysis, these same phenomena are free from all ontological extremes and are beyond the range of conceptual construction. The masters who followed him are called Svatantrikas or Prasangikas according to whether they emphasize the middle way of meditative equipoise or the middle way of postmeditation. To say, however, that the Svatantrikas failed to elucidate the meaning of the sutras and shastras properly is incorrect. For if one fails to take support of the Madhyamaka of the postmeditation, where the two truths are distinguished, one renders the Madhyamaka of meditative equipoise impossible to attain, for one has removed the cause of such an attainment. As it is said in the *Madhyamakavatara:*

> Conventional reality therefore becomes the means,
> And by this means, the ultimate is reached.[162]

And it is said that "without relying on the conventional, it is impossible to realize the ultimate."

Now the so-called conventional is not simply the relative understood in contrast with the approximate ultimate. The conventional covers all that is known, spoken of, and manipulated; it is the domain of thought and word, in which the two truths appear as separate. It follows therefore that the approximate ultimate also belongs to the conventional; it is part of the relative. And it is through an understanding based on this differentiation of the two truths on the conventional level that one comes to a realization of their union. This union is beyond formulation; it is the great Madhyamaka, which dwells in no extreme. It is a freedom from all conceptual constructs, the sphere beyond the intellect. This is what is referred to as the ultimate or supreme truth, the ultimate truth in itself.

People who devote themselves to much study and reflection encounter all sorts of terms used to describe the ultimate truth. Owing to their habituation with the Dharma-language of the two truths employed in the scriptures, it is easy for them to understand that what is implied amounts to no more than a nonimplicative negation. Since there is room for error here, it is important to examine whether a given term refers to the approximate ultimate or to the actual ultimate truth. For there is indeed more than one ultimate: the great, actual ultimate and the lesser, conceptual ultimate—the ultimate in itself and the approximate ultimate—just as there are different kinds of Arhat and different kinds of nirvana. One should ascertain such terms as "absence of origin" and "emptiness" accordingly.

The great ultimate, beyond all formulations and assertions, is emphasized in the extraordinary tradition of the Prasangikas. But the *Madhyamakalankara* also teaches it and with great clarity. As it is said in the autocommentary: "Even the absence of production and so on are located within the unmistaken relative."[163] And when explaining stanza 71 ("Production and the rest have no reality . . ."), the same commentary says: "Why is this? Because it is taught that this is not the actual ultimate . . . ," and "The ultimate is beyond both thing (*dngos po*) and nonthing (*dngos med*). It is beyond both production and the absence of production, beyond emptiness and nonemptiness. It utterly transcends the fabric of thought. Nevertheless, because the absence of production and so forth is an approach to the actual ultimate (being consonant with it), it is also referred to as ultimate." This then is how the *Madhyamakalankara* may be considered an ornament for the entire Madhyamaka.

Some people may object, saying that the Prasangika and Svatantrika masters explain the thought of Nagarjuna differently and that therefore they should be kept apart. In fact, the reverse is true. These same views should be expounded in a unified manner. For this is very necessary for intelligent people who have the capacity to understand that the views of the great charioteers Nagarjuna and Asanga are not in conflict.

In conclusion, the title of Shantarakshita's work concludes with the specification "stanzas." This refers to the fact that it is composed in verses, that is, in line and meter, as distinct from prose.

2. The homage of the translator

The Tibetan text begins with the words "Homage to Manjushri the youthful!" inserted by the great translator Yeshe De before beginning his work.[164] This was in accordance with the edict of the king Tri Ralpachen and indicates that the work in question belongs to the Abhidharma of the ultimate teachings.[165] The mind of Manjushri, like the dharmadhatu itself, is exempt from every affliction due to conceptual construction. He is therefore mild and gentle (*manju*). At the same time, his wisdom body, endowed with twofold knowledge, ceaselessly, universally, and spontaneously accomplishes the benefit of beings to the very limits of space itself.[166] He is thus glorious (*shri*) with the riches of the twofold purpose; he is also youthful (*kumara*) because, even though he is, by his very nature, the nonconceptual wisdom of all the Buddhas, he takes the form of a great Bodhisattva on the tenth ground, with a youthful body, firm and unchanging, ageless and free from all degeneration, remaining for as long as samsara lasts. It is to him indeed that the translator pays homage in his thoughts, words, and deeds.

2. The text itself

The text is divided into two parts: an investigation and establishment of the two truths as objects of knowledge, followed by a summary in the form of a eulogy of the approach adopted. The first part, the establishment of the two truths, consists of three sections. First of all, the two truths are identified, then objections are countered, and finally a review is made of the benefits that this knowledge bestows. With regard to the first topic, the identification of the two truths shows that whereas on the ultimate level entities do not exist, on the conventional level they do. The consideration of the ultimate level is again subdivided into the main argument and the proof of its validity.

3. An examination and establishment of the two truths
4. The two truths identified
5. A demonstration that no entities exist on the ultimate level
6. The main argument of the *Madhyamakalankara*

> 1
> The entities that our and other schools affirm,
> Since they exist inherently in neither singular nor plural,
> In ultimate reality are without intrinsic being;
> They are like reflections.

Systems of philosophy, both Buddhist and non-Buddhist, posit the true existence[167] of certain entities. But when all are examined as to their ultimate status, one finds neither a single truly existent entity nor a plurality of such entities. Such entities, in other words, enjoy not the slightest degree of inherent being. They are just like forms reflected in a mirror, which appear and yet are not "true." The content of this stanza may be formulated as a probative argument[168] in the following way: "The subject,[169] that is, outer and inner entities, said by certain Buddhist and non-Buddhist schools to exist inherently, have no existence on the ultimate level, because there is neither one truly existent entity nor are there many such entities. Outer and inner entities are like images seen in a mirror."

"Entities" here refers either to the five aggregates and so on, asserted by the Buddhists, or to entities like prakriti, of which the non-Buddhists speak. If any "truly existent entities" really occur, it follows that there must be either one of them or more than one of them. Now, "singular" and "plural" ("one" and "more than one") are mutually exclusive terms, and aside from these two categories, it is impossible to find, among objects of knowledge, a third category of truly existent things. Consequently, the probative sign[170] of the argument is contradictory evidence consisting of the nonobservation [of one truly existent entity or many such entities], which pervades all things affirmed to be truly existent.[171]

Let us explore this topic a little further. Three things should be considered: the subject of the probative argument, the reasoning employed, and the nature of the analogy.

7. An investigation of the subject of the probative argument

One may well ask how the mere refutation of entities affirmed by philosophical tenets is able to invalidate the inborn apprehension of, and clinging to, the self—something we have grown accustomed to from beginningless time. The answer is that eternal realities and compounded things, the person, pervasive entities, extended objects and subtle things, consciousness, and so forth—in other words, all phenomena as asserted by both Buddhist and non-Buddhist tenet systems—may be made the subject of probative arguments. And if, by force of reasoning, we are able to show that true existence is enjoyed by none of them (permanent and impermanent, outer and inner, subject and object, pervasive and nonpervasive entities, gross and subtle, the knowing mind and the things it knows), it will be possible for us to uproot our inborn clinging to the two kinds of self.

Generally speaking, because of the ignorance innately present in their minds, beings apprehend objects—pots, for instance—as being really existent. And it is in relation to such things that they conceive of (that is, produce names for) nonthings, or pseudoentities. Things and nonthings are thus cognized, and clung to, as real. And in dependence on the five aggregates, which make up their continua, and in the absence of analytical investigation, beings conceive of "I." It is their inborn tendency to identify their perishable aggregates as a self. Phenomena and the person, which are assumed to exist truly just as they appear, do indeed have a basis of labeling: the five aggregates and the rest.[172] Furthermore, thanks to their defective reasoning, ingenuous beings ascribe reality and permanence to the atman and so on—which is not real even on the conventional level. They are thus entangled in the threads of assumption and clinging.

We may deal with the question whether or not the refutation of one of these two selves (coemergent or imputed) entails the annulment of the other. Although objects conceived to be real and permanent[173] are refuted by reasoning, the coemergent apprehension of, and clinging to, the ego is not abolished thereby, for such objects are not the basis of this apprehension. On the other hand, if one understands that that which seems to be the object of innate clinging to self (namely, the aggregates) is not the "I," all imputations concerning the permanent atman, the creator, and so forth, are annulled. When one realizes that the child of a barren woman does not exist, one is equally convinced that the child's color does not exist. Therefore, once it is established that persons and compounded and uncompounded phenomena are without inherent existence (because they are neither one nor many), there can be no further apprehension of, or clinging to, these two kinds of self. For it will have been shown that *all* objects of knowledge are without inherent existence. Therefore, all imputed objects and apprehended objects relating to the coemergent selves[174] may be taken as the subject of this argument. This subject is not limited to things appearing to the normally functioning consciousness; it also covers the entities imputed by non-Buddhists.

7. An investigation of the argument

In this section, three questions are to be considered: (1) Is the argument just mentioned a Prasangika or a Svatantrika argument? (2) Does the argument establish the predicated property in itself, or does it do no more than establish the predicated term?[175] (3) Does it constitute an implicative negation or a nonimplicative negation?

8. A Prasangika or a Svatantrika argument?

The question may be asked whether the argument put forward in the first stanza is Prasangika or Svatantrika. If it were a Prasangika argument, the sign or reason would have to derive from the assertion of an opponent.

But since this reason (that there is neither one nor are there many truly existent things) is not asserted by an opponent, it follows that the argument cannot be a consequence (*prasanga*). If, on the other hand, the argument were Svatantrika, the sign must be validly established with all three conditions complete.[176] In the present case, however, since the logical subject (a permanent atman or an eternal Deity, and the indivisible particle of matter or moment of consciousness) is not established,[177] the argument itself has no (real) subject. Since there is no subject, it is impossible to establish the sign as being a property of the subject.[178] This being so, it will be objected, the required three conditions of the sign are incomplete.

Our answer to this is that there have been scholars in both India and Tibet who have said that entities that are imputed by non-Buddhists and are not part of the common consensus should be dealt with using the Prasangika method, whereas phenomena that are encountered empirically may be dealt with by either the Prasangika or Svatantrika approach. The *Madhyamakaloka* and other texts declare, however, that this distinction is unnecessary and that both kinds of entities (empirically encountered and otherwise) may be refuted by Prasangika and Svatantrika arguments equally.

Suppose we were to approach this question in the manner of the Prasangikas. The opponents do not actually say that entities are neither one nor many. On the other hand, they do assert a predicate with regard to entities, namely, that they exist truly. This implies an entailment [that truly existent things must be either singular or plural], an entailment that can be set out and established as a consequence.[179] This being so, the Prasangikas need only adduce the argument of neither one nor many; no other strategy is required. For example, Ishvara is said to be eternal, in the sense of unchanging.[180] But if it is asserted that Ishvara's creation is multiple, the plurality of his created effects is sufficient to show that he is not a single, truly existent entity. When his being one is refuted, his being many is also refuted. In fact, the sign (many created effects) adduced by the disputant establishes that Ishvara is not a single, undivided entity. For when his products are shown to be many, it is simultaneously proved that he is not a truly single, undivided entity. This reasoning may be similarly applied to all other assertions.[181]

Alternatively, the demonstration may be formulated in terms of a Svatantrika argument. Although it is impossible actually to have an eternal Ishvara and so on as the subject of the proposition, the idea of it does occur to the mind by means of an "other elimination," namely, the reverse of what is not an eternal Ishvara.[182] And since this idea is the designation of something that does not exist in fact, the assumption that there is an eternal Ishvara existing outside the mind is refuted. It is perfectly admissible for a refutation to apply to something that is merely mentally posited—as when permanent sound is taken as the logical subject of debate. All logical processes of affirmation and negation apply to whatever one apprehends as the blend of two elements: appearances as they occur in the outer world, and their denominations, which are merely apprehended by the mind through other-elimination. This is common to all pramana traditions.[183] Logical subjects that cannot possibly exist as actual things lack the specific characteristics of objects suitable for analysis. Nevertheless, one clings to them as if they were really existent. By establishing that such "appearing objects" are mere designations of what lacks true existence, it will be possible to understand that they do not exist in fact.

8. Does the "neither one nor many" argument serve to establish the predicated property in itself, or does it simply establish the term predicated?

It may be objected that if this argument is establishing the predicated property in itself, it follows that the absence of inherent existence as a predicated property constitutes no more than a nonimplicative negative. It simply negates truly existent phenomena, and nothing else is suggested in place of the refuted thing. And if this alone is what the argument establishes, it follows that the logical subject (phenomena taken as the basis of the discussion) is not found. It is simply nonexistent, like a flower growing in the sky. With this kind of argument, the subject and its predicated property cannot be differentiated.[184] On the other hand, one may consider that the argument establishes the term predicated and say that when the ascription "lacking inherent existence" is shown to pertain (positively) to things, it follows that phenomena lack inherent existence in the same way that one can speak of a place being without pots.[185]

Our reply is that even though the argument establishes the predicated property in itself (namely, the *fact* that phenomena are without inherent existence), it does not follow that phenomena—the locus of the predicated property—simply become nothing. The argument is simply saying that the things that, as a result of our beginningless clinging, we take to exist truly as they appear in fact have no such inherent reality. Not the slightest speck of inherently existent, observable reality is established. Nevertheless, on the basis of appearances, which are fully apprehended as real in empirical experience, it is quite acceptable to speak, on the one hand, in terms of a logical subject that lacks inherent existence and, on the other hand, of its predicated property.

When considering physical and mental phenomena (illusory apparitions, which are nevertheless accepted in the way that they appear), if one takes them as the subject of argument, correct evidence will establish their lack of inherent existence as a term that is merely mentally predicated—just as when the name "buffalo" is applied to a group of characteristics (hump and so forth). But however much one calls to mind terms that one recognizes (and knows) with certainty, or however much, with the help of correct reasoning, one evaluates terms the meaning of which is uncertain, the predicated property (lack of true existence) and the logical subject (things) do not become distinct and separate in reality.[186] The subject is not divided from its property. It is not a contradiction for phenomena to appear even though they lack inherent existence, for such is the very nature of phenomena themselves.

The example used to illustrate our two replies is the image of the moon reflected in water. When discussing this question, all other texts argue in one or another of the two directions just described.[187] But it is very important and helpful to understand the matter in the manner just outlined. This is true generally, but particularly so with regard to the present text.

8. Are the object of refutation and the sign nonimplicative negatives or implicative negatives?

If the object of refutation and the sign are nonimplicative negatives (*med dgag*), it might be thought that the object of refutation (true existence) is simply denied, and to what is simply negated nothing can be said to relate. The predicated property cannot constitute something knowable, nor can the sign or evidence be considered something that conveys knowledge. On the other hand, the objection continues, if the evidential sign adduced constitutes an implicative negative (*ma yin dgag*), the question then is, why is nothing asserted in place of what is negated?

This question has given rise to a great deal of scholarly discussion. For my part, I would say this: The sign or reason (that there is neither one truly existent thing nor are there many truly existent things) and the property to be proven (lack of true existence) are both nonimplicative negatives. However, although "true existence," the object of refutation, is simply not there—being completely ruled out—this does not mean that there is no relation between the sign and property. The property "lack of inherent existence" and the sign "neither one nor many" are *conceptual* distinguishers, arrived at through other-elimination. By their nature they are the same in being without inherent existence. They are linked by a relation of single nature.[188] There are indeed a great many wearisome demonstrations and refutations connected with the different views on this matter (of whether the argument is an implicative or a nonimplicative negation). Every uncertainty will be removed, however, if one makes a clear distinction between appearance and "elimination."[189] Without this, no matter how much one investigates, it is difficult to come to a decisive conclusion.[190]

In general, it is important to be familiar with the teachings on probative signs and reasoning and, within that context, the notions of other-elimination, the three conditions of the correct sign, and all the methods of proof or refutation. None of this will be discussed here, however, for fear of making the book too long. One should acquire a detailed understanding of these matters from the texts on pramana.

7. The nature of the analogy

Reflections and so forth are the examples used to illustrate how things appear without truly existing. It is said in the *Pitaputrasamagama-sutra:*

> *Just as in a clear, unclouded glass,*
> *The shapes of forms appear*
> *Though they are substanceless,*
> *'Tis thus, O Jönpa, you should understand all things.*

Even ordinary people say that the shapes and so forth seen in a reflection have no real existence even though they do indeed appear. Using such examples, one may understand by means of reasoning that all phenomena have a similar character. When one looks in a mirror, the reflection of one's face appears, and one can observe directly and distinctly all its features of color and shape. If one leaves it just as it is, without further investigation, no difference whatever will be found between it and one's real face. And yet, if one examines it, the reflection will be found to contain not even an atom of an actual face. Furthermore, even though the appearance is perceived and cannot be denied, if one examines it, the very reflection will not be found in the place where it is seen. It is neither inside nor outside the mirror (nor somewhere in between). Neither is it found between the object and the consciousness, nor within the consciousness itself. But where else can it be located? It is unreasonable to cling to the existence of something when it is *nowhere* to be found. Otherwise, why not accept the existence of a barren woman's son?

This then is how one should understand that phenomena appear even though they do not exist truly. They are like reflections. As the *Samadhirajasutra* says:

> For when at night the moon, reflected on the stream,
> Shines brightly and within the spotless water seems to be,
> The water-moon is empty, substanceless; there is no thing to
>   grasp.
> Now understand: 'Tis thus that all things are.

We may, at this point, dismiss a few misconceptions regarding this example. The Mimamsakas, followers of Jaimini, account for the phenomenon of reflection by saying that rays of light emanate from the eyes and strike the surface of a mirror.[191] They then return and one observes one's likeness. This occurrence, they say, is described as a reflection, but the use of the term "reflection" is, according to them, based on the particular way of seeing just described, and apart from that, the reflection and the form itself are linked in a relationship of single nature. This is unacceptable. If the surface of the mirror is turned to the north, the reflection will not be facing south, as the actual face does. Thus form and reflection are turned in opposite directions. They are also of a different size, since a large face may seem tiny when reflected in a small mirror. Their location is also different because the reflection seems to be inside the mirror. Similarly, the peaks and branches of the mountains and trees reflected in a lake will appear to be pointing downward; thus there is a difference of position. Consequently, the consciousness that apprehends the actual form and the consciousness apprehending the form's reflection in fact observe different objects. Their fields of action are distinct—as different as the sound consciousness is from the sight consciousness. It should be understood therefore that the actual face is not perceived by the same consciousness that apprehends the reflection.

The Vaibhashikas, for their part, consider that a reflection is a distinct, extremely subtle form manifesting within the mirror. This, however, is untenable, for material forms, which are by their nature composed of infinitesimal particles, necessarily obstruct and prevent one another from appearing in the same place. They mutually exclude each other. Otherwise, if they were to occupy the same position, they would necessarily intermingle beyond the possibility of differentiation, and consequently they could only be said to be one and the same. In the present case, a reflection is observed on the surface of the mirror. If, as the Vaibhashikas affirm, a reflection is a material form, there would be two forms in the same place. This is impossible, just as it is impossible for two pots to coincide exactly on the same spot. The example given by the Vaibhashikas, of air and sunlight, does not affect our argument. For the particles of air and sunlight are mingled together in the same way that dust may be mixed with flour. The particles, each in their individual positions, are mutually exclusive of each other; they are not one.

The followers of Jaimini and the Vaibhashikas both believe that reflections are material forms. If this theory of theirs is not disproved, however, the example of a reflection, given in the root stanza, relating to both the property to be established (absence of true existence) and the evidential sign (the reason of "neither one nor many") cannot stand. This is why we have refuted it. By contrast, the Sautrantikas and others consider that a reflection is consciousness. They say that it is owing to the inconceivable power of things that, thanks to the presence of a mirror, consciousness simply appears in the aspect of a reflection. But if they believe that a reflection is not an object but simply consciousness appearing like a reflection, why do they not also hold that material forms, which they believe to be truly existent, merely appear while being nonexistent? For indeed, they say that the perceived appearances of both material forms and their reflections are merely mental aspects. To this they may answer that a reflection cannot be described as an "object that casts a mental aspect" (*rnam pa gtod byed kyi yul*), since it has no real existence. It is not an object; it is no more than consciousness. To this we reply that all objects (material forms, sounds, and so on), which they say exist outside the mind and do create mental aspects, are not established even on the level of their infinitesimal particles. The [Chittamatra] arguments that refute the existence of particles also disprove outer objects. It follows therefore that there is no difference between outer objects and reflections. And it is said that this also holds for the examples of illusions, dreams, mirages, castles in the clouds, and the impression of a circle created by a whirling firebrand.

Others, such as Zhönumalen,[192] consider that illusions and suchlike are not untrue. For the term "illusion" refers either to the lump of clay (that the magician uses as a basis for his illusory display) or to the cognition that appears in that form. In the first case, the illusion is a material form; in the second, it is a cognition. And thus it is not proved that the illusory horses and oxen are nonexistent. The same applies to dreams and so on. Their cause is either a truly existent material form or a consciousness, and for this reason it is inappropriate to adduce such illusory things as examples for the lack of true existence.

This is a mistake. Whether the appearance of an illusion (such as a magic elephant) is believed to be a perception of a mental aspect, as in the case of the Sakaravadins,[193] or a direct apprehension of an object, as in the case of the Nirakaravadins,[194] it is the observed object—an illusory elephant perceived by the mind—that is designated as the illusion. It is not the cause (the ball of clay, for example) by itself that receives the designation of illusion. For if this were so, one's eyes and so forth—since they too are the cause of the illusion—would be an illusion also. But the observed illusion and the cause of such an illusion are distinct entities. Consequently, although the causes of illusion—namely, material form (clay, for example) and consciousness—are present, they are not used as an example. If there is a ball of clay and it is not observed as a horse or elephant, it will not be designated as an illusory appearance and cannot be used as an example. But when a ball of clay is perceived as a horse or elephant, we call it an illusion, and such an experience may be used as an example.

Furthermore, since the outer object and the consciousness are established as being without true existence, the cause of an illusion cannot be established as truly existent either. And even if one does regard as true the object and consciousness that are for the time being the causes of illusion, the perceived illusion cannot be considered true. People who perceive an elephant, while knowing that it is an illusion, will not experience even the slightest conviction that there is an elephant present in the clay. Conversely, whereas clay, eyes, the magician, and so on are considered to exist as the causal basis for the illusion of an elephant, the elephant itself is not considered true. Even though the illusion does appear to exist truly just where it is, it is recognized as not existing in the way that it appears and is perceived. It is therefore cited by Shantarakshita as an example, and it is not unfounded. All these examples, which are given in the autocommentary, are clearly explained here.

6. A demonstration of the validity of the argument
7. A demonstration that the sign fulfills the condition of being the property of the logical subject

8. Establishing that there is no such thing as a truly existent entity that is one
9. A refutation of a single, truly existent, pervasive entity
10. A refutation of a single, truly existent, particular pervasive entity
11. A refutation of a single, truly existent, permanent pervasive entity
12. A refutation of a truly existent, permanent entity as presented by non-Buddhist schools

> 2
> Producing their effects sequentially,
> Eternal entities cannot be "one."
> If each of their effects is different from the others,
> These entities can have no permanence.

It is said that the three conditions of the sign must be fulfilled in order to establish that the property is correctly predicated. These three conditions may be described as follows: (1) As was generally described above, the sign or reason of neither one nor many is established as pertaining to the logical subject (entities postulated by Buddhists or non-Buddhists as real). This is the first condition. The so-called sign or reason belongs to, or is a property of, the subject under consideration (*phyogs chos*). (2) If the reason of neither one nor many is applicable, the property to be proved[195] (the absence of true existence) is necessarily established. This is the second condition, forward pervasion or positive concomitance (*rjes khyab*). (3) If the absence of true existence is not the property to be established, the sign of neither one nor many is also excluded (rendered inapplicable). This is the third condition, the reverse pervasion or negative concomitance (*ldog khyab*).[196]

When the property to be proved and the sign or reason are specifically related by virtue of both positive and negative concomitance, the property is pervaded by the reason, or, to put it another way, the reason establishes the property with certainty. This is the meaning of the term "pervasion" or concomitance (*khyab pa*).[197] If the sign or probative reason, by which the property is pervaded, is known to be present in the logical subject, the predicated property is incontrovertibly proved. The theories stating that the reason must fulfill fewer or more conditions than the three given (that is, from two to as many as six) are thus refuted. It is therefore said that "from a sign that fulfills the three conditions, one is able to 'see' the property predicated," and similarly that "the [reason as the] property of the subject is utterly pervading."

The way in which the sign of neither one nor many, given in the main argument of the root verses, is established as the property of all entities affirmed by Buddhist and non-Buddhist schools will be explained in stages. In the autocommentary, in the passage preceding the explanation of this stanza, it is said that one should not think that this sign is unproven. But the question is, how is it proved? To begin with, it is shown that there is no such thing as a truly existent entity that is single or one. And if it is impossible for one such entity to exist, it stands to reason that there cannot be a plurality of such entities—given that an individual item is the basis of a collection. Consequently, it is first of all established that there is no such thing as a single, truly existent entity.

Broadly speaking, if, within the field of phenomena, a single, truly existent entity could be found, it would be impossible to divide it into aspects (parts, for example, that are visible and parts that are invisible). Such an entity would have to be uniformly *one,* irrespective of spatial direction and the passage of time.[198] But if such were the case, the separate manifestation of all knowledge-objects contained within the whole of time and space would be impossible. All would necessarily become a single, undivided thing, like space. This, however, is not the case. For we do perceive an infinite variety of appearances existing in terms of spatial extension (directions) and temporal duration, and these can only appear because there is no such thing as a single, truly existent entity.[199] It is therefore clear that the reason of neither one nor many applies to all knowledge-objects that may be encountered within the ambit of phenomenal existence, whether of samsara or nirvana.

This being so, it can be gradually shown how the sign (or reason of neither one nor many) is established as the property of the subject under consideration, namely, entities commonly accepted as real by Buddhists and non-Buddhists. And here, depending on the division of subject matter adopted, these entities may be organized into twin categories of permanent and impermanent things, external apprehended objects and the internal apprehending mind, or the known object and the knowing subject. In the present commentary, we will follow the explanation given in Kamalashila's *Madhyamakalankara-panjika* (*Commentary on Difficult Points*), which makes a distinction between "pervasive entities" (the self, space, and so forth) and "impermanent or nonpervasive entities."

We will therefore consider such putatively truly existent phenomena to be divided into the categories of pervasive and nonpervasive entities. Since a permanent, truly existent entity[200] and the self or atman—as described by those schools that assert their reality—cannot be grasped in isolation from things, they are categorized as "pervasive entities." But when, in his auto-commentary on stanza 10, Shantarakshita distinguishes between pervasive and nonpervasive, it is evident that he is speaking from the standpoint of authentic, actual pervasiveness.[201] To the first category—particular, pervasive phenomena—belong the permanent, truly existent entities affirmed by the non-Buddhists. The way to demonstrate that such entities have no true existence as single realities is set out in the second stanza of the root text.

Certain non-Buddhists declare that Ishvara the Almighty, and so on, is by nature eternal. They say too that he is an active power and does not, like space and so on, lack causal efficiency. He is, in other words, a causally effective entity. Although Ishvara is said to be eternal, being unchanging in the three times, he is acknowledged as the creator. For he is the author of all things—the world and all it contains—in the same way that a potter is the maker of his pots.

Now, it is at no time possible for all the objects that compose the world to manifest simultaneously. They arise in succession, with the result that it must be admitted that their creation is gradual. Since, therefore, the divine cause, which the non-Buddhists say is eternal, does not produce its effects all at once—for the latter are perceived to arise one after the other—it follows that such a cause, namely, the putatively eternal Ishvara or whatever, can have no existence as a single, truly existent entity. Indeed, if the cause (of creation) is eternal and one—an undivided, single whole—and if this cause produces all things, it follows that it must always retain an unwavering power to produce the multiplicity of its effects. Why then do these effects (happiness, suffering, indifference, and so on) not appear simultaneously and all together? Effects cannot arise when there is a deficiency in the cause. But since the potency of the divine cause is eternally present, how is it that its effects are delayed?[202] If they do not arise all at once, they cannot be said to follow (or be related to) the divine cause, and for this reason, they cannot be described as its effects.

To this our opponents might answer that the fact that the effects are not produced in one instant is due to various cooperative conditions. But since that which is eternal can never be other than what it is in the first place, it cannot be affected by cooperative conditions. Such conditions can have no bearing on it, any more than paint can be applied to space. If, on the other hand, the divine creator is dependent on conditions and can change, it follows that he is not eternally unchanging. For if it is conceded that he is dependent on conditions, the question must be asked whether there is a difference between the eternal, truly existent divine cause accompanied by such conditions and the same cause divested of them. If there is a difference, this detracts from its eternity. If, on the other hand, there is no difference, it follows that in the earlier and subsequent phases, the cooperative conditions are not separable from the main cause. They are pulled along as though tied to Ishvara's neck with a string! Since the cause of previously produced effects remains always complete, these same effects can never cease. By this same means is refuted the opponent's assertion that the term "cooperative conditions" is merely a name for the potency implicit in the cause, namely, Ishvara, and that it is this potency that accounts for the gradual production of effects. For if the creator and his potency are distinct, "potency" is just another word for the cooperative causes. If they are not distinct, then as we have just explained, the opponent's position is invalidated by the fact that the created effects ought to be unstoppable.

It should therefore be understood that as long as it is asserted that created effects are produced gradually, there can be no such thing as an eternal cause of any kind that is truly one. A sequence or continuity is not a truly existent, single entity. Consequently, it is certain that the above-mentioned cause is not eternal.

When they perceive this inescapable defect in their argument, our opponents may try to retain the eternal immutability of the cause while granting that it is not a single entity. But if they believe that for every effect there is a distinct aspect successively within the cause, how is it possible for Ishvara, as an eternal entity, not to be disproved? For he modulates from one condition to another.

Again the opponent may reply that this is not problematic. For even though the divine cause is not a single entity, its nature or continuum is one. It is therefore quite acceptable to say that such a cause is eternal (that is, immutable, ever-enduring), even though it passes through different phases. It is rather like an actor, who remains one and the same person while assuming a different demeanor in the morning and in the afternoon.

If this theory is examined, it will be found that something that is not a partless and aspectless entity cannot be permanent. Therefore, the first half of the second stanza refutes the idea of a single, truly existent entity for those disposed to believe that such a thing is permanent. The second half of the stanza refutes the permanence of entities that are not single. There have been several interpretations of this stanza, but the one just set out is the only one that correctly fits with the meaning of Shantarakshita's text. The nature or continuity (of several aspects of a thing) is designated as one, or as a single whole, on account of the continuous similarity of the object's aspects. But such a thing never actually exists as a single, truly existent entity. If it did exist, it would not be beyond the faulty consequence just mentioned.[203] The ascription of oneness is not being refuted here. This has no real existence and therefore cannot be posited as permanent.

As long as there are distinct phases,[204] there can be no single, truly existent entity. Something that can be analyzed into parts or aspects can never be described as permanently *one*.

12. A refutation of a truly existent, permanent entity as posited by Buddhist schools
13. A brief presentation of the refuting argument

> 3
> And also in the schools that say the uncompounded
> Is cognized by wisdom that results from meditation,
> This selfsame object is not one,
> For it is linked with knowing instants that arise in
>   sequence.

The Buddhist Vaibhashika school asserts three uncompounded entities, which are truly existent and permanent (*rtag dngos*). The first of these is space. The second is nonanalytical cessation, or absence. This term refers not to a cessation that occurs through the application of analysis or understanding but to the fact that when something is not present, owing to the absence of some of the natural conditions that would normally produce it, this very absence is regarded as an uncompounded entity that precludes the appearance of the thing in question. And this is therefore called a nonanalytical cessation or absence (*brtags min 'gog pa*) The Vaibhashikas claim that this uncompounded entity is a really existent thing.[205] The third uncompounded entity is analytical cessation—the cessation that arises through analysis or understanding (*so sor brtags 'gog pa*), referring to the absence of defilements that results from the practice of the path. The Vaibhashikas ascribe real, "substantial" existence to this as well.[206] Of these three, the present text refutes only analytical cessation as a truly existent, single entity, because the same reasoning also disproves the other two uncompounded entities.

Now, the Vaibhashikas say that this uncompounded entity (analytical cessation or absence), which is the object of yogic perception acquired through meditation and is free from every characteristic of compoundedness, constitutes an ultimate truth. Being the object of the yogi's supreme wisdom, it enjoys ultimate existence. Its natural condition is known only through yogic perception. On the other hand, the Vaibhashikas say, this uncompounded entity does not give rise to the consciousness that observes it. For the production of effects belongs to things that are compounded, whereas analytical cessation is uncompounded. This then is what they assert. They consider that although it is an object, it is not considered to be the cause of the arising of consciousness.[207] Therefore, even though yogic perception perceives this uncompounded object in successive moments, the Vaibhashikas believe that analytical cessation, because in itself it is unrelated to the perceiving consciousness, remains uncompounded and is a permanent, single, truly existent entity.

It is said [in the autocommentary]: "When the uncompounded entity, that is, the analytical cessation (cognized by yogic perception acquired through meditation), which the Vaibhashikas consider to be truly existent, is subjected to rational inquiry, it is not found to be a truly existent, single entity. This is so because this same uncompounded object is related to a succession of cognitive instants in the manner of known and knower."

The word "also" appears in the root verse to indicate the untenability not only of the eternal entity, said by non-Buddhists to be the producer of all effects, but also of the inherently permanent entities, asserted in the Vaibhashika system, which do not produce effects. The word "also" thus associates these permanent entities with non-Buddhist beliefs and implies that, regardless of whether such entities produce effects or not, they cannot truly exist by any means.

The Vaibhashikas consider that since the object itself is permanent (meaning a truly existent, single entity), it cannot be linked with the cognizing subject in a relationship of a single nature. The two are related merely in terms of knower and known. Why, they ask, should the object become impermanent and multiple simply on account of the knowing subject?

This indeed is the innermost conviction of those who assert the existence of permanent objects. On the one hand, there are our own Buddhist schools that believe in a permanent, ultimate reality or nature of things.[208] On the other hand, there are the non-Buddhists, who consider that objects such as pots are, and remain, permanent until such time as they are destroyed. They believe, for example, that the pot that we saw yesterday and the pot we see today are one and the same thing, even though the consciousness (the knowing subject) is not the same. But if the knowing subjects (that is, the moments of consciousness) are not the same, it is impossible for the object of those subjects to exist truly as one. This point requires a more extensive explanation.

13. A detailed explanation of the argument
14. The assertion that the object of a past moment of consciousness is also the object of a subsequent moment of consciousness is untenable

> 4
> If, already known to earlier consciousness,
> It continues to be present to a later consciousness,
> The earlier consciousness becomes the later;
> The later too becomes the earlier.

Here we must put a question to the proponents of a permanent, uncompounded entity. Does the actual uncompounded entity itself, previously the object of the earlier moment of consciousness, become the object of the later moment of consciousness, or does it not? Our opponents have affirmed the existence of an uncompounded object. This same object must be observed by a consciousness, otherwise all valid cognition of it is impossible. Now, all consciousnesses that observe objects are necessarily sequences of cognitive instants; and with regard to such sequences, only two assertions can be made: The object of the preceding moment either continues to be present to the subsequent moments or it does not. The Vaibhashikas say that the actual uncompounded object (namely, an analytical cessation), which is the known object of the preceding moment of consciousness, continues to be present to the subsequent moments of cognition. In other words, it exists and is observed in subsequent moments.

If this is the case, however, then given that not even the slightest difference is discernible in the said object, and that the different moments of consciousness observe one and the same thing, it follows that there can be no distinction in the apprehending mind either (in terms of distinct sequential instants). A consciousness is posited in relation to what it cognizes, and indeed consciousness cannot be differentiated in any other way.[209] Consequently, in one moment[210] of consciousness apprehending a pot, arising in the mind stream of a single person, several different perceptions of a pot do not occur. And it is the earlier moment of consciousness, observing the uncompounded thing as its exclusive object, that is properly posited as the consciousness of the uncompounded. Since this same consciousness cannot be regarded as a consciousness of other aspects or things, it follows that this consciousness cannot be divided into two. And since, in the present case, the single object of two successive moments is truly existent in itself, it necessarily follows that *the earlier consciousness becomes the later; the later too becomes the earlier.* Thus it is also illogical to say that the uncompounded entity as the object of a past moment of consciousness continues to exist in subsequent moments while the past moment of consciousness has itself ceased to exist, or to say that the object of the subsequent moment of consciousness also existed previously while the same consciousness (of the later moment) did not.

Again our opponents may insist that if this object *were* differentiated in terms of temporal sequence, it could not be one. But the object is undifferentiated—even though the cognizing subject is momentary—and therefore the different moments of this sequence repeatedly observe a single thing.

But if the object observed by the present consciousness existed also in the past (in the absence of the present knowing subject), and if it exists later on (when the present moment of consciousness has ceased), why is the cognitive subject of those earlier and later moments not also present?[211] For if the objects observed in distinct moments are unrelated to the observing consciousness, it is nonsense to speak of the perception of outer objects.[212] The only truly existent, single entity is one that is not the object of different instants of consciousness. For if such an entity existed, it would follow that it is not the object of momentary consciousness. Accordingly, it should be understood that it is impossible to establish uncompounded cessation as one truly existent entity.

A single thing may be apprehended by a succession of conscious instants. It cannot, however, be so apprehended if it is a *single, truly existent thing.* When one perceives an individual thing, a vase, for instance, as being the same vase observed yesterday and today, the illusion (that it is the same vase) is based on the uninterrupted succession of instants that cognize, in a similar way, the specific characteristics of the vase. "Single vase," in this sense, is no more than a mental ascription. Any thought that the vase really is one and the same may be disproved by the present argument. This point is easily established by many lines of reasoning such as the argument of nondependency (*ltos med*)[213] and the argument of invalidation (*gnod pa can*).

Thus any claim that a compounded or uncompounded entity truly exists as one is refuted by the present reasoning that proves that such a thing cannot be observed by a sequence of cognitive instants. This same argument, however, does not refute the mere ascription of singularity or plurality, which the Madhyamikas themselves also accept. It is therefore important to appreciate the difference between these two kinds of "oneness." In the *Pramanavarttika*, Dharmakirti adopts a similar method to refute truly existent permanent entities. He says:

> *Granted that a diamond or some other changeless thing*
> *Existed independently of other things,*
> *The consciousness of everyone*
> *Would take its mental aspect constantly.*
> *But granted that conditions have their part to play,*
> *And diamonds are experienced in successive instants,*
> *They're said to be, in every moment, different.*

The establishment of an object as truly existent and one necessarily involves its being observed by a mind. Now, if observation has occurred, this means that the object-condition[214] has given rise to a consciousness apprehending that very object. But since the object, which cannot be divided into different aspects of time or of space, is a wholly independent, truly existent entity, it is impossible for it ever to generate a succession of knowing subjects (moments of cognition). Although the arguments explained above are well able to prove this point, one may still, in one's confusion, have the lingering impression that there is no contradiction involved in thinking that a single, truly existent entity may be observed by a sequence of conscious moments—in the same way that a single pot may be observed by the minds of several different people. Since it is difficult to eradicate this notion, I will explain the foregoing argument in greater detail.

The question to be addressed is this: Is the object of knowledge, which existed at the time of the earlier moment of consciousness, perceived by the subsequent moment of consciousness (at the time when it is known by the earlier consciousness) or not? It cannot possibly be so, since at that time, the later moment of consciousness has not yet arisen. But if it is not so known, it remains (exclusively) the object of the past consciousness, and of necessity, it cannot be the object of the later instant of consciousness. If one accepts this, the object cannot be known in following moments. For it is accepted that the object is permanent, truly existent, and one. As the object is in the first moment, so should it be in later moments. If it is different, this detracts from its permanence and partlessness.[215] Furthermore, by investigating whether or not the past moment of consciousness knows the object at the time of the subsequent moment of consciousness, the notion that the earlier and later objects are one and the same is also refuted. The two objects, namely, of past and future moments of cognition, are different. The object of the past consciousness is not known by the later consciousness, and the object of the later consciousness is not known by the earlier consciousness. Such is the difference between the two objects.

If a distinction is not made between these two occasions, it follows that the later moment of consciousness knows the object of the earlier consciousness, and the earlier moment of consciousness knows the object of the later one. Since the earlier consciousness is the knower of the object of the later consciousness, the earlier consciousness *becomes* the later consciousness. And vice versa: since the later consciousness is the knower of the object of the earlier consciousness, it becomes the earlier one. This means that all notion of successive instants of cognition—of past and future, as well as of object and subject—collapses. So one should understand that if there were such a thing as a truly existent phenomenon, indivisible into parts or aspects, the mind observing it would also have to be single. It could not be multiple.

Some extremely foolish people believe that the object in itself remains one even though the mind perceives it differently. This is wrong. [In point of fact] it contradicts the Vaibhashika doctrine according to which objects are apprehended without the mediation of mental aspects. Non-Buddhist proponents of permanent entities might advocate such a theory, but given that the outer entity that is casting the aspects is one, how does it happen that the aspects appear to perception so differently? It ought not to happen.

The people just referred to will object that since it is possible for the minds of several persons to have a single pot as their object of observation, what contradiction is there in saying that different moments of cognition have as their object one and the same thing? Our answer to this is that what we refer to as "one pot" is the conventional label "pot" ascribed by the conceptual mind (by elimination of all that is not "pot") to what appears in the aspect of a bulbous (potlike) object. A specifically characterized phenomenon (a particular object), which itself is but the gathering of many (atomic) particles, is merely designated as one thing. But it is not one in itself; its oneness is a mere imputation. If it were truly one, it could not be observed by the minds of different people. For this reason, the example used in the objection is disqualified.

In short, when distinct consciousnesses, differentiated in terms of space and time, perceive a single compounded object, one assumes that what is but the conglomeration of many particles, instants, and so on, constitutes a single thing, and it is thus that one claims to be observing it. When, however, it is a case of several minds referring to a single uncompounded phenomenon, what happens is that, by excluding all things, the aspect of what is a nonthing, or absence of thing, is conceptually achieved. Thus even though the uncompounded thing does not exist (as the object of cognition), the mind nevertheless arrives at the designation of uncompoundedness and so on through other-elimination, whereby (compounded) "things" are excluded. And the name or notion, thus achieved, is assumed to be the object. And whenever this notion is recalled, the mental objects in question seem to be the same, and one assumes that they constitute one truly existent entity.

The opinion of the learned is that there is no argument more effective than this in undermining the belief in the *permanent and truly existent* ultimate nature of phenomena (which is revealed through gradual purification of obscuring stains and is the object of successive moments of cognition). To be sure, even though it is ultimate reality, any notion that it is permanent and truly existing is powerfully refuted by the great abbot's argument. Nevertheless, on account of their empty nature, the qualities of the Sugata, namely, the kayas and wisdoms (than which there is certainly nothing greater among all knowledge-objects), as well as all other enlightened attributes, which pervade unlimited time and space, may be posited just as they are described. They are invulnerable to logical refutation.

In the *Madhyamakalankara,* the true existence of an uncompounded entity is refuted simply by showing that whatever is related in time (that is, as an object of successive instants of consciousness) cannot be established as one truly existent entity. In fact, an investigation into whether any knowledge-object is or is not the object of any consciousness related to different places and moments disproves its true existence, regardless of whether it is said to be compounded or uncompounded and even if it is said to be neither.

Whenever anything related spatially and chronologically to something else is said to be "one," its true existence as a single entity is in fact ruled out. All we have is the label "one" attached to a composite phenomenon. It is by a process of exclusion of all that is not a knowledge-object that a knowledge-object is posited. In the same way, by excluding things, one posits a nonthing, and by excluding nonthings, one is able to affirm "thing." In short, words and concepts, which exclude all that is not what they refer to, do indeed produce the notion of a single thing. But every "single thing" may be broken down into segments, each of which may receive the ascription of "one." Indeed, until such time as one actually arrives at the indivisible particle of matter or instant of consciousness, everything may be further divided into myriad parts and no single thing can ever be found. And even the partless particle and partless instant (of mind and matter), inasmuch as they are observed, cannot be established as truly existent, single entities. Therefore, when investigated, whatever is designated as "one" will not be found to possess any oneness; it is a mere imputation on the conventional level. When therefore the Vaibhashikas talk about an uncompounded thing being the single object of earlier and later cognitions, they merely ascribe the notion of oneness to a manifold of momentary aspects. Moreover, when one says, "What you see, I also see," meaning that, when an object of several cognitions (occurring at the same time but from different perspectives) is apprehended as a single entity, it is the several characteristics of the ground of labeling of that very object that are being designated as "one"—and nothing else. In sum, no object of any consciousness differentiated in terms of space and time can be a truly existing, single entity.

Some people might object that a nonthing or absence is indivisible. In general, however, "nonthing" may be broken down into its various instances, such as "nonpot" (absence of pot) or "complete nothingness." And even a specific instance of nonthing ("nonpot" or absence of pot) can be further divided into as many categories as the corresponding thing itself possesses (for example, a "non–golden pot" or "absence of golden pot"). For this is just the conceptual aspect of a particular nonthing, perceived by the mind, which is arrived at simply by excluding the particular thing itself. "Nonthing" is, as it were, an "object appearing to the mind"—and nothing more. It does not have the slightest degree of extramental existence in its own right. It should therefore be understood that as long as phenomena, whether things or nonthings, are the objects of different consciousnesses, they are not truly established. That is, they are not truly existent, single things. If, for the sake of argument, we accept that the infinitesimal particle is truly existent as "one," no particle can be truly superadded to it in the position that it occupies, for of necessity it is indivisible in relation to any other thing placed upon it. This inevitably means that there can only ever be that one particle, and other (extended) knowledge-objects cannot arise. The same is true of everything in the whole range of phenomena that are considered to be truly existent.

A particle posited as a truly existent, single entity may be broken down into segments in terms of spatial direction and time. First, in terms of space, if this particle is not observed from one side or other by some consciousnesses, it ought to be categorized accordingly into the same number of unobserved phenomena (particles). Then, in terms of time, if, out of the limitless cognitions (extending for moments, days, months, years, and kalpas) of all living beings, there are moments of nonobservation of this particle, it follows that this particle can be categorized into the same amount of "nonobserved particles," according to the number of moments in question. And for as many knowable aspects attributable to a particle in terms of what it is not (for instance, that it is not a consciousness or a pot), so too may the particle be categorized. And conversely, if the particle is observed by a consciousness in time or space, it is appropriate to consider it multiple, on the understanding that such and such a particle is observed by this or that consciousness. For to the extent that aspects that can be mentally ascribed to a particle (as being subtle or small or as being a knowledge-object, for example), to that extent is the particle multiple. It dissolves into multiplicity.

Therefore, of all these different aspects, which aspect is to be identified as the truly existent, single particle? And is it not just empty words to claim that the truly existent, single particle is none of these but stands apart from them—that the truly existent, single particle is what cannot be known by any consciousness related to time and space? All such particles are endlessly divisible. How can there be one particle that is in itself truly existent? Out of all of them, it is impossible to identify a single one that cannot be further divided, for all can be categorized into a multiplicity of features. They are not single entities. It is impossible to appeal to their indivisibility as a basis

for asserting their truly existent individuality. And it will surely be difficult
to find any other criterion for thus positing them.

To sum up: If, out of the entire range of knowledge-objects, there were
a single, truly existent entity, all consciousnesses related to time and place
would of necessity be observing that one thing and no other. Inevitably,
therefore, in terms of time and place, there could be no other phenomenon
aside from that very thing. Finally, and equally inescapably, the knowing
subject, the very consciousness that separately observes such a single entity,
must likewise disappear. For if there were a knowing subject, an aspect
could be distinguished in that putative single entity that is not the entity itself.[216] If, on the other hand, there is no consciousness as subject of the
object cognized, there is no percept (that is, thing apprehended by consciousness) either, for what is there to observe the object, even if it is truly
existent and one? And if observation is ruled out, the entire varied spectrum of knowable phenomena would be reduced to nothing, like a rabbit's
horns. On the other hand, the appearances occurring in time and space can
be perceived in all their varied clarity—precisely because, within the range
of knowledge-objects, there is not, has not been, and never will be any such
thing as a truly existent, single entity.

> If, of all the things that may be known,
> There were but one existing truly,
> No object of cognition could we ever see.
> But since no knowledge-object—no, not even one—
> Has such a true existence,
> A bright, unbounded world of things appears
> As objects to be known.

Ema! How inconceivable and wonderful is the nature of phenomena!
This nature is known by the Tathagata, and it is by listening to his lion's
roar, whereby he expounds the equal status of all things, that the strength
of one's intelligence grows—until one is able to swallow, as it were in a single mouthful, the infinity of space.[217] Brandishing the sword of Manjushri,
the blade of profound reasoning difficult to fathom, which instantly shears
through the webs of our concepts about phenomenal existence, we should
have perfect confidence that emptiness manifests as dependent arising. It is
because not even one phenomenon is truly existent that phenomena are
able to appear. By enlarging on the reasoning given here in the *Madhyamakalankara*, I have, for the sake of my fortunate readers and according to

my own understanding of the matter, explained the reasoning that demonstrates the great emptiness of true existence.

14. To deny that the object continues coexisting with consciousness is also untenable
15. For if it does not coexist, if follows that the uncompounded object is momentary

> 5
> And if the uncompounded is not present
> In conscious moments earlier and later,
> This very uncompounded, you should know,
> Is momentary, like consciousness itself.

If, on the other hand, it is said by the Vaibhashikas that the same uncompounded object does not indeed arise in both earlier and later moments of consciousness, it follows that the uncompounded object of the preceding consciousness is not present to the subsequent consciousness, and the object of the latter does not exist at the time of the previous consciousness. In short, the object of distinct moments of consciousness is different. It should be clear to any intelligent person that if the object of one moment of consciousness does not continue to coexist with the following moment of consciousness, this same object (even if considered to be uncompounded) is just as momentary as consciousness, which ceases as soon as it arises.

15. What is wrong with the assertion that the object does not continue to coexist with different moments of consciousness?
16. If the uncompounded is dependent on conditions, it is compounded

> 6
> Should it arise by force of moments
> That occur in sequence one by one,
> It is not uncompounded.
> It is like the mind and mental factors.

If an uncompounded cessation is the object of different knowing subjects, it is established as distinct (in different moments) and is proved to be momentary. If our opponents still insist that this object is uncompounded, we shall ask them whether this uncompounded entity that is said to be the object of different conscious subjects (precedent and subsequent) is dependent on conditions or not. In the first case, if it is dependent, and it is thought that the earlier instants of the uncompounded give rise to the later moments of the uncompounded thing, it is clear that this same object is a thing, arising through causes and conditions, in which case it is not uncompounded. It is, for example, like the mind and mental factors.

16. If the uncompounded does not depend on conditions, it must be either forever existent or forever nonexistent

> 7
> If you consider that in all these moments
> The uncompounded, wholly on its own, occurs,
> It must forever be or never be,
> For there is no dependence upon something else.

In the second case, it may be considered by the Vaibhashikas that in these different instants, the uncompounded object is independent of all conditioning factors, namely, the preceding moments of consciousness. Instead, it arises in its own right and is not dependent in the slightest way. If this is so, the uncompounded object either must always exist or must never exist, for it is unaffected by any external causes.

Why must the assertion that a thing is uncaused entail either its permanent existence or its permanent nonexistence? If, for the sake of argument, we accept that a thing can exist uncaused, how could it be otherwise than that it should endure constantly without ever being overthrown? In the case of other things, which exist at one moment but not the next, these states of existence and nonexistence are possible in dependence on the presence or absence of causes. In other words, if there is a cause, there is an effect; if there is no cause, there is no effect. By contrast, since the object in question has no cause, it cannot cease. Given that it exists, there is no overturning it even at a later stage. There cannot be a time when it does not arise. In the case of other things, however, when they are not produced, their nonappearance is due to the fact that their causes are not complete. But an uncaused thing by definition has no need of causes for its manifestation, in which case, why should it not exist always? And by the same token, there is no reason it should not exist everywhere.

Moreover, all existing things are produced from their respective causes. If the seeds are not sown, the crop does not appear and is not enjoyed. Conversely, if seeds are sown, the crop is apt to appear. Cause-dependent entities do indeed appear in reality, and they do so by the power of their causes. On the other hand, since "uncaused things" follow from no cause at all, they cannot ever appear in reality; they are not apt to exist. They are to be compared with a rabbit's horns and the other stock examples.

For fear that their "momentary uncompounded entities" might turn out to be compounded, those who claim that the uncompounded is independent of conditions are forced to the conclusion that the *momentary* uncompounded entity has *permanent* existence or nonexistence—and there is no statement more contradictory or ridiculous.

The so-called uncompounded object, a conceptual reflection or aspect arrived at through the elimination of all causally efficient things, is merely assumed to exist as a truly existent, single entity. But since this object (the uncompounded cessation) is not causally efficient even conventionally, how could it possibly exist on the ultimate level! It is appropriate to conceive of functional entities that appear directly to the undamaged senses as being this or that. But it is highly inappropriate to rely on something assumed to be permanent and truly existent but which is not perceived and is not established by valid reasoning.

12. A summary of the refutation of permanent, truly existent entities

8
What purpose does it serve to pin your fond beliefs
On what is destitute of causal potency?
What use for lustful girls to estimate
The charms or defects of a neutered male?

The eternal atman, the almighty Ishvara, uncompounded cessation, and so forth, are but the claims of dogmatism. In themselves they have not the slightest degree of causal capacity.[218] What is to be gained by ascribing existence to such entities, claiming that they are the creator, and so on? For women who desire love, it serves no purpose to look upon a eunuch and to assess his beauty or otherwise. For the eunuch is in no position to satisfy their passion. If the ladies wish for intercourse, their hopes are destined for frustration, since the eunuch is unable to do the required deed! In just the same way, putative eternal entities are by definition destitute of any causal efficiency. And whatever one may say to the contrary, nothing will ever be gained from such assertions. Intelligent people make assertions that prove or disprove functioning entities; they do not waste their strength establishing anything about nonexistent figments (which are no more than names), however pressingly they may be asserted. For this reason, just as a healthy person has no need of medicine, there is no need for such fantasies to be refuted. One can simply ignore them.[219]

It could of course be objected that this is the reverse of what we have just done. For have we not ourselves just refuted the existence of eternal entities? In fact, we have done no more than disprove the misconceptions of our opponents; if they had not made such assertions, there would have been no need for us to refute them. For it should be understood that this refutation of ours is solely in response to the opposing position.[220] The learned define causal efficiency as a characteristic of *things*. They demonstrate that in respect of such things, namely persons and phenomena, both kinds of valid cognition unerringly establish their lack of self[221] and refute their contraries: things the putative existence of which is no more than a misconception. When people take causally efficient things as a basis for examination using valid reasoning, proving or disproving them as the case may be, they will invariably achieve their aims. Such people are like passionate women considering suitable partners.

To this it may be objected that, since it is only things (*dngos po*) that are shown to be without self, not all phenomena (*chos*) are included in this demonstration of the nonexistence of self. But this is not true. The word "all" refers to whatever one wishes to express; and what one wishes to express in the present case is causally efficient things. If it is understood that such things are without self, why should we not also understand nonthings in the same light? For these nonthings are simply the exclusions of (causally efficient) things; they are nonimplicative negations. We may be sure, therefore, even by the force of conventional reasoning, that what is devoid of causal capacity has not the slightest degree of independent existence. And if is it shown that nonthings (which cannot be posited as self-sufficient) are incapable of proof or refutation, what need is there to say that they are unestablished on the ultimate level?

It is within the context of an examination of "things" that whatever is found not to be such is called a nonthing. Apart from this, it is never possible for so-called nonthings to arise in their own right, independently. This being so, how could any instructed person consider that nonthings have a self-sufficient existence of their own? And if they are not so considered, what need is there to refute them?[222] Even if one were to establish them, *what* exactly would be established? They are mere figments, like a barren woman's child, and can be left out of the count. Of course, the *term* "nonthing" exists, and it is so defined in relation to "things." And it takes no great effort to establish or refute it (it being just a term).

Consequently, relative phenomena are posited only as things that are causally efficient, and since they function as such, they are necessarily momentary. For whatever is not momentary is disqualified from any kind of function on a gradual and momentary basis. This manner of understanding constitutes a crucial point when explaining the relative. According to the Vaibhashika system, which, when discussing the conventional, regards "substantially" existing entities (*rdzas*) as the relative, whatever is merely an imputation has no existence as a self-sufficient entity. It is therefore unnecessary to consider the imputation a separate, permanent object in itself—in just the same way that the universal or general idea "pot" is not separable from the (individual, concrete) pot.

On the ultimate level, things are established as neither permanent nor impermanent. On the relative level, however, they are certainly impermanent, and it should be understood that when one calls something permanent, one does so merely in contrast with (obviously) impermanent things, ascribing permanence to what is in fact an uninterrupted continuity of momentary things of the same kind (*rigs 'dra rgyun mi 'chad pa*). For when one searches phenomena for their ultimate status, one finds that they are but dependent imputations. And these dependently originated appearances— just as they are not established—cannot be refuted. They are like the reflection of the moon in water. For this very reason, they have no true existence as single entities.

Whereas the argument of neither one nor many refutes truly existent, single entities at all times and from all points of view, it should not be thought that it refutes the mere designation of oneness. For this is a mere name ascribed to something that is in fact manifold and does not exist as one. Understood in this way, the single entity is not refuted by the argument of neither one nor many. It is important therefore to make a clear distinction between true existence as an absolutely single entity and the merely conventional imputation of singularity. For if one does not directly ascertain on what level one is speaking, it is as when one hears, out of context, a word like *sendha* that has several meanings (salt, chariot, and so on). However much one may study and reflect upon the texts, one will be hopelessly entangled in confusion and will fail to understand. The different levels are to be properly distinguished.

11. A refutation of the person considered as a truly existent, single entity

> 9
> The person is not able to be pointed out
> As other than existing momentarily;
> It should be clearly noted
> That it has no true existence in the singular or plural.

The continuum of sentient beings, the ground that is said to be either fettered or liberated and extends from life to life in samsara, is assumed to be a single entity and is called a person.[223] When it is said that a "person" wanders in samsara and attains nirvana, many successive (conscious) instants are brought together and are so designated. The conceptual mind refers to this as a "self," a "man," and so forth. People do not examine what it is that constitutes their uninterrupted continuum[224] and simply take it for their "self" and think, "I am." The non-Buddhist Samkhyas define the self, or purusha, as a permanent, truly existent entity, the enjoyer of manifestation, of which, however, it is not the creator. They believe that this self is by nature unoriginated and has always existed. Other non-Buddhists believe that the self is all-pervading, while others deny this. Some think that it is inanimate, some that it is conscious, and so on. It is thus that their tenets fasten the iron bands of the innate sense of self with the nails of the imputed self.

The Vatsiputriyas[225] consider that the self is a real thing and is the basis upon which the karmic process unfolds. They believe, however, that the self is indefinable: It cannot be regarded as either identical with or different from the aggregates; nor can it be said to be permanent or impermanent. All those within the Dharma who uphold authentically Buddhist tenets believe that the sense of "I" arises merely in relation to the collection and continuity of the five aggregates; it has no existence from its own side, a fact that can be demonstrated by reasoning. Since the five aggregates, which perpetuate the experience of the samsaric world (*nyer len gyi phung po*), arise and disintegrate moment by moment, they are not the self. And since it is impossible to point out the existence of even an atom of the so-called person in some other way that accords with reason, it is concluded that the "person" is no more than a figment imputed on its ground of designation, namely, the aggregates. Other than that, the wise have understood with the greatest clarity that, in truth, it has no inherent existence in either the singular or plural. The self cannot be shown to exist in separation from the aggregates. But since the aggregates are many and impermanent, the self cannot be a single, truly existent entity. On the other hand, if the self is momentary, it is subject to constant change and is thus manifold, in which case, the perpetrator of actions and the experiencer of their results are different entities. But if the self is not momentary, the past self does not disintegrate and the subsequent self does not arise—for the self is a permanent and single entity. In that case, there can be no question of bondage and freedom, suffering and bliss, and so on. Being unborn, it cannot exist as a thing; it has no more reality than a barren woman's child. Speaking broadly, such a permanent self is refuted by the arguments that negate the existence of permanent, truly existent entities. As for the "inexpressible self," since no pervading sign or proof (*khyab byed*) of its true existence can be found, how could such an inexpressible self (the probandum, or *khyab bya*) ever enjoy true existence? Since it is neither identical with, nor distinct from, the aggregates, it is not very difficult to establish that it is as nonexistent as a flower growing in the sky. For if indeed it is something that exists on the relative level, it must be posited as either the same or different in relation to other things. But since this is not at all a feature of the self (as propounded by the Vatsiputriyas), to say that it is a "real" entity—a thesis in which a probandum is asserted without any proof—is extremely foolish. It is like someone believing that junipers are still present even when it has been shown that there are no trees.

The Lord Buddha has said:

> For it is in relation to collected parts
> That we may designate the so-called chariot.
> And likewise on the basis of a continuity of aggregates,
> We relatively designate a living being.

In accordance with this scripture then, although on the ultimate level there is no such thing as a truly existent person (for it has no inherent existence in either the singular or the plural), on the conventional level of the relative truth, the uninterrupted continuity of the five aggregates is referred to as a self. It is only when the five aggregates are not distinguished and are taken all together as a single thing that the term "person" is applied to them. Similarly, it is when the instants that make up the continuity of the aggregates are regarded as one entity that one speaks of a "continuum." And by designating as a single item all the phenomena pertaining to this continuum,[226] without dividing them in terms of space and time, it is possible to say that a certain person passes away in a given moment here and will take birth at a later stage there.

Inborn ego-clinging has for its referent object a mere "I" imputed in dependence on the five aggregates. Its referent is not the five aggregates clearly distinguished. This ego-clinging, wherein the objective referent (that is, the five aggregates) and the subjective sense of "I" are not clearly differentiated, comes about by the strength of habit. Nevertheless, if an analysis is made and the objective referent is distinguished from the subjective sense of "I," it must be said that since the ground of designation of the imputed person is the five aggregates, the aggregates are what is labeled as the person. This is the same as saying that the mind that apprehends a pot observes the specific characteristics (shape and so on) of its basis of designation, although it has for its referent object no more than the imputation (or name) "pot."

Consequently, when, in a bid to find out what it really is, an examination is made of the self as being that which underpins the karmic process of cause and effect, some consider that it is constituted by the mental continuum, others by the continuum of all the aggregates, and so on. Indeed, the karmic consequences of an action fall upon the perpetrator of that action; they cannot ripen elsewhere. But this so-called perpetrator is also something made up of manifold elements to which the imputation of a single, individual "doer" is simply attached. On the ultimate level, there is no truly existent agent of action; neither is there a truly existent karmic process of cause and effect, nor anything else for that matter. It is on account of this crucial fact that the effects of actions once performed will be inevitably experienced, and one never encounters the effect of actions that one has not performed.[227]

Now, if the agent of an action really existed (as opposed to being a simple imputation), and if this agent were a permanent entity, it would be incapable of action; neither could it experience the results of actions. On the other hand, if the agent were impermanent, it would follow that the doer of an action and the experiencer of its effect would be distinct, and it would be incorrect to say that the agent experiences the result. Therefore, only the "I" that, as a single entity, is merely imputed to a manifold of aggregates can be admitted as the doer of an action and the experiencer of its consequences: "Before, I did this. Now, I am planting these seeds. Later, in the autumn, I shall eat the fruits." Making no distinctions of time and so on, one simply assumes that one has a single identity or is a single individual. And it is in the context of this mere, unexamined "I" that one claims that an action is done by oneself. But since on the ultimate level this mere "I" of present experience is said not to exist, there is no need to locate the basis of the karmic process by a process of rational investigation.

When we think that we have suffered in the past but that now we are happy, we make no distinction between the five aggregates existing in the past and the five aggregates now present. We label them all as a single being. Likewise in the midst of samsaric existence, which is without beginning or end, we impute upon the aggregates a single entity and think, "It is I." It is on the strength of this that, in the absence of any investigation and any distinction of time and place, it is acceptable to say that the mere "I" is the basis for the karmic process. If, on the other hand, one does make such distinctions (in connection with this "I"), since cause and effect cannot coincide, the perpetrator of an action cannot be established as the experiencer of its result. That which did an action in the past and that which becomes the present and future experiencer is merely designated by imputation as a single entity or self—no more than a label affixed to a collection of many items. If one considers well, the past, present, and future aggregates are but a succession of momentary constituents. They cannot be one. But within the same analysis, because they are imputed to a single continuum, the perpetrator and the experiencer are said to constitute just one mindstream. There is indeed no contradiction in such an estimate. However, if one also subjects the aggregates themselves (of the said continuum) to an investigation, they too are found to be no more than imputations. And in the final analysis, no truly existent, single entity can be found that is not an imputation ascribed to a multiplicity. To sum up, it is important to understand that a person cannot be a truly existent, single entity, and that therefore it is the person merely imputed upon a multiplicity of aggregates that can be regarded as the support and basis of the karmic process and so on. The purpose of the investigation, at this point, is to identify the so-called basis of the karmic process, that is, the self mentioned in the teachings as that which reaps the effects of actions performed. This self, however, should not be understood in the sense of a ground for habitual tendencies.[228]

10. A refutation of pervasive universals as being truly existent, single entities

> 10a
> How can a pervasive thing be one?
> For it is linked with things in different places.

Broadly speaking, there are two kinds of pervaders or pervasive entities. On the one hand, there is a universal pervader that is concomitant with a plurality of things. This is the case, for instance, of universals, which pervade their particular instances by being of the same nature as they. On the other hand, there are pervaders that coexist with, and permeate, individual things (until they disintegrate) while yet being of a different nature than they, as when cloth is saturated by dye. Of these, universal pervaders such as space, time, and direction, which are considered great and unlimited, are assumed by various non-Buddhist systems to be really existent entities. Of these, time, for example, is said to be the cause of phenomena. The Vaisheshikas and others believe that universals (*spyi*) are concomitant with their particular instances (*rang gis gsal ba*), that is, a multiplicity of particular things (*bye brag*). They pervade them; they are permanent and invisible realities and are what join together all the particular instances (of a single class), like a rope used to tie a herd of cows together. The Vaisheshikas believe that great universals such as "existence" pervade all phenomena, while lesser ones correspond to more restricted universals (*spyi nyi tshe ba*) such as "cowness." The Samkhyas, for their part, believe that the universal and its particular instance are of the same substance. The argument given in stanza 10, however, refutes all universal, pervasive entities of any kind. For since they are associated with different objects, such as trees, which exist in various directions (locations), how can universals (even a universal like space), which are believed to pervade things, be truly existent, single entities? If space and other generally pervasive entities[229] are not connected with what they pervade, namely, things existing in space and time, they cannot be called pervasive. But if they *are* connected with them, can the pervader of the tree in the east be the same as the pervader of the tree in the west? If it is the same, it follows that the pervasive entity is all one and the same, and by the same token that the things pervaded—for example, the trees (in different directions or locations)—blend indivisibly with the universal and cannot be differentiated. They all become identical. Such a view is further invalidated by the consequence that if a particular item, such as a tree, grows, other trees different from it in time and space must of necessity grow with it. On the other hand, if the various instances are not one, how can the pervasive entity be a single item? For it must be multiple, in accordance with the number of its particular instances.

There are several different ways of defining the universal and the particular, but in sum, if the two are unconnected, they cannot be described as pervader and pervaded. If, on the other hand, they are connected, this argument alone is sufficient to show that the universal is not a truly existent, single entity.

What we have referred to as a pervasive universal is an "elimination of other," the conceptual result of the exclusion of everything that is other than what is being referred to. In reality, it has no existence of its own. For example, when one catches sight of something with branches and leaves, the conceptual mind excludes all that is not that thing and attaches to the manifold of items a general name "tree."[230] This name is also applied to (is concomitant with) all the different instances (of tree) irrespective of space and time. The conceptual mind identifies the universal (generally characterized) with the specifically characterized thing (the individual object), mixing the appearance with the ascribed name. In the logical process of proving and disproving, when a universal is refuted, the particular is also refuted, and this procedure is free of the faults that would be entailed if one were to consider, as in certain non-Buddhist systems, that the two are substantially the same or different.[231] In this process, the single primary conceptual distinguisher or isolate, which appears as the reverse of all that is other than a given object, is the universal. A secondary distinguisher is the distinguisher of a distinguisher, which isolates an object from other items in the same class[232] and actually points to a specifically characterized phenomenon, a particular object. Both universals and particulars, however, are pluralities of phenomena onto which a single identity is imputed. Thus they cannot be truly existent, single entities. The argument disproving the real existence of space is given later.

9. A refutation of nonpervasive entities regarded as single and truly existent

10. A refutation of external objects
11. A refutation of extended objects regarded as single and truly existent

> 10b
> Things extended, likewise, are not one;
> For instance, they can be both hidden and revealed.

The gross, extended objects referred to are nothing but agglomerations of many infinitesimal particles. This is true, for example, of our bodies as well as of the appearances of other objects, from pots and cloths to houses, mountains, continents, Mount Meru, and all the vast reaches of the three-thousandfold universe. Since they exist distinctly as things that are partly visible and partly invisible (as in the case of a body partially concealed by clothing), extended objects are not established as truly existent, single entities. The body, for instance, has parts that are covered by clothes and parts that are not so covered. And the expression "for instance" in the root text indicates that a body may have parts that move and parts that do not move, parts that are painted and parts that are unpainted, parts that are burned and parts that are not burned. Since it possesses many conflicting features, how could such a body be truly one?[233]

One may object that only portions of the body, such as the legs, are covered or uncovered—not the body as a whole, namely, the possessor of the parts. But then we must ask: Is the body, taken as a whole, the same as its parts or not? If it is the same, it is clear that the body is a collection of many different phenomena (and not a simple, indivisible whole). If, on the other hand, the body is not the same as its parts, it should be perceptible as different from them. But this is obviously not the case, since no such body is perceived. Furthermore, the two items—body and parts—would be as unconnected from each other as a pot and a pillar.

It may be objected that the body and its parts are bound in a "relation of inherence,"[234] on account of which they are not to be observed separately. To this we reply that if the relation of inherence between the body and the legs is not the same as the relation of inherence between the body and the arms, the body as an extended object cannot be "one." And if they are the same, they are in manifest contradiction since they are observed as manifold. Thus when one speaks of "one body," this is but a gathering of many parts that is assumed to be a single entity. Oneness is a mere imputation; the body does not truly exist as one. One may talk about the body in this way, but if there is such a thing as a body truly existing as a single entity, one is bound to ask whether it is identical with or different from its parts.

11. A refutation of the indivisible particle as a truly existent, single entity
12. A presentation of the refutation
13. The position of the opponent

> 11a
> Joining or surrounding,
> Or disposed without interstices—

The five objects of sense and the five sense powers (otherwise known as the ten dhatus endowed with form)[235] appear as coarse (extended) objects, but they may be broken down into many parts. They are seen to be aggregations composed of many elements, which are mutually exclusive in the sense that they cannot occupy the same location. These parts can be further fragmented, down to the level of infinitesimal particles. For example, an earthenware pot can be smashed in pieces. These pieces can in turn be reduced to smaller fragments and thence to fine dust. Because everything endowed with form (that is, everything material) can be broken down into separate parts, they are termed *gzugs*, in Tibetan, which simply means "breakable." In fact, "material form" is understood as that which obstructs or offers resistance on contact. Unlike consciousness, it is something that can be taken hold of and damaged. This then is the definition of the term *gzugs*, or form, which can also be further explained as that which can be pierced,[236] as with a knife. It may be objected that this does not apply in the case of the infinitesimal particle, but the point being made is that gross extended objects are able to disintegrate, and so there is no fault. Also, in the case of the imperceptible form,[237] this too is so named because its support, namely, the body, is itself subject to damage. For in general, a term may be (1) a description, (2) a mere name in the sense of a conventional designation, or (3) a name that is also a description. These are the three ways of classifying terms.[238] Consequently, even imperceptible forms can be defined as breakable "forms."[239] On the other hand, gross extended objects visible to the eyes are a particular instance of the category "form."

When a material object (*bems po*) is divided into fragments, the smallest particle, which cannot be further divided, is referred to as an infinitesimal particle (*rdul phra rab*). It is so called because no further reduction is possible; it is the finest particle. Seven of these infinitesimal particles constitute one "small particle" (*rdul phran*). Gradually, by a process of aggregation in multiples of seven, one arrives at the so-called iron particle; water particle; rabbit particle; sheep particle; ox particle; sun-ray particle; particles the size of louse eggs, lice, and barley grains; and particles of a finger's width.[240] It should be understood that, in the desire realm, the smallest particle perceptible to the senses is a gathering of eight infinitesimal particles.[241] This does not include the particles of sound and the auditive sense power, which, if they were included, would result in a larger agglomeration. One arrives at the final, indivisible particles by conceptually separating out the individual particles of the elements and the senses. In themselves, however, these particles do not have individual aspects. It is further said that the quantity of infinitesimal particles gathered in gross extended objects corresponds to the size of those same objects. There were certain authorities in Tibet who said that it is impossible to posit such infinitesimal particles. This theory, however, is untenable, being invalidated by the fact that the composition of extended objects would be otherwise impossible. In short, granted that extended objects can be divided into smaller and smaller parts, it was thought that if the infinitesimal particle were to vanish it would be impossible for gross objects to exist. It was therefore concluded that there must exist infinitesimal particles, which cannot be made smaller. This is the general idea behind the atomic theory.[242] Non-Buddhists believe that the infinitesimal particle is permanent; Buddhists, by contrast, consider it to be momentary.

Now, when these infinitesimal particles combine to form extended objects, there must either be a space between them or not. With regard to this point, three theories were advanced. The followers of Kanada (the Vaisheshikas) say that in order for an agglomeration to be formed, the particles must touch. For if the particles do not touch, the occurrence of even one extended object would be ruled out. Therefore, the particles are joined one to one.

But if this is so, the indivisible particles are joined in different directions, with some sides joined and some sides not joined. This means that the particles have parts and therefore are not indivisible. On the other hand, if they have no parts that are not joined, how can two particles be differentiated? They would completely coincide and become one. But this cannot be correct, for in that case even Mount Meru, the king of mountains, would be no more than a single indivisible particle!

On the whole, schools like the Vaibhashikas and certain others say that the particles cohere and do not drift apart owing to a reciprocal energy. They reject the earlier belief that the particles are joined and say that a central particle is surrounded by other particles, all of which are separated by space like the hairs in a yak's tail or the blades of grass in a lawn. But this is not acceptable either. If the particles are separated by space, it follows that other particles—of light (in the daytime) or of darkness (at night)—are able to interpose themselves. And since even the particles of light and dark cannot be in mutual contact, there must of necessity be other particles coming in between. And in the end, between two infinitesimal particles, even the three worlds could be placed!

The Sautrantikas and others think that the particles "touch but are not joined." They consider that the previous two beliefs, to the effect that particles either join or do not join, are equally untenable. They therefore say that though the multitude of particles are not joined one to one, nevertheless there is no space between them, and this is why they are perceived as being in contact. But this is just the same as saying that they are joined, for they touch and there is no space between them. There is not the slightest difference in the two positions. As long as the particles do not become one, it is impossible for there not to be a space between them. The Sautrantika theory of contact and the Vaisheshika theory of joining come to the same thing. This was proved also by the great charioteers of the Doctrine. If the particles touch or if there is no space between them, they cannot be other than joined. If they are not joined, they cannot touch and must be separated by a space, as has been shown in the previous discussion.

It is stated that these three opinions concerning infinitesimal particles regarded as the building blocks of extended phenomena (that they are joined together; that they are grouped together without joining, being separated by interstitial space; or that they do not join but are without interstitial space) are all refuted by arguments that consider their directional parts.

13. A refutation of infinitesimal particles as truly existent entities
14. If a particle has no parts, extended objects are ruled out

> 11b
> The particle that has a central place
> Is turned exclusively toward a single particle.

12
If you insist that this is truly so
(Though it must also face the other particles),
How is it then that earth and water
And all other things extend—or maybe they do not?

The problem of directional parts is to be investigated as follows. When gross extended objects are formed, the particles concerned must congregate on all sides, around a central particle, which is like a house (with an east-facing side and other sides facing in the other directions). When an extended object is formed through the aggregation of numerous particles, it may be affirmed (by an opponent) that the central particle only faces the eastern particle, for it has no other parts or aspects than this. Consequently, although the central particle must face the particles in the other directions, it may be maintained that this central particle is wholly one-sided and east-facing. But if this is what the opponent is saying, how can the extension of gross objects, such as earth and water, ever be accounted for?[243] Or is the opponent saying that they are not extended? If it *is* believed that it is by the accumulation of particles that earth and water gradually extend, the assertion that the side facing one particle is also the side that faces the other particles[244] is to be rejected, since it is a contradiction. How so? When a gross extended object is formed and the central particle is simultaneously surrounded by ten particles in the ten directions, it follows that, since the central particle is not divisible into parts, all the other particles necessarily occupy the position of the particle located in one direction only. All the other directions are devoid of meaning; they all become a single direction. And however many particles may be put together, there can be no advance on the earlier state, and the formation of extended objects becomes impossible.

We might continue this investigation in still finer detail. If we consider all the particles occurring in the position of a single particle,[245] we can see that unless all the earlier parts are pervaded by all the later parts, the particles themselves cannot be indivisible, for it would follow that they have parts that are pervaded and parts that are not pervaded. On the other hand, if the particles pervade each other completely, they become one, there being not the slightest gap between them. If they are one, there is no extension. Conversely, if there is extension, the particles are not indivisible.[246] Thus it is impossible for an indivisible particle to pervade another particle. If therefore an indivisible particle truly exists as a single entity, the vast array of particles composing the immense mandala of the earth and the great oceans could never extend in accordance with the quantity of their particles; they would only ever be the extent of a single particle. It should be understood that the word for "particle" (*rdul phran*) used in this context refers to the smallest, indivisible particle (*rdul phra rab*). It does not refer to the particle that is a sevenfold aggregation. There is, generally speaking, a difference between the particle (*rdul phran*) and the infinitesimal or fine particle (*rdul phra rab*). Normally "particle" refers to the sevenfold grouping, whereas the infinitesimal particle is considered the finest or ultimate particle. The Tibetan word *rdul phran,* which is a contraction of *rdul phra mo,* is in fact a general term, with the result that it is necessary to distinguish the particular instances to which the term is applied.

14. If a particle has parts, it cannot be infinitesimal

> 13
> If you say the sides that face
> The different particles are different,
> How comes it that the finest particle is one:
> A single entity devoid of parts?

If, alarmed by the above investigation, our opponent admits that it is not the same side of the central particle that faces all the other directions, but that the particle has other sides turned to the other particles, how can it be maintained that this infinitesimal particle is a single, truly existent, partless entity? Indeed, it now has ten directional parts! It should therefore be understood that even subtle phenomena (in this case infinitesimal particles) are posited in dependence on extended phenomena, and that even the basis of imputation of the infinitesimal particle itself is posited in reference to the gathering of a multiplicity. It is impossible for the particle to be a specifically characterized, truly single, and partless entity.

12. A demonstration that the refutation of the existence of infinitesimal particles also entails the refutation of manifold phenomena
13. A presentation of the argument

> 14
> The particle, it's proved, does not exist inherently.
> And therefore it is clear that eyes or substance and the rest,

The many things proposed by our and other schools,
Have no intrinsic being.

Given that the infinitesimal particle is shown to be without inherent existence, it is clear that manifold phenomena—the visual organ, for example, posited by the Buddhists, or the substances in which the non-Buddhists believe—are also devoid of inherent existence. To be sure, if there is no clay, there is no possibility of earthenware vessels. In this respect, certain Buddhist schools consider that the visual and other sense powers, together with form and the consciousness generated in the aspect of form, all have an ultimate existence. For their part, the disciples of Kanada and other non-Buddhist schools believe that substance, properties, and the rest also exist in an ultimate sense.

13. Establishing the validity of the pervasion

> 15
> The former are their nature, or they constitute them.
> The latter are the properties of particles, themselves the
>   agents of all action.
> Universals and instantiated things
> Are only their agglomeration.

How does it follow that because there are no partless particles, objects such as eyes have no inherent existence? The Buddhist schools say that the ten dhatus endowed with form (that is, the five sense powers and their objects) are but accumulations of particles; the latter are their (innermost) nature. Non-Buddhists say that the joining of two and more particles results, directly and indirectly, in the formation of wholes. Form, smell, taste, and so on are the qualities or properties of the particle. The action of walking, for example, the lifting and lowering of the feet, the bending and stretching of the limbs—since they are based on the possession of a body—are, in principle, the activity of the particles. Moreover, the particles are also linked with, or are the support of, universal ideas: the great universals such as existence or the more restricted universals such as "cow." And they are also linked with particulars such as the elements, earth and so on. Thus the particle is the universal and the particular instance of things. Now, given that it is believed that all things are the agglomeration of particles, it follows that if the particles do not exist, everything that is either directly or indirectly related to them cannot exist either—for they are rooted in the particles. Since the infinitesimal particle does not exist, neither do the ten dhatus endowed with form (the five senses and their objects). Therefore, the five consciousnesses produced by the dominant condition (*bdag rkyen*) of the five sense organs and the object-condition (*dmigs rkyen*) of the five sense objects cannot exist truly. And if these consciousnesses do not exist, neither does the mental consciousness, which is the outcome of the immediately preceding condition (*de ma thag rkyen,* namely, the preceding moment of consciousness). If the six consciousnesses do not exist, neither does the immediately preceding mind. And if the mind does not truly exist, neither do the mental factors, such as perception, feeling, and intention,[247] which are coterminous (*grub bde rdzas gcig*) with the mind. All this can be understood without difficulty.

Furthermore, nonassociated conditioning factors,[248] directly or indirectly connected with form and so forth, have no true existence either. They have no reality in themselves, for they are no more than mental imputations. The learned have dissected and destroyed them time and time again—no need to assail once more what is already defunct! It is also clear that imperceptible forms have no existence. For they are said to be established on the causal basis of the elements (earth, water, and so on); and since the elements have no existence, imperceptible forms are likewise nonexistent. As for uncompounded entities like space, these have already been refuted.

Therefore, since it is evident that even the eighteen dhatus[249] have no inherent existence, all the many items postulated by the Buddhist schools are clearly shown to be without true existence. And as for the many entities propounded by non-Buddhists, their existence is disproved by the fact that they are but aggregations of two or more particles, designated as wholes. If the particles—the building blocks—do not exist, then the whole does not exist either. With the exception of sound (which is regarded as a quality or property of space), form and the other sense objects are said to be the qualities of the other four elements. If the four elements have no true existence, the same applies to form and the rest. The action of walking is dependent on the possession of a body. If the particles of which the body is constructed have no existence, it is evident that the action of walking has no existence either. Great universals (like space) and restricted universals (like cow) are associated with forms and so on. Thus universals are themselves based on particles. Individual items (that instantiate the universals) such as trees, earth, and so forth, are likewise all included in form. They too are dependent on the particles, in the relation of supporter and supported. In addition, all those things that are said to be mutually inherent are also, for the most part, dependent on particles. It is thus that all the claims of the non-Buddhist doctrines are disproved. If one examines the matter well, one can see—owing to the crucial fact that consciousness and knowledge-objects are interdependent—that the existence of extramental matter is not proved (because the particle can be shown not to exist) and that therefore the (observing) mind is also without true existence. In the final analysis, one is able to dismantle the assumed true existence of all phenomena. It is like removing one twig from a bundle; the remainder will not hold together so tightly and will gradually come apart.

11. The refutation of consciousness as a truly existent, single entity
12. A refutation of consciousness as a truly existent, single entity as propounded in the system that ascribes existence to outer objects
13. A refutation of specific beliefs
14. A refutation of the two Buddhist schools
15. A refutation of the Vaibhashikas, who hold that external objects are perceived without the mediation of a mental aspect
16. Valid proof of the self-knowing mind
17. What is the self-knowing mind?

> 16
> Consciousness arises as the contrary
> Of matter, gross, inanimate.
> By nature mind is immaterial
> And it is self-aware.

Broadly speaking, there are those who assert the existence of outer (nonmental) objects and those who deny them. To the first category belong the Vaibhashikas, who deny the existence of mental aspects, and the Sautrantikas, who assert them. The position of the Vaibhashikas is that external objects do indeed exist and are apprehended by the sense organs. Consciousness is like a crystal sphere and does not grasp the aspects of objects. On the contrary, the object (such as material form) is apprehended directly, "nakedly," by the sense organ itself, supplied with its support.[250]

What need is there, they ask, for a mental aspect to act as the connecting link between the subject and object? The Vaibhashikas consider that when one sees a pot, for example, one beholds directly and nakedly the specific characteristics of the pot precisely in the location occupied by the object in question. Their view[251] corresponds closely with what people usually think. When they say, "I see a pot with my eyes," they believe that the seeing eye and the pot seen are truly existent, and they think that their eyes directly observe the object, the pot, as it really appears. They believe that if a hundred other people were to look at the pot, it would be exactly the same pot that they all see.

By contrast, in their examination of perception, the Sautrantikas and others say that objects are only apprehended when they appear *in the mind*. If objects are not apprehended by consciousness, they ask, how can we be conscious of them? For it is impossible for matter to know objects. Consequently, it is not the *eye* that sees. Being inanimate, the eye is not the subject of the act of seeing. Moreover, if something transparent (such as a glass) is interposed between the eyes and the object, one sees the object.[252] Accordingly, all objects are seen and known by consciousness. They are *cognized*—and how can a thing be cognized in the absence of a cognizing consciousness? It is impossible. The sense organ is no more than the dominant condition for engagement in the object by the visual consciousness. It is a kind of faculty for apprehending the object, and the corresponding consciousness arises or does not arise depending on the presence or otherwise of this faculty. Thus, for example, when the reflection of something appears in a mirror, it is the semblance of the thing that appears, not the actual thing itself. Similarly, all the things that appear to the mind are but the mind itself appearing in the aspect of those things. When a hundred people look at one pot, their individual minds assume the aspect of the pot, in exactly the same way that the images of a single pot might appear in a hundred mirrors. If this were not the case—if in the minds of each of the hundred persons there were no appearing or known aspect of the pot—the pot could in no way be cognized. On the other hand, since these aspects appear in different minds, the aspect occurring in the mind of one person cannot be the same aspect occurring in the mind of someone else, for the simple reason that their mind streams are distinct. Thus, whatever appears to one person is necessarily the particular experience of that person's own mind. This does not mean, however, that such appearing aspects arise uncaused.[253] There are indeed external things that cast or impress their aspects upon the mind (*rnam pa gtod byed kyi phyi don*), like the shape left in wax by a seal or a reflected form arising from the form itself. When something appears in a mirror—even though it is impossible for the thing itself to appear—the image created arises in perfect resemblance of the thing itself. Likewise, although whatever appears to one's mind is no more than the mental aspect of the outer object, all the features of the former,[254] neither more nor less, are necessarily present in the outer object itself. The aspect that appears in the mind and the actual outer object that casts the aspect are misconceived as being the same thing. In fact, however, what we perceive is a mental aspect and not the object itself. The actual outer thing is concealed (*lkog na mo*) and not perceived; it is concealed beneath the mental aspect, so to speak, with the result that it is never directly cognized. Wherever the existence of the outer world is asserted, there is no epistemology more coherent than this, or more tenable.

The Sautrantikas say that when one has a perception of a crystal that has taken on the color of something else, it is the crystal that is perceived, whereas the color is apprehended in the manner of a reflection.[255] In the same way, the Sautrantikas consider that what is perceived is only consciousness, appearing in the shape and color of the outer object (which is itself different from consciousness and is composed of particles). Therefore, it is the conscious mind, and not the sense organ, that cognizes the object.

Given then that outer objects are wholly unperceived, certain commentators[256] ask why it is that consciousness does not also observe aspects projected by (normally invisible things like) spirits. For pots and spirits are on a level in being hidden objects (*lkog gyur*). However, in saying that outer objects are perceived in the first moment of perception, after which they become hidden, such commentators reveal an imperfect understanding of the Sautrantika view. For if the object is perceived in an unmediated manner in the first instant, why should it not continue to be so in the second and so on? Moreover, although pots and spirits are both hidden, it is only possible to apprehend the aspect of an "aspect-projecting" object. In other words, although it is never possible for an actual thing to appear in a mirror, it is not possible for the mirror to reflect anything other than what is placed before it. This example of the mirror is given in the present context simply as an aid to understanding.

The Sautrantikas, who assert the theory of the mental aspect, are like the Chittamatrins. The sole difference lies in the assertion or denial of the existence of the external object. When an examination is made of the cognized aspect and the cognizing consciousness, as given in the Sautrantika system, there are three kinds of possible relation. All this will be explained later. For the moment, we will consider which of these three possible relations is asserted in the *Madhyamakalankara*.

The opinion of Gelugpa scholars is that, according to pramana and in harmony (as they believe) with the teaching of the *Madhyamakalankara*, the relation in question is one of perceptual imparity (*sna tshogs gnyis med pa*).[257] Generally speaking, it is only when considering the mind stream in terms of apperception or self-awareness (*rang rig*), understood as the inward-looking aspect of cognition (*kha nang lta rang rig*), that one can speak of perceptual imparity.[258] It is not correct, however, in the present context when the three possible relations between the apprehended mental aspect and the apprehending conscious subject are under review. For here it must be understood that the way in which the aspects are grasped is in the manner of twin counterparts,[259] and therefore the theory of perceptual imparity is wholly unacceptable.

According to the theory of perceptual parity (*gzung 'dzin grangs mnyam pa*), a numerical equality is observed between cognized aspects and cognizing consciousnesses. Since this is established irrefutably by conventional reasoning, it is only on that level that I also maintain it. This also corresponds to the view of the *Madhyamakalankara*.[260] Regarding this point, when Shantarakshita refutes, in this same text, the theory of perceptual parity of the Chittamatra,[261] he shows (in the autocommentary) how the opinion of certain earlier authorities[262]—to the effect that several consciousnesses of the same kind (for instance, the cognitions of the color blue) can occur simultaneously—contradicts the scriptures. For the Buddha said that two cognitions can occur only in chronological sequence. He said too that every being is but a single stream of consciousness. In order to ward off this difficulty, it may be claimed that quotations like these refer only to the alayavijnana. This, however, is untenable. For since the alaya also occurs in a variety of aspects (of places, persons, and sense objects), it follows that it too is manifold. Moreover, from the point of view of scriptural authority, the earlier master Dharmakirti explained the meaning of the sutra in certain passages where he excluded the possibility of the simultaneous appearance of two cognitions of a similar type. But since the interpretation referred to earlier fails to take this into account, I shall give a clear and reasoned explanation of the meaning of these quotations.

When the Buddha said that two cognitions do not arise simultaneously, he was thinking in terms of contraries or opposing aspects.[263] And when he said that there is *one* mind stream, he did not mean this numerically. His meaning was restrictive in the sense of *only,* and he was referring to the fact that there is only the mind. There is no outer object; there is no "I" or "mine," no subject or object. It is thus that the meaning of such passages may be explained. To this it may be retorted that although it is not wrong to interpret such passages in this way, nothing is gained by it. But we reply that by thus interpreting the above passages, we avoid the fault of having to conclude that because the alayavijnana has different aspects (as when it appears in a variety of forms, as places, bodies, and objects), there are different alayavijnanas. This shows that ours is a better interpretation than that of our opponents.

Of course, even given that the contrary positions are refuted and the theory of perceptual parity asserted, the question may well be asked whether the latter fares any better and is faultless. In reply, we would point out that Shantarakshita himself admits [in the autocommentary] that the theory is not without its defects. He sets out the arguments disproving perceptual parity (on the ultimate level); and when refuting perceptual parity as present in other [that is, Chittamatra] tenet systems, he naturally demonstrates his own way of asserting the position (on the relative level).

As for the theory of the split-eggists (*sgo nga phyed tshal*), this is defective on both the ultimate and the relative levels.[264] The refutation of the theory of perceptual imparity, which is dismissed with the rhetorical question whether it is the doctrine of the naked ascetics, applies also on the conventional level. By contrast, the argument that refutes the theory of perceptual parity does so only ultimately; it does not apply on the conventional level. For this reason, this account may be accepted.

In this connection, the functions of the conceptual and nonconceptual consciousnesses are habitually confused,[265] and it is rare to find the matter correctly expounded. In point of fact, for nonconceptual consciousness, different aspects do not appear as one, and it is impossible for one aspect to appear as many. For if this happens, the mind is not in conformity with its object (and is mistaken). Therefore, in whichever way the object presents itself, consciousness must appear likewise. For example, when the characteristics of a pot are seen, its spatial and temporal aspects are necessarily perceived distinctly and without any confusion. The mouth of the pot, its belly, and its base are apprehended separately, in accordance with the parts that impress their aspects on the mind. It is impossible for them to be apprehended blended together as a single thing. The consciousness that apprehends the mouth and the consciousness that apprehends the base cannot be one and the same. Thus consciousness is necessarily considered multiple; how could it possibly be regarded as only one?

However, that which binds all these aspects together and apprehends them as one is the (conceptual) consciousness that cognizes "pot" and regards all these aspects as belonging exclusively to the same ground of designation.[266] But the particular consciousness apprehending the mouth of the pot conforms only to its object, namely, the mouth, and not to the other parts. And as for the mouth itself, it too has distinct parts, above and below, which are different, and it is perfectly possible to take them as the exclusive bases of designation for the consciousness that apprehends the pot's mouth. Since this is the case for all the parts of the pot, two consciousnesses of the same kind are never produced simultaneously. If when an object such as a pot is seen, two nonconceptual consciousnesses of the same kind—or if two conceptual consciousnesses (for example, pot-apprehending)—are simultaneously produced, one is necessarily in the presence of two different subjects and consequently two distinct mind streams. But however many *dissimilar* kinds of consciousness are produced, it is perfectly clear to everyone that one is not in the presence of different mind streams and different consciousnesses. On the other hand, one wanders into a considerable error if one supposes that the cognition of the mouth of the pot is the same as the cognition of the pot in its entirety, or that the cognition of the pot's belly is the cognition of the pot.[267] Therefore, if one posits the "pot-apprehending" consciousness as that which synthesizes all the cognitions observing the pot's parts (the cognition of the pot's mouth and the cognition of the pot's belly), the sum total will not be a mass of different consciousnesses. It is just as when the wheels and so forth are designated as the chariot: The parts are not identical with the chariot, but on the other hand the chariot is not separate from them. When the thought arises "This is a pot," this cannot be done without the exclusion of all that is not pot.[268] Consequently, there cannot be another concept simultaneously accompanying that very concept of pot. Similarly, one should understand that as long as the conceptual mind distinguishes between a many-colored surface as a whole and a blue color that forms part of it—and can home in on the central part of the blue patch as a fragment of the wider color—there will be conceptual cognitions in accordance with these distinctions.

It is in this way that one speaks of *one* mind stream and *one* object. On the other hand, if one were to interpret this as meaning that they are without a multiplicity of inner parts, how could this be sustained—unless one were to say that the mind and object are truly partless? That is something to think about!

Furthermore, if it is claimed that since the mouth and belly of the pot do not belong to different objects, the cognitions (that is, the knowing subjects) are not of dissimilar kind, it follows that the cognition apprehending the pot and the cognition apprehending the water that the pot contains are identical.[269] And in the last analysis, since all subjects are one and the same in being simply consciousness, the consciousness of form and the consciousness of sound and so on all become identical. In that case, consciousnesses of dissimilar kinds are ruled out, and the distinction made by our teachers[270] between similar and dissimilar classes of cognitions is rendered meaningless.

According to the proponents of perceptual parity, it is possible to observe all the colors of a butterfly's wing all together and at once.[271] Perception is not possible otherwise. The split-eggists say that the colors are observed successively. This position is disproved by the so-called *lata* argument.[272] Finally, the theory of perceptual imparity is quite unacceptable because, even though the colors are observed all at once, the fact that the different colors are not individually apprehended leads to the unwanted consequence that the consciousness is unrelated to the perceived aspects.[273] In conclusion, since even a single appearing object, such as a patch of blue color, may be differentiated into its central part, edges, and so forth, it is impossible for the epistemic subject perceiving all these different aspects to be itself deprived of distinct aspects.[274] If the reverse were true, it would follow that an object consisting of parts could be *validly* cognized as being partless, which is untenable. However, following the account of the proponents of perceptual parity, according to which a plurality of apprehending consciousnesses is asserted on the conventional level, it is correct to maintain that the consciousness apprehending its object is a valid cognition. This is similar to the case of those who do not assert a (unitary) partless pot because—having first seen that it has aspects—they are able to conclude that it is composed of many infinitesimal particles.

According to the proponents of perceptual parity, two consciousnesses of the same kind [either two apprehended aspects or two apprehending aspects] are not produced simultaneously.[275] These same two aspects (apprehended and apprehending) are but imputed designations distinguished on the conventional level. In fact, they are not distinct.[276] Although I have not seen this corroborated in other texts, I have personally no hesitation in affirming that it is this system of perceptual parity alone that should be asserted on the conventional level. This indeed accords with the final position propounded by the glorious Dharmakirti. For intelligent scholars, well versed in the writings of Tibet and India, it will be clear where the correct approach lies. There is a great deal more to be said on this subject, but for the moment, I have covered only the essential points.

It is necessary to demonstrate the extreme incoherence of the systems that deny the mental aspect. To this end, one must first provide a valid proof of apperception or self-awareness. The proponents of these systems object that since the aspect appearing as the apprehended object is consciousness, and since the apprehending aspect is also consciousness, these two aspects partake of the same nature—with the result that the mind is acting upon itself. This, they say, is intrinsically contradictory;[277] therefore self-cognition is inadmissible.

Our reply to this is that the two aspects, apprehended and apprehending, are posited only according to the way that things appear—that is, objects (the appearances of the manifold of knowledge-objects) seem different from the subjects that apprehend them. In reality, however, these two aspects are nothing but consciousness arising as the reverse of inert matter (for example, chariots or walls), devoid of clarity and knowing, the defining characteristics of consciousness. Thus it is specified (in the root stanza) that consciousness is immaterial and that it is, by its own nature, autocognizant, or self-aware, and self-illuminating.[278]

17. It is admissible for consciousness to be designated as self-knowing

17
A mind that is by nature one and without parts
Cannot possess a threefold character;
Self-awareness thus does not entail
An object and an agent as real entities.

18a
Because this is its very nature,
Consciousness is apt for self-cognition.

By excluding all that it is not (namely, all other things), "self-cognizing" consciousness constitutes a single entity. This being so, it is necessarily without aspects that are different from itself. It is therefore unacceptable to say that it really has a threefold nature composed of an object of knowledge (the cause of positing the knower), the knower itself (arising in response to the object), and the act of knowing (which is the result). Therefore, when it is said that consciousness is self-knowing, this is not meant in the sense of an ax chopping wood. It does not mean that consciousness apprehends itself as something really other than itself, or that consciousness as the subject and consciousness as the object of the act of cognition are being considered as real and separate entities. To know is simply the nature of consciousness, and for this reason it is acceptable and correct to consider that consciousness is autocognizing.[279]

The belief that this so-called self-knowing mind has in fact a twofold nature—subject and object, in the sense of productive cause and produced effect—is untenable. If a thing produces itself, does it produce itself as born or unborn?[280] The first of these alternatives is impossible. Since, prior to its existence, this (self-producing) thing has no being, it lacks the capacity to produce.[281] If, on the other hand, it is produced while being already existent, this means that at the very moment that it is able to be born (self-produced), it is already existing alongside itself, sharing the same nature. But there is an inconsistency in having, in this sense, something acting upon itself—it is like saying that the knife cuts itself.

Objects like pots, being material, are devoid of clarity and awareness. For them to be cognized, it is necessary to rely on something that is quite different from them, namely, the luminous and knowing mind. The nature of consciousness, on the other hand, is unlike matter. For it to be known, it depends on no condition other than itself. Therefore, it is perfectly acceptable to say that it is self-cognizant. In the very instant that consciousness arises, the factors of clarity and knowing are present to it. And although other things are known by it, it is not itself known by something else and is never without self-awareness (it is never "self-unaware"). It is like a boatman taking himself over the river at the same time as his boat, or the lamp that is self-revealing as it shines. Although it renders a pot visible in a dark room, it has no need of another source of light for itself to be seen. This is what is meant by the expression "self-illuminating lamp." It does not mean that the lamp makes itself visible as its own object.

Consequently, all experience, which has the nature of clarity and knowing, is called self-awareness.[282] Broadly speaking, and by its nature, every consciousness entails self-cognition. But it should be understood that when one differentiates the apprehended and apprehending aspects (conceptually, that is, from the point of view of their distinguishers or isolates), this is not the case. Only the apprehending aspect is then posited as self-cognizing.[283]

If one understands that so-called self-cognition is established as a mere conventionality, it follows that it is logically coherent on the relative level and there can be no objection to it. All the arguments to the effect that if consciousness knows itself, it is like the eye seeing itself or the acrobat standing on his own shoulders, and if the lamp is self-illuminating, darkness is self-obscuring, and so on, apply only if self-awareness is asserted as a truly existent entity. In such a case, if consciousness is subject, it is not object. If it is object, it is not subject. And if these two, subject and object, do not exclude each other, then it does follow that darkness is self-obscuring and the rest. All such objections would be unavoidable. But when, in the experience of an object, one speaks of the apprehending (subject) aspect and the apprehended (object) aspect, the fact is that these two aspects are not distinct,[284] and from this point of view there is no fault at all in speaking of (reflexive) self-awareness. It is just as when in a dream horses and oxen may appear as if existing externally, while the apprehending mind and sense power may appear to be within. In fact, all is just the luminous aspect of consciousness. That which appears as the apprehended factor and that which appears as the apprehending factor are none other than consciousness itself; and because they are experienced clearly, it is acceptable to speak of consciousness as self-knowing. Likewise, although a thing cannot in reality have a relationship with itself, the aspects of the distinct conceptual distinguishers of that thing may be said to be linked to it in a "relation of a single nature." All that is experienced as aspects of knowledge-objects arises in the clarity and knowing of the experience; it is therefore admissible to say that consciousness experiences *all* objects on the conventional level.[285] And since subject and object are mere interdependent imputations, it is perfectly acceptable to say that consciousness knows itself.

Moreover, valid inference depends, in the final analysis, on perception. And the perception of an object comes in the end to reflexive self-awareness, whereby the object is clearly experienced. Therefore, if a conventional valid cognition is posited, it cannot be without reflexive self-awareness. The refutation of theories that do not affirm reflexive self-awareness[286] and the manner whereby the latter is correctly established are all to be found in the writings of Dharmakirti, with which it is important to be familiar.

16. It is untenable to say that consciousness can perceive external objects

> 18b
> But how can consciousness cognize
> Those things of nature foreign to itself?

> 19
> The nature of the mind is absent from nonmental
>   things.
> How then could self-cognizing consciousness
> Know other things? For you have said
> That known and knower are two different entities.

Since consciousness is luminous and aware, it is knowable to itself. But how is consciousness able to know things that are by nature different from itself and that lack these qualities of clarity and awareness? They are completely alien to it. Clear and knowing experience, the defining feature of consciousness, is wholly absent from the nonmental things that are foreign to it. How therefore can consciousness, which is self-cognizing, have a direct experience and knowledge of other things? For indeed those who affirm the existence of external objects and the knowing mind do say that consciousness and the object to be cognized are two quite different natures. The so-called detection of the object (*yul yongs su gcod pa*) is an extraordinary feature of consciousness. This is like the mind's experience of happiness and so on—which cannot be a feature of external objects.[287] To the extent that something is experienced by consciousness or appears to consciousness, this same experience can only be due to the clarity and knowing of the mind. How can there be an awareness of anything in the absence of clarity and knowing?

Let us consider the position according to which the clear appearance of a pot to a pot-apprehending consciousness is not the mind but an extramental material object. Since inert matter does not occur in consciousness and since mental phenomena do not occur in inert matter—that is, since the one is clear and knowing and the other not—it is evident that consciousness and inert matter are mutually exclusive and thus wholly different. How is it possible for a thing to experience something different from itself when the two things are by their nature wholly foreign to each other?

They are as unconnected as light and dark. Since consciousness is never anything other than mere clarity and knowing, when could it ever have the occasion to experience something devoid of such clarity and knowing? It is therefore impossible that the aspect of a pot, appearing to a pot-appre-hending consciousness, should be different in nature from clear and know-ing consciousness. If there is no link between the consciousness and the object, there can be no experience of the one by the other. On the other hand, if the detected object is connected to consciousness in the same na-ture of the clear and knowing experience, then consciousness becomes aware of the thing. By contrast, in the system of those whose minds are in-fected by their clinging to the true existence of phenomena, this is impos-sible. For they affirm that object and consciousness are two different entities; and for as long as there is no relation of a single nature between them, there can be no experience of the object by consciousness. For what-ever appears to the mind and is vividly experienced by it must share the mind's clear and knowing nature.

The experience of an object cannot be merely the effect of causation (exerted by the object upon the mind), for if it were, the simultaneously oc-curring visual organ ought also to be seen [since it too is a cause of vision]. And since for the Vaibhashikas and others there are no mental aspects pro-duced as the effects of the object that is the cause, what is it that is pro-duced? The effect is ruled out. As for those non-Buddhists who not only deny the conscious nature of the object's aspect but even go so far as to deny the existence of self-awareness, even the terms "object" and "con-sciousness" are devoid of meaning. Given that consciousness is necessarily clarity, it follows that if its object is not clarity, it becomes impossible to have an experience even of the (material) object in front of oneself—for the ob-ject and the consciousness are unconnected, just as someone else's percep-tion cannot become one's own perception. Therefore, since in one's perception of a pot, one's mind is not hidden from itself, it follows that the mind is self-aware. Indeed, if the mind were not self-aware, every mental perception or experience of objects would be rendered impossible. Thus the theory of self-awareness is highly tenable.

16. A demonstration that the Vaibhashika view of perception without the mediation of mental aspects is unacceptable
17. The perception of objects by means of aspects is tenable only on the relative level

> 20
> According to the theory of the mental aspect,
> Mind and object are in fact distinct.
> But since the aspect is akin to a reflection,
> It's by such means that things may be experienced.

According to the view of the Sautrantikas, who have a theory of mental aspects but assert the existence of the outer object, consciousness and the outer object are regarded as different from each other. Nevertheless, the outer object and the mental aspect are related to each other in the manner of a thing and its reflection. Since the aspect is simply the image of the object, it is possible to say that consciousness knows or experiences outer things by virtue of their representations or aspects.[288] Although consciousness does not indeed have direct access to the object, it experiences the object's likeness, and thus it is permissible to speak in terms of "seeing a pot," "hearing a sound," and so on.

17. The belief in perception without the mediation of mental aspects is an inferior view because with such a view it is impossible to explain the perception of objects even conventionally

> 21
> For those who disallow that consciousness
> Is modified by aspects of nonmental things—
> There can be no perception
> Of external objects.

The Vaibhashikas and others do not accept that consciousness is modified by the mental aspect of outer things. But if this is the case, it is impossible for there to be a link between the mind and its object. Consequently, aspects identified as blue, yellow, and so on, and asserted to be outer phenomena can never be perceived. For example, if a crystal ball is not susceptible to modification by color, then no matter how many colored cloths are placed in front of it, the crystal will not reflect them and will not diverge from its own color. In the same way, these tenet systems say that outer objects are inert and without perception, whereas consciousness is aware. Mind and matter are thus separated by an enormous gulf, which renders it impossible for there to be a direct, unmediated experience of the one by the other. And since these systems do not accept even a reflectionlike aspect to act as a link between the mind and outer objects, all talk of seeing, hearing, and so on, is disqualified even on the conventional level.

If the Sautrantika system, which accepts aspects, is examined well, however, it will be found that here too (since the existence of extramental objects is asserted) there is no link between the mind and outer things either.[289] Nevertheless, the Vaibhashika system now being considered is far inferior, for it in fact amounts to a denial of perception. It may be thought that perception occurs without the mental aspect, but reasoning shows that without it there can be no experience.

Now that it has been shown that there is no knowledge without the mediation of mental aspects, the root text goes on to prove, by reasoned argument according to the different systems,[290] that consciousness endowed with manifold aspects has no existence as a truly existent, single entity.

15. A refutation of the Sautrantika view
16. A refutation of the system of perceptual imparity
17. The first unwanted consequence: just as there is only one consciousness, there must be only one apprehended aspect

> 22
> Since they are not different from the consciousness con-
>   sidered to be one,
> The aspects in themselves cannot be manifold.
> And therefore it cannot be said
> That it is through their power that things are known.

In the systems that propound perceptual aspects, the question alluded to above may be understood in three different ways. First, some say that there is only one apprehended aspect.[291] By contrast, it may be thought that there are many such aspects and that the apprehending consciousness is either one or manifold. This being so, the second way of understanding the above question is to say that one consciousness cognizes many aspects,[292] whereas the third way is to say that there are equal numbers of apprehending consciousnesses and apprehended aspects.[293] These are the only three alternatives possible.

Beginning with the second interpretation, there are those who say that though there are many apprehended aspects, the cognition or consciousness that apprehends them is one. When, for example, something blue is apprehended, its various other aspects (fabricatedness, impermanence, and so on), which are coterminous with it, all arise. Nonetheless, the cognition as the knowing subject arises exclusively in the aspect of the blue object. When furthermore a single consciousness apprehends a multicolored object, despite the fact that the object casts many aspects of blue, yellow, and so on, the visual consciousness does not arise in a corresponding number of aspects but only in a single aspect and apprehends the multicolored thing as a whole. Since, according to this point of view, the apprehended aspects are many, whereas the subject, the apprehending consciousness, is one, one speaks of *perceptual imparity*.

Because, according to this system, the cognizing aspect and the cognized aspects are not regarded as separate substances,[294] the unwanted consequence follows that there can be only one (globally) cognized object-aspect. There cannot be a plurality of object-aspects corresponding to the different colors, blue, yellow, white, red, and so on. But if the object is without multiple aspects, the affirmation that distinct outer objects, such as blue and yellow, may be perceived owing to their distinctive individual aspects is reduced to nothing. In other words, if when one sees a painting one's mind does not apprehend individually the various colors—blue, yellow, and so on—appearing in the picture, the mind does not concord with the object and it becomes impossible even to say, "This is blue" or "This is yellow." For there are no causes (that is, distinctly apprehended aspects) for such designations.

17. The second unwanted consequence: if the apprehended aspects are multiple, it follows that the consciousness must be also

> 23a
> But since it is not separate from a manifold of aspects,
> Consciousness itself cannot be one.

In response, our opponents may say that they do not indeed claim that there is no variety of aspects in an object. For this would do away with conventional phenomena, and in any case the evidence of perception is to the contrary. It follows from this, however, that if consciousness is accompanied by a variety of cognized aspects (in the object), it is not a single entity; it becomes as multiple as the object-aspects.

17. To deny this drives a wedge between consciousness and the aspects

23b
If this is not the case, you must explain
What you intend in saying that these two are one.

In short, if the opponents say at one moment that both consciousness and the object-aspects are one, and then go on to claim that whereas consciousness is one, the aspects are manifold, it is clear from the reasoning given earlier that they must either abandon the belief that there is a multiplicity of aspects or give up their assertion that consciousness is a single entity. The proponents of such an assertion must either abandon their theory or supply an explanation of what they mean when they say that consciousness and its apprehended aspects are identical. For since consciousness is one, and since the object-aspects are multiple, it is clear that they exhibit conflicting characteristics. And if they can still be regarded as identical, it is clear that nothing is impossible for such theorists. Even a barren woman's son can exist for them!

16. A refutation of the theory of the split-eggists
17. An explanation of their theory

24
The color white, you say, and other features
Consciousness cognizes step by step,
But owing to the speed with which this happens
Foolish people think that they are known at once.

In the opinion of those who affirm that, like the cognition, the apprehended aspect is one, a blue object casts the aspect of blueness alone. It does not cast its other aspects individually distinguished, such as fabricatedness or impermanence, which are equally coterminous with the blue object. Similarly, the produced consciousness arises solely in the aspect of apprehending blueness. Even in cases where the eye consciousness detects a multicolored object, the latter merely casts the aspect of something multicolored; the different factors of blue, yellow, and so on do not create their different aspects simultaneously. Likewise, the subject consciousness is also produced merely in the aspect of apprehending (globally) something multicolored. The proponents of this system say that, in one consciousness, a single apprehended aspect is directly confronted by a single apprehending consciousness. They are like the two sides of an egg that has been divided in two. Hence the system's name.[295]

One might have thought that the split-eggist position would be invalidated by the fact that the eye consciousness can take in all at once the many colors of a butterfly's wing or the many colors of a painting. But the split-eggists could perhaps defend themselves by saying that the subject consciousness engages the different features—white, yellow, and so on—of the multicolored object not instantaneously but separately and successively. However, because the consciousness acts with such speed, this process is perceived as instantaneous, rather as when a pin is driven through a stack of a hundred lotus petals. A simple, unreflecting person might therefore conclude that the different colors and so on are all perceived simultaneously. It is the same, the split-eggists might contend, with a firebrand whirled rapidly in the air. It looks like a wheel of fire. But since the firebrand is no more than a point of light, it cannot actually be appearing uninterruptedly in all directions. It appears in the way it does simply because the mind joins together all the successive moments in which the firebrand is observed.

The position of the split-eggists is, nevertheless, incorrect.

17. A refutation of the split-eggist theory
18. The actual refutation
19. Showing that the theory is inconclusive by an appeal to the manner in which sound is observed

> 25
> But when cognitions such as those of words like *lata*
> Are produced at extreme speed,
> And therefore seem to be perceived at once,
> How is it that such words do not correctly manifest?

If, as they say, it is merely on account of speed that a "clear" appearance[296] of a multicolored object is observed completely and all at once, when the cognizing moments of sounds like *lata* manifest with great rapidity, and on account of such rapidity seem to be perceived all at once, how is it that the word (*lata*) does not manifest as it should?[297] The principle of successive but rapid observation as applied to a blue and yellow object ought also to apply in the case of an object like sound. With regard to the impression of instantaneous completion arising from the rapid, successive cognition by the mind of the syllabic components of the word *lata*, which means a twig, and *tala*, which is the name of a kind of tree, the difference between the first syllable of the word *lata* and the first syllable of the word *tala* (in the order of syllables) is annihilated. And inasmuch as no clear chronological order is detectable—so that it is as though the two syllables are like the colors yellow and blue in a picture, observed simultaneously and not successively—the consciousness observing the word *lata* may be mistaken for the consciousness observing the word *tala*, and vice versa. The syllabic order of the two words is thus rendered meaningless, and neither term ought to be discernible. It is just the same with words like *sara* (ocean) and *rasa* (taste). When they are repeated one after the other, they turn into something indeterminate in which either word could be understood. For no matter how the words are pronounced, no clear order is discernible. Since it would be difficult to perceive and indicate a sequence more rapid than the moments of consciousness that clearly observe the separate syllables of the words *sara* and *rasa*, it is pointless simply to claim that there is such a sequence beyond the reach of experience. And even if the moments of consciousness (of sights and sounds) do arise in a similarly rapid manner, since they do not result in the complete, instantaneous perception of the object, such an object cannot be posited as the cause of the apprehending consciousness.[298] For an effect is necessarily consequent upon a cause. Where there is no cause, there is no effect.

19. Showing that the split-eggist theory is inconclusive by an appeal to the way in which conceptual cognition engages its object

> 26
> In the mind that is exclusively conceptual,
> There is no sequence of cognition either.
> Since none of them remains for very long,
> Cognitions are alike by virtue of their swift arising.

Only the conceptual mind is able to think about an object, examine its features, or take the mind itself as its object. This conceptual consciousness is not mixed with nonconceptual perceptions and it manifests uninterruptedly. Furthermore, for such a conceptual mind, the knowledge of past and subsequent moments of consciousness is instantaneous in its appearance; it is not sequential. The reason for this is simply that such moments have only slight duration because they manifest and cease on the instant. All cognitions, both conceptual and nonconceptual, are the same in arising at great speed. There is no difference between them. The Sautrantika tradition that asserts the existence of outer objects also says that all perceptions decay rapidly.

19. Showing that the split-eggist theory is inconclusive by an appeal to the character of all cognitions

> 27
> Accordingly, there are no objects
> That are grasped sequentially.
> But like their different aspects, it is thus
> That objects are perceived—grasped all at once.

All cognitions are similar in that they arise with great rapidity. There is no difference between them on that score. For this reason, it follows that they do not know their objects in a sequential manner. And just as the different aspects of a thing—for example, blue or yellow colors—seem to be apprehended all at once, in just the same way their apprehending cognitions occur at once and instantaneously. Although the colors of a painting all coexist, the split-eggists say that the mind engages with them in sequence and not all at once. But this leads to the same conclusion as with the observation of sound, as we have just seen. In fact, as far as mental engagement is concerned, it is at the moment when the foregoing moment ceases that the subsequent moment is born. The mind is instantaneous; it does not perdure. A good understanding of this matter may be achieved by asking whether there is in fact a link between the past and subsequent moments of consciousness.[299] As long as something is perceived by the mind as appearing in sequence, its instantaneous appearance is refuted; and what appears all at once cannot be observed as arising in a temporal sequence. Therefore, a thing appearing *all at once* to a sequential mind will never be established by perception. And since no knowledge-object can ever exceed this restriction, no inferential argument or example can be found to establish it either.

18. A refutation of the example of the firebrand
19. The formulation of the argument

28
Since it is the firebrand itself
(Mistaken, in the instant, as a wheel of fire)
That clearly is perceived by visual consciousness,
It's not the latter that connects the separate instants.

The example that the split-eggists supply is also unacceptable. The impression produced by a firebrand of a single, simultaneous wheel of fire is a misapprehension, an illusion arising in the conceptual mind. It is the firebrand itself that is clearly seen, and therefore perceived, by a nonconceptual consciousness. But visual perception is unable to connect preceding and subsequent moments (of the perception) and fuse them into one. Therefore, it is impossible for the moments to be connected. Through the quick rotation of the actual firebrand, an illusion is produced whereby the trail of light appears clearly in the instant as an actual circle of fire. But this is just a hallucination. And it should be understood that it is not the (visual) consciousness that joins the many earlier and later moments of the sequence and mistakes them for a wheel of flame.

19. Establishing the pervasion
20. The object that is remembered and the object that is seen are incompatible

29
Thus the joining of these moments
Is the work of memory.
The visual sense does not accomplish it,
For sight does not perceive the object that has passed.

One may wonder whether clear, vivid perception is incompatible with the joining together of different moments of cognition. It is indeed! For it is memory that joins together past and subsequent moments. To be sure, what is not recalled cannot be linked to what is present, and therefore this linking is accomplished by recollection and not the perception of the present moment. The latter is concerned only with what is actually happening; it cannot apprehend past objects.

20. If there is a joining together of past and subsequent moments (through memory), vivid, clear perception is impossible

30
All that is the object of our memory
Is dead and gone; it is not manifest.
Thus what is now appearing as a wheel of flame
Should not indeed be clearly seen.

If, as the split-eggists believe, the appearance of the fire-wheel is the result of the joining together of successive instants that consequently come to appear as a single object, such an amalgam could only be the product of memory. But whatever is the object of memory is already annihilated in the past; it is merely recalled and cannot be clearly experienced. Memory is associated only with past objects; it does not perceive the object confronting the mind in the present moment, for it is not associated with it. For this reason, if memory is what connects the successive moments of the firebrand, the wheel of fire that we see in the present ought not to be clear—being no more than an object of memory. It could not at all be like the bright circle of fire that we do indeed perceive in front of us. The (individual) piercing of a hundred lotus petals—like the perception of the firebrand—is not perceived clearly in the instant. Yet it is impossible for a hundred petals to be pierced simultaneously; any intelligent person can see that the process must be gradual. When someone pierces many copper plates placed one on top of the other, it cannot be validly claimed that they are pierced all at once. The same is to be inferred in the case of a man driving a pin through a pile of a hundred lotus petals.

16. A refutation of the view of the proponents of perceptual parity
17. A presentation of the view of perceptual parity

31
And if the claim is made
That when a painting is beheld,
The many mental states that apprehend its aspects
Arise together, all at once,

According to this system of perceptual parity, it is believed that there are as many apprehending cognitions as there are apprehended aspects. For instance a blue-colored object has many characteristics that are coterminous with it (*grub bde rdzas gcig*), such as being impermanent and fabricated. The object casts its aspects accordingly. And no matter how many aspects are cast, the same number of apprehending aspects are produced in the mind. Furthermore, the proponents of perceptual parity say that, in the case of a multicolored object, an equal number of apprehending aspects will occur in the visual consciousness as there are features of blue, yellow, and so on, cast by the object onto that same consciousness. For example, when a colored picture is seen, there will be as many consciousnesses—all produced simultaneously—as there are aspects of blue, yellow, and so on. And by saying "If the claim is made," Shantarakshita sets aside (with a certain emphasis) his opponents' assertion.

A thorough examination of this position yields the following points. Cognitions arise in a number equal to the number of aspects (of color, shape, and so on) occurring in the appearing, substantial object. On the other hand, since the object's conceptual distinguishers[300] are not distinct from the substantial object itself, when the object appears and is not misconceived (as permanent or unfabricated), these distinguishers produce the same distinctions in the apprehending aspects of the subject, namely, consciousness.[301]

The majority of proponents of perceptual parity (that is, those who say that there is a numerical equivalence between apprehended aspects and apprehending cognitions) think that though all cognitions are of the same nature,[302] there is no contradiction involved in saying that the same number of dissimilar aspects of consciousness can arise as there are dissimilar aspects in the object. But it is impossible for several consciousnesses of the same kind to arise simultaneously. Though there may be several apprehending aspects, they are not of the same kind. This has already been explained in the exposition of our own position.[303]

17. The refutation of the view of perceptual parity
18. All consciousnesses have many aspects

> 32
> In that case, even the cognition
> Of a single aspect such as "white"
> Becomes a manifold array,
> With up and down and middle parts distinct!

According to the point of view just explained, when a multicolored object is observed, it has many aspects, blue, yellow, and so on. In exactly the same way, when a particular part of the colored thing—a white patch, for example—is seen, the perception of it will be just as manifold as there are aspects in it: a top and a bottom, a "this side" and a "that side," a middle and edges. The perception cannot be truly one.

18. Demonstrating that the true existence of one indivisible moment of consciousness is impossible
19. When an inanimate object is analyzed, it cannot be referred to as a single entity

> 33
> The finest particle of something white
> That's one by nature and devoid of parts,
> Appearing as it is, to consciousness—
> That's something I have surely never seen!

If an aspect can be subdivided into a multiplicity of parts, it cannot be a single entity. It might be objected that the infinitesimal particle, which cannot be subdivided, constitutes a single aspect that is observable. But, says Shantarakshita, however much he has searched for it, and with painstaking effort, he has certainly never come across an infinitesimal particle of white and so forth, by nature isolated and unmixed with other things, indivisible into its different directions and appearing to all cognitions.[304] He says, in short, that the infinitesimal, partless particle can never be the object of experience. The learned accept that something is to be regarded as existent when it is observed by valid cognition. But to affirm the existence of something when it is not observed is no more than self-deception. Consequently, just as manufactured things like a colored cloth or naturally occurring things like iridescent butterflies have many aspects, the perception of them likewise has no existence as a truly existent, single entity.

19. An analysis of the apprehending mind shows that there are no indivisible moments of cognition

> 34
> The five sense consciousnesses have observing aspects.
> These regard compounded things.

And it is called the sixth that has
The mind and mental factors for its object.

Also the knowing subject, namely, the five sense consciousnesses (of sight and so forth), have many aspects whereby their particular objects, composed of particles, are observed. As a result, the sense consciousnesses are themselves multiple in accordance with the number of aspects in their objects. The mental consciousness resembles the sense consciousnesses, for it is coterminous with the aspects of its objects. As for mental phenomena (without overlooking imperceptible forms and uncompounded phenomena), these are mere imputations—nominal objects in the sense of being names arising by virtue of an exclusion. They have the nature exclusively of the three aggregates of feeling, perception, and conditioning factors. Now the mental consciousness that observes mental phenomena does not apprehend mental factors alone; it observes the entire group of mind and mental factors together. Consequently the object of that which is posited as the mental or sixth consciousness is considered to be the amalgam of main mind and mental factors.[305]

This then is an explanation of the Buddhist views, wherein we may see that the observation of a truly existent, single thing by a single consciousness is impossible.

14. A refutation of the non-Buddhist schools
15. A general refutation

35
And also in the texts of those outside the Doctrine,
Consciousness does not appear as one,
For it is said to observe entities
That are endowed with sundry properties.

The followers of masters such as Kanada and Kapila, who do not adhere to the Buddhist teachings, are referred to as "outsiders," in other words, tirthikas or extremists. Since there is no limit to the false understanding of beings, there is no limit either to the individual cases of defective view as enshrined in false tenet systems. Generally speaking, however, all such views fall into the two opposing categories of eternalism and nihilism.[306] There are many different brands of eternalism; they can be classified into three hundred sixty views, sixty-two false positions, eleven systems, and so on. All can, however, be condensed into the five tarka, or speculative systems. Although when its meaning is explained, the word "extremist" is found to apply to all proponents of real existence, Buddhist and non-Buddhist, it is mostly used to refer to non-Buddhists and especially—when the word is explained—to proponents of eternalism. Similarly, the name Charvaka may be understood as referring to non-Buddhists in general and to the proponents of nihilism in particular. Likewise names like Samkhya may be understood in a general or specific sense. In any given scripture, such names may be understood to refer to either one or even several different schools. There are many possibilities. It is important to be aware of the subtle distinctions between a general class and its particular instances, just as one should understand whether the name embodies a real description or is being used in the manner of a conventional designation.[307] If, on the other hand, one is unclear of the names and fails to grasp the meanings according to the proper context, the explanation of the text will be muddled and nothing will be correctly identified. It is essential to get the meaning of the terms straight.

In the system of the master Kanada and his followers, otherwise known as Vaisheshikas, "Owlists," or Logicians, phenomena are divided into six categories (padartha; tshig don). They speak of (1) nine substances (dravya; rdzas), such as earth; (2) twenty-four properties or qualities (guna; yon tan), such as form; (3) five actions (karma; las), such as stretching and bending; (4) universals (samanya; spyi), great and small, which pervade the previous three categories; (5) individual cases or instantiations (vishesha; bye brag) of the universals; and (6) inherence (samavaya; 'du ba), whether in terms of difference (such as the inclusion of horns on an animal's head) or in terms of identity (as in the case of the whiteness or roundness of a conch). All phenomena, so the Vaisheshikas believe, are included in these six categories. It is said that once, when Kanada was practicing austerities and meditating on Ishvara, an owl came and perched on the stone lingam that he was using as the support of his concentration. Kanada took the owl to be a manifestation of Ishvara and asked it six questions (corresponding to the six categories): "Does substance exist?" and so on. At each question, the owl was seen to nod its head, after which it flew away. Thus Kanada believed that he had received confirmation of the six phenomenal categories of his system.

Kanada's followers take Ishvara as their god and believe that he is possessed of five qualities (such as permanence) or else eight qualities (such as subtlety and lightness). They believe also that he resides in the dimension called Paranirmita-vashavarttina.[308] They say furthermore that knowledge of and meditation upon the six categories of phenomena leads to liberation, a state in which the self abides beyond both existence and nonexistence. In accordance with their scriptures, the *zhi ba'i rgyud* and others, they hold that the self or atman is both inert and permanent.

The nine substances of which the Vaisheshikas speak are: five permanent substances (the self, time, direction, space, and the infinitesimal particle) and four impermanent substances (earth, air, fire, and water).

The twenty-four properties comprise the six properties common to all phenomena, which are number (enumeration), dimension (length and so on), contact, separation, difference, and nondifference; and the five properties that are the aspects of the various elements (sound as the property of space, touch as the property of air, form as the property of fire, taste as the property of water, and smell as the property of earth). They say that although sound dwells permanently in space, it is not constantly heard because it is enveloped in moist wind. For example, when a man utters the syllable *Om*, he expels air from his chest cavity and thus the sound is heard. But when the wind returns inside his chest, the sound becomes inaudible. In addition to the eleven properties just mentioned, there are the thirteen properties of the self. These are the five sense perceptions such as sight, together with joy, sorrow, desire, hatred, virtue, and vice, to which are added the property of effort and the compounding faculty. All these are the properties of the self, and the fact that they are available to observation is proof of the self's existence.

The five actions of which the Vaisheshikas speak apply to all physical phenomena. They are: extension, contraction, lifting, motion, and the transportation of objects from place to place.

Whereas the bases of both properties and actions are material substances, these are pervaded by universals, which group individual things together by name and concept according to their kind. Individual things are the instances of the universals that pervade them. Universals and instances are mutually connected by means of inherence or inclusion. The Vaisheshikas consider also that pleasure and so on are inner, nonmental substances residing in the self. Whereas the Samkhyas say that pleasure and so forth are the property of external things like cloth (with the result that, for them, pleasure is an external substance), the Vaisheshikas say that one may have the impression that pleasure and the other sensations are experienced by one's self, but in fact the feelings are mixed with consciousness in such a way that they are experienced without any sense of separation. In fact, they say that the self is unconscious but that we have the impression of knowing because the properties of the self are intermingled with consciousness.[309] When these non-Buddhists talk about unconscious matter (*bems po*), they are not just referring to something composed of atomic particles. Since they necessarily understand it generally as all that is not mind, the self that the Vaisheshikas assert is pervasive—like space, direction, and so on—and lacks the nature of a knowing thing.

Shantarakshita consequently concludes that according to the non-Buddhist texts also, consciousness cannot be regarded as a single phenomenon. For the non-Buddhists also believe that it observes substances endowed with properties, actions, members, modulations, body, and so forth. Given therefore that in the non-Buddhist scriptures, it is said that observed objects, such as substances, have many specific aspects, such as properties, and that none can appear as a single entity, neither can there be a single entity of consciousness.

15. Specific refutations of the different systems
16. A refutation of the Jain and Mimamsaka views

> 36
> Some say the aggregate of things is like
> The multicolored onyx stone.
> The mind that grasps it must be just the same,
> And as a single entity it cannot manifest.

The Jains are followers of the brahmin Jina and take scriptures like the *rgyal byed* as authoritative. They are known by other names, for example, the Exhausters (of their sins), the Naked, the Pure, and the Wanderers. They recognize Brahma as their god, and since they consider that the sole cause of bondage and freedom is action, they believe that when action is exhausted, liberation ensues. They classify all phenomena into the seven categories mentioned in their scriptures: austerity, vows, defilements, bondage, freedom, life, and lifelessness. Their austerities consist of, for example, going naked, abstaining from food, the practice of sitting in the middle of five fires, and the "ascesis of beasts."[310] By vows they mean that, in order to halt negative emotion and not to accumulate new karma, they practice the ten virtues. For fear that they may tread upon and kill insects, they tie little bells to their feet. They refrain from cutting trees and do not drink water unless it is offered to them, even when they find themselves in unpopulated regions. For fear of speaking untruths, they keep silence and so on. Defilements refer to the three poisons and so forth, which are the antitheses of the vows. Bondage is the name they give to the condition of abiding in samsara owing to unexhausted karma. Freedom is liberation from samsara, following the exhaustion of karma. They say that the place of liberation is like an inverted umbrella at the summit of the universe. It is round and white like curd or snow or the tagara flower. All life, they believe, possesses mind. They say too that the four elements are possessed of consciousness and the sense of touch. The plantain tree, they say, has an auditive sense because it grows when it hears thunder. Similarly, the other trees are said to possess different sense faculties. They believe that worms and oysters have the sense of touch and taste; fireflies, ants, and so on, have the senses of touch, smell, and taste; honeybees and insects that drink nectar have all the senses except that of sight; whereas horses, humans, and so on, possess all five senses. Whatever is lifeless is without mind. This includes sound, odor, taste, light, space, shadow, iridescence, reflection, and so on.

The Jains also have another system of nine categories. These are: life, afflictions, vows, aging, bondage, action, negative action, merit, and liberation. These, however, are the equivalent of the seven categories mentioned earlier because aging, being a form of bodily suffering, is included in austerity. Similarly, action (further classified into future action, name, clan, and life span) is for the most part identical with bondage. Afflictions are in turn identified with defilements. Likewise merit and vows are the same, while negative actions may be grouped with afflictions and bondage. The Jains consider that although knowledge-objects generally differ in terms of place, direction, time, and number, they are all, by nature, one.

The Mimamsakas are followers of the brahmin Jaimini. They are devotees of Vishnu and have as their scriptures such texts as *rtog pa la phan pa'i yal ga lo ma can gyi gsang tshig*. They are also known as the Ritualists, Upholders of the Vedas, Vaishnavas, and so on. The Grammarians are counted as a subschool of the Mimamsakas. As for their many beliefs, deriving from the Vedas, the goal of the Mimamsakas is to attain the state of immortality, which occurs when the vision of the purusha, of which the Vedas speak, is achieved. This purusha is like the sun, full of light. He dwells in the mandala of darkness, far beyond the mandala of earth, and is many-colored: white, blue, red, yellow, tumeric, deep orange, azure, pink, and kapijala, or speckled brown. Purusha is also referred to as Brahma,

Atman, Ishvara, the Omnipresent, and the Eternal. The Mimamsakas pay
tribute to Brahma, Ishvara, and Vishnu, whom they take to be the creator
of the universe. As for their spiritual practice, they make peaceful and
wrathful offerings, are adepts of pranayoga, and practice meditative absorption and so forth.

As to their principal beliefs, they have ten tenets through which liberation is accomplished. These are: (1) that Vishnu and his ten avatars are God;
(2) that the Vedas, which are not of human origin, are a source of valid
knowledge; (3) that bathing in the Ganges purifies their sins; (4) that
women should give birth to male children, for it is thus that they attain a
happy rebirth; (5) that waging war is meritorious and that if one dies in bat-
tle, one is reborn in the higher realms (they therefore wage war enthusias-
tically, regarding it as a means of purification); (6) that life is of the highest
importance and is to be protected, so that, if one is starving, for example, it
is good and wholesome to steal food; (7) that nonthings are produced uncaused; (8) that it is virtuous (purificatory) to kill those who harm the brahmins, the Vedas, or one's spiritual teacher, for it is thus that religion is
protected; (9) that to be born in the land of Kuru (the birthplace of Rama)
or even to touch the dust thereof is a sure way to attain rebirth in the higher
realms; and (10) that consciousness is not self-knowing.

These non-Buddhist schools give credence to their scriptures and defend
their contents with specious arguments. And though one may demonstrate
the contradictory nature of the assertions of those who base themselves on
the secret instructions of an evil brahmin,[311] they insist that the words of
sages who can see beyond the world are not to be invalidated by logical inference—thereby revealing their own extreme foolishness.

The fine distinctions that separate the beliefs of the non-Buddhist
schools are exceedingly numerous, and it might be of great benefit to one's
understanding if the reasons for their misconceptions and ensuing tenet
systems were explained. But although it would be possible to give a clear
exposition of the Samkhya and other systems, this would make for a very
long book, and I have therefore omitted it. However, since, in the complete
absence of all explanation of the tenets, the reader may run the risk of not
knowing to which schools Shantarakshita is referring, it is desirable that the
views of the five tarka systems, together with that of the Vedantists, be
briefly indicated.

At this point, Shantarakshita is mainly concerned with the refutation of
non-Buddhist theories of perception: the various ways in which the mind is
thought to engage its object. In this respect, the views of the Jains and Mi-

mamsakas are similar. They both say, for instance, that just as the nature of a multicolored onyx is one, so too is the nature of all the various aspects of different things. In other words, they bring together all the different aspects of different objects and simply assume that they form a single thing. But the different cognitions that apprehend a variety of different objects cannot be a single consciousness. If a variegated object is not apprehended as such by different apprehending aspects of consciousness, how can consciousness be in accord with its object? And if there is a discrepancy between them, it is impossible to say that the object is known. These schools believe that all objects of knowledge form a single whole, and they use the onyx stone with its different colors as an illustration of what they mean. But if this were true, everyone would have the same knowledge.

The Jains and Mimamsakas of course deny this and try to prove their theory by an appeal to linguistic practices and the mode of mental apprehension. In the first case, they say, suppose we wish to point out a single composite object and to allude to its manifold character, asserting thereby its different features of blue, yellow, and so forth. We can allude to the multiplicity of the object all at once by simply referring to its "many different aspects" or to "all its aspects." Alternatively, we can enumerate its different characteristics one after the other, specifically referring to the thing's features: its shape, the sound it makes, and so on. There is no other way. Consequently, whether one details the different particulars of the object gradually or all at once, the fact is that one is (all the time) speaking about *a single thing.* And this same thing is valid for mental apprehension. For example, a multicolored object constitutes a single thing. If one wishes, however, one may apprehend its particular colors separately, with the result that the thing is not single but multiple. Thus the mind can apprehend it either as a single undifferentiated unit or as a composite of many elements. This is what the Jains and others say, and their view is stated, as the autocommentary remarks, in the first two lines of the root stanza.

Thus, according to them, a multicolored thing is a single entity. But a thing cannot be multicolored without having different colors. In other words, when they speak about a multicolored thing being a single entity—and similarly for all other variegated phenomena—they fail to understand that such a "single entity" is no more than an imputation. They think of it as a truly existent, single thing. But if a single, truly existent thing can be many, then everything is possible! The sharp blades of a hundred arguments can instantly demolish such a position.

Some commentators have interpreted the "onyx stone" of the root stanza as illustrating the opponent's belief that the object is multiple. But this is untenable since it does not correspond to the opponent's thesis.[312]

16. A refutation of the Charvaka view

37
And also in the doctrine of the ones who say
That objects and the senses that detect them
Are but gatherings of earth and other elements,
There are no single things nor consciousnesses that ac-
    cord with them.

It is said that once upon a time, a war was fought between the gods and the asuras. The gods, being religiously inclined, were reluctant to fight and were therefore threatened with defeat. As a solution to this state of affairs, the god Brihaspati (*lha phur bu*) is said to have composed a treatise in which he denied the reality of past and future lives.[313] This system of thought spread to the human realm through the agency of such teachers as the rishi Drokarwa (*grog mkhar ba*). Those who accept this teaching as a trustworthy source of valid knowledge are known as Barhaspatyas (the disciples of Brihaspati), or as Charvakas, or as Hedonists. Briefly, they deny the reality of past and future lives, the karmic principle of cause and effect, the possibility of omniscience, and the existence of any beings that they cannot see. They may propitiate Indra or the deities of the sun and moon, but this is solely in order to secure advantage in this present life.[314] They accept the scripture *lta ba'i snying po* and the six tantras of Brihaspati as a source of true knowledge.

Their tenet system is to be understood by means of a single argument, three examples, and four modes. Past and future lives and so forth have no reality because they are not available to sense perception. This is their one argument. As for their three examples, the spontaneous production of mushrooms growing in the fields illustrates the fact that there are no such things as causes; the scattering of ashes in the wind illustrates that there are no such things as effects; and finally the facts that the sun rises, that water falls, and that peas are round and thorns sharp all illustrate that things are simply what they are, arising by themselves. The four modes are: (1) that pleasure and pain simply occur in this life, without reference to past and future existences; (2) that the self arises spontaneously when the body comes into being (there is nothing that passes from one life to another); (3) that consciousness arises anew, produced simply by the gathering of the physical elements, which thus have the capacity to produce awareness, just as the fermentation of grain gives rise to the power to intoxicate; and (4) that there is no such thing as the karmic principle of cause and effect: liberation is not attained by training on the path and the practice of austerities, and death itself is the state of universal release.[315] If one understands all this, the Charvakas say, their teachings will not have been in vain, and one will not weary oneself for the sake of gaining liberation. Such are the beliefs of the Charvakas.

The root of their belief system is the notion that since life after death is not directly perceived, there is no such thing. Only the present life has any reality. Alas, silly people who deny the existence of what they cannot directly perceive have no reason even to prepare their own food, for tomorrow and the day after have no existence. But though postmortem existence is not directly perceived, its nonexistence is not evident either. So how can they claim that there is nothing? Despite the fact that they refuse inference as a source of valid cognition, here they are upholding defective inferences! This is so pathetic, one hardly knows whether to laugh in amazement or weep with compassion.

Shantarakshita considers this philosophical position in the root text. In the view of those who believe that the five senses and their objects are no more than the gathering of the four elements (earth, air, fire, and water— all of which have, so they think, an ultimate existence), this so-called gathering is a composite aggregate. It follows therefore that the consciousness that apprehends this compounded object is also multiple, for there are no single things or individual truly existent consciousnesses that would accord with them.

16. A demonstration that it is impossible for conciousness to be one and truly existent, as the Samkhya system affirms
17. The refutation

> 38
> For those who say that sound and other things
> Are by their nature *sattva* and the rest,
> Consciousness cannot appear as one,
> For it perceives an object with a threefold nature.

The sage Kapila, who in the reign of King Rashtrapala lived on the snowy mountain of Kailash, acquired certain spiritual powers through the practice of austerities. He was accomplished in samadhi and, in accordance with his experience, composed treatises such as *The Sixty Tantras of Lord Krishna* and *The Fifty Definitions,* as well as texts that teach the three sources of valid knowledge and the seven exegetical methods. Those who accept the authority of these scriptures are known as followers of Kapila, or Samkhyas. They consider that all knowledge-objects are accounted for in terms of twenty-five principles, which include both matter and consciousness. Of these, the self, or purusha, is consciousness and is endowed with five features, such as being a permanent entity. By contrast, prakriti is the source of all material things.[316] It is one and permanent and is devoid of consciousness. It is the creative origin of matter, but it is not that which "enjoys" or experiences it. Its nature, which is the perfect equilibrium of the three gunas, or attributes (*rajas, tamas,* and *sattva*) is difficult to realize. Rajas is suffering, sattva is pleasure, and tamas is indifference. When these attributes or qualities are perfectly balanced without any one of them predominating, this is prakriti in its natural state. It is the principal cause (in the sense of clay being the cause of earthenware objects). The Samkhyas say that twenty-three manifestations or modulations derive from it. From prakriti there arises mahat, the great principle or intellect. This is like a limpid mirror. On its outer surface, so to speak, arise the reflections of objects. From within, there arises the reflection of purusha. The great principle is thus the medium or interface in which purusha experiences and enjoys outer objects. As the three gunas evolve, there emerges from *mahat* the threefold *ahamkara,* in other words, individuation or the sense of self. There is an ahamkara that is subject to change (rajasa), an ahamkara that is luminous (sattvika), and an ahamkara that is dark (tamasa). These three kinds of ahamkara together constitute one of the twenty-three modulations.

From the first of the three ahamkaras (that is, in the rajasa aspect) derive the five subtle or simple elements (*tanmatra*). These are the principles of sound, touch, taste, form, and smell. From these, there subsequently arise the five gross elements such as space. The gross elements are said to be caused by the subtle or simple elements, whether alone or together, up to the combination of all five (in the way that milk may be said to have its form, taste, and so on). From ahamkara in its sattvika aspect manifest the eleven organs of sense. These are the five organs of perception (sight, hearing, smell, taste, and touch), the five organs of motion (the voice whereby we have the power of speech, the hands wherewith to give and take, the legs with which to walk, the anus for the expulsion of excrement, and the genitalia for the procuring of pleasure). Finally, there is the mental organ, which has power over all the others. Ahamkara in its dark or tamasa aspect plays a subsidiary role to the other two aspects.

As long as the knowing subject is bonded with an object, like a worm encased in its cocoon, the individual being wanders in samsara. But when one understands the defects of the object and stays in a state of one-pointed meditation, one attains, and is able to utilize, the "eye of samadhi." It is then that prakriti withdraws all its modulations, almost as if it were ashamed. Unconnected with any object that is the source of its bondage, purusha thus abides alone. This is liberation according to the theory of the Samkhyas.

It has been said that the view of the Samkhyas is very similar to the tenet of those Chittamatrins who deny the reality of mental aspects (namely, the False Aspectarians). Here, the alaya could be mistaken for the prakriti and the mental consciousness for purusha. In addition, the way in which manifestations are said to emerge from the expanse of prakriti is similar to the way in which this subschool describes the arising of the various consciousnesses.

This view of the Samkhyas is the best of all non-Buddhist views. And within the limits of its own tenet system, it has some excellent points to make.

The followers of Kapila thus believe that all objects are the manifestations of the three gunas. This is what Shantarakshita is referring to when he says that for those who say that the observed objects, the modulations of sound, touch, and so forth, are by nature sattva and the other gunas, consciousness cannot arise or appear as a single thing. This is so because the Samkhyas are saying that the object that consciousness perceives has the nature of the three gunas. For according to them, all objects necessarily have this tripartite nature. And whatever observes three things cannot itself be a truly existent, single entity.

17. A refutation of the Samkhya reply to our objection

> 39
> The thing is threefold, they will say,
> But consciousness is one. Now, does this mean
> Perception is discordant with its object?
> But how, if so, can consciousness be said to grasp it?

The Samkhyas say that the object of consciousness has the nature of the three gunas; nevertheless, consciousness itself manifests as a single entity. But do the Samkhyas then believe that the object is perceived in such a way that the knowing subject is not in accord with its object? In that case, how can they claim that this consciousness is the knowing subject, the apprehender of a threefold object? This is impossible.

The Samkhyas may defend themselves by saying that although the object has a tripartite nature, nevertheless, when it is observed, only the predominant guna is perceived, so that, for all intents and purposes, the object of observation is a single entity. This is unacceptable. It is owing to their differences of character, various preoccupations, and spiritual practices that different beings may individually identify the same phenomenon (such as sound) as pleasant or mournful. This is enough to show that the three gunas cannot be present in different proportions[317] in a given object. The Samkhyas may say that the weak gunas do not appear, with the result that consciousness does not detect them. But to this we would answer that it is only a consciousness that perceives an object in conformity with the way it actually is that can be said to know its object. If the consciousness does not accord with an object, it is unsuitable to say that it apprehends that object. For example, when a consciousness is apprehending something blue, it cannot be regarded as a consciousness of a multicolored object. Therefore, according to the Samkhya scheme of things, consciousness of sound cannot be apprehending *sound*. For sound is threefold, whereas consciousness is one—with the result that there is no apprehension of the object.

This then is a general exposition of the five tarka, or intellectual theories. These systems are referred to in this way because they are the speculative opinions of ordinary people whose vision of things falls short of perfect primordial wisdom.

16. A refutation of the Vedanta system

> 40
> External things do not exist; it is the mind, they say,
> Appearing variously while yet being permanent.
> But whether it arises all at once or in succession,
> It's very hard to say that consciousness is one.

The Vedanta is the system that propounds the end of the Vedas. Although it is considered to belong to the Vedas,[318] it is the final hidden teaching and the profound and essential message of these scriptures. It therefore contains many special assertions (uncommon to the rest of the Vedas). In particular, whereas all the five tarka systems mentioned above maintain that subject and object exist separately, the Vedanta asserts the opposite and maintains that everything is a single, undivided whole. Consequently, for this system too it is necessary to show that consciousness cannot be a single, truly existent entity. In saying that all is one, the Vedantins are in agreement with the Vedas, but with the difference that, basing themselves on scriptures such as the *dran par byed pa bslab pa'i khor lo,* they propound a self that, like space, pervades all knowledge-objects, with the result that the latter assume a single nature. This self is said to have nine characteristics. It is said that (1) its very nature is consciousness and (2) it is endowed with a body. It is (3) all-pervading, (4) permanent, and (5) one. It is (6) the basis of all arising and destruction and (7) unmodified by the defects or qualities of corporeal beings. (8) It is not the object of thought, and (9) it is inexpressible. Even though it appears embodied, it is not by nature corporeal but is pure knowledge and awareness. The Vedantins say that all things, the physical universe and the beings that inhabit it (all of which is the basis of our delusion), constitute a single reality in that they all have simply the nature of knowledge-objects. And basing themselves on this oneness, which is no more than their imagined imputation, they call it the self. And to this they ascribe a multiplicity of characteristics.

With regard to bodily form, this self has the zenith for his head, the nadir for his feet. The airy regions are his belly; the four directions are his arms, the planets and stars his hair. Mount Meru is his chest; the Ganges and other rivers are his nadis; the forests are his nails and the hair upon his body. The higher realms are his back, and the heaven of the Pure is his forehead. Virtue is his right eyebrow, nonvirtue his left eyebrow. His frown is the Lord of Death, while the sun and moon are his right and left eyes. His breath is the wind and Sarasvati his tongue. When his eyes are open, it is day; when they are closed, it is night. All men are his right side; all women are his left. His legs are Vishnu. All colors are his blood. All worldly things are his right breast, and all that is beyond the world is his left breast. Prajapati (the lord of creatures) is the nature of his joy. And so on.[319] It is thus that everything arises from the self, everything abides within the self, and everything dissolves into it. It is the one and only reality, immutable and permanent consciousness.

Although the nature of this self pervades all things without differentiation, it is in, and by virtue of, phenomena that it is manifest individually and distinctly—like space contained in various vases. The failure to recognize, on the absolute level, this one and only entity of the self—which is by nature knowledge and awareness, is neither unliberated nor liberated, and is endless and beginningless—is what is meant by delusion, as when one mistakes a rope for a snake. The duality of subject and object appears and phenomenal existence is perceived, all of which is like a dream, a mirage, or a castle in the clouds. Some conceive of the self as (outer) elements; others think of it as inner qualities.[320] But whether the self appears as pure or impure, it is like the sky, which may be covered by the clouds or free of them. When one realizes that the self is truly real, and when one dwells in a state of no-thought, mental consciousness ceases and even dualistic perception is halted. All this is taken from the autocommentary wherein Shantarakshita expounds the teaching of the Vedanta.[321]

Failure to realize the self means to wander in samsara. On the other hand, for those who realize the above doctrines, all things have the same taste: simple people and learned masters, good and evil, brahmins and outcastes. All are equal; and those who have this realization are stained neither by virtue nor by sin.[322] And when adepts dissolve into this great self, they are never again reborn. Therefore, the yogis settle (without thinking or expressing anything) in the nature of all knowledge-objects, the void state of the indestructible self. It is thus that they gain liberation from the two kinds of misconception: the misconception arising from innate ignorance, which is naturally present even in the minds of birds, beasts, and so on, and the misconception arising from an ignorance contrived through the assimilation of teachings at variance with the ultimate reality just described. Subsequently, just as when a vessel is broken, the little space that it contained is mingled in one taste with the great space outside it, these yogis dissolve into the great self beyond all duality. It is thus, so the Vedantins say, that liberation is attained.

If one focuses on the nature of the mind as a permanent and pervasive entity (that is, if one does not arrive, through investigation, at the certainty that it is wholly lacking in true existence), one's position is in fact very close to the tenet just described. It is therefore good to make such an investigation having imbibed and reflected upon the stainless teachings of Nagarjuna and Asanga. It is said, however, that even if, on the basis of their mere nominal designations, one assumes that the dharmadhatu and the primordial wisdom of buddhahood truly exist,[323] the fact that one is nevertheless focusing on buddhahood is not without benefit. And for this reason, we would never dare to say that such a view is no different from that of the

Hindus, for the karmic law of cause and effect is beyond our power to conceive. What we can say, however, both through reason and by quotation from scripture, is that such a clinging to real existence is not the authentic path pleasing to the Buddhas.

Pressed to its logical conclusions, the Vedanta tenets entail the consequence that if one person gains liberation, everyone is liberated, and if one person fails to gain it, everyone does likewise. It follows too that the path is rendered meaningless. For, assuming that there is a difference between things that are to be discarded and their antidotes, if the negative factors to be eliminated exist within the nature of the self, they cannot possibly be abandoned. Conversely, if the unmistaken primordial wisdom is already fully contained in the self, it is unnecessary to cultivate it. Neither is the self admissible in terms of different aspects of objects and time. In brief, all these unwanted consequences follow for the simple reason that the self is said to be one, permanent, and truly existent. In addition, the example of space as used by the Vedantins can also be negated by the arguments that disprove permanent, truly existent entities.

In this system, wherein the subject (consciousness considered to be by nature permanent and one) is said to arise as a variety of objects, consciousness cannot be a single, truly existent entity. This is demonstrated by the following argument. Since external objects are said not to exist separately from consciousness, and since consciousness, which is the one and only reality, appears as a variety of objects, all things make up a single whole. This has the nature of the self, which is consciousness and is forever permanent and unchanging. This self therefore is asserted as being the one and only reality. But whether the variety of appearances arises all at once or in sequence, it is impossible to posit a truly existing, single consciousness. If many things appear at once, cognition must be manifold, for it cannot be different (in this respect) from the many things that it observes. And if they appear sequentially, how can consciousness be other than manifold, endowed with the different aspects of form, sound, and so on? Furthermore, given that objects appear in sequence, since the first cognition (for instance, an appearance of blue) and the subsequent cognition (an appearance of red) are not different, it follows that even in the first instant of cognition, the subsequent cognition appears. For these are identical in the nature of a single, permanent, and unchanging consciousness (the conscious self). If consciousness does not become multiple, in accordance with manifold appearance, it is impossible to assert that these two (consciousness and objects) are one and the same.

The Vedantins assert a consciousness that is all-pervading. Nevertheless, in the present text, they are discussed in the section dealing with the refutation of nonpervasive entities. There is no contradiction in this, since their position is being reviewed from the point of view of the condition of (outer) things. In addition, even though the Vedanta asserts that outer phenomena are (manifestations of) consciousness, there is an advantage in placing them in the section dealing with those who assert the real existence of an external world, for they can then be discussed together with the other non-Buddhist systems.

The beliefs of the five tarka systems and of the Vedanta are knitted together in a web of darkness. But no one in the world, not even a god, is able to overturn the ultimate nature of things. No words, no theories can conceal this nature, any more than dry tinder wrapped around a piece of incandescent metal. The ultimate nature itself destroys all false tenets. By contrast, those who follow reasoning based on the evidence of phenomena are like lions; they move through the world undaunted and fearless. On the other hand, those who embark on their researches in an independent and freelance manner, without reference to the teachings of masters possessed of authentic primordial wisdom (and which are proved, moreover, by the three sources of valid knowledge), have been led, are led, and will continue to be led into many errors, the outcome of ordinary worldly opinions. For indeed misconceptions will proliferate for as long as minds are active. But since, within the very nature of knowledge-objects, there is no such thing as a single, truly existent entity, there cannot under any circumstances or at any time be found a tenet system able to prove successfully such an entity. It was in order to demonstrate this fact that we have given the above explanation.

Of the non-Buddhist systems described here, most are based on experiences gained in meditative absorption. Some rely on rational investigation, and many are the deceitful compositions of malicious brahmins aiming only to further their own interests. In Tibet, moreover, before the Dharma was disseminated there, there arose a religion called Bön, the origins of which have been ascribed to a Tibetan child who, possessed by spirits, displayed a spontaneous knowledge of how the gods and spiritual powers were to be propitiated. From such beginnings, it gradually spread. In our day, it is no more than the Buddhist teachings themselves disguised as Bön. Some say that the Bön and Nyingma teachings are very close, and indeed there are many similarities on the level of Dharma terminology and so forth. How could it be otherwise, given that the Bönpos have composed their teachings in accordance with the Buddhadharma? A similar situation was found in India, it is said, where there existed a doctrine called Vyava-harika (*tha snyad pa*), which resembled the Buddhist tenets of the Shravakas. And there were other doctrines similar to the tenets of the Pratyekabuddhas, the Chittamatra school, the Kriya, Upa, and Yoga, and also the Father, Mother, and nondual tantras. Likewise in Tibet, the Bön religion has imitations of all the Buddhist texts of Madhyamaka, Prajnaparamita, Vinaya, Abhidharma, and Secret Mantra, and also yidams like Chakrasamvara, Yamantaka, and Kila, together with all the instructions on the tummo fire, Mahamudra, and Dzogchen. These teachings were not Bön in origin; they were simply adopted by the Bönpos, and there is no need for us to refute them. And since Cha, their god of luck, and Shen and all their mantras appear to bring them benefit within the context of this present life, it is quite possible that they embody the activity of the Buddhas and Bodhisattvas, together with the teachings of their emanations. For the field of action of the Buddhas and Bodhisattvas, skilled in means, is inconceivable, as we can see from the life story of the wandering ascetic, the Speaker of the Truth. Whether the Bönpos have recourse to the Buddha, the teacher of such doctrines, or whether they adhere self-sufficiently to an independent teaching of their own, they could equally well be called to account by Buddhist scholars in reasoned debate. On the other hand, if their teachings are examined, they and their arguments turn out to be of no account. They are no more than simplistic deceptions done up into tenets, and it would be inappropriate either to accept or to reprove them. It is said furthermore that these parallels, which we find in India between Buddhists and Hindus, or in Tibet between Buddhists and Bönpos (there being no Hindus in Tibet), or in China between the so-called Hashang and Hoshang, are all manifestations of a certain connecting pattern in things (*rten 'brel*). Consequently, with regard to other traditions, if they do no harm to the Buddhadharma, they should simply be left alone. As it is said in the *Chandrapradipa-sutra*:

> Have no hatred for the nonbelievers
> That you find established in this world.
> Instead regard them with compassion.
> Let this be the first sign of your forbearance.

On the other hand, one should not delight in them, for then one would be like an idiot preferring brackish water to the amrita of the gods. Especially for those who sincerely uphold the tradition of the great abbot

Shantarakshita, the teachings of the Buddha Shakyamuni, it would be quite out of place to show enthusiasm for them. For Shantarakshita was the one who proscribed the teachings of the Bönpos, and they consequently looked upon him as their enemy.[324]

13. General conclusion
14. A refutation of the view that there are outer objects that are truly existent, single entities

> 41
> Of space and suchlike,
> Names are all that mind experiences.
> Because these names consist of many sounds,
> 'Tis clear that they're perceived as manifold.

It may be thought that since extramental objects like space and so forth are partless, the consciousness observing them must be a single entity. This however is not the case. In fact, a consciousness cognizing a nothing (i.e., a privation) such as space never has the direct, naked experience of an object. For these nonthings are nothing more than conceptual representations or reflections arising in connection with their names. And since names are perceived as consisting of a multiplicity of sounds, it is evident that they are perceived as manifold. The name "space" is superimposed on what is merely the absence of obstructive contact with material forms; and whenever one thinks "space," it is recalled together with its name. Unlike objects such as pots, space can never be adverted to without the admixture of its name. Since space is not a specifically characterized phenomenon, it can never be observed by sense consciousness. It is the same as with the horns of a rabbit, which, in the absence of the verbal expression, can never appear to the mind.

Names are not part and parcel of objects; they are merely designations, adventitious to the things they designate.[325] However, when these objects are referred to, they must be indicated by names and sounds. Now, all nonthings—a rabbit's horns and the like—are similar in being no more than "eliminations" (sel cha), that is, the exclusions of (actual) things. In the case of space, however, an empty area, which (on account of there being no obstructing wall in front) one can see to have a specific shape owing to its being demarcated by surrounded walls, forms the basis of the mistaken notion that space exists. If this is well examined, however, it will be found that space is no more than the absence of visible form; it is not an existent thing in itself. The space observed inside a cavity cannot be used to prove the existence of space (as a positive entity). The azure firmament above our heads, which is known as ornamental space, is not space in the sense just referred to; it is a form obtained through the effect of the sun's rays striking Mount Meru.[326]

14. A refutation of consciousness as truly existent and one

> 42
> Even if it is allowed that there are some cognitions
> That appear without diversity of object,
> Ultimately it is wrong to posit them.
> For thus defined, we see that they're disproved.

The claim may be made that there do exist certain cognitions that appear in the absence of a diversity of object. But even if we do accept them, they are no more than imputations, and it is incorrect to posit them as truly existent entities in an ultimate sense. The reason for this is that consciousness defined as (or possessing the features of) a truly existent, single entity is undeniably invalidated by reasoned argument.

If there is a truly existent, single consciousness, it must be devoid of all capacity to function (as Shantarakshita explained when dealing with truly existent, permanent entities). But this cannot be said of any consciousness. Consequently, in whichever way the tenet systems examine and envisage this consciousness, and in whichever way they express it, they are unable to establish a truly existent, single consciousness that is universally valid always and everywhere. Anyone wishing to sustain such a thesis is therefore destined to fail.

14. Concluding reflection on the previous two topics

> 43
> Therefore, consciousness appearing variously
> At all times in accordance with the aspects of its object—
> This is inadmissible
> As something that is truly one.

When this matter is investigated according to the explanation given above, it is found that, since a truly existent, single object is impossible, consciousness appearing in a variety of aspects, according to the different characteristics of the observed object, cannot be taken as a truly existent and single entity. The word "object" in the root text may be understood in the sense of "situation" or "context." This constitutes Shantarakshita's concluding summary of the refutation of outer objects and inner consciousness as truly existent, single entities.

12. A refutation of the Chittamatra system, which denies the existence of extramental objects
13. The Chittamatra position

> 44
> Within the mental stream without beginning,
> Through maturation of habitual tendencies,
> Things manifest, yet these appearances
> Are miragelike and due to the delusion of the mind.

The intelligent and learned masters of the Buddhist Chittamatra school have disproved the theories of various systems regarding the manifold appearance of external objects and which are themselves of varying degrees of excellence. On the one hand, there is the Shravaka theory that extramental objects are composed of infinitesimal particles; on the other, there is the Vaisheshika theory that the extramental world consists of (real) substances, properties, and actions.

The proof of the nonexistence of extramental objects, that is, the refutation of the belief that the subject and object of perception are different substances, is called by the Chittamatrins "the argument disproving concordant production" (*skyes la 'dra ba 'gog pa'i rigs pa*). It is so called because this reasoning rejects as untenable the assertion that perceptions are triggered by outer objects that they then resemble. In texts like the *Mahayanasamgraha,* many arguments are put forward to this effect. Chiefly, however, as in the argument cited above, they show that the mere fact of production (of perception) is no proof that outer objects exist. This is shown by the inconclusive character of the argument from production, as illustrated by the appearance of a double moon and so on,[327] and also by the fact that it is impossible to establish (explain in rational terms) the existence of gross objects on either the coarse or subtle level. It is impossible to maintain that partless infinitesimal particles, which are not of course objects of sense consciousness, are able to combine and form extended phenomena.

And in thus demonstrating the nonexistence of outer objects, the Chittamatrins prove that the subject and object of perception are not two different substances. Their principal argument used to prove this is called "the generation of all appearances in the clear and knowing nature of consciousness" (*snang ba thams cad shes pa gsal rig gi ngo bor skyes pa*). They also use the argument of "certainty of simultaneous occurrence" of percept and perception (*lhan cig dmigs nges*). For it is correctly observed that the color blue and the cognition apprehending it occur together, at the same time. Far from being a sporadic occurrence, moreover, this is an invariable fact. The Chittamatrins therefore affirm that the object (for example, the color blue) and the subject (the "blue-apprehending cognition") are not different substances. For it is definite that they are simultaneous—as simultaneous as the appearance of two moons in the example.[328]

How can we be sure that simultaneity necessarily implies unity of substance? If phenomena are not of a single substance, they must be distinct substances. However, the sign or evidence adduced (namely, that of simultaneous occurrence) cannot apply to things that are substantially different (*rdzas tha dad*), like the colors blue and yellow. Although different objects (such as the colors blue and yellow) may occasionally be observed simultaneously, it does not follow that while one of them is constantly observed, the other one is necessarily observed as well. But in the case of a blue object and the consciousness observing the blue object, it is impossible that while one of them is not observed, the other occurs in isolation. On the other hand, if the two were separate substances, it ought to be possible for one or the other occasionally to occur in isolation.

In the present context, it would help to have a more detailed account of how the Chittamatrins respond to the charge that there are three defects in their position (such as the fact that the sign is not proved). But I have confined myself to the key issues.

To express the matter briefly, the decisive conclusion of all these arguments (such as the certainty of simultaneous occurrence), which prove that the object and subject of perception are one and the same substance, is that if something appears to consciousness, it must itself be consciousness. If it is not cognized, we can have no experience of it. Once this single crucial point is grasped, a hundred other arguments (including that of simultaneity of occurrence) will at once be understood. In this way, the entire Chittamatra tenet is exhaustively encapsulated in stanza 91 of the *Madhyamakalankara* when it says: "And all that this [i.e., consciousness] establishes abides in consciousness." But this will be explained when we reach that section.

The state of consciousness that is mere clarity and knowing, which does not veer off into an active sense cognition, and which is the support of habitual tendencies, is called the alayavijnana, the consciousness that is the universal ground (*kun gzhi rnam shes*). The Chittamatrins consider that this is essentially neutral, neither positive nor negative. It is an awareness of the mere presence of objects and it arises in a continuity of instants. It is attended by the "five omnipresent mental factors," such as contact. It does not have a specific object of focus but observes the world and beings in a general, overall manner. Finally, the alayavijnana may be divided into a "seed aspect" and a "maturation aspect." The reason for its being so described (in terms of nature, attendant mental factors, object of focus, and so on) is that when the key point is grasped that this consciousness is a mere clarity and knowing, not caught up in any of the active sense consciousnesses, it is easy to understand all the different features of the alaya. If, on the other hand, the nature and object of the alaya are explained and understood differently, it will be difficult to achieve an understanding of its essence even if one reflects upon it for an entire kalpa.

The fine details of the Chittamatra position should be studied in other texts. Within the universal ground consciousness, which is like an immense ocean, there is a potential (a power source) for the seven kinds of consciousness and their attendant mental factors, which rise and fall like waves on the sea. This potential is supplied by habitual tendencies. In brief, if the potential stored in the alaya is not yet ready to bring forth its subsequent result, it remains in the universal ground consciousness like a seed. When this ripens, however, it gives rise to the appearance of all sorts of things: bodies, places, and experiences. There are no outer objects. It is simply through the strength of habitual tendencies that various appearances are experienced, just as in the case of a dream consciousness or when the mind, habituated by meditation upon repulsive objects, perceives the ground strewn with bones. Such are the assertions of the Chittamatrins.

If one accepts that appearances are the mind, one is necessarily committed to a belief in the alaya. For the active sense consciousnesses necessarily gravitate to their respective objects. It is therefore impossible for them individually to act as the common ground of all—of places, bodies, experiences, and so on. When it is said that the whole variety of appearances are mind only, the mind in question must be the support of all things, cognitions, and beings; it cannot be other than mere clarity and knowing.[329]

Intending to sum up this system briefly, Shantarakshita says in the root stanza that, owing to the complete ripening of different habitual tendencies (associated with the belief in the true existence of things) lodged in the beginningless, streamlike continuum of our minds, there manifest the appearances of objects, forms, and so on. But although the perceiver and the object of perception have not even the slightest existence as two separate entities, they nevertheless appear as subject and object because of the mind's deluded condition. They appear though they do not exist. They are like illusions, dreams, castles in the air, circles of light created by whirling firebrands, phantoms, the moon reflected on the water, and so forth. All this is the Chittamatra position.

13. An examination of the Chittamatra tenet
14. A consideration of its strengths and weaknesses

45
This view indeed is excellent. But is this mind of theirs
An ultimate existent?
Or do they say that it is only satisfactory
When left unanalyzed? This we shall consider.

The Chittamatra tenet system is proved by using conventional reasoning, and it is the perfect antidote for dispelling the wrong view that the subject and object of perception are different entities. The excellence of the Chittamatra system is attested to by the *Lankavatara-sutra* and the other authoritative and authentic scriptures on which it is based. But the question to be asked is whether this mind of theirs, appearing in a variety of aspects, exists ultimately. Or are the Chittamatrins saying that the existence of the mind is satisfactory (that is, acceptable) only in the absence of analysis? This is the issue that must now be considered, and the truth of the matter is that the Chittamatrins do not say that consciousness is a conventional appearance existing only in the absence of analysis. On the contrary, they claim that this consciousness exists by its nature even on the level of the ultimate truth. They thus ascribe an ultimate reality to it.

14. A refutation of the true existence of consciousness, the weak point
of this tenet system
15. A refutation of the True Aspectarians
16. A refutation of the split-eggist system
17. A demonstration that such a position is inherently contradictory

> 46
> If consciousness is ultimately real,
> It must be manifold, or else its aspects are all one.
> Failing this, the mind and object are at variance
> And there's no doubt that they diverge.

When consciousness is examined to see whether it exists ultimately or
only conventionally as we have just mentioned, there are some who believe
that consciousness exists in an absolute sense. This is the general position
of the Chittamatra school, and Shantarakshita indicates that it is to be refuted. There are in fact two subschools within the Chittamatra tenet system, both of which consider that the mind is ultimately existent. Whereas
the True Aspectarians (*rnam bden pa*) say that the appearing aspects truly
exist as mind, the False Aspectarians (*rnam brdzun pa*) deny this. There are
no other interpretations possible aside from these two.

In the case of the True Aspectarians, there are three possible ways in
which the mental aspects and consciousness may be said quantitatively to
relate. This is similar to the situation with the Sautrantikas, except that
whereas the latter affirm the existence of outer objects and say that they
cast their aspects on the mind, the Chittamatrins simply consider that the
object is an appearing mental aspect and deny the existence of extramental
entities. This is the only point on which the Sautrantikas and Chittamatrins
disagree. Since the three alternatives in question have already been discussed in the section dealing with the Sautrantikas, there is no need to explain them separately here.

Of these three accounts (considered in the Chittamatra context), the
theory of the split-eggists is untenable. Given that the cognition and the
object-aspect are the same in being one, and since it is contrary to reason
for a single partless aspect to appear, consciousness must be as manifold as
there are multiple aspects. Or, if consciousness is one, the multiple aspects
must also form a single thing; they cannot possibly be perceived as many.
Otherwise one is singular and the other plural, with the result that consciousness and aspects are necessarily in contradiction. Consequently, there

is no doubt that they diverge and it is absurd to say that they are equal in being one.

Generally speaking, as far as (apprehended) aspects are concerned, not just one but many aspects appear in different ways. This is an undeniable fact of experience, and the Chittamatrins also certainly accept this. They believe, however, that consciousness is truly existent. But if it is truly existent, there must be either one consciousness or many consciousnesses. Now a truly existent plural is necessarily grounded in a truly existent singular. If therefore consciousness truly exists, it must, in the final analysis, be truly single. This is the general principle. Therefore, in the present context, the fact that there are many aspects is enough to prove that consciousness is not a single, truly existent entity. It is not necessary to refute it by distinguishing the instantaneous nature of consciousness from its sequential order. Single cognitions can perceive single aspects successively, but earlier and later aspects are not one and the same. Therefore, the consciousness that perceives them is not established as a single and truly existent entity. We are at this point refuting the ultimate existence of a truly existent, single, momentary consciousness. We have already demonstrated (in the section dealing with the Sautrantikas) that the existence of a one-to-one aspect is untenable even conventionally. The opinion of those who assert the existence of an outer world has already been refuted—that is to say, those who think that although blue and yellow exist simultaneously in a multicolored object, the two colors are perceived by consciousness only sequentially—that is, the split-eggists. Now, since the Chittamatrins, who do not assert the existence of outer objects, establish that blue and other colors, as aspects of a multicolored object (which are the full maturation of habitual tendencies in the alaya) necessarily exist simultaneously—the very fact of aspectual multiplicity is enough refute the idea of a single consciousness. Consequently, the only peculiarity of the split-eggist approach of the Chittamatrins is that the latter believe that the apprehended items of (the experience of) a multicolored object all form a single multicolored aspect. However, we will now explain the weakness of this theory—for a multicolored aspect cannot be a single entity. In general, if consciousness is not established as a single entity even on the conventional level, it is unnecessary to mention the ultimate. No need to murder the newborn child if it has already died in its mother's womb!

17. The Chittamatrins are unable to circumvent this contradiction
18. The unwanted consequence

47
If the aspects are not different,
Moving and unmoving parts and so forth—all are one.
All must be in motion or at rest!
It's hard to give an answer to this consequence.

The statement given above concerning the unwanted consequence, made as it is in terms of consciousness and the aspects, unavoidably applies when one believes that consciousness is truly existent and that a single aspect is perceived by a single cognition. The proponents of the split-eggist system may claim that a multiplicity of aspects does not involve difference but rather that they are all bound up together in a single thing. But if this is so, it follows that the moving and unmoving parts of something, or the painted and unpainted parts, are all one and the same. This being so, all the other parts must be moving or unmoving as the case may be. In short, it follows that in whichever way one aspect is seen, all the other aspects must appear likewise. Since the Chittamatrins have already said that the aspects (of an appearance) are not different, they cannot now say that they are different—that some aspects are moving and some are not. It is hard to sidestep such a consequence. If a multicolored aspect is not just imputed—labeled—as being single, but is regarded as an entity that is truly one, it follows that if one colors a white part of it, the whole must appear colored too. For something that is truly one has no parts. But no one could possibly hold such an opinion. Therefore, if the aspects are distinct, the aforementioned consequence is unavoidable. There is not the slightest need for further arguments.

18. The same unwanted consequence is found in the theory of the proponents of aspects who assert the existence of outer objects

48
And even in the case of outer things,
Since these are not devoid of aspects,
All such features are contained in one:
A consequence that no one can gainsay.

This consequence is here applied to the aspects themselves, in the sense asserted by the Chittamatrins, who deny the existence of extramental objects. This is not to say, however, that this same consequence does not apply equally to the external phenomena propounded by those who believe in the existence of an extramental world. Insofar as things are believed to exist apart from the mind, if one says as the Chittamatrins do (mutatis mutandis) that these things have many simultaneous aspects, and if these aspects are said to form a single reality, it follows that within any given part of the outer object (which causes the perception of the aspects) all the features of the other parts are present. There is no avoiding this consequence. Shantarakshita says that if all the aspects corresponding perfectly to the outer object constitute a single aspect, why is the outer object not a truly existent, single entity also? If one applies white paint to a multicolored thing, all the other parts (blue-colored, for instance) should also become white. Accordingly, it is important to understand the general point that different aspects cannot constitute a single, truly existent entity. It may be possible to entertain all sorts of mistaken ideas to the effect that something multiple constitutes a single thing, but it can be logically shown that a single, truly existent entity cannot possibly appear or be perceived as multiple. On the other hand, something that is merely labeled or imagined as "one" can so appear. In the same way, a truly existent multiplicity cannot be posited as a single entity, whereas something that is merely imagined or labeled a multiplicity may also be labeled "one." In this treatise, from beginning to end, the most important thing is to be sure of the difference between what actually is (*dngos*) and what is only imputed or imagined (*btags*), and to realize that that which is only imputed or imagined can be designated either as one or as many.

16. The refutation of the system of perceptual parity

49
If you say cognitions are as many
As the mental aspects,
They can be examined like the partless particle,
And it is hard to circumvent such scrutiny.

The assertion of certain earlier Vijnanavada (i.e., Chittamatra) masters to the effect that several consciousnesses of a same kind can be produced all together and at once cannot be sustained even on the conventional level. In Shantarakshita's system of perceptual parity,[330] where consciousness is considered to have as many cognizing aspects as there are cognized items, the cognizing aspects are not said to be of the same kind. For several consciousnesses of the same kind can never occur simultaneously. As was briefly explained earlier, a distinction is made between consciousnesses in terms of conceptual and nonconceptual activity.[331] In accordance with the specific position of Shantarakshita's system, therefore, it is perfectly in order to speak of perceptual parity provided that it is understood as being no more than an imputation. This indeed is one of the beauties of the Madhyamaka system.

But when the Chittamatrins say that there are as many cognitions as there are mental aspects, consciousness, which in their view is truly existent, cannot be established. When something appears as multiple, each of its many aspects is also perceived as possessed of parts in terms of spatial direction (center, extremities, etc.). In other words, each aspect has many parts, in just the same way as when the infinitesimal particle is investigated. The Chittamatrins cannot say that such an investigation applies only to the particles and not to consciousness, for the particles and consciousness are not at all different from the point of view of their appearance.[332] Therefore, it is said that it is hard to sidestep such an investigation—indeed, it is impossible to do so.

According to Shantarakshita, when it is said that there are as many cognitions as there are cognized aspects, the multiplicity in question is no more than imputed or ascribed (*btags pa*). But this does not prevent aspects from *appearing* as multiple, for this is due simply to their dependent arising. For example, although a single object, such as a pot, is made up of several parts, which are themselves composed of many particles—particles that themselves have no real oneness—the pot nevertheless appears to us and is so designated. It is posited undeniably, possessed of all its functions. The same is true for the entire endless array of knowledge-objects.

Let us say that we perceive a multicolored object. If the central portion of an individual patch of blue (taken in isolation from the other colors) appears to be surrounded without interstice by other features (*rnam pa*), and if this portion has only one dimension (side) facing in different directions, it follows that the different directional aspects become one and the same aspect.[333] On the other hand, if the central portion has different sides, it follows that the consciousness of it must also be multiple. When many particles of the same kind, without interstice, are apprehended, it is said that their conglomeration is mistaken for a single unitary entity. Similarly, the consciousness of blue, for example, whose many aspects are experienced as an uninterrupted continuum, is said to be mistaken for a single aspect. What is the difference between these two mistakes? The first is made by those who say that blue (appearing as an uninterrupted expanse) has the nature of the infinitesimal particle. The second mistake belongs to those who say that blue has the nature of consciousness. Other than this, there is no difference between them. For both parties, there appear directional parts (whether in terms of a particle or of consciousness), and no one can claim that different directions are one and the same. Both positions, when investigated, exhibit the same fault. Whether the aspects are of the similar or dissimilar kind, the same method of investigation applies to all aspects appearing uninterruptedly within a given object.

16. A refutation of the system of perceptual imparity
17. The refutation itself

> 50
> If various aspects form a single entity,
> Is not this the teaching of the sky-clad yogis?
> Variety is not a truly single entity
> But is like various gems and other things.

Some may say that a single consciousness apprehends a variety of aspects in just the same way that it apprehends an onyx [a multicolored stone]. But if, despite the fact that the aspects are various, it is said that they all form a single entity, being of the nature of consciousness, it may be asked whether this is the same theory as that of the Jains, who consider multiplicity to be a single entity. (The Jains are referred to as "sky-clad" on account of their going naked.) But since things are said to be multiple, on account of their being various, how can consciousness be described as one? A "variety" does not truly exist as a single entity. A variety is just like gold, silver, coral, sapphire, and so on—simply different precious substances (the phrase "and other things" in the root stanza refers to the different cognitions present in the mind stream).

The proponents of perceptual imparity are like the Jains in considering that different things can be regarded as a single entity. Likewise the Vedantins say that everything has the nature of consciousness (i.e., the self). For their part, the Chittamatrins propound not one but eight kinds of consciousness, each of which is said to be momentary and present within the mind stream of different beings. The only difference between the Chittamatrins and the Vedantins is that the latter believe that consciousness (the self) is single and permanent and exists in all beings without distinction. Consequently, the present refutation is said to apply to all such schools.

In the language of debate, this argument may be formulated in two stages as follows. *Whatever appears as variegated is necessarily not one truly existent entity, just like a heap of different jewels. As for consciousness, it is also variegated.*[334] The sign (reason), which is seen to contradict true oneness, is the observed variety (the antithesis of inherent singularity). Variety is set forth as the sign. Kamalashila has pointed out that the example of precious stones applies to the Jains, not to the Chittamatrins. For the latter, Shantarakshita gives the example of "different cognitions in the mind stream." However, according to the appearing mode of things, there is no contradiction in giving "different precious stones" as the example.

17. Demonstrating the validity of the refutation

> 51
> If various items form one thing inherently existent,
> How do they appear to us as various?
> For some are hidden, some are not.
> Now how can they be so distinct?

If all the multifarious aspects of things exist inherently as a single entity, how is it that they appear so different and various? Some are concealed, some are manifest, some are produced, some disintegrated. How can they appear so unalike and separate? If, for example, in an onyx stone, different features were all blended into a single entity, how would it be possible to observe them as distinct? Things that appear distinct to an unimpaired consciousness are unmistakenly established as distinct phenomena, just as different precious substances are established as being separate. If they are not different, the consequence follows that when one perceives one, one is perceiving them all; when one of them moves, they must all be in motion; when one is produced, all are produced, and so on.

15. A refutation of the False Aspectarians
16. A presentation of their view

52
Since, they say, in consciousness itself
There are no mental aspects,
The mind, which in reality is aspectless,
Appears with aspects only through delusion.

Some may believe that within the very nature of consciousness, there are no mental aspects and that consciousness itself is essentially free of all such aspects, like a sphere of pure crystal. And yet, is it not the case that different aspects appear to the mind? The False Aspectarians reply that they do indeed appear. But in reality, such aspects are not in the mind; it is owing to a delusion, a mere mistake, that consciousness seems to be "aspected." Such aspects are, for instance, like the horses and oxen seen in a ball of clay by those whose sight has been disturbed by the power of magical incantations and so on. In this way, the False Aspectarians reject the idea that the aspects are part and parcel of consciousness. For them, these aspects are false, just like the optical illusion of hairs floating in the air. Consequently, the mind does not possess different apprehending aspects equal in number to the aspects apprehended. If such (apprehending) aspects truly existed, this would contradict the fact that consciousness is one truly existent entity. But since these aspects are false illusions, there is no conflict between the singularity of consciousness and the plurality of the aspects. Consequently, the False Aspectarians consider that the faults just attributed to the True Aspectarians do not apply to them; on the contrary, they believe that they are quite correct in upholding the true existence of consciousness, which is clear and knowing.

16. A refutation of their theory
17. A brief demonstration

53
But if these aspects are without existence,
How do we experience them so clearly?
Indeed there is no consciousness
That from the aspects stands apart.

If these aspects do not exist, how is it that everyone, from simple people to learned masters, all experience them directly and clearly and in a wholly

undeceptive and incontrovertible manner? How could it be possible? Whatever is nonexistent is necessarily outside experience. One cannot be gored
by a rabbit's horns; one cannot smell the perfume of flowers growing in the
sky or look upon the form of a barren woman's child. It is impossible to experience such things.

Since the False Aspectarians are unable to deny the arising of perceptual
aspects, they cannot claim that they are unperceived. They believe that
though these aspects do not exist, they can still be experienced, and they illustrate their contention by saying that hairs can still be perceived floating
in the air, even though they are not there. But this idea is untenable. If the
matter is well examined, it will be found that all appearances manifest
within the mind; they cannot appear elsewhere. Therefore, to be sure, consciousness and aspects are both alike in being the mind. It is when they are
differentiated in respect of each other that one speaks of an apprehending
consciousness and an apprehended aspect. The two notions are mutually
dependent distinctions. Essentially, however, they are one and the same
thing. They cannot therefore be distinguished in terms of good and bad,
true and false, existent and nonexistent. If one of the two is absent, the
other is necessarily absent also. But the False Aspectarians say that although
consciousness exists, the aspects do not. They therefore distinguish them in
terms of existence and nonexistence.

According to the Chittamatra system generally, to say that something
is substantially different from consciousness is a violation of the Mind
Only tenet. Consequently, the Chittamatrins never make such an assertion, since, for them, all phenomena necessarily exist within the nature of
consciousness. Given, therefore, that the False Aspectarians deny that the
aspects share the same nature as (the cognizing) consciousness, they say
that the aspects are nonexistent. To do otherwise would be to imply that
the aspects and consciousness are not substantially different. But then, if
consciousness and aspects are substantially the same, there is nothing to
distinguish False Aspectarians from True Aspectarians. This is why the former deny the existence of the aspects, or say that they have no true existence within the nature of consciousness, or say that they are false. They
affirm, however, that consciousness is truly existent. But even if we assume with the False Aspectarians that the aspects are nonexistent, how is
it possible that within consciousness, which the False Aspectarians consider to exist and to stand alone and unsupported like a pure crystal
sphere, there manifest a variety of experienced features? If there are no as-

pects, is it feasible that consciousness should be generated in the likeness of what it observes? That is something for the False Aspectarians to think about. They may well give the example of hairs appearing in the air and say that though there are no hairs present when hairs are perceived, consciousness is appearing in the aspect of hairs. To be sure, the nonexistence of the hairs does not preclude the mere experience of such a perception. But if, in addition, it is said that the aspects appearing as floating hairs do not exist either, it follows that the experience (which consists of the mind's being generated in the aspect of floating hairs) must likewise be completely nonexistent also! Consequently, in the present context, to say that the aspects do not exist is the same as saying that no aspect can arise at all; if nothing arises at all, the aspects do not exist. If, on the other hand, an aspect does arise, inasmuch as it is aspect, it is also consciousness. That it is consciousness cannot be denied. If the aspect is not consciousness, it lies outside the range of cognition—like the color of a barren woman's child. It cannot become the object of any consciousness. All this constitutes the general refutation. Nothing is gained by saying that what is clearly experienced is false, but what is not experienced is true!

In brief, consciousness and the aspects are differentiated only reciprocally. They can never be differentiated in *fact*, with the specification that one is existent and the other is not. "Aspect" cannot be classified as anything other than a feature of the clarity and knowing of the consciousness that cognizes individual objects. This is why it is never possible for consciousness to be something that stands separate from the aspect. It is therefore important to reflect carefully on the consequence that if the aspect has no existence whatever, it cannot appear. Otherwise, if one fails to do so and considers, without more ado, that the aspects just do not exist, this position will eventually turn against one and one will stray very far from the subtle position of the Madhyamaka path.

Therefore, the authentic Chittamatra is the system of the True Aspectarians (who are authors of excellent treatises). On the other hand, in saying that the outer object is not even truly existent as the mind, the False Aspectarians are a little closer to the understanding that things are empty of true existence[335] and thus provide, in a manner of speaking, a bridge to the Madhyamaka. Although in the correct ordering of things the False Aspectarians are, as a result, placed higher on the scale of views, nevertheless, because the system exhibits many inconsistencies on the level of the conventional truth, the conventional should be expounded according to the system of the True Aspectarians. Once this key point is grasped, it will be easy to understand the refutations that follow.

17. A detailed exposition of the refutation
18. It is inadmissible to say that the aspects are nonexistent
19. This is so when one reflects about the manner in which the object is cognized
20. A general demonstration

> 54
> Therefore, where there's nothing present,
> Absent also is cognizing consciousness.
> Likewise misery cannot be known as bliss,
> Nor white cognized as something that's not white.

Objects and subjects are differentiated in relation to each other. If, in a given place, there is no thing present, without such an object (appearing through its own power) there can be no subject consciousness cognizing it. For example, as indicated by the words of the root stanza, "misery cannot be known as bliss," joy cannot be cognized as suffering, and a white object cannot be cognized as something black and not white. This is the general demonstration set forth in the root text.

20. A specific demonstration
21. Unmediated cognition is untenable

> 55
> Unmediated knowledge of the aspects
> Is untenable.
> Because they are themselves not consciousness,
> These aspects are like blossoms in the sky and all the
>   rest.

There are only two ways in which consciousness can cognize objects: either in an unmediated manner (*dngos su shes pa*) or by means of representations or aspects (*btags pa'i tshul gyis shes pa*). Unmediated cognition means that consciousness, which is the antithesis of inert matter, is itself generated, clear and knowing, in the aspect of the object in question.[336] For those who affirm the existence of an extramental world, consciousness does not cognize objects like pots directly or unmediatedly. Instead, through the influence of outer things, consciousness arises in their likeness, and this is designated as the knowledge or perception of objects.

By contrast, for those who deny the reality of the aspects (the False Aspectarians), neither of these explanations is possible. To begin with, unmediated perception and knowledge of clearly experienced aspects like colors is untenable; these aspects cannot be perceived and cognized as this or that. Unmediated cognition necessarily implies that the object is known in a manner that partakes of (or is at one with) the nature of consciousness. The False Aspectarians say, however, that the aspects are not consciousness. But if they are not of the nature of consciousness, how can they be directly experienced? In the same way, it is impossible to have perceptual experience of the color of a sky-flower or of a barren woman's child.

21. Cognition by means of representations or aspects is also untenable

> 56
> What does not exist is without potency,
> Unfit for aspects, like a horse's horns.
> Nonexistents thus can have no power
> To cause cognitions that resemble them.

It may be said that existent things cannot be straightforwardly experienced in an unmediated manner, but rather that objects that cast their aspects have the power to produce consciousnesses appearing in their guise. And it is the arising of consciousness in the likeness of a thing that we call the seeing or knowing of that thing. By contrast, nonexistent things have no power to produce cognitions that resemble them. Accordingly, it is improper to say that such objects are experienced or known as specific things—even by means of mere representations. As in the case of a horse, a horse's horns have no power to produce a consciousness appearing as a horse's horns. Therefore, even on the level of conventional reality, it is impossible for there to be a consciousness that grasps their characteristics by identifying their specific aspects. In accordance with this example, if even the aspects do not exist, there is no power whereby a consciousness appearing, say, in the likeness of blue or yellow can be produced, enabling one to say that it is like this or like that. The False Aspectarian Chittamatrins do not indeed say that objects exist separate from the mind and that they are cognized and experienced by the mind by means of representations that resemble these same objects. Nevertheless, since in their system objects are not experienced unmediatedly (*dngos su*) or by means of a representations (*btags*), and since there is no other alternative, it follows that there can be no such thing as a consciousness that experiences aspects—a consequence that the foregoing argument is intended to demonstrate.[337]

19. An examination of the relation between consciousness and its object shows that denial of the aspects is untenable

> 57
> But since these aspects are, and are indeed experienced,
> How do they relate with consciousness?
> Nonexistent aspects cannot share the latter's nature,
> Nor indeed can they arise from it.

There must of necessity be a link or relation between an object and the consciousness that experiences it. Without such a connection there can be no experience. Now, since, as a matter of fact, aspects such as colors are experienced by consciousness (the knowing subject), the question remains how, in the system of the False Aspectarians, are such unceasing appearances connected with consciousness? The answer is that they cannot be connected at all, for the simple reason that, according to the False Aspectarians, the aspects do not exist whereas consciousness does—which means that they cannot be related through their partaking of the same nature. If the aspects are linked with consciousness through their having the same nature, it undoubtedly follows that either consciousness is nonexistent like the aspects or the aspects are existent like consciousness. Neither can it be said that the aspects are the product of consciousness. For nonexistent things cannot be the result of something that exists. And even if one were to accept that aspects arise from consciousness, they could never be perceived simultaneously with it, since cause and effect occur at different moments, one earlier, one later. These and innumerable other faults would ensue, all of which concern the fact that, in general, the simple relation of provenance (between aspects and consciousness) precludes the experience of objects. It is in the context of this relation that this matter should be investigated, but since the False Aspectarians cannot assert that aspects and consciousness are linked with each other in a relation of provenance, there is no need to consider this matter here. As a result, the False Aspectarians are necessarily saying that though the aspects are experienced, there is no link between them and consciousness—which is a very considerable inconsistency.

Things can be said to be related when there is no incompatibility between them. Non-Buddhists make a distinction between relations of possession, relations of inherence, and so on, but the reasoning supporting these different categories is unproven. On the other hand, the glorious Dharmakirti has set forth only two relations. Since phenomena must be either of the same or of different nature, the relation between them must be that of a single nature (*bdag gcig 'brel ba*) in the first case, or of provenance (*de byung 'brel ba*) in the second.

A basis of properties, such as a vase, is said to be impermanent by eliminating the contrary concept of permanence. It is said to be fabricated by eliminating the concept of unfabricatedness; and it is said to be a (causally efficient) thing by eliminating the concept of nonthing. Such aspects exist individually (in the mind) through other-elimination, which excludes the misconceived ideas that are opposed to them, and it is by means of their specific names that they can be understood, not otherwise. As a result, they are individually posited as the objects of speech and thought. They are one with the nature of the pot. Consequently, fabricatedness and impermanence are said to share a relation of same nature with the pot. This relation exists through the discerning power of the conceptual mind, occurring through other-elimination. But since they are one and the same entity, it is impossible for the thing and its aspects to be linked in a subject-object relation—just as it is impossible for a fingertip to touch itself.

With regard to the relation of provenance, this is simply the relation of cause and effect. Causes are of two kinds: main causes (*nyer len gyi rgyu*) and cooperative causes (*lhan cig byed pa'i rgyu*). One should be aware that in other texts, effects are said to be the product of six causes and four conditions and so forth. In general, causes are defined as fivefold, although in fact all may be subsumed in two categories: (1) causes for the positing of something (*rnam par bzhag 'jog gi rgyu*)[338] and (2) causes of production (*skyed byed kyi rgyu*). The definition of a cause is "that in whose absence an effect is not produced."

It may be said in passing that there are two kinds of antithesis or contradiction (*'gal ba*). First, there is the antithesis of simultaneous incompatibility (*lhan cig mi gnas 'gal*), as when two things are mutually counteractive and cannot possibly be concomitant in terms either of continuity or efficacy.[339] Second, there is the antithesis of mutual exclusion (*phan tshun spang* '*gal*), in which the opposing factor of a thing is the absence of that thing (as in the case of blue and nonblue). Of these two kinds of antithesis, the first may be further subdivided into (a) factual opposites (*don 'gal*), such as light and darkness, and (b) mental or attitudinal opposites (*blo 'gal*), such as self-grasping and the realization of no-self. In addition, the antithesis of mutual exclusion may also be subdivided into (a) direct antithesis (*dngos 'gal*) and (b) indirect antithesis (*brgyud 'gal*). In the case of direct antithesis, the two things in question are clean contraries, as in the case of permanence and impermanence. As for indirect antithesis, the two factors are not directly or mutually opposed, but since the reverse of the first element pervades (or is concomitant with) the second, it follows that the two elements cannot co-exist. This is illustrated by the concepts of fabricatedness and permanence. Permanence is pervaded by unfabricatedness (all permanent things are nec-essarily unfabricated). It is very important to grasp these different kinds of relation and antithesis correctly. For fear of being overly verbose, I shall leave the matter here. However, since these issues are entailed in every kind of argument, I have touched on them by way of indication.

19. An examination of causes shows that denial of the aspects is untenable

> 58
> And if they are without a cause,
> How is it that they can arise sporadically?
> But if instead they have a cause,
> Why are they not "dependent nature"?

When one asks, "Are aspects like blue, yellow, and so on, caused or not?" only two replies are possible. One may claim that aspects are uncaused; but in that case, how is it that they are neither constantly existent nor constantly nonexistent but are present at some moments and not at others? How is such occasional manifestation possible? As we have already explained, that which is independent of causes cannot appear sporadically. If, on the other hand, aspects *are* caused, this means that they are produced subject to con-ditions. And since, in that case, the aspects are produced interdependently, they constitute "dependent nature." How can the False Aspectarians deny such a conclusion? To be sure, it is undeniable.

If aspects arise owing to conditions, they must exist. The Chittamatrins do not assert any cause other than consciousness. It therefore follows that the aspect does not belong to the imputed nature but is of the dependent nature. This is an undeniable consequence.

18. A demonstration that the apprehending aspect standing on its own is untenable

> 59
> And if they don't exist, then consciousness
> Itself will be devoid of aspect
> Like a sphere of purest crystal.
> Such consciousness is surely undetectable.

If the object-aspect does not exist, it follows that the subject conscious-ness is all alone. This being so, it follows that consciousness, which is con-sidered to possess the aspect of being empty of the duality of subject and object and the aspect of being self-illuminating, should experience itself in an entirely aspectless manner. But though the epistemic subject—con-sciousness in isolation—ought, in that case, to be experienced on its own, like a pure crystal sphere unaffected by the color of the object, the fact is that it is not at all observed in this way; it is not experienced or perceived.

In this general context, "consciousness" refers to the awareness of any objects and their specific aspects. If no aspect of form is in any way ob-served, one cannot point to the occurrence of a visual consciousness. In the same way, there can be no experiencing of consciousness alone, de-void of any aspect. The Chittamatrins say of this consciousness that it is "mere clarity and knowing, similar to a pure crystal sphere." But in point of fact, they are referring to the aspects of this consciousness taken as an object. If one observes this consciousness as being like a pure crystal sphere, it necessarily arises as that thing equipped with the aspects in ques-tion. If, however, there are no aspects produced, to talk about conscious-ness as being like this or like that is nothing but empty words—no more meaningful than saying that the barren woman's son is white. Therefore, since a consciousness devoid of aspects (which is supposed to be experi-enced) is not experienced, we may conclude that it does not exist. There is no reason at all for its being unobservable. If the [False Aspectarian] Chit-tamatrins believe that the aspects (whereby consciousness is modified or colored) have not the slightest existence, either outside or inside the mind, how is it that this nondual consciousness itself, like a sphere of pure crys-tal, is not experienced? And how is it that the conceptual mind does not ascertain it if it is experienced? For there exists no other altering cause that might render it uncertain.

The Chittamatrins may say that the experience of aspects occurs in the same way that the aspect of water is experienced in a mirage: It is seen but is not there. They consequently regard our argument as inconclusive. But the argument is not inconclusive, since a comparable investigation can be applied to the optical illusion as well. For even if we allow that there is no outer aspect of water in the optical illusion, if there is no illusory aspect of water within consciousness, how can there be an experience of something that is completely nothing? It is impossible.

17. A refutation of the Chittamatra replies to this objection

> 60
> It may be said that it is through delusion that they are
>   cognized.
> But whether they depend upon delusion
> Or arise by reason of delusion's power,
> Such aspects are indeed dependent nature.

In answer to our demonstration that in the absence of aspects there can be no experience, the False Aspectarians may say that the absence of aspects does not necessarily rule out experience in the conventional sense. There are no aspects, they say, but because of mistaken habitual tendencies or delusion, it is thus that the mind perceives—just as when a victim of jaundice sees a white shell as yellow. In the same way, the False Aspectarians believe that it is through the conditioning of deluded habitual tendencies that aspects such as yellowness and so on appear to be true, even though they do not exist. But is the aspect found to be dependent on delusion in the sense of sharing in its nature, or does it arise by the power of delusion, in which case aspect and delusion are linked in a relation of provenance? However they may be related, the aspects can only be the dependent nature.

When one speaks of delusion ('khrul pa), one is referring to either (1) the habitual tendencies that are the cause of delusion or (2) the actual delusion itself, which is the result of these same tendencies. Now, habitual tendencies, considered as the cause of the delusion, cannot be linked with the mental aspect (as their effect) in a relation of same nature. At the stage of habitual tendencies, their effect (the mental aspect) is yet to manifest—and it is thus untenable to say that the aspect is experienced. Neither can the aspect be linked in a relation of provenance to the delusion in the sense of result (of habitual tendencies). For there would follow the faulty consequence that the aspect and the delusion would not, in that case, be simultaneous.[340]

If therefore the aspect appearing because of delusion is necessarily related to habitual tendencies in terms of provenance, and to the delusion in terms of same nature, it can only be that the aspect is none other than the dependent nature, because what the Chittamatrins call the dependent nature is not in the slightest degree separate from pure and impure dependent arising. Therefore, what they call "perception due to illusion" cannot occur in the absence of aspects. And if such a perception occurs, there is necessarily a relation between aspect and delusion, with the result that the aspect partakes of the dependent nature and is not nonexistent. On the other hand, if there is no relation whatsoever between them, there can be no such thing as a perception arising from a delusion—any more than we can speak of the color of a barren woman's child.

Another example that the False Aspectarians give in reply (to the demonstration that without aspect there is no experience) is that something small may appear to be large at a distance. They also answer it by quoting the master Shubhagupta (*dge srung*), who says:

> *Consciousness is just awareness.*
> *When this is disturbed through the power of deluded habit,*
> *Aspects, nothing more, arise and are experienced—*
> *Colors such as blue and other things.*
> *We then think, "This is blue" (or something else),*
> *And yet it's not a real, existent blue.*
> *It's only in delusion that we think*
> *That there is blue external to the mind.*

Accordingly, the False Aspectarians may consider that the aspects of blue and so on are (in the absence of an object) no more than the apprehending aspects of consciousness. They are not the aspects of the observed object. Therefore, since the consciousness of ordinary beings is not actually modified by the aspects of (an external) blue object and so on, they believe that their position—namely, that there is a single, aspectless consciousness—is not invalidated.

In answer to this, we may say that if aspects such as blue are apprehended, there is an object of perception. But if this object has no existence, either as an external fact or as (a feature of) inner consciousness, no experience can occur, whether unmediated (*dngos*) or through a representation or aspect (*btags*). And the notion that mental aspects (of objects) merely appear by the power of delusion was disproved during our investigation of their relations. Our adversaries may differ in the way they formulate their theories, but they are all the same as to their meaning, as well as in their inability to prove the nonexistence of aspects.

When it is demonstrated (with the help of dreams and the perception of blue as an object-universal) to those who assert the nonexistence of aspects that their theory is inconclusive, they answer that though aspects do not exist, they appear to do so through the power of delusion. But it should be understood that all such responses are invalidated by our earlier arguments.

Again, other Chittamatrins may accept that when operating at the level of impure perception, consciousness appearing as a variety of objects is fallacious. At the level of pure perception,[341] however, they may think that consciousness becomes single and nondual, and the arguments designed to refute a single, truly existent consciousness lose their certainty and are thus invalid. To this we reply that, granted the possibility that all aspects come to a halt at the level of pure perception, the conclusion of the theory of the False Aspectarians is different. For even if delusion is arrested, the aspects (as they describe them) cannot come to a halt. For, since they believe that the aspects (though appearing) do not exist, they cannot be connected with either the delusion or the habitual tendency to delusion—just as the absence of horses does not exclude the possibility of cows.[342] Another weakness in their position is that if they consider that, at the level of impure perception, consciousness is fallacious (illusory), whereas at the level of pure perception, consciousness (being devoid of manifold aspects) is established as a single, truly existent entity, they must now explain the cause of this truly existent consciousness, which previously did not exist. It cannot have been produced from the previously false consciousness, because a false entity (the contrary of a true entity) has no power to produce a truly existent consciousness. For if it has such a power, it is not false. On the other hand, if the (previous) consciousness has this power while nevertheless being without true existence, it follows that even if they say that the (later) consciousness *is* truly existent, it cannot be. A consciousness that is truly existent at the level of pure perception[343] cannot be without a cause, for in that case it would follow that the consciousness is always either existent or nonexistent. It is impossible to establish nondual consciousness as a truly existent, single entity, for in that case all the unwanted consequences of the earlier and subsequent arguments, which refute, for example, the existence of truly permanent entities such as Ishvara, would apply here as well.

It may be said that this consciousness is produced through the power of the previous moment of consciousness, but this is out of place with regard to a consciousness truly existing on the ultimate level. Causally related things cannot be ultimately existent. If two moments are simultaneous, to posit a relation between them of cause and effect is untenable. This is so because there is no cause prior to the production of the effect and therefore no productive power, and because when the cause is present and equipped with productive power, the effect is also already there. Thus the two moments of consciousness cannot be posited as cause and effect. Even if the previous and subsequent moments of consciousness are different, it is untenable to claim that they constitute a truly existent cause and effect. For an effect cannot be produced from what is chronologically either separated or not separated from it. If there is a time gap, there must occur a disintegrated cause intervening between the cause and effect. And if the cause does not disintegrate, no gap is possible. Consequently, an effect must be produced from the disintegration, that is, the disintegrated cause. But this too is untenable. For a disintegration constitutes a nonexistence, and that which does not exist is devoid of all power. Disintegration is characterized or defined in terms of nonexistence. Otherwise, how could one speak of the cause disintegrating? For it could not do so. If disintegration were a positive, causally efficient thing (*zhig pa dngos po*), how is it that past things such as incinerated wood do not continue to exist in the present? Since, aside from their disintegration, there is no other reason for describing things as being now nonexistent, it would follow that everything would be permanent. And if the cause does not cease, there can be no producing of effects, and the latter are ruled out. It would follow too that disintegration itself becomes something not produced from causes, and so on. There are innumerable ways to invalidate such a notion.

What we call disintegration is merely a part of nonexistence and occurs when a cause disintegrates. In itself, however, disintegration is not in the slightest way a positive, causally efficient entity. If it were, it would be impossible for nonthings or absences of things to be counted as objects of knowledge. The label "nonthing" is applied to what is the negation or absence of a thing. Aside from this, the nonthing has no separate existence whatsoever. For if a nonthing is not the reverse of a thing, this means that, in the end, affirmation and negation, thing and nonthing, existence and nonexistence no longer have a mutually exclusive character. Everything will be confused and the categories of knowledge-objects will collapse. Therefore, so-called disintegration is the aspect of the disintegration of a cause; it is a mere nonimplicative negative (i.e., a simple absence, nonexistence). In itself, it has no potency in any way. And since (when disintegration occurs) a cause no longer exists, its effect cannot be produced, as it were, from the intervening gap. This refutation is similar in meaning to the demonstration that production is untenable when there is no contact between cause and effect. For to say that effects are produced from disintegration (that is, disintegrated causes) is to say that effects are produced without being in contact with their causes. If cause and effect are not separated by a lapse of time, they become simultaneous. For two partless instants without a gap between them necessarily coincide in the same moment. Without a space between them, they become one, and it is untenable to say that something is producing itself, for in that case, with regard to time, an entire kalpa becomes no more than an instant.

If the link between cause and effect is untenable, does this not mean that cause and effect are also untenable on the relative level? Not at all. Although cause and effect appear, they cannot withstand analysis. This is why they are referred to as relative. If cause and effect *were* resistant to analysis, they would be ultimately existent—how could they be relative? But analysis on the ultimate level is not the same as investigation on the relative level. These points have been briefly elucidated according to the explanation given in Kamalashila's *Commentary on Difficult Points*.

Now, if effects cannot be produced regardless of whether there is contact between cause and effect, does not the assertion of causality once again become untenable? The answer is no. The reason is that, for those who say that the cause and the effect are truly existent, such truly existent things must resist analysis. In that case, cause and effect either meet or do not meet. Either there is a gap between them or there is not. There is no other possibility and effects can only be produced in one of these two ways. And because there is no causal production possible apart from these two situations, the process of causality is untenable. For those, however, who do not assert a truly existent cause and effect, it is enough to say that a cause is "that without which a certain effect would not arise" and that this is just the way things are. There is no need for them to specify that effects are produced either by being in contact or by not being in contact with causes. And the fact that they make no such assertions does not mean that causality becomes untenable—quite the reverse, it becomes extremely tenable! This will be explained in the sequel when Shantarakshita explains the relative truth in stanza 65: "Based upon foregoing causes, things arise as though they were the causes' subsequent effects."

The arguments disproving the position of the False Aspectarians are very powerful and of extraordinary profundity. If one is able to assimilate them correctly, they will bring one to the heart of the Chittamatra tenet and reveal the secret key point of the Madhyamaka. There is nothing more important than these arguments in the whole of Shantarakshita's system, uniting as it does the twin approaches of the Mind Only and the Middle Way.

8. Establishing the absence of many truly existent entities

61
No matter what we may investigate,
A single entity cannot be found.
And since there is no "one,"
Indeed there is no "many" either.

When all things asserted by both Buddhist and non-Buddhist schools—permanent or impermanent, pervasive or nonpervasive, infinitesimal particles or extended objects, consciousness or objects of consciousness—are investigated to find out whether or not they can be established as single entities, however much they may appear to be single wholes when left unexamined, they all fall apart like bursting bubbles. They cannot support the weight of such investigation, which is greater than that of a hundred thousand mountains of adamant. Not even a single infinitesimal particle can withstand investigation. All things disintegrate into shards, shards into a hundred fragments. Everything scatters. Not a single thing can be established as an entity that is truly one. Now "many" is necessarily a collection of "ones." Therefore, where there is no singular, there is also no plural. If there is not one tree, there cannot be a forest. As it is said in the *Lankavatara-sutra:*

> *When the mind examines things,*
> *These same things in themselves cannot be grasped.*
> *And so they're said to be unspeakable,*
> *Devoid of all inherent nature.*

When the mind examines and investigates,
There's no dependent, no imputed, nature,
And there's no nature that exists completely!
How then does the mind conceive them thus?

There's no inherent nature and no consciousness;
There are no things; there is no alaya.
Inferior thinkers, lifeless and naïve,
Believe and take them all as real.

But all such features, entities and mind
(All movements of the intellect),
My offspring Bodhisattvas utterly transcend,
Enjoying thus the state beyond all thought.

When they are subjected to the mind's investigation, no single, truly existent entity and no multiplicities of these same entities can be apprehended or found. They cannot therefore be said to be truly existent in the singular or the plural. Neither can they be grasped as such by the mind. They do not exist in and of themselves. Therefore, as the first stanza of the above quotation shows, external objects have no existence. Then, in the second stanza, in order to show that the same is true for knowledge-objects considered as inner (mental) phenomena, the sutra says that when investigated by the mind, the three realities of dependent nature, imputed nature, and completely existent nature[344] have no existence whatever. How therefore can the mind conceive them so?

To the qualm that if they were nonexistent, how is it that there is a common consensus with regard to the experience of outer and inner phenomena, the sutra goes on to say (in the third stanza) that outer forms and so on have no inherent existence. Likewise, the experiencing subject—that is, consciousnesses (such as the eye consciousness)—does not exist. The outer and inner things that appear as the environment, beings, and experiences do not exist. Neither does the alaya, the container of the seeds of such phenomena, exist. Nevertheless, the naïve (who, in lacking the primordial wisdom of awareness that realizes the ultimate nature, or rather the wisdom that discerns authentic, ultimate reality as it is, are like lifeless corpses) experience all these things in the common manner, victims of their faulty discursive processes. They regard them all as truly existent, whereas ultimately this is not the case.

And if we were to ask in what state of mind the learned abide who know the ultimate nature of things, the Buddha goes on to say that his offspring (the Bodhisattvas) transcend all conceptual constructs: characteristics like color, the senses, and sense-fields; the consciousnesses like the eye consciousness; and all thoughts, which are the movements of the dependent nature. The learned and expert remain in a state beyond thought.

Moreover, the spotlessly intelligent master Dharmakirti has said:

> *When anything is scrutinized and ascertained,*
> *Ultimately it is found to be unreal.*
> *Thus no single thing is found*
> *And no pluralities of things discovered.*

> *If all the different things*
> *Cannot be properly described as singular,*
> *Consciousness of these likewise appears as various;*
> *For how could it be one, a single thing?*

> *To the extent one thinks of all such features,*
> *To that extent they are deprived of them.*
> *And thus being empty of the same,*
> *They're said to lack inherent nature.*

> *All that the learned have explained*
> *Will be most clearly understood.*

7. Establishing the pervasion

62
A thing cannot exist unless it be in singular or plural—
Aside from this, no other mode of being can it have.
For singular and plural
Are mutually excluding contraries.

Some people may think that although the sign or reason is established as belonging to the logical subject of the argument and as being concomitant with the concordant example, and though there is neither one truly existent entity nor many truly existent entities, there might still be something that exists truly. Such people are in doubt perhaps regarding the mode of the reverse pervasion (in which the sign is absent from the discordant case)[345] and think the validity of the sign is not conclusive. But their expectations are futile and entirely deceptive.

If it were possible for something to exist neither in the singular nor the plural, then even granted that the two categories of "one" and "many" contain nothing that is truly existent, the conclusion would not indeed follow that all phenomena are necessarily without true existence. But no "thing" can exist in any way other than in the singular or the plural, for these two categories are mutually exclusive [and form a dichotomy]. There is no third possibility. Therefore, since the evidential sign of "there being neither one truly existent entity nor many truly existent entities" is established as being the property of the logical subject—all knowable phenomena accepted by Buddhist and non-Buddhist schools—and since the pervasions (forward and reverse) are also definitely valid, it follows that all phenomena are established as lacking inherent existence.

But here some may object that whereas "one phenomenon" and "many phenomena" are counted as things, their contrary (neither one phenomenon nor many phenomena) is a nonthing. This being so, it follows that the predicated property and the sign or proof are not different from each other, in that both are nonthings. Therefore, if the predicated property, that is, the lack of inherent existence, is not established as belonging to the subject of the proposition, it follows that the sign or proof (which is by nature indistinguishable from the predicated property) is not established either. On the other hand, if the sign *is* established, the predicated property, namely, that all dharmas are without inherent existence, is (automatically) established as well. For example, having ascertained the argument of neither one nor many, no one will claim that the rabbit's horns are (efficient) things. Accordingly, those who make this objection say that the sign and predicate amount to exactly the same thing.[346]

This, however, is not the case. Although phenomena do lack inherent existence, beings fail to recognize this owing to their beginningless ignorance. The argument of neither one nor many is designed to bring them understanding. It is just like saying to someone who is unaware that certain collected features are characteristic of an ox, "Since this animal possesses a hump, a dewlap, and so on, it is an ox." Or else it is like saying to someone, "There is no vase here in front of you for you to see and touch. For if there were, you would see it, but you can't." For those who do not know about the absence of true existence, it can be demonstrated to them with respect to the logical subject appearing to them (i.e., everything that is said to exist) that, just as "where there are no trees, there are no junipers," it follows that since there is neither one truly existent thing nor many truly existent things (this being the pervasive sign with regard to true existence), it follows that there are no truly existent things (this is the probandum pervaded by the sign). Thus the way in which the probandum and the way in which the probative sign are understood are not the same. The sign proves that the logical subject is without true existence. Similarly, when it is demonstrated by means of the sign that the vase lacks true existence, the sign and the predicated property are not the same. Therefore, this reasoning brings knowledge to those who do not understand and refreshes the memory of those who have done so.[347] This argument has the power to dispel all misconceptions contrary to the fact that things have no inherent existence.

5. A demonstration that things exist on the relative level
6. Identification of the relative as mere appearance, empty of true existence

> 63
> Therefore, all these things possess
> Defining features only in the relative.
> And if I thought that in their essence they existed truly,
> What would be the point of all my labors?

Things believed to exist truly in either the singular or the plural are unable to withstand analysis. Therefore, like the men, horses, and oxen that one might see in an illusory display, phenomena enjoy a "satisfactory" existence—only so long as one refrains from investigating them. They possess characteristics only in a relative sense. If Shantarakshita thought that the defining features with which they are endowed were not illusory and relative, and believed that, in their essence, they truly existed as they appear, what would be the point of all his refutation? The nature of a thing is simply the way it is; it cannot be changed in the slightest way by the wishes of others. If the illusory horses and oxen really existed in the way that they appear, it would simply be incorrect to say that they are deceptive or illusory. "Whether or not the Buddhas appear in the world, the nature of things simply is what it is." And, in accordance with the meaning of this citation, the mode of being of phenomena is not to be changed by the theories that the mind entertains about them. If the mind is in tune with the way things really are, the mind is correct or unmistaken. If the mind is not so attuned, then whatever it conceives with regard to its object, it misconceives. The object does not follow the wishful thinking of the mind. Consequently, since the mode of being of things is simply what it is (and cannot be altered by anything extraneous to itself), it is their very nature, their way of abiding, or their essence, spontaneous and uncontrived. No one can ever change this nature into something else. It is thus said to be without hooks, or to be free of hooks. A hook allows one to catch hold of something, and the meaning of the expression is that theories can find no purchase in the nature of things. For example, fire is simply hot, and no one is able to establish that it is otherwise.

Here, the words of the root stanza *kun rdzob kho na* ("only in the relative") refer (in the distinction between the real[348] and unreal) to what is unreal or false. Things are never found to be truly existent. Thus the words of the stanza preclude their true existence. In some editions of the text, the words *'di bdag* ("in their essence") in the third line of the stanza, are replaced by *'di dag* (the plural marker), but the omission of the prefix *ba* is a mistake. In the ancient texts, which are extremely accurate, the spelling is *'di bdag,* and it is in this sense that the root text is to be understood.

With regard to the last two lines of the stanza, there are some commentators who consider that they do not refute the valid establishment of relative phenomena. In general, in the context of the exposition of the approximate ultimate truth, the principal concern of the Svatantrikas is to establish, through conventional valid cognition, the specific characteristics of relative phenomena and to deny their true existence on the ultimate level. It is therefore indeed true that the Svatantrikas do not refute the valid establishment of conventionalities. But this is not the correct interpretation of the root text here. I will not, however, expatiate upon this point.

This stanza is extremely important and pregnant with meaning. But though there is a great deal that needs to be said about it, I shall give no more than an outline here. Certain words in the stanza may be understood in very different ways. The words in question are "therefore" (*de phyir*) in the first line, "only" (*kho na*) in the second line (which on account of the translation is assimilated in some editions to "very" or "itself"),[349] and "if" (*gal te*) in the third line. All the refutations that use investigation aiming at the ultimate status of things are means to understanding what exactly the relative is. And all the variegated appearances of the relative are means to realizing the ultimate truth. It should thus be understood that they mutually assist each other.

The relative is mere appearance, empty of true existence. Were something to exist exactly as it appears, it would not be relative. In that case, there would be no such thing as ultimate truth either. But since whatever appears to us is not established, it is accounted relative, and by the same token, the ultimate is also established. And since there is neither one truly existent thing nor many such things, all things lack inherent existence in an ultimate sense. Wherefore, their mere appearance is defined as the relative. The two truths reveal each other. How could they be in opposition? All the minute explanations both above and in the sequel come together on this point: Emptiness and dependent arising are mutually supportive. If one of them were missing, the other could not be. There is no effort more important than striving by every means to understand and assimilate this truth.

What therefore is the actual mode of being of things? Although they appear in their various aspects, they are lacking in inherent existence. Therefore, by examining phenomena as to their lack of intrinsic being, the ideas that misconceive things exactly opposite to the way in which they are, are dispelled, and the true nature of the relative is revealed. If appearance and emptiness do not merge, the mode of being of phenomena is not recognized. Conversely, if one understands that the two are inseparable, one has grasped the nature of things. This may be illustrated by illusory horses and oxen seen in a mirage. They are the combination of the appearance, which is perceived as horses and oxen, and their lack of true existence, which is their illusoriness. This has been perfectly explained by the Bhagavan Buddhas, who know the ultimate nature of things. It is said in the *Dharmasangiti-sutra:* "A Bodhisattva should understand the ten classes of conventional teachings set forth by the Tathagata, the perfect Buddha, who has vanquished all foes. These ten classes are the teachings on the aggregates, dhatus, ayatanas, and so forth." And the *Ratnamegha-sutra* adds, "Child of my lineage, if Bodhisattvas possess these ten teachings, they know the relative truth. What are these ten? That which is labeled as form, being not found as form in the ultimate truth, is not regarded as truly existent." And the text goes on to say the same for feeling and the other skandhas. The *Akshayamati-sutra* also says: "When we say 'correct,' this means that all phenomena are without self. It is thus by reasoning that phenomena are seen through." And the *Prajnaparamita-sutra,* the progenitrix of all the Conquerors, declares: "Since the nature of everything is emptiness, everything, including consciousness, is empty of itself."

The Chittamatrins may object that this teaching on emptiness applies to the emptiness of the imputed nature. This is quite true. But we also believe that what they consider to be ultimately existent consciousness is also an imputed reality. Although they establish that the nature of the dependent reality is truly existent, and that imputed reality is but the mere dualistic appearance of subject and object, their ultimately existent consciousness is disproved by the reasoning previously set forth. Consequently, it too is established as being imputed reality. As it is said in the *Hastikakshya-sutra:* "'Shariputra, what do you think? When the nature of phenomena is understood, does it exist or not?' And Shariputra answered, 'Lord, all these existing phenomena do not exist! And why? Because the Lord has taught that phenomena are illusionlike by nature. Whatever is like an illusion does not exist. For so it is. Existent phenomena do not exist. And why? Because on the ultimate level, no phenomena are observed.'"

Consequently, dependently arising appearances and the lack of inherent existence are inseparably united. They are like the moon reflected in the water; they are empty and yet they appear. When, on developing an extraordinary certainty in this, the mind is focused on and remains steadily attentive to it, one has what is called the illusionlike certainty of one who abides in perception. Such an apprehension of phenomena is in accordance with their ultimate nature. Nonetheless, it is no more than an apprehension in which the mind has associated phenomena, the locus of emptiness, with their lack of inherent existence. Since the conceived objects, or notions, that deny and affirm (true existence and appearance respectively) can themselves be refuted by reasoning that aims at the ultimate status of things, it is still possible to improve on this position. For this is an apprehension of the ultimate that is still dependent on concepts and is therefore classified as relative. Meditation on the *ultimate nature as it is,* however, is free from all conceptual constructs of either negation or affirmation. This is the "spacelike meditative equipoise of one who abides in nonperception."

Regarding freedom from conceptual constructs, there is no difference between the system that holds that meditative equipoise is perceptual and the system that says that it is nonperceptual.

6. Discerning the nature of the relative truth
7. Mere appearances exist incontrovertibly
8. The manner in which they appear

64
Only satisfactory when left unscrutinized,
Subject both to birth and to destruction,
Possessing causal potency:
Thus we understand the all-concealing relative.

When we say "relative," the question is, are we referring to something that is no more than a name, as when we speak of a rabbit's horns or an eternal Ishvara? Or do we mean a dependently produced thing equipped with infallible causal efficiency and empirically experienced in the common consensus, even by the simplest and least instructed? In answer to this we say that the relative is not a nonthing, that is, something posited only nominally, like a rabbit's horns—which we cannot see and which are wholly without effect. By contrast, although dependently arising things, when examined, cannot withstand analysis, when they are left to themselves, unquestioned, they appear to us directly nevertheless, and exist well enough and to our satisfaction. They act as causes and they are effects, subject to arising and cessation from moment to moment. They are the things we perceive; and they are unfailingly able to perform a function. It should be understood that all such things constitute what we call the relative. Now, it is said that it is through exclusion[350] (*rnam bcad*) that relative things are shown to have three defining characteristics, whereas it is by virtue of detection (*yongs gcod*) that these three characteristics are established as being one.[351]

The relative is defined as "satisfactory when left unscrutinized, subject both to birth and to destruction, and possessing causal potency."

The threefold definition of the relative is as follows.

1. *Phenomena are satisfactory when left unscrutinized.* As a way of countering the idea that relative things without true existence are unable to appear, these same things are said to be "satisfactory" if left unexamined. If they are examined, they are not found; but they appear uninterruptedly to anyone who leaves them uninvestigated. It is thus that they are like the reflection of the moon in water. This may be ascertained by means of the arguments expounded above, which establish that all such undeniable appearances are without true existence.

2. *Phenomena are subject both to birth and to destruction.* In order to counteract the idea that relative phenomena are not momentary, they are shown to be subject to production and to cessation. This was shown clearly by the reasoning that refutes truly existent, permanent entities, but it may be worth considering it a little further.

There are two arguments that prove the momentariness of things. First, there is the argument of nondependency and, second, the argument of invalidation. The argument of nondependency may be formally stated thus: *Whatever is causally efficient is necessarily self-disintegrating at every instant, independent of any external agent of destruction, like a flash of lightning or a flame. As for sound, it is also considered to be causally efficient.* Some people think that things like vases are permanent until they encounter something that causes their destruction. As long as the vase is not smashed to pieces by a hammer or something else, it is assumed that yesterday's vase is today's vase and that today's vase will also be tomorrow's vase. In this context, the Tibetan word *'jig* (destroy, destruction, disintegration) applies both to a thing, which is liable to destruction, and also to the nonthing, namely, the actual destruction or disintegration of the item in question. But in either case, no external cause of destruction is required. In the first case, no other cause of disintegration is needed aside from the mere fact that the vase has been produced; and in the second case, no cause of destruction is possible at all. Let us take the example of a vase, which for a hundred instants after its production does not meet a cause of its destruction. It is then destroyed by some external force. There must be one *instance-of-vase* in the first moment after its production, and there must be a second instance-of-vase in the second moment, and so on sequentially. If this were not so, if all the momentary instances of the vase occurring in successive points in time constituted one and the same vase-instance, it would follow that the two vases—the one in the first moment immediately after its production and the one occurring in the actual moment of its destruction—would be the same vase. Therefore, the vase must be disintegrating at every moment; a single identical vase does not perdure for a hundred instants. Again, if even one of the intervening vase-moments were not individually distinct, these (hundred) moments would be incomplete. Moreover, these so-called vase-moments are not different from the vase itself. You cannot count the vase-moments while the vase remains permanent.

The same is true of all compounded things. However long their duration, be it days, years, or kalpas, they are all established as momentary. For a thing like a year cannot be, except it be an accumulation of instants. When we say that something has lasted for a century, we tally the count with a hundred separate years. And a year itself cannot be, unless it be composed of a complement of twelve months. A month is composed of thirty days; a day comprises sixty spans.[352] Each span has sixty measures, every measure six breaths. A breath is composed of an inhalation and an exhalation, and each of these has many instants. And just as a pin pierces a stack of a hundred lotus petals progressively, all instants arise in orderly succession, not otherwise. If an instant were to be missing from this succession, the duration of the process would be shortened. If the thing in the first instant and the thing in the second instant are the same thing, it is meaningless even to mention a second instant. If a thing does not stir from its state in the first instant and does not disintegrate, all change is ruled out. It would in short be impossible to observe anything other than what is observed in the first instant. Of necessity, there would be no perceptible difference between old and new, between what has existed in the past and what exists in the present. And the causally efficient and the causally inefficient would necessarily be indistinguishable. But none of this is true, for it is certain that the subsequent instant of a thing occurs when the past instant of the thing has ceased. For example, if the vase that in the past was empty of water and the vase that in the present is now containing water were one and the same, the past instant of the vase (empty of water) must contain water. But this is impossible. It should be understood that the past instant of the vase without water has ceased. If it does not cease, there can never occur an instant when the vase contains water. In the same way, if all things that appear to be causally efficient do not cease as the instants pass, they will not occur in the instants that follow. Therefore, both the arising and the cessation of things are propelled by one cause,[353] and one should understand that no other cause of cessation is needed.

Things arise and disintegrate moment by moment, but because they manifest continuously in a similar fashion, they are mistakenly considered to constitute one and the same entity. One may, for instance, believe that one crossed a certain river last year and that one will do the same next year. One may think that the river last year, the river this year, and the river next year are one and the same river. But if one examines the river even at this very moment (to say nothing of last year or next year), there is not a single drop of the river that was there this morning. It is all brand-new water.

One may think that the vase is destroyed by a hammer. But in fact it is the interruption of the stream of continually arising vase-instants (which might otherwise have persisted in the future) that is referred to as the "destruction of the vase." The hammer is not the *direct* cause of the vase's destruction. As to what the hammer actually does, there are three possibilities. The hammer could be said to be producing itself, or producing the potsherds, or doing something else. But when one considers the present case, this cannot be an instance of the hammer producing itself. As for the potsherds, these are produced by the vase as the substantial cause and by the hammer as the cooperative cause. But whereas this may account for the production of the potsherds, how is the vase itself destroyed? It may be thought that, in one and the same instant, the hammer reduces the vase to nonentity and gives entity to the potsherds. But an entity and a nonentity cannot be the objects of the same action. And if the hammer produces something other than potsherds, it follows that the vase itself is not destroyed—any more than it would be destroyed by the production of a pillar. Again one might think that when the hammer destroys the vase, the potsherds just come naturally, like ash when there is a fire. But in that case the absurd consequence follows that the potter destroys the clay but does not produce the pots. Thus, to say that the nonentity, disintegration, is produced by a cause is to assert in fact that the cause does not produce anything at all. This is just like the expressions "to look at nothing" and "to have nothing to look at." They have a similar meaning.

The second of the two arguments that prove the momentariness of things is the argument of invalidation. Some people may think that although crows are usually black, there might be some that are white. In the same way, phenomena are mostly impermanent, but there might be some things, such as Ishvara, that are truly immutable and enduring. If something is eternal and immutable, in the sense of being empty of any causal efficiency (in terms of gradual succession of effects or their production all together and at once), it is not a real thing but is like space. Since Ishvara is eternal, it follows that he too is devoid of any causal efficiency. If something is causally efficient, it can only be gradual and momentary. But change is inadmissible in a permanent entity, because a permanent entity is empty of causal capacity. And whatever is empty of the capacity to function cannot be a thing. In short, permanence is incompatible with causally efficient things; and causally efficient things are incompatible with permanence. It should be understood that there are no objects of knowledge that are both permanent and causally efficient. Therefore, since it is proven that there are no permanent, functioning things, and that all existent things have no need of any external agency to bring about their destruction, it is clear that among all knowledge-objects, there exists not one single permanent entity. Space and other things that have no causal efficiency do not in fact exist. They are just names superimposed on the mere absence of causally efficient things. Against this, one might refer to the example of permanent space and so on, but in fact space is said to be permanent only in contradistinction to impermanent phenomena; it can in no way be established as a truly permanent entity.

To understand thus how production or birth itself means disintegration or destruction is a crucially important item of conventional reasoning. Thanks to it, one may grasp the unmistaken principle of the cause and effect of actions, and the mode of being of conventional phenomena. All clinging to existence, and all mistaken notions of eternal entities, will come to a halt. And one will, without difficulty, be able to penetrate emptiness, which is the absence of thinghood. This understanding therefore is the root of all the positive qualities of Purity.[354] As the Buddha said, "Just as the traces of the elephant's foot are the greatest of all traces, so is the understanding of impermanence supreme among all understandings."

3. *Relative phenomena possess causal potency.* Relative things are defined by their causal efficiency. On the other hand, figments, like the horns of a rabbit, are not real but have only a nominal existence. And all nonthings are the same. They are mere negations of things and do not have the slightest degree of independent existence. Conventional valid cognition does not establish the existence of space and so forth, which is devoid of causal efficiency. One must therefore conclude that it does not exist in fact. The only things that people involve themselves with, or else avoid, are specifically characterized conventional phenomena endowed with causal efficiency. These, in the present text, are regarded as the relative. As it is said, "If the (causally efficient) thing is established, this is the basis of everything; and all other nonthings are left aside, that is, they are of no importance."[355] Accordingly, the basis of knowledge is causally efficient things, which are experienced and accepted by everyone, from the learned down to the very simple. They are things that can be perceived by unimpaired senses as being endowed with specific characteristics, and they are able to produce their own future effects. Such are the proper objects to be assessed by conventional valid reasoning. Based on them, there arise and are named countless classes of things and nonthings—affirmation and negation, universals and their instances, relation and antithesis, substance (actual things) and conceptual distinguisher (or isolate), signifier and signified, appearance and conceptual representation through other-elimination (*sel 'jug*), and so on. Therefore, the true referent of the term "relative" is exclusively the causally effective thing.

It may be thought that the thing in its final moment, when its continuity is severed, is not characterized by causal efficiency. Our answer is as follows. It is taught that, given that the thing in its final moment has this capacity when it meets with certain conditions, the above fault is not present. But we will add that even when it does not meet with such conditions and indeed is unable to produce the effect of its own subsequent continuation, this does not generally mean that the object in question is without causal efficiency.[356]

It must be said at this point that in certain other scriptures, the relative is designated either as mistaken or as unmistaken.[357] According to the way things appear (kun rdzob kyi snang tshul), no contradiction is involved in so designating it. However, since in the Madhyamakalankara, the abiding mode of the conventional level (tha snyad kyi gnas tshul) is posited by means of investigation with valid reasoning, this must be done in accordance with the treatises on pramana. Given that even on the conventional level things devoid of causal efficiency cannot be posited as the proper objects of investigation by conventional valid reasoning, it is things that *have* this capacity that must be regarded as relative. As for appearing objects that are mistakenly assumed to exist (as for instance in the perception of two moons), their appearance is but consciousness appearing in their aspect, and therefore the fault of their not being accounted for in the relative is not incurred. And if we consider whether such apparent objects exist in themselves, as they appear, it will be found that they are simply nothing. Some people, however, considering that such things exist in fact, may think that, since they are not endowed with the characteristics of the relative, they constitute a third category of phenomena that are not accounted for in the two truths. If, however, they say that such appearing objects exist and are not momentary, this can only mean that these same objects become permanent appearances and are not false or deceptive! It follows too that there exists no commonly perceived example that proves the absence of true existence of phenomena. But those who say this have become almost like cattle—even more ignorant than worldly people. They pretend to debate with the most learned of those who understand the nature of phenomena, and make a laughable spectacle of themselves as a result. This same understanding [as in the case of appearing objects mistakenly assumed to exist] should also be applied to the apprehension (by other-elimination) of the aspects of nonthings (that is, names), which, as it is said, are empty in themselves.[358]

Those who have not yet perfectly assimilated the treatises on pramana can easily understand the division of the relative into mistaken and unmistaken. However, the assertion found in the Madhyamakalankara that the relative necessarily entails causal efficiency evokes extremely profound key points of conventional logic, the field of those who are long familiar with the system of Dharmakirti.

Although it is said that from the point of view of exclusion, or identification (*rnam bcad*), relative phenomena possess three defining characteristics, from the point of view of detection (*yongs gcod*), these characteristics necessarily coalesce within the same entity of the relative phenomenon itself. The latter is what is repeatedly defined as "the finding of conventional valid cognition (pramana)," or as "specifically characterized things that can be perceived and are universally accepted within empirical experience," or as "things that appear though they do not exist."

Exclusion and detection may be summarily explained as follows. As their Tibetan names [the elements *bcad* and *gcod*] indicate, they proceed by eliminating everything that is other (*gzhan sel*) than the thing in question. This elimination occurs in two ways. There is an other-elimination that constitutes a nonimplicative negation (as when one says, "The vase does not exist"), and there is an other-elimination that is an implicative negation (as when one says, "This is not a vase"). In the first case, to know something for what it is, by eliminating everything that is other than it, constitutes an exclusion. In the second case, when something is known because, by presenting itself, it eliminates all that is not itself, this is detection.[359] Consequently, when all that the thing is not is excluded and removed, the thing itself is established either by detection or, on the contrary, by exclusion. In an overall manner, therefore, it should be understood that there are two ways in which things are established.[360]

If we consider the matter in greater detail, it may be said that there are two kinds of exclusion: word-exclusion and meaning-exclusion.[361] Let us take word-exclusion first. Every word or name is the subject of other-elimination (*gzhan sel*). Owing to the fact that words exclude (*rnam bcad*), or isolate from, whatever they do not signify, we have the impression that what they refer to is established by detection (*yongs gcod*). In this connection, there is obviously no need to mention words that refer to actual things, but even in the case of an expression like "a rabbit's horns," which does not correspond to anything real, if its sense is not established by excluding all that is not rabbit and all that is not horn, one could derive no meaning from the expression. And without that, it would be impossible to determine that a rabbit's horns are entirely nonexistent. Although it seems that the meaning of the expression is established in detection, "a rabbit's horns" are entirely imaginary objects conjured up by the simple power of words. Other than that, rabbits' horns in themselves do not exist even conventionally. If they did, they would have to be established by both exclusion and detection.

The meaning-exclusion consists of both kinds of establishment: detection and exclusion. In the case of nonthings (*dngos med*), however, these are rooted purely in the exclusion of things. Although it seems that, in dependence on the exclusion of the object of negation (things), nonthings are established by means of detection on the level of their names, in fact they are established only by means of exclusion and are not even slightly established in and of themselves by way of detection. In the case of a given causally efficient thing (*dngos po*), this is established in and of itself by detection, and it is by virtue of this that all that is not that thing is removed by means of exclusion. It is thus that efficient things are established by both processes. Even so, it is mainly through detection that they are established—which then implies their establishment through exclusion.[362]

Consequently, if the word-exclusion and the meaning-exclusion are not differentiated, it is impossible to ascertain whether the knowledge-objects expressed by words are conventionally existent or not.[363] And furthermore, if one does not distinguish whether the object of knowledge is established by exclusion or detection, it will be impossible to discern whether the object in question is a thing or a nonthing. Therefore, these two kinds of distinction are extremely important. In this connection, a specific property (*khyad chos*) may be established as belonging to a specific basis (*khyad gzhi*)—that is, a given phenomenon—in a twofold manner. First, the property is established as belonging to *this* phenomenon by excluding all properties that do not belong to it; and second, it is established as belonging to it by excluding properties that belong to other phenomena. This approach may be applied to a definition or defining characteristic (*mtshan nyid*) of a thing. And it is said that the definition is perfect when the three kinds of preclusion (*rnam gcod*) eliminate its three possible defects (of being impossible of application, too narrow, or too broad).

The first preclusion is called preclusion of what is not possible (*mi srid rnam gcod*). This eliminates a definition that is wholly impossible (for example, a definition of the mind as something made of particles) and sets forth a definition that is possible. The second preclusion is called the preclusion of what does not belong to the totality of the thing (*mi ldan rnam gcod*). One might define the mind, for instance, as the awareness of objects produced in dependence on the visual sense. This is admissible for the visual consciousness but not for the other kinds of consciousness. Therefore, this preclusion excludes whatever does not belong to the totality of consciousness, and sets forth a definition embracing the whole phenomenon. The third preclusion is called the preclusion of what belongs to other phenomena (*gzhan ldan rnam gcod*). One may, for example, define the mind as an object of knowledge. Though this definition covers the mind, it also pervades to a great extent other phenomena, the definition of which is not intended here. This preclusion therefore excludes whatever belongs to other phenomena and sets forth a definition that pertains only to the mind.

Therefore, all particular properties as belonging to specific bases (according to whatever it is one wishes to speak about) are established by means of two kinds of preclusion: of whatever does not belong to the totality of the phenomenon in question and of whatever belongs to other phenomena. Consequently, from the point of view of conceptual distinguishers of whatever may be predicated of a given basis, an equal number of aspect-exclusions may be distinguished. The thing itself, however, which is the exclusion of all that is not that very thing, constitutes a detection and is a single entity. Thus, according to the distinction between a specific basis and its specific properties, there is a conceptual distinguisher of the specific object (for example, a patch of blue) and the distinguishers of the predicated properties of the blue patch, such as fabricatedness and impermanence.

If we consider the differentiation made between a definition or defining characteristic (*mtshan nyid*), the name (*mtshon bya*), and the basis of definition (*mtshan gzhi*),[364] the distinguishers associated with these three items are respectively the meaning-distinguisher (*don ldog*), the own-distinguisher (*rang ldog*), and the basis-distinguisher (*gzhi ldog*). In short, all distinguishers are posited from the standpoint of the exclusion or elimination of what is other than themselves. The two kinds of exclusion are expounded very clearly here.

When the three properties previously mentioned in the root stanza (to have "satisfactory" existence, to be subject to origin and cessation, and to possess causal efficiency) are cited as the necessary criteria of a relative phenomenon, some may object that these same properties are untenable. This is so, they say, because if this is the case, it follows that the subject, an unpleasant sensation, if left unexamined, is satisfactory (*nyams dga' ba*), because it is a relative phenomenon. This, however, cannot be said, because it is not satisfactory.

To this we might (ironically) reply, "It follows that the subject, all the pleasures of existence experienced by Brahma, Indra, and the

Chakravartins, is suffering, for all that is stained by the emotions is suffering. This, however, cannot be said, because they are pleasures." There are many such arguments. If our opponents wish to follow such an interpretation, so can we!

There is a further objection: "It follows that the subject, emptiness that is just a nonimplicative negation, is momentary because it is relative." (The sign adduced is valid, for Shantarakshita says in the autocommentary that since the so-called relative is based on the discursive mind, absence of production and so on is part of the relative and is not the ultimate truth. It is like any object-universal, for example, "tree." And it is said by the same authority that the absence of production and so on pertains to the unmistaken relative. This cannot be said, however, because emptiness as a nonimplicative negation is a nonthing, a mere absence.)

To this we could reply (following the above argument and showing its absurd consequence): "It follows that the subject, emptiness that is a nonimplicative negation, cannot be conceived or expressed by our opponents, because for them it is the ultimate truth." (The evidence for this is valid because it is taught in the scriptures that the ultimate truth is inconceivable, to say nothing about the possibility of its expression. But it cannot be said that emptiness as a nonimplicative negation is the ultimate truth, since this is evidently contradictory [because a nonimplicative negation is conceived and expressed].)

Again there is another objection to the effect that "It follows that the subject, an uncompounded entity such as space, is causally efficient because it is relative." (The evidential sign is valid, because all knowledge-objects are certainly included within the two truths, and space is not an ultimate reality. But one cannot say that space is relative because it has no causal capacity.)

We reply that, instead of comprehending what the evidential sign actually means, these debaters are playing with words. But if space is on a level with the barren woman's son, which has no existence in the world even conventionally, it should be concluded that space too is completely nonexistent. For all nonthings are the same in being no more than names and do not correspond to actual things. Once again, if our opponents adopt such a line of interpretation, so can we!

Of course they will argue that the two cases are not the same. For space and the child of a barren woman are different in being conventionally existent and conventionally nonexistent respectively. But since they cannot be established as having any property as specifically characterized things, they are established only through the process of exclusion. And when one examines their ultimate status, they are all the same.

This little string of consequences is set out in a lighthearted manner, but the meaning conveyed thereby is to be understood as follows.

The expression "satisfactory when left unscrutinized" can be construed in the sense of "appearing as really existent"—like any perception of an illusion when the latter is left alone and is not investigated. It does not mean that all illusory appearances are therefore "satisfactory." Fearful appearances can also arise. Therefore, when, in the absence of analysis, consciousness apprehends something as if it were really existent, this appearance deceives the mind, leaving it with a feeling that the thing is sound and really there. This is why it is termed "satisfactory." The expression is not to be understood literally as relating to pleasant physical and mental sensations.

The first of these three objections is of no great significance, being no more than a piece of verbal trickery. The second and third objections, however, are more important.

In relation to the authentic ultimate truth beyond all assertions, emptiness as a nonimplicative negation is posited as belonging to the relative. How then can this relative be the relative that is the counterpart of the approximate ultimate truth? For according to the latter relative, emptiness as a nonimplicative negation is indeed the ultimate. It is therefore necessary to discern the conventional and ultimate truths according to their different categories. In the explanation of the *Madhyamakalankara,* this distinction is like one's very eyes; one cannot get anywhere without it.

Turning now to the third objection, it must be said that space and so on are nonthings or absences. "Space" has no more than nominal existence. We conceive of it through the exclusion of its opposite, namely, things. Given that this is so, although generally speaking it is sometimes denied that space is an object of knowledge and that it is only a name, it should not be thought that it belongs to neither of the two truths just because it is not included in the relative. The assertion that the so-called inconceivable self[365] is found in neither permanent nor impermanent knowledge-objects has no bearing on the division of knowledge-objects into permanent and impermanent. It is thus that one should understand the claim that space and so on are not found either in the relative or the ultimate. For space is no more than a way of referring to the mere absence of material contact or obstruction. So although one might say that space exists only conventionally, whereas the child of a barren woman does not exist conventionally, if one analyzes both these notions, no difference will be found between them as to their existence or nonexistence as specifically characterized phenomena. Both are nonexistent. Consequently, when one says "the rabbit's horns," it seems as though the mind observes them—by virtue of the verbal expression that excludes all that is not "the rabbit's horns." But since rabbit horns—as specifically characterized things—cannot be knowledge-objects, one can say of them that they are not objects of cognition. Otherwise, if it were by observing no more than a mere name that one had access to a knowledge-object, it would follow that even rabbit horns would be such. And the final conclusion would be that there is nothing that is not a knowledge-object, and there would be nothing that is not possible.

Therefore, when one adverts to nonthings, or absences—space and so on—one is adverting to mere labels. Since such entities have no objective reality in fact, it is correct to say that space does not exist. Also in other (Madhyamaka) texts it is said, "Space is like the child of a barren woman."

Now, it may be objected that the nonexistence of space contradicts the fact that space is numbered among the five elements and is used as an example in the scriptures. But in such contexts, space is so described from the point of view of those who do not investigate what is in fact no more than a label used to indicate the absence of contact or obstruction, as we have explained. On investigation, however, no sort of valid cognition can prove the existence of space. Since space is devoid of specific characteristics, it cannot be validly established by perception, whether by the visual or by any other sense consciousness. For if it were established in this way, it would become a form (to be seen, a sound to be heard, an odor to be smelled, and so on). And if it were established by the self-knowing mind, it would become a kind of consciousness.

Again, it may be thought that since space is experienced, this very fact establishes its existence. But space is simply the "nonencountering" of contact or obstruction. If something may be observed, it cannot be space. To what is nonexistent the two kinds of relation cannot apply. Therefore, space cannot be established by inference. Consequently, space is no more than a name. If one has this understanding, it will be clear why space is given as an example for the fact that phenomena are no more than the deposit of thought (*rtog pa'i dbang gis bzhag pa tsam*);[366] they do not exist in themselves. As it is written:

> *People say, "I see a space";*
> *They certainly express themselves in words like these.*
> *But how can space be seen? Examine what this means.*

Ornamental space, namely, the blue sky, and the space contained in a cavity cannot be accepted as proofs of the existence of space. This we have already shown above. Therefore, if it is understood by means of conventional reasoning that space has no existence in itself and is no more than an imputed name, there is no need for further demonstrations of its nonexistence, using valid reasoning on the ultimate level. This is similar to the hierarchy of lower and higher tenet systems.[367]

Therefore, things that are causally efficient may be unerringly proved or disproved; and the two kinds of self, the misconceptions superimposed on these things, may be dispelled. It is just as when someone with healthy eyesight contemplates the fair form of a youthful person.[368] On the other hand, nonthings, which are the absence of causally efficient things, are established as mental objects. So-called nonthings have no other basis for their affirmation or negation. However much one may talk about what are just names, it is as if one were discussing flowers grown in the sky.

Now, regarding the bases of definition, or instances, of the relative, these are the twelve ayatanas, wherein all knowledge-objects are accounted for. We generally speak of the six inner ayatanas, or senses, and the six outer ayatanas, or sense objects. Their definitions may be supplied progressively as follows. The inner ayatana of the visual sense, for example, is the extraordinary dominant condition of the visual consciousness that apprehends form. The outer ayatana of form is the objective condition of the visual consciousness. Similar definitions can be given mutatis mutandis for the other ayatanas, up to and including the mental object, which is the objective condition for the mental consciousness. Consciousness itself is defined as clarity and knowing, and it may be classified into eight kinds, which are defined as the awareness of objects produced in dependence on the dominant condition of the visual organ (and so on for the other consciousnesses, including the mental consciousness). The alaya, as the basis for the different habitual tendencies, is defined as mere clarity and knowing, whereas the defiled emotional mind is a clinging to the continuum of consciousness as being the self.

A so-called definition or defining characteristic is the cause of positing the name of a given, causally efficient thing (*mtshon bya rnam 'jog gi rgyu*). In order to distinguish the meaning-distinguisher (definition or defining characteristic) from the own-distinguisher (name) and to avoid being mistaken about the object and its designation, it is said, for instance, that a vase is defined as "something bulbous-shaped." But thinking that it is necessary to eliminate in a single formulation all possible misconceptions that might arise in the mind owing to a definition in which words are used that might also apply to other things, some people pile up their words with great glee. But rather than doing this, it is far more important to grasp the meaning of the definitions as taught in the sutras and the great treatises. Alas! The silly people of our day fail to grasp the words and their meaning. As a result, they fret and worry whether the definitions are correct and even come close to saying that the Buddha's words are mistaken!

The vital point is to understand the meaning of the definition. If, on the other hand, definitions are spun out with additional verbiage, such additions are usually completely pointless—no more significant than the patterns made by the smoke of Indian incense. Satisfied with words and formulas expressed by others, some people just parrot them, committing them to memory like brahmins with their mantras—and treat with scorn even the sublime masters of the past. It is really quite amazing. And in the same way that it is important to understand the sense of the definition, instead of sticking slavishly to the words, one should go for the meaning intended when the specification "on the ultimate level"[369] is added or not added [to the object of refutation].

If the meaning that one wishes to express is incorrect, words alone will not remove the fault. Mere verbal formulation is like a lasso held in one's hand. It corresponds to the level of one's own intelligence and follows the import of what one wants to say. When the learned debate on the basis of sound evidence, they rely on the meaning, not just on formulas. But the debates of silly children are no more than words. Since they lack the hook of powerful understanding, words become for them like drunken elephants beyond their control—they inevitably land them in very alarming situations! Such people, who spend all their time gawping at terms, will have to wait for a considerable increase in their intelligence before they can be considered learned! For when people are principally concerned with verbal formulations, whether in teaching, debate, or composition, the net result is a great deal of prattle of only meager substance; the birth of understanding is inevitably slow. Therefore, those who are wise go for the meaning and take as their main objective the genuine understanding of all the great texts.

Having thus gained mastery of profound wisdom, they are naturally skilled in the manipulation of its verbal expression. And by elaborating all the crucial points of the treatises into sequences of consequentialist arguments, they likewise become expert in overcoming the errors of their opponents.

Let us consider briefly what constitutes a correct or clear-cut definition. The meaning-distinguisher, that is, the definition applied to a name like "vase," is the cause whereby the term "vase" is posited. If "something bulbous" is taken to be the definition of vase, it is this definition that is the cause for positing the term "vase"—whereas "that which supports a beam" does not. In the same way, when the basis-distinguisher (that is, an actual specific vase) and the own-distinguisher (the term "vase") are not confused and are correctly ascertained within the definition itself, the definition is faultless. When these are so grasped, the definition is free from the three defects of being too narrow (*ma khyab*), too broad (*khyab ches*), or impossible (*mi srid*). It will, in other words, exclude characteristics that are not possessed by the totality of the thing to be defined, those that belong to other things, and those that are impossible. When the link between the definition and the name to be defined is ascertained with certainty, it is by virtue of the meaning-exclusion (*don gyi rnam bcad*) that the remaining defects of the definition (excessive broadness, excessive narrowness, or impossibility) are obviated. And the meaning is grasped without excessive verbosity, and this is sufficient. For example, when someone says, "Give me the stick," by virtue of the meaning-exclusion, one will understand that reference is being made to the stick present in front of oneself. There is no need to specify its kind and every feature pertaining to its individual existence in place and time.

If one is unable to grasp the connection between the definition and the name, then no matter how many words one uses, they will serve no purpose. For example, on seeing a precious, transparent crystal, a man might ask, "Is it a sapphire?" In reply, another might say, "No, a sapphire is blue." On reflection, the first might ask, "Well, is this blue cloth a sapphire?" to which the second will reply, "No, a sapphire is a blue jewel." Again the first man might say, "Well, is this blue diamond a sapphire?" to which the second will respond, "No, a sapphire is less precious." "Is it blue glass?" "No, sapphires are worth much more than ordinary glass." The conversation could go on indefinitely, and even if all the characteristics of the sapphire were enumerated, the sapphire might still not be properly identified. It is like trying to describe an elephant to a man born blind. But if, when it is said "The sapphire is blue," one understands the connection between "blue" as the defining property of the given object and "sapphire," the key point of its definition is grasped,[370] which is as if one were eliminating all misconceptions regarding that very object. In this way, one will automatically be able to ascertain all the particular features of the thing defined and eliminate all the doubts related to it. It is just as when life comes to an end, all the senses come to an end as well. It is therefore important to become skilled in identifying the crux of a definition. It is important to focus one's mind on a correct understanding of the meaning-exclusion. For example, when someone says "vase," the bulbous-shaped object comes to mind, and it is impossible to mistake it for other things that have a bulbous shape. On what basis is a name like "vase" established, posited according to its defining characteristic? If "vase" is not identified in an actual vase—a specific vase, for example, a golden vase—the name and its basis (the actual golden vase) will not arise in their different aspects and the basis-distinguisher will not be identified. If the basis of the definition is a golden vase, it must necessarily be the basis of both the definition and the name. Thus the golden vase must of necessity be both a bulbous thing and a "vase." But this does not necessarily apply to the vase's ground of imputation (*gdags gzhi*). The aspects of spout, belly, base, as well as the form and the particles, are the ground of vase-imputation, but the definition of the name "vase" does not apply to each of these aspects individually.

Now, regarding the basis of definition (that is, a specific object), one may come upon a bulbous object (that is, a vase) but not know its name. In such a situation one constructs a probative argument equipped with a correct sign (that is, the definition) that establishes the name.[371] And since the golden vase, as the actual object, and the term "vase" produce a concordant mental understanding of "vase" (inasmuch as only the distinguisher "vase" is concerned), one can then easily understand that this golden bulbous object with a narrow base, which functions in that it holds water, is the basis of definition of the term "vase." In other words, it is an actual vase. The process is the same in all similar cases. For instance, this is like taking for the basis of definition of "pillar" "the object at the eastern end of the house able to support the beam."[372]

In the case of sound, however, used as the basis of definition for impermanence, since the terms are different [but refer in fact to the same reality], it is not necessary to consider the different aspects of impermanence, such as impermanence in the south and so on. For the meaning of all the profound and subtle terminology of logic, it is necessary to consult the appropriate literature.

What we call the relative—defined in the threefold way (as revealed by a process of exclusion)—appears ineluctably and incontrovertibly to conventional valid cognition. Yet none of it can be established, even to the slightest degree, as truly existent. Its appearing aspect is the relative; its empty aspect is the ultimate. Thus the relative is defined as dependent arising. As the noble Nagarjuna has said:

> *Whatever shall arise dependently,*
> *The same shall be defined as emptiness.*
> *Because of relative, we speak of ultimate.*
> *The Middle Way is simply this.*

8. An explanation of the cause of mere appearance

65
Satisfactory if not examined,
Based upon foregoing causes,
Things arise as though they were
The causes' subsequent effects.

One may well ask what is the cause of the unceasing appearances of relative phenomena defined in the threefold way. In order to show that they have no cause other than dependent arising, this root verse declares that, though appearing satisfactorily enough if left unexamined, things have no extraneous cause.[373] Yet based on foregoing causes, they arise as though they were their subsequent effects. Whatever is not dependent on anything else cannot appear, any more than a flower growing in the sky. And whatever is an object of knowledge is necessarily pervaded by dependence on something else. All things are dependent arising and nothing more, and all nonthings or absences are exclusively dependent imputations. But how do they dependently arise? It is possible to speak of the dependent arising of both outer and inner phenomena. In the case of outer phenomena, these are dependently produced just as a shoot is produced from a seed. As for inner phenomena, these are produced in an uninterrupted sequence of cause and effect, in the manner of the twelvefold chain of interdependent production. In this context, *ignorance* is the failure to recognize the intrinsic nature of phenomena. It is not simply an absence of knowledge. The mental factor of ignorance is the reverse of the primordial wisdom that cognizes in an unmediated way. It is its antithesis. Out of ignorance, and on account of false mental processes that apprehend one's own self and that of others as intrinsically existent, actions are performed. These are *conditioning karmic factors,* which besmirch consciousness with habitual tendencies. And when the latter are actualized, *consciousness* is produced as the propelled effect. Based on consciousness, the five aggregates occur—the fourfold *name and* the single *form*[374] (the inchoate form of the fetus in the womb and so on). On the basis of name-and-form, there arise the six *inner sense powers,* such as the visual organ of the eyes. Once the six organs exist, *contact* with the six sense objects is bound to ensue. When contact occurs, it is definite that *feeling* will arise, whether pleasant, unpleasant, or neutral. Once there is feeling, it will be impossible to remain indifferent to this, and as a result there will be *craving.* When there is craving, it is impossible to leave the object just as it is. Being involved with the object, one will experience the impulse to seize it, and thus *grasping* will manifest. Owing to the impulse to seize, actions will be performed, and this constitutes *becoming.* The effects of action are not exhausted in the bardo state, and consequently one will be born in the lower or higher realms according to one's white or black actions. This is *birth,* and from that moment onward, there follows the gradual and continuous process of *aging,* which is brought to an end by *death.* Aging and death are alike in being both manifestations of impermanence. These twelve links may be condensed into the three groups of defiled emotions, karma, and suffering. Owing to their reciprocal interplay of cause and effect, the cycle of existence revolves uninterruptedly; it is like the wheel of fire produced by a whirling firebrand.

Although things are able to appear, their appearance is not based on causes that are not themselves empty. As it is said:

> From things that are but empty,
> Empty things arise and that is all!
> Like recitation, flame, and looking glass,
> Or seal or lens, seed, sound, astringent taste,
> The aggregates continue in their seamless course,
> Yet nothing is transferred, and this the wise should know.

If someone recites a text and this is memorized by someone else, it is not that the text has moved from one mind to another. The text that is now in the mind of the hearer has simply manifested on the basis of the sound of the recitation pronounced by the person who knew it. It is not uncaused. Likewise, the previous aggregates do not transfer into the subsequent aggregates, for this would result in their being permanent. The later aggregates do not manifest without their being based on previous aggregates, for this would mean that they are uncaused. It is the same with the other examples. From one flame there manifests another; thanks to a mirror, a reflection arises; from a seal there comes an imprint; a lens gives rise to fire; seeds give rise to shoots; an astringent taste provokes the production of saliva; and from sound there comes an echo. So it is with cause and effect. The cause does not pass into the effect, and they do not have one and the same nature. On the other hand, it is not that the effect manifests without relying on its previous causes. For without a cause, an effect cannot be produced, and if all the causes are complete, it is impossible for effects not to appear. They are produced in dependence. Such is the unmistaken explanation of how things are. This is the unsurpassable and unique teaching of the Lord Buddha, victorious, virtuous, and transcendent.

As to the manner in which causes produce their respective individual effects, this is due to the inconceivable power of things. It is simply their nature. On the ultimate level, however, there is neither productive cause nor produced effect; there is nothing but the coincidence of appearance and emptiness. For if cause and effect meet, production is untenable; it is untenable also if they do not meet. And to be sure, there is no other kind of production possible aside from these two. But on the other hand, the invariable appearance of cause and effect is highly acceptable, provided one says no more than that "from this cause this effect invariably arises." This alone is sufficient. If a thing is produced, there is no need to wonder how it is produced, nor is it necessary to question the reason for production and so on. The nature of fire is simply to be hot. There is no need to prove the validity of this by trying to find out the reason for its being hot. That which is to be assessed is the mode of being of things. And such an assessment, in agreement with its object, is valid cognition, or valid reasoning. As far as the latter is concerned, viewed from the standpoint of the assessment of an object's causes, its effects, and its nature, three principles of reasoning are set forth. These are respectively: reasoning with regard to efficient function, dependence, and the nature (or evidence) of things. In addition, there is the principle of valid proof,[375] which, through affirmation or denial in a logical manner, eliminates misconceptions about the object of assessment. The principle of valid proof is twofold. First, there is the valid cognition of perception, which assesses manifest objects. Second, there is the valid cognition through inference, whereby hidden objects are ascertained. Given that inference is able to assess hidden objects by means of a valid apprehension of (manifest) causally produced phenomena, inference is reducible to perception. And perception itself necessarily boils down to the nature (that is, evidence) of phenomena. Therefore, since the efficient function of a thing and its dependence on causes are the very character of that thing, these two principles of reasoning related to them are themselves contained within the wider principle of the nature or evidence of things. It is therefore the reasoning concerned with the nature or evidence of things that captures and supersedes all other principles of reasoning. When one has reached this point, no other valid proofs are necessary—just as there is no need to explain the reason for a fire's heat. "Reasoning based on the evidence of things" (dngos po stobs zhugs kyi rigs pa) is reasoning attuned to the nature of phenomena. Since it unmistakenly assesses the mode of being of things, this kind of reasoning cannot be surpassed by any other form of argument. Conventional and ultimate reasonings are both referred to as reasoning based on the evidence of things. The relative nature or mode of being of fire is that it throws out heat; the ultimate nature or mode of being of fire is that it lacks inherent existence. Thus a thing's mode of being is established without mistake by both valid cognitions (conventional and ultimate) together, and not by only one of them in isolation. The Buddha's doctrine, from the exposition of the two truths onward, unerroneously sets forth the mode of being of things as it is. And the followers of the Buddha must establish this accordingly, through the use of reasoning. Such is the unerring tradition of Shakyamuni. On the other hand, to claim that analytical investigation in general and the inner science of pramana, or logic, in particular are unnecessary is a terrible and evil spell, the aim of which is to prevent the perfect assimilation, through valid reasoning, of the Buddha's words—a teaching that threefold investigation[376] demonstrates to be utterly pure.

It is therefore essential to know how reasoning judges its objects. This is most important when the two kinds of valid cognition are used[377] and should be acknowledged as a general principle. Now, with regard to our investigation of cause and effect, some may wonder how causes are related to their effects when there occurs a large hiatus between the conclusion of a given action and the appearance of its result.[378] Those who believe in the true existence of phenomena say causes and their effects are linked by a kind of entity known as an "obtention," or by a kind of indelible substance.[379] The Madhyamikas, however, who consider that cause and effect are merely dependently related, have no use for any substance to act as a link between a cause and its effect. A past action will ripen and give a result in that mind stream in which all causes and conditions are gathered. There is no way that the result is not experienced. Thus, for the Madhyamikas, the principle of causality makes a great deal of sense logically speaking. If, on the one hand, effects manifest immediately after their causes, without any intervening gap, like seeds and shoots, this is unproblematic for them. But *real* effects cannot be produced when there is contact with *real* causes.[380] Therefore, just like shoots arising from seeds, phenomena that simply manifest, without interstice, after their causes, are quite admissible as being in a causal relationship, when viewed in the light of dependent arising. If, on the other hand, effects arise from their causes only after an interval, like karmic action and its effect, once again it is perfectly acceptable to consider them causally linked. Here it is of the highest importance to understand that, from the standpoint of dependent arising, these two alternatives come to the same point.

Consequently, the notion that the seed produces a shoot belongs to the reasoning of efficient function. It also refers to the nature of the seed, understood in the same way that heat is considered to be the nature of fire. The power of the cause, left unobstructed, cannot fail to produce its proper effect. Neither can it produce its effects in a chaotic manner,[381] nor can it produce effects ad infinitum. Such is the nature of things.

Whether the shoot is produced from a seed that is destroyed or from a seed that is not destroyed, both cases are in fact untenable. The shoot is simply produced from the earlier foregoing moment, now gone, which was that of the seed. The preceding moment of the seed, which is over and done with, is designated the productive cause of the shoot. But if one examines such a cause (the seed) to see whether it is an undisintegrated thing or a disintegrated nonthing, one will find that the production of the shoot is impossible in both cases. The cause of the shoot is simply the seed. The seed's form or its other aspects,[382] which make of it a thing, cannot individually be posited as the cause of the shoot. If the seed's particular spatial and temporal aspects[383] were posited as the cause of the shoot, the result would be that all conventional assertions would collapse, since only these specifically identified features of the seed, and nothing else, could be admitted as the cause. This would be like saying that what we call a vase is nothing but its form and particles. Therefore, although the cause cannot be either in contact with its effect or otherwise, it is in the nature of things that the cause produces its proper effect without fail. This can be illustrated by the fact that within the reflection of the sun and moon appearing on the surface of the water, all the aspects of these heavenly bodies appear, and these are perceived—even though it cannot be admitted either that the form and its reflection are in contact or that they are not. The same is true of the causal process, whereby the production of an effect occurs in the manner of dependent arising. As it was said, if one does not keep to the nature of things, namely, their interdependence (that is, the power of the cause producing its effect), one's assertion will always be untenable no matter how one asserts production. One can say no more than that the seed produces the shoot and that action gives rise to an effect. On the other hand, no examination of whether the seed disintegrates or not will lead to a coherent account of causality. If the seed does not disintegrate, the unwanted consequence will be as we have already explained: Cause and effect will be simultaneous. On the other hand, if the shoot is produced from a seed that has disintegrated, since in between the seed and the shoot there will be a gap corresponding to the momentary entity of disintegration, the unwanted consequence will be that no process of causality can occur.[384] If between cause and effect there is no interstice arising through the momentary (entity of) disintegration, how could the cause ever disintegrate? Either the shoot is produced at a point in which the first moment of the seed's disintegration has not perished, or else it is produced after this moment. In the first case, the disintegrated seed, as cause, and the shoot, as the result, are simultaneous, which is impossible. In the second case, when the first moment of disintegration has gone, the second moment of disintegration occurs and so on.[385] But if this moment is simultaneous with the shoot, cause and effect are simultaneous, and this is untenable. Therefore, the shoot cannot be said to be produced from any moment of disintegration. And if disintegration is not momentary, if follows that it is either the same as the permanent entity or else it is destitute of any causal efficiency. In that case, how can it be a cause that produces its effect? Even if it is considered that the seed ceases to exist or is destroyed, the (successive) moments of its disintegration would prevent any possibility for the shoot ever to eventuate, and the moments of its disintegration would necessarily be produced until the end of existence. Moreover, there could be no such thing as the causal process, and all knowledge-objects would be reduced to nothing.

Therefore, as Kamalashila explains in his *Commentary on Difficult Points,* since it is impossible for the shoot to be produced either from disintegrated or undisintegrated seeds, one should trust only the reasoning based on the nature or evidence of things, namely, that effects manifest from causes. When, for example, with regard to seed and shoot, it is said that conventionally the effect is produced when the seed has disintegrated or no longer exists, this is said simply because at the time of the effect, the cause is no longer there. There is simply production and there is simply cessation, without there being any gap, filled by some other entity, between the cessation of the cause-moment and the arising of the effect-moment. On the other hand, if these moments are examined, nothing is found. Apart from the foregoing cause, there is absolutely no "disintegration as an entity able to produce an effect." After the disintegration of the cause, no "disintegration" remains as a positive, causally efficient entity. Effects are produced from their foregoing causes that have disappeared. On the other hand, one should understand that the so-called past cause now disappeared is not an entity able to produce effects different from the cause itself.

7. A conclusive demonstration that the ground of appearance is itself empty of true existence

66
Thus it's incorrect to say that in the absence of
A (true existing) cause, the relative could not appear.
And if the latter's cause is ultimately true,
This you should indeed declare!

While they do not exist inherently, appearances manifest unceasingly in the manner of causes and effects. Thus, phenomena appear although they are without inherent existence. Nevertheless, the proponents of substantial existence say that if this relative level, which is perceived and experienced, is without a true cause or ground of appearance, it could not appear. But here they are mistaken. If they believe that the ground of appearance, or the cause of relative phenomena, is an ultimate existent, they should say so clearly. And if reasoning is able to establish it unassailably, we will certainly accept that it is the cause of the relative. But since the arguments explained earlier show that all knowledge-objects are wholly without true existence, these same causes[386] cannot be posited as truly existent. This is demonstrated by Nagarjuna in the *Vyavaharasiddhi*, where, in the verse beginning "Without a syllable there is no mantra," he establishes dependent arising, using the examples of mantra, medicine, illusion, and so forth.

The proponents of substantial existence think that relative phenomena could never appear if there were no cause for their appearance—just as a cloth could not appear in the absence of threads. They therefore assert the particle and the instant of consciousness, or else the nondual mind and so forth, as being the cause or basis of appearance. They say that, just as the Buddha taught that on the basis of the chariot's parts we speak of "chariot," it is on the basis of the aggregates that we talk about "beings." But the Madhyamikas know that it is because there is nothing truly existent as the ground of appearance that appearances arise unceasingly. They believe that all phenomena manifest naturally within the state of emptiness, and they illustrate this using the example of the mirror image, which though empty nevertheless appears to the sight.

For ordinary people, beginners in the practice, appearance and emptiness (in other words, existence and nonexistence) are mutually exclusive and negate each other. This is the only way that they can conceive of them. It is hard for beginners to realize the union of appearance and emptiness. Nevertheless, we may say of this union that when one uses the argument of neither one nor many to examine a thing such as a vase placed in front of oneself, it is possible to understand that there is not even a particle of the vase that is inherently existent. When this conclusion is reached, it is not as though the emptiness of the vase suddenly occurs, having been nonexistent beforehand. Throughout its three stages of production, duration, and cessation, the vase never stirs from its lack of inherent existence. It appears as a vase while all the time being empty. The union of its appearance and emptiness is the vase's natural state. We must be absolutely certain of this.

In general, it is easy to come to an understanding of emptiness through the application of reasoning aimed at establishing the absence of true existence. It is more difficult to understand and be convinced of the fact that emptiness consists in dependent arising. Once acquired, however, such a conviction constitutes the foundation of the view of all the sutras and tantras. To be convinced that things, the bases of appearance, are "untrue," inasmuch as they are without inherent existence, and to see how dependently arising appearances manifest infallibly, is the greatest of all wonders. It is to this that the present stanza alludes.

4. Answers to objections made to this distinction of the two truths
5. A brief demonstration that no faults are incurred
6. Our reasoning is able to vanquish all opposition

> 67
> By following the path of reasoning
> That's based upon the nature of phenomena,
> All other doctrines are dispelled.
> No room is left for false positions.

When one follows the unmistaken nature of things, that is, the reasoning based on the evidence of phenomena, all incorrect beliefs concerning the nature of things, as put forward by the Samkhyas and others (who assert either the existence or nonexistence of effects) are dispelled. This kind of reasoning leaves no scope for the false positions of our adversaries; it is able to destroy them all, just as the sun, riding high in a cloudless sky, leaves no room for darkness. The Samkhyas say that the effect is inherently present [in the cause]; the Vaisheshikas believe that it is not; while the Jains for their part consider that it both is and is not present. Since none of these assertions accords with the nature of things as it really is, none of them constitutes valid knowledge. But the Madhyamikas possess a reasoning that is based on the evidence of things. They are thus able to refute easily and with great force all such assertions and opinions.

6. This approach is completely unassailable

> 68
> "It is," "It is not," "It is both"—
> If from all such statements one abstains,
> One cannot be the object of attack
> Despite the fervor of one's adversaries.

The unfailing dependent arising of mere appearances—which is experienced by ordinary people right through until the primordial wisdom of omniscience is experienced, is not denied by the Madhyamikas. And yet these phenomena are devoid of intrinsic existence. Therefore, anyone who refrains from asserting any of the four extreme positions (existence, nonexistence, both existence and nonexistence, and neither existence nor nonexistence) is invulnerable to attack, even though people may be very eager and persistent in assailing them. Attacking a Madhyamika is like trying to punch the sky. Having overcome all views that have a specific target [in considering phenomena to be truly existent], the Madhyamikas abide on the path of the Middle Way. They are completely free of all theories. It may be thought that if phenomena did not really exist, they would be like flowers growing in the sky and this would contradict the fact that various particular phenomena are seen and heard both by ordinary beings and indeed by Aryas. It would be in conflict with all the categories of convention and of philosophical theory. But such a criticism is no more than empty words. Aryadeva has said:

> *Those who do not postulate*
> *Existence, nonexistence, both, or neither*
> *Cannot be reproached by any censure,*
> *Even though they may be long assailed.*

5. A detailed explanation
6. Elimination of objections concerning the ultimate truth
7. The ultimate truth beyond conceptual constructs is free from all assertions
8. An explanation of the approximate ultimate together with its assertions
9. Establishing the approximate ultimate by means of reasoning and scripture

> 69
> Therefore, there is no such thing
> That ultimately can be proved to be.
> And thus the Tathagatas all have taught
> That all phenomena are unproduced.

The reasoning previously set forth has established that neither is there one truly existent entity nor are there many such entities. Consequently, on the level of the ultimate truth, no entities are truly established. So it is that the Tathagatas, the perfect Buddhas, have said that all phenomena are unproduced. It is in this way that they expound the true condition of things. It is said in the *Sagaramatinirdesha-sutra*:

> *Everything arising by dependence,*
> *No "thingness" does it have in any sense.*
> *And all that is devoid of entity*
> *Does not in any way arise.*

Likewise the *Hastikakshya-sutra* says:

> *A thing that in itself is truly born*
> *Is utterly beyond our observation.*
> *And all these things that have no origin,*
> *Simple folk believe that they arise.*

Again, the *Ratnakara-sutra* says:

> *All things are devoid of entity.*
> *Lacking it, how can there be extraneous conditions?*
> *And being without entity, how can things come through*
> *   something else?*
> *Thus the Sugata has reasoned.*

Finally, the *Pitaputrasamagama-sutra* says:

> When one enters dependent arising, one enters the dharma-dhatu. This the Teacher has set forth. The Buddha has taught at length that ignorance itself is empty of ignorance.

Elsewhere in the same sutra it is also said:

> All phenomena are equal within the equality of the three times. In the past also, phenomena were wholly lacking in inherent existence. . . . All phenomena are empty by their nature; and that which has no inherent existence had no existence in the past and will not exist in the future . . .

Phenomena that occur through dependent arising are without reality in the past, the present, and the future. Therefore, it was said:

> *Protector, when you turned the Dharma wheel,*
> *You said that things are peace and unproduced primordially.*

They are by very nature out of reach of sorrow.
'Tis thus you have proclaimed phenomena.

We may say, as an explanation of the above stanza, that since phenomena are without inherent existence, they are peace primordially and forever. Manifesting in the present, they are without origin, for they are without any true identity. And in the past also, they were always naturally beyond suffering—once again because they were without any true identity. It is thus that all things are said to be equal throughout the three times. Therefore, that which is established by reasoning corresponds also to what the Buddha has proclaimed in accordance with reality. And that which the Buddha has proclaimed corresponds with what is established by authentic reasoning.

9. The meaning of the expression "approximate ultimate"

70a
Since with the ultimate this is attuned,
It is referred to as the ultimate.

Mere nonexistence is the counterpart, the simple negation, of true existence. It definitely belongs to the conventional or relative level. It is not the ultimate and natural condition of phenomena. Since, however, it is in agreement with ultimate truth (that is, the authentic ultimate state of things), this mere absence of true existence, the conceptual opposite of true existence, is called "ultimate truth," in much the same way that the name of a result is given to its cause. This is the approximate or conceptual (*btags pa ba*) ultimate.

The authentic ultimate truth is not just nonexistence; it is freedom from all of the four conceptual extremes. Nevertheless, if one fails to understand the mere lack of true existence of all phenomena (which is a mental object reached through the process of conceptual other-elimination)—that is, if one fails to understand the approximate ultimate—there can be no understanding of the great and authentic ultimate. Given therefore that the approximate ultimate is the means or cause whereby the great ultimate is understood, it is included as part of the ultimate and is accordingly so called. The *Madhyamakahridaya* says:

> *Those who spurn the ladders of conventionality*
> *But try to scale the pinnacles,*

> The roofs and gables of the palace
> Of the ultimate, are fools indeed!

According to this tradition, the aspect of emptiness of true existence (that is, the nonimplicative negation that simply negates its object, namely, true existence) and the aspect of dependent arising are separate and unmixed realities. This being so, to approach the matter in this way involves dualistic clinging as well as the making of assertions. If, however, such a lack of true existence is the ultimate condition of phenomena, and the mind observing this is in agreement with the ultimate state, it follows that the ground, or ultimate nature, of phenomena is not the union of appearance and emptiness. And it falls into the extreme of mere emptiness. Similarly, the mind, or knowing subject, cannot be beyond the sphere of dualistic clinging or discursive thought.

On the other hand, if phenomena are left unrefuted after they have been emptied of "true existence" by the appropriate reasoning that negates this, it cannot be denied that they possess specific characteristics. And if something that exists according to its characteristics is left unrefuted, three unwanted consequences ensue, and these will invalidate such a position. First, it would mean that the conventional truth resists analysis. Second, it would mean that the ultimate truth is unable to negate production. Third, it would mean that the meditative equipoise of the Aryas would bring about the destruction of phenomena.[387] Consequently, the assertions that things exist according to their characteristics and that they are empty of true existence belong only to the conventional level. For on the ultimate level, appearance and emptiness are inseparable.

The intelligent should ask themselves sincerely whether they would be able to realize the profound view of the glorious Chandrakirti (the Middle Way of primordial wisdom in meditative equipoise) without relying on the path set forth according to the present approach.

8. An explanation of the actual ultimate, free from all assertions
9. A brief explanation

70b
And yet the actual ultimate is free
From constructs and elaborations.

To the foregoing remarks, the following objection may be made: How is it that the ultimate that negates the existence of phenomena (that is, the nonimplicative negative) is not the authentic ultimate? And what indeed is this authentic ultimate that cannot in any way be superseded?

The negation of the existence of phenomena (the object of negation) is simply a conceptual representation or reflection (*rtog pa'i gzugs brnyan*), reached through a process of other-elimination, the exclusion of phenomenal existence. It is thus part of conceptuality. But on the ultimate level, the authentic ultimate truth is utterly free from all conceptual constructs, all clinging to existence, nonexistence, both, or neither. This is what Shantarakshita is briefly referring to in this stanza.

9. A detailed explanation of the actual ultimate[388]
10. The ultimate truth is the object of neither thought nor word

71
Production and the rest have no reality,
Thus nonproduction and the rest are equally impossible.
In and of themselves, both are disproved,
And therefore names cannot express them.

72a
Where there are no objects,
There can be no arguments refuting them.

The ultimate truth is wholly untouched by the webs of such conceptual distinctions as "thing" and "nonthing," "production" and "nonproduction," "empty" and "not empty," and so on. Since therefore there is no such thing as origin, abiding, or cessation, their contraries ("no origin," "no abiding," and "no cessation") can have no reality either. Since truly existent production and truly nonexistent production and so forth have all been disproved in and of themselves, neither can there be any words (signifiers of such signified entities) that express them or point them out. There are in fact no such objects to be refuted and therefore no arguments able to refute them. All is false. Whatever one is refuting (be it existence, nonexistence, both, or neither), since the object of the refutation is primordially unborn, the arguments used in the refutation (all the words of which the arguments are composed and the mental processes that they express) are no different from the words and sentences used when claiming that the child of a barren woman has been killed. They are no more than conceptual acrobatics. They make no contact with the nature of things.

Consequently, the arguments used in nonimplicative negations (negating the existence of things) do no more than remove one concept by replacing it with another. It is just as when one is dreaming that a child born in the dream has died, with the result that one suffers thinking that the child is no more. All such arguments merely prove the nonexistence of things, demonstrating that things that are assumed to exist (through a misconception of their nature) do not in fact do so. This mere nonexistence of things is no more than conceptually posited. For no one can prove that the ultimate nature of things is simply their nonexistence.[389]

As Shantideva says:

> If there is no object for analysis,
> There can be no grasping at its nonexistence.
> Thus for deceptive objects of whatever kind
> There will be absences that likewise are deceptive.
>
> When therefore in one's dream one's son has died,
> The state of mind that thinks he is no more
> Supplants the thought that he is living still.
> And yet both thoughts are equally deceptive.[390]

And again in the same text:

> If phenomena are truly analyzed,
> No basis for analysis remains.
> Deprived of every basis, they subside.
> That indeed is said to be nirvana.[391]

As long as there are movements in the field of thought and word, one is within the sphere of the relative and of designations. Nevertheless, it is on the basis of thoughts that the primordial wisdom of nonconceptuality arises. It is necessarily on the basis of the conventional that the ultimate is reached, and it is on the basis of a wisdom that makes distinctions that nondual primordial wisdom is attained.

Since therefore the ultimate nature of things is beyond all the conceptual constructs of the four extreme positions, there is no way to give verbal expression to this nature. Neither can one observe or refer to it by means of the intellect. As it is said, "No name, no thought, no explanation is there for the Wisdom That Has Gone Beyond." This ultimate nature falls neither to the side of appearance nor to that of emptiness. It is beyond all notion of origin or cessation; its nature expresses itself as perfect peace and luminosity. As it is said, "Unceasing and unborn, the very nature of the open sky." Though it transcends the relative fields of words and of the conceptual mind, it is able to dissolve all wrong views that grasp at extreme ontological positions. The primordial wisdom of self-awareness (*so sor rang rig pa'i ye shes*), as this is experienced by a yogi, beholds the ultimate nature in a "nonseeing" manner.[392] And the yogis remain in it in a manner of "nonremaining." This is not at all to be compared with a state of unconsciousness or of profound sleep. As it is said, "It is the domain of the wisdom of self-awareness."

When it is said therefore that the ultimate truth is not within the domain of the conceptual mind, it is important to understand as follows. The approximate ultimate, which does no more than negate the true existence of things, is an object of the intellect and is expressible verbally. In addition, when the authentic ultimate truth is referred to in terms of not falling into the separate camps of either appearance or emptiness—that is, when it is said to be the union of appearance and emptiness, the Middle Way beyond all conceptual constructs—this is just a mere indication, rather as when one uses one's finger to point at the moon. To be sure, the ultimate in itself is utterly beyond thought and word.

However, when reasoning has investigated and refuted all conceived objects of these extreme ontological positions, one will accede, without the addition or subtraction of anything[393]—now that the nets of concepts have been removed—to ultimate reality beyond all assertion or denial. This is the actual practice of the paramita of wisdom. As it is said, "There is nothing to refute, and there is nothing to assert. Through the perfect watching of the ultimate, the ultimate is seen and one is freed."

In the present context, this "seeing" may be expressed negatively, as when one says, "I did not see anything," or positively, as when one says, "I saw nothing." There is, however, no difference in meaning, because even the latter statement does not indicate that there is something (a "nothing") to see. Likewise, there is no difference in meaning between the statements "The ultimate is beyond the reach of intellect," "The ultimate is not the object of the intellect," and "The ultimate is the object of no-thought." Since the state of no-thought is identified as the halting of all concepts and the absence of all duality between the perceiver and the perceived, it does not mean that the ultimate can be "detected" as the object of no-thought. Rather, it is detected or observed in the manner described in the *Madhyamakavatara:*

> *Suchness is unborn, and mind itself is also free from birth.*
> *And when the mind is tuned to this, it is as though it knows*
> *the ultimate reality.*[394]

If the ultimate truth *were* established as the observed object of the non-conceptual mind, in the same way that a form is an object not of the olfactory but of the visual consciousness, the state of no-thought and the absence of duality of subject and object would be brought to nothing; it would no longer be tenable.[395] Thus the affirmation that the ultimate is beyond the intellect can never be invalidated. The sutras have explained at great length how the ultimate cannot even be the object of the primordial wisdom of emptiness.

We can see therefore that the ordinary consciousness of worldly beings, which knows relative phenomena, is not a valid means of knowledge when it comes to the direct assessment of the ultimate truth that transcends all conventionalities. Such a consciousness is produced in dependence on a support.[396] It is thus unable to observe the dharmadhatu, which is not based on anything and which is the field of primal, world-transcending wisdom. For, as it is said in the sutras, it would be like a newborn baby looking at the sun (blinded and unable to see anything) or like a man blind from birth turning his eyes to a form. A support-dependent consciousness may take as its object of reference the notion of existence or nonexistence (of the dharmadhatu), and consider that such an object of focus constitutes ultimate reality. But this is a mistake. Madhyamaka reasoning forcefully eliminates every kind of mental target.[397] Since the reasoning based on the nature of things applies to all phenomena without distinction, it effectively prevents any object of reference (of people who cling to the characteristics of such objects) from being posited as ultimate reality. When their boat (namely, clinging to reality) is shipwrecked in the ocean of emptiness beyond all conceptual extremes, the merchants (the mind that clings to the cage of all the characteristics of various objects of reference) panic and in their terror clutch at any object that might present itself as their support. But no such supports are stable. This is just the way phenomena are. When, in the unbounded ocean of the dharmadhatu beyond all extremes, all discursive thought, by which we have been bound to samsara from beginningless time, subsides—who could not rejoice? Because primordial, nonconceptual wisdom (which is what actualizes the dharmakaya: nirvana that dwells in no extremes) is thereby brought to birth, those who aspire to the profound view are not alarmed but extremely happy.

Although all the Madhyamaka treatises demonstrate that phenomena are without inherent or true existence, the lack of inherent existence—that is, emptiness—can be understood in the sense of the approximate ultimate or in the sense of the ultimate itself. From the standpoint of the ultimate in itself, conceptual constructs are no more. As the sutra says, the word "emptiness" is just a way of saying that nothing is seen. One must be convinced of this—without allowing the expression "lack of inherent existence" to lead one into any kind of clinging. For all such formulas were set forth precisely for the purpose of bringing conceptual constructs to an end. It is as Chandrakirti says in the *Prasannapada:* When someone says to a beggar, "I have nothing to give you," if the beggar replies, "Well, give me your nothing!" how is one to explain to the beggar that one is without anything to give? We should understand that "clinging to emptiness" is just like this.

In brief, one must clearly distinguish the lack of inherent existence apprehended as a mental object (the approximate ultimate) from the ultimate that is beyond all assertion and concept. This distinction, however, cannot be made merely on the strength of words and expressions like "absence of inherent existence" and so on.

Consequently, the explanatory methods of the Prasangikas and the Svatantrikas converge. As far as the ultimate view, the absence of all conceptual constructs, is concerned, they are the same. But when distinctions are made in the postmeditation period, it is easier to divide the ultimate truth into two categories as the Svatantrikas do. When, in meditative equipoise, one penetrates nonconceptual primordial wisdom, there will be no further need to divide it, and a great freedom from all conceptual constructs will be accomplished. If one understands this, one will grasp the final vital point of the Madhyamaka. It is difficult to do so otherwise.

According to the approximate ultimate truth, what we call "production" and "absence of production" are posited merely in dependence on each other. If both are investigated with reasoning, they are on a level in being impossible to establish. Reasoning is able to eliminate these conceived objects, but if, on the other hand, one is unable to abandon all *clinging* to the absence of production as being real in itself, this shows that one's reasoning based on the nature of things is not yet strong enough, with the result that clinging to production and the rest, as existing in and of themselves, is not avoided.

For example, some may think that there can be no apprehension of the nonexistence of a pot without having the aspect of the "pot as the object of negation" on the one hand and the thought that negates it on the other. But this thought (whereby the pot is eliminated) is a merely mental negation. In a place that is empty of pots, for example, there are no pots even conventionally. Consequently, in such a case, these thinkers say, one cannot speak of the union of emptiness and dependent arising. Nevertheless—they continue—there is production and so on conventionally, but there is no *truly existent* production, and this, for them, is the union of emptiness and dependent arising. And they claim that since the mind accords with this absence of production, its apprehension can never be averted and disappear.

This is a mistake. If this were the union of emptiness and dependent arising, it would be beyond words and formulations. But the kind of union we have just mentioned *can* be observed as an object! If, just on the level of thought, one brings together emptiness and appearance and *conceives* of their union, this does not mean that one's mind is attuned to the ultimate nature of things.[398] If an investigation is performed with ultimate reasoning, neither conventional production (which some say is not to be refuted) nor the absence of truly existent production is found. They are both on a level. Within the context of the ultimate in itself, the Prasangikas and Svatantrikas have an identical view and realization.

Some may think that if discursive thought (which mixes the name with the object and apprehends the "lack of inherent existence" of things) is arrested, there is no way for the nature of things to be perceived. But if this is true, it follows that when they are in their meditative equipoise, free of all discursiveness, the Aryas cannot directly see it either. And even if the people we are referring to think that for ordinary beings, meditation is incorrect unless it be conceptual, what is to stop ordinary people from *trying* to cultivate a state of nonconceptuality that is attuned to that of the Aryas? But our opponents may object that, as ordinary beings, we are unable to cultivate this, and therefore we should not, for the time being, discard the mental apprehension of the lack of inherent existence. Of course, we cannot simply force ourselves to shake it off. However, it is necessary to generate confidence in ultimate reality, which is inconceivable.[399]

One may insist that profound emptiness must be the object of discursive thought. But to make the sphere of supreme primordial wisdom the object of ordinary consciousness is to corrupt the very essence of the Doctrine of the Tathagatas. One should not therefore simply adopt what is easy to understand at the expense of the profound teachings. If one trains for a long time in the union of the two truths, the stage of acceptance (on the path of joining), which is attuned to primordial wisdom, will arise. By thus acquiring a certain conviction in that which surpasses intellectual knowledge, and by training in it, one will eventually actualize it. This is precisely how the Buddhas and the Bodhisattvas have said that liberation is to be gained. It is important to mull this over. And we should not only abandon the fond hope that strenuous mental effort in the ordinary sense of the word can achieve profound emptiness, but we should also avoid any kind of depressed discouragement, thinking that it is unattainable. We must enter inconceivable primordial wisdom by gradual degrees. As it is said in the *Lankavatara-sutra*:

> *Nonexistence is evoked by existence, its counterpart;*
> *And existence by nonexistence is in turn evoked.*
> *So do not say that things do not exist,*
> *And as existent, do not think of them.*
>
> *Whatever has not come to birth*
> *Can never, for that reason, cease to be.*
> *You see that things within the world are empty:*
> *They do not exist; they are not nonexistent.*

The assertion that nonexistence depends upon existence as its counterpart is similar to three (the first, second, and fourth) of the four kinds of nonexistence postulated by Zhönumalen. Certain non-Buddhists, of whom Zhönumalen is one, postulate four kinds of nonexistence and believe that these are related to phenomenal transformation. The first of these is the nonexistence of what is not previously present (for example, the nonexistence of curd in milk). The second is the nonexistence of what has been destroyed (the absence of milk in curd). The third is utter nonexistence (the absence of horns on a rabbit's head). The fourth is the nonexistence of mutual exclusion (in the cow there is no horse).

Consequently, even a nonthing (absence) is posited in dependence on its counterpart: a causally efficient thing. If there were no certainty that barren women and children existed, it would be impossible to derive any meaning from the expression "a barren woman's child." It is through the understanding that this expression evokes that one uses it as an example of nonexistence. And the rabbit's horns are similar.

Conversely, existence depends upon its counterpart, nonexistence. One speaks for instance of the birth, or coming into being, of something, because this something did not exist in the past. If it existed already, its present existence would render impossible any ulterior entry into existence. If something that were already existent could come into being, it would never stop coming into existence (which is absurd). Therefore, existence and nonexistence, truth and falsity, emptiness and nonemptiness—all such things are only the positings of thought. None of these categories corresponds to the ultimate nature, for the latter is beyond all conceptual elaborations. It should be understood that when one has achieved the primordial nonconceptal wisdom and abides in a state of freedom from all conceptual constructs, far from the lair of the demon of moving thoughts, one has entered the path pleasing to the Conquerors. As it is said in the *Avatamsaka*:

> *Subtle, hard to fathom is the mighty Sage's path.*
> *'Tis not a concept nor the object of conception; it is*
> *   hard to see.*
> *Peaceful is its nature, neither ceasing nor arising,*
> *Known and understood by clear and learned minds.*

> *This nature, void and peaceful, is removal of all sorrow,*
> *Freedom from the mind's continuum, dwelling evenly beyond*
> *   all pain,*
> *It has no center and no limit; nothing can describe it.*
> *Like space, it is not past, not present, and is not to come.*

And the *Ratnakuta* says: "In the ultimate truth, in the presence of the supreme knowledge and primordial wisdom of the Aryas, there are no phenomena to be known, none to be rejected, and none to be meditated upon or actualized."

In the *Sagaranagaraja-paripriccha-sutra* we find:

> *Time past is void and future time likewise;*
> *Arising, dwelling, and subsiding, all are empty of themselves.*
> *There are neither things nor nonthings—*
> *All is by its nature empty.*

The *Sagaramatinirdesha-sutra* says: "O Brahma, no phenomenon can be established. Do not say that phenomena exist; do not say that they do not exist."

The *Jnanalokalankara-sutra* says:

> Those who know the ultimate
> Do not assert that it exists, and its existence they do not deny.
> No answers do they give; no statements do they make.
> To you who are beyond dependency I bow.

The *Condensed Prajnaparamita* in the chapter entitled "The Digest of Precious Qualities" says:

> If in ignorance the Bodhisattvas think
> That form and feeling, consciousness, perception
> Are their aggregates—though they may think them empty—
> They stay within the sphere of signs and of the unborn nature
>   they are not convinced.

It is thereby shown that one ought not to cling either to things or to their absences (nonthings). Similarly, in the same text it is said:

> Things that are not found are said not to exist;
> Observing them, the simple say that they exist or otherwise.
> Existence is unreal, and nonexistence too.
> The Bodhisattvas, knowing this, are certainly set free.

This shows how by training in the prajnaparamita free from all extremes (of existence and nonexistence), the Bodhisattvas are freed from all theories. It is also said:

> When one has no thought of "born" or of "unborn,"
> One practices the highest wisdom gone beyond.

The *Ghanavyuha-sutra* says:

> The teachings upon emptiness were given
> That all the views that living beings hold,

Whatever they may be,
Might be relinquished and dismissed.

But if the view of emptiness thus heard
Is not itself refuted and destroyed,
There is no remedy for such a view,
And one is like the sick forsaken by their nurse.

But just as with a fire that does not stay
Once all there is to burn has been consumed,
When it has burned the tinder wood of views,
The fire of emptiness itself goes out.

And when such views are thus removed,
The fire of perfect wisdom springs,
Defilements are consumed, afflictions burned away,
And then the mind, in all its beauty, manifests.

As it is said in the *Akshayamatinirdesha-sutra:* "What is the relative truth? It is defined as all conventional phenomena, sounds, languages, and names. As for the ultimate truth, since there is no mental movement, what need is there to speak of words?" Here, the relative is regarded as something existent. It is constituted by the world (that is, beings and their environment), the objects of experience or cognition (form and so on). In addition, it is the experience itself, the cognition, of happiness and other states. In short, it is all that manifests (whether as appearing as the world itself or as spoken of in the texts). All that can be pointed out with words like "This is consciousness; this is something to be recognized; this exists; this does not exist," and so on—all that can be expressed in the written or spoken word—is the relative. On the ultimate level, however, there exist neither the inner expressions of the mind nor the outer expressions of speech. But what is the inner expression of the mind like? It is as when the Buddha bestowed, telepathically from mind to mind, the Abhidharma teachings on Indra, or like the verse responses by the Buddha given in the sutras.

As it is said in the *Mahaparinirvana-sutra:* "Maitreya, son of my lineage! That which is neither existent nor nonexistent is beyond the fathoming of Shravakas and Pratyekabuddhas!"

And the *Samadhyagrottama-sutra* says:

When in a past life our Teacher the Buddha was a learned master, he contended with Manjushri. Manjushri propounded a doctrine of existence, whereas the Buddha championed the doctrine of nonexistence. There was no resolution to the dispute. After their deaths, and for countless ages, they were born in hell and were obliged to consume balls of burning iron. When they were liberated from this infernal existence, they encountered the Buddha Kashyapa, who instructed them as follows on the truth of existence and nonexistence. "The nature of phenomena cannot be ascertained in a one-sided manner. You hold it for either existence or nonexistence, but it is not so. And why? Because phenomena are empty; their nature is peace. And as for the union of the two truths, it is neither existence nor nonexistence. All your knowledge is no more than the knowledge of words; you have no idea of the profound meaning. In this regard, you are like men blind and deaf from birth. How can you ever understand and realize the profound truth?" On hearing these words, they spent seven days in solitary meditation and realized emptiness.

As it is said, it is truly excellent if one meditates on the Middle Path beyond all extremes, where appearance and emptiness coincide and are united. In Tibet, nevertheless, there are many who understand that the dharmadhatu, emptiness beyond extremes, is either existent or nonexistent. And they quarrel among each other about their opinions as though they were sworn enemies. Fortunate indeed are those who, without falling into partiality, proceed straightforwardly on the path of the Sugatas!

This very view, set forth in the sutras, is also explained by the noble Nagarjuna, sublime of intellect:

> If things be not established,
> Neither can their absences be proved.
> When things transform to something else,
> It's said that they exist no longer.

As Nagarjuna says, when things change into something else, it is said by worldly people that they cease to exist. This is similar to the nonexistence of what is not previously present and the other types of nonexistence (as expounded by Zhönumalen) mentioned earlier. Nagarjuna also says in the *Mulamadhyamaka-karika*:

> *Those of slight intelligence believe*
> *That things exist or that they don't exist.*
> *By viewing things in such a way,*
> *They'll never see the peace of Perfect Peace.*

And again:

> *What is called "existence" is but clinging to things'*
>   *permanence;*
> *And "nonexistence" is but nothingness.*
> *And thus the wise and learned do not rest*
> *In either "This thing is" or "It is not."*

And again:

> *All is real, all is unreal;*
> *All is both unreal and real;*
> *Things are not unreal nor are they real:*
> *Thus by steps the Buddha taught.*

And again:

> *Those who see the entity of self, the entity of other,*
> *Who see things and the absence of such things,*
> *All such people fail to see aright*
> *The teaching that the Buddha has set forth.*

And again:

> *Those who say that things arise dependently,*
> *And like the moon reflected in a pool*
> *Do not exist and are not nonexistent,*
> *Can never be assailed by other views.*

And again:

> *Things are not impermanent or permanent.*
> *If they were permanent,*

> They would exist forever.
> How could they ever cease to be?
>
> We should perceive that everything—
> Whatever may be said—is empty by its nature.
> So-called emptiness is empty too,
> And therefore there is nothing that's not empty.

And again:

> Those for whom this voidness manifests
> Will clearly understand all things.
> Those for whom no voidness manifests,
> Nothing will they ever understand.

And again:

> The Conquerors have all discoursed on
>   emptiness
> That every view might be destroyed.
> They said that those who make a view of
>   emptiness
> Will fail to gain accomplishment.

And again:

> Karma and defilements manifest
> Through movement of discursive thought.
> This is stopped by emptiness.

And again:

> Nothing is there now to say,
> For thoughts, the mind's activity, are stilled.
> Unproduced, beyond cessation,
> Such is the reality beyond all pain.

And finally:

Not known through other sources, it is peace,
And not by concepts can it be conceived.
Unthinkable, beyond diversity,
This indeed is how it is defined.

10. Words and concepts lie within the scope of the relative truth

72b
Even "nonproduction," entertained conceptually,
Is relative and is not ultimate.

The ultimate nature is not the object of language or conceptuality. Nevertheless, one speaks of phenomena as being "unproduced" and so on in order to generate within the mind an understanding of the ultimate status of these same phenomena, which ineluctably appear owing to habituation accumulating from beginningless time. These phenomena are taken as objects to be either affirmed or denied and, on the basis of discursive thought, are regarded as existent or nonexistent.

However, the mere notion that an object does or does not exist does not constitute the nature of the object in question; it is no more than a conceptual reflection (*rtog pa'i gzugs brnyan*). It has no reality apart from the mind. And consciousness has already been shown to be without ultimate reality, has it not? Moreover, the intellect, which does not see the ultimate condition of things, is the very essence of the relative. And so the objects that lie within its ken—that is, the things that are misconceived (as existent or nonexistent) belong to the relative. Therefore, concepts and words like "nonproduction" and so on pertain to the relative also; they are not the ultimate in itself—in the same way that the word "tree" only *refers* to an actual tree.

Phenomena arise dependently. They have no true existence. In phenomena, appearance and emptiness coincide. They are beyond the reach of conceptual construction. Although this is so, simply adverting to and grasping at the sense of these expressions does not constitute the realization of the ultimate nature of phenomena. For wisdom that is beyond thought, whereby conceptual construction is arrested, is to be elicited by the *experience* (direct or concordant) of that to which these words refer. As Shantideva has said:

The ultimate is not within the reach of intellect,
For intellect is grounded in the relative.

To say that phenomena have no inherent existence is a nonimplicative negation, whereas an implicative negation establishes the presence of something else. Now mere juxtaposition (emptiness on the one hand, phenomena on the other) is not what is meant by union. For if one talks about phenomena being without inherent existence, but understands that phenomena are empty of something separate from themselves, this is an implicative negation, however much one may claim that it is nonimplicative. Phenomena are unreal but nevertheless appear, and *this* is the union of the two truths and is a great wonder. Since the indivisibility of appearance and emptiness lies beyond all formulation, the ultimate truth is not something that can be either affirmed or denied. It does not lie within the scope of the ordinary mind. The sutras explain in detail that when the ultimate truth is brought within the sphere of body, speech, and mind, it becomes relative and is no longer ultimate. The ultimate nature that is discerned in relation to various phenomena, when the latter are conceptually negated, is a lesser kind of ultimate, conditioned as it is by different aspects of time and place. This kind of ultimate nature is just a conceptual imputation. It does not transcend the relative and the duality of subject and object. It does not qualify as "equality": the "even" nature of the dharmadhatu. Since phenomena are primordially beyond production, cessation, and so on, they are one and the same in the expanse beyond conceptual construction. Their equal taste (their equal nature), in which it is impossible to make any distinction or dualistic division, is called the dharmadhatu, the one and only "thatness itself."

7. Answers to objections
8. If phenomena are empty of inherent existence, this ought to be evident to everyone
9. The objection

73
Because things are perceived,
Their nature also should appear to us directly.
Then why do simple, uninstructed folk
Not see the nature of phenomena likewise?

It may be objected that when one has a perception of a location in which there are no pots, one perceives the absence of pots in that very place. In the same way, given that the nature of all phenomena is emptiness, that is, a state unaffected by whatever misconceptions may be entertained in their regard, it follows that when one has a perception of a pot, its nature too should also be apparent. For this nature cannot exist separately from the thing itself. This being so, how is it that the naïve (whose view is mistaken) and the unlearned (who have no skill in reasoning) do not perceive the nature of things? Since they do not perceive it, this can only mean that emptiness is not the nature of phenomena. For if it were the nature of phenomena, it could not be imperceptible.

9. A reply to the objection

74
Their mental stream, beginningless,
Is governed by their false belief that things are real.
All living beings therefore fail
To see the nature of phenomena.

Although the nature of phenomena is indeed emptiness, this is not perceived by everyone. The reason for this is as follows. No beginning or end can be assigned to samsaric existence, beyond which it is possible to say that there is nothing. And within this state, the mind streams of beings have taken birth repeatedly. In all that time, the minds of beings have been suffused with a poisonous clinging to the real existence of entities. They have become addicted to such an attitude, and their habit is exceedingly strong, with the result that it is hard to abandon. Therefore, in perceiving concrete objects like pots, beings are quite unable to discern their nature. They are overpowered by false discursive thought, which mistakenly takes such objects to be truly existent things. It is for this reason that all living beings fail to perceive the nature of phenomena—that is, their emptiness. In exactly the same way, it is by continuously observing a thing that looks the same from moment to moment that the mind is dulled and fails to notice the thing's momentary nature. Although people never actually *perceive* anything as "unempty" (that is, truly existent)—for this would run counter to the very nature of phenomena, which is emptiness—nevertheless, their minds are hampered by their mistaken thoughts and they *apprehend* things amiss.[400] Emptiness therefore is not invalidated by perception.

Our apprehension of appearances, inasmuch as it is imbued with the assumption that these phenomena are real, is mistaken because it is an apprehension of what does not exist. This does indeed appear to be a counterintuitive and astonishing thing to say, whereas there is nothing very extraordinary in assuming the true existence of what is perceived. But the false theories of Kapila and Kanada are far stranger. For when they clearly see the shapes of objects, such as cows or pots—objects that are themselves empty of universals (*spyi*) such as "cowhood" or "pothood"—they consider to be real not the thing seen but the unseen universal instead![401]

8. A reply to the second objection (if the emptiness of phenomena is not apparent, it is perceptible to no one and the reasoning given is consequently pointless)

> 75
> Those who sound the nature of phenomena with
>   reasoning
> That cuts through misconception and brings under-
>   standing
> Know this nature. It is known by powerful yogis also,
> Through their clear, direct experience.

The root verses here are an answer to the implied objection that even if emptiness is the nature of all phenomena, if it is not ascertained, what difference does it make—for no one can possibly perceive it? But this is not the case. The argument of neither one nor many explained above cuts through and eliminates all misconceptions concerning the nature of things and brings one to an understanding that is free from error. Moreover, those on the paths of accumulation and joining who hear this argument and then discover its true meaning, thanks to the wisdom resulting from reflection, will come to a correct understanding of the way that phenomena are empty by their nature in the manner of an object-universal (*don spyi*). Powerful yogis who profoundly habituate themselves to this will, with the eye of unerring wisdom, clearly see, by direct (nonconceptual) perception, the ultimate nature of phenomena, that is, their equal status. And when transmundane, primordial wisdom directly and nonconceptually perceives the equal status of phenomena, this constitutes the first ground of realization. Subsequently, the aspect of luminous appearance of the dharmadhatu gradually increases until ultimate reality as it truly is finally manifests perfectly and completely. This is the state of Tathagata, buddhahood itself. Primordial wisdom, manifesting through the concentration wherein the equality of all phenomena is discerned, and which is free from the defilement of discursive thought, fully realizes that outer and inner phenomena, which appear acceptable in the absence of analysis, are, like the trunk of a plantain tree, wholly without pith or reality. Not even the seed of misapprehension with regard to their true existence can now develop. As it is said in the *Mahakarunavatara-sutra:*

> *Just as with the living plantain tree—*
> *We may dissect it, seeking for its core,*
> *Yet fail to find it, outside or within.*
> *'Tis thus that we should know that all things are.*

It is also said in the *Udanavarga:*

> *Not finding any substance in the realms of being—*
> *As though he searched in vain for blossoms on the udumbara*
> *   flower—*
> *The monk leaves this and journeys to the other shore,*
> *Just as a snake will shed its old and worn-out skin.*

The udumbara lotus does not always have flowers, and when it does not have them, it is not that they are too small to be seen. They are not visible because they are not there. Similarly, when one sees that this world of existence is wholly unreal, one reaches its far shore, that is, nirvana. In other words, one delivers oneself from samsara.

These two stanzas of the root text (74 and 75), which supply the answers to certain objections, in fact set forth the following teaching. It is difficult to reverse our clinging to the true existence of things, an assumption to which we are beginninglessly accustomed. The only possible solution is to conduct an investigation through the use of reasoning. If one trains oneself in this, it will be possible to rid oneself of defilement; it will be impossible if one fails to do so. We should therefore be assiduous in making this the core of our practice. It is difficult to give up all at once even habits that we have acquired on the basis of chance occurrences; what need is there to speak of the emotional afflictions that have become instinctive from time without beginning? Knowledge of the Dharma should bring about a remedy for fear, suffering, and defilement. If it does not, the entire purpose of the Dharma has been lost. It is just like someone dying of hunger through refusing to eat the delicious food specially prepared to remedy his plight. Since dry, intellectual understanding of the empty nature of phenomena, arrived at through analysis, by itself leads nowhere, those who practice should rest in concentrated meditative equipoise in order to bring their understanding into a living experience. For those who have understood the teachings, this is the only thing worth doing. It is said in the *Udanavarga:*

> *The man who speaks with many reasoned arguments*
> *But carelessly neglects to act accordingly*
> *Fails to win his share of virtue.*
> *He is like a herdsman counting cattle of another's herd.*

> *Those who, though they give but little reasoned teaching,*
> *Practice Dharma as the Dharma says*
> *Will gain indeed their share of virtue*
> *And free themselves from hatred, lust, and ignorance.*

If one does not strive with many methods and by way of a hundred reasonings in the subtle and profound paths of the Buddha, one will not gain the conviction that is in harmony with the ultimate nature of things. The wisdom that results from hearing the teachings and reflecting on their meaning must be like a forest fire, stirred up by the winds of diligence. The reasoning that is based on the evidence of phenomena themselves must utterly consume the thick undergrowth of misconception, leaving nothing behind.

Not allowing oneself to drowse in the gloom of foolish meditations, nor to be carried away by the gale of erudition that is nothing but words, nor to get lost in ordinary concerns, one must savor all the different teachings within the palace of the supreme vehicle. One should attend an authentic spiritual master and act in a manner pleasing to him. One should keep the company of good friends. One should likewise nurture a powerful devotion for one's yidam deity and a loving heart for all who wander in samsara. If then one is able to enjoy the illusory display of phenomenal existence, as though it were a spectacle put on for one's entertainment, one's learning and reflection on the teachings will have been brought to term. Such is the aspiration and conduct that we should have, following in the footsteps of the holy beings of the past. As Shantarakshita has said in the concluding verses of his autocommentary:

> *May I too taste this object's riches,*[402] *scattering the darkness*
> *of my sleep of ignorance.*
> *May I rely upon a perfect master and with perfect reasons rea-*
> *son, assisted by good friends,*
> *And focused single-mindedly on others' good, may I with utter*
> *veneration place*
> *Upon my head the lotus of Manjushri's foot.*

Let us, at this point, pause to consider briefly the kind of yogic perception that clearly apprehends the absence of self. We will consider first its essence: what it is; second, its categories; third, the etymology of the term; and fourth, any objections made concerning it, to which we will then give answers.

1. In the present context, the essence of yogic perception consists in the clear perception that all objects are without self, or intrinsic being. Generally, yogic perception is defined as a nonconceptual cognition that is free from error and arises on the basis of meditation.

2. From the point of view of its general divisions, yogic perception is classified threefold, in relation to the Shravakas, the Pratyekabuddhas, and the noble beings of the Mahayana. Going into greater detail, it may be classified fivefold in that the Shravakas and the noble beings of the Mahayana are divided into those who are on the path of learning and those who are on the path of no-more-learning. The Pratyekabuddhas on the path of learning are not regarded as a separate category because it is said, "When they attain the final samadhi, they cross all (five) paths 'on one seat.'" Some tenet systems say, however, that there is a separate category for the Pratyekabuddhas on the path of learning. But given that these are included among either the Shravakas or the noble beings of the Mahayana, the Pratyekabuddhas are considered here only as belonging to a single class, those on the path of no-more-learning.

The five classes of yogic perception turn into ten when classified first in terms of the postmeditation state (in which phenomena appear), and then in terms of the meditative state (in which there are no appearances). Of course, for Buddhas, there is indeed no distinction between meditation and postmeditation. Nevertheless, their yogic perception may be categorized from the standpoint of either the wisdom that sees phenomena in their actual nature or the wisdom that sees phenomena in all their multiplicity (that is to say, in terms of meditation or postmeditation). Yogic perception with appearances is a perception that occurs through the power of preternatural knowledge. With regard to the latter, we may refer to scriptural citations such as:

> Foe-destroyers, the rhinoceros-like,[403] and all the Buddhas
> See respectively two or three worlds or countless thousandfold.

Yogic perception without appearances is the seeing, by the Shravakas, of the personal no-self; by the Pratyekabuddhas, of the personal no-self and half of the phenomenal no-self (the realization of the absence of the inherent existence of form); and the complete realization of the unreality of both the personal and phenomenal selves by the noble beings of the Mahayana—as well as the primordial wisdom free from all habitual tendencies that is the preserve of the Buddhas.

3. With regard to the etymology of the expression "yogic perception," it may be said that the Tibetan word *rnal 'byor* (yoga or yogic) alludes to the fact that the mind dwells on, or in union with (*'byor*), its object as it actually is.[404] *Mngon sum* means clear perception or appearance. The equivalent in Sanskrit is *pratyaksha*, which comes from the conjunction of *prati* and *aksha*. The word *prati* in fact has numerous meanings, including "different" or "distinct." The word *aksha* means "sense power." Consequently, *pratyaksha* refers to what is based on a distinct sense power or sense powers.

Now, this term may be considered according to three possible alternatives. Either the name is a description of what it refers to (*sgra bshad*) or it is just a conventional designation (*sgra 'jug*). For example, in Tibetan, a lotus is sometimes designated by the term *mtsho skye* (water born). When this term is used to designate a lotus that is actually growing in water, the term is both a conventional name and a description (*sgra bshad 'jug*). When, however, it is applied to the kind of lotus that grows on dry land, it is only a conventional name (*sgra 'jug*) and not a description of the flower indicated. Similarly, the expression "water born" may be used to refer to frogs and fishes, creatures that are actually born in the water. But this is not an accepted conventional name for them and remains no more than a description of one of their characteristics. Accordingly, if the term *pratyaksha* is descriptive, it refers to what is based on the sense powers. But if it is just a conventional term, it applies to all cognitions that apprehend specific characteristics. *Pratyaksha*, both as a descriptive and as a merely conventional name, applies to both sensory and mental perceptions.[405] In the case of the perception involved in self-awareness and yogic perception, the term is only conventional, not descriptive. In the case of deluded sense cognition, *pratyaksha* is descriptive only, for it is not its conventional appellation.

4. The refutation of objections regarding the yogic perception of no-self is both general and particular. Generally speaking, there is a possible objection concerning the cause of yogic perception and an objection concerning its result. The objection about the cause is subdivided into an objection concerning its nature and an objection concerning its function (*byed pa*).

Yogic perception has been questioned from the point of view of its cause. Certain non-Buddhists contend that even if one meditates on no-self, it is impossible to have an utterly clear perception of it. To this we may reply in terms of a probative argument: The subject, a meditation equipped with the means of training in primordial wisdom that fully realizes the emptiness of true existence, is able to come to a perfectly clear perception of no-self. For such a meditation has a sure foundation, and habituation with no-self naturally strengthens—just as in the case of the habitual mental states of craving and fear. The expression "sure foundation" means "unbroken continuity" in the sense that the power of the previous meditation informs the subsequent one, with the result that the second is stronger than the first. In other words, the earlier state of meditation cannot but support and improve the one that follows. Charvakas and other materialists say that the evidence for this contention is not established. They believe that there is no past life and no life to come and that therefore it is impossible for the process of meditative habituation to have a "sure foundation." This, however, will be refuted in the sequel. As long as meditation has a sure foundation, familiarization with no-self will become increasingly clear. This is established by experience and is similar to the mental states of desiring and fearing.

Furthermore, an objection to the yogic perception of no-self has been made with regard to its function. Granted it is possible to grow used to the absence of self, it is argued that the yogic perception of no-self is powerless to undermine the world of existence. But, on the contrary, it *is* able to do so, for effects can never arise in the absence of their respective causes. But what is the cause of samsara? Most non-Buddhist schools accept that the source of samsara is the combination of karma, body, and mind. If one of these is neutralized, the result, samsara, will not be generated—just as with seeds deprived of water and manure. And the adepts of these schools say that karma and the body are to be exhausted through the practice of austerities.

It is, however, impossible to rid oneself of karma, for this is limitless. And even supposing that karma is abandoned, if self-clinging is not overcome, it will reassert itself. Without cutting the root, it is useless to chop off the branches. On the other hand, if self-clinging is abandoned, karma will naturally subside, like a fire going out for want of fuel. It is pointless, therefore, to try to eliminate karma separately, on its own. Consequently, existence cannot be overturned by the practices of such (non-Buddhist) paths.

The root of samsara is ignorance: ignorance of the nature of phenomena and especially that inborn ignorance entertained with regard to the "transitory composite," the sense of self. As long as there is a sense of self, afflictive emotion, karma, and suffering, which are grounded in it, will arise. On the other hand, it stands to reason (*dngos po stobs zhugs kyis rigs pa*) that if this self-sense is overturned, the other factors will not manifest. The roots of karma and suffering are the defiled emotions. As it has been said:

> Defiled emotion here is like a seed,
> Like naga, grass, and tree.[406]

The root of all affliction is the view of self. As the saying goes: "It is the root of every ill."

To the question whether it is possible to eliminate such a root, the answer is yes, for the sense of self is no more than a misconception superimposed on what is truly the case. Now the remedy that dismantles this self-clinging cannot be meditation on love, for example, or the unattractive nature of objects of desire. For these are themselves concomitant with the belief in self and do not call it into question. By contrast, the wisdom that realizes the absence of self is wholly in opposition to it, just as light is the reverse of darkness.

Falsehood may be eliminated by truth, and therefore it stands to reason that there does exist a path that can cut the root of samsara. For even if a seed has no beginning, it may be burned by fire and therefore have an end. Beginningless as samsara may be, if one has the realization of the absence of self, which blocks the proliferation of samsara, there will be no further birth, and samsara will cease.

We now come to a twofold objection regarding the effect of yogic perception. First, there is the claim that yogic perception fails to bring liberation. Certain non-Buddhists affirm that since it is the nature of the mind to be defiled, defilements cannot be removed. Even if it were possible, the objection continues, ordinary people do not know how to accomplish it. And even if they did know, and even if they succeeded in such an enterprise, defilements would return just like the body's odor. Such an elimination is therefore unstable. Consequently, an everlasting deliverance, that is, the definitive absence of defilement, is completely impossible.

But defilement is *not* the nature of the mind. Defilement consists of adventitious thoughts, whereas the nature of the mind is clear luminosity. And since we know that there is a method to eliminate defilement, namely, the realization of no-self; and since, when the cause of defilement is completely abandoned, the latter can never return (like the fire that goes out for want of fuel), liberation is indeed possible.

Second, it is said that yogic perception is powerless to effect the realization of primordial wisdom. Once again, certain non-Buddhists contend that no matter how much the mind is trained and becomes habituated to emptiness and compassion, the latter can never be unbounded and the mind can never actually *become* them. It is just as when one trains in jumping; no matter how much one does so, it is impossible to arrive at the point where the jump becomes endless. However much one boils water, it can never become fire. However much one melts gold, it will always, in the absence of heat, solidify again. But these examples are inappropriate. For although training in jumping does depend on effort, the reason the jump cannot increase indefinitely is that there is a limit to one's physical strength. By contrast, because the nature of the mind is limitless, the qualities of love and so on will develop to the extent that training in it is continued, just as seeds endlessly derive from previous seeds. Similarly, although water does boil away and nothing remains, the power of the earlier mental state increases in the subsequent one and actually assumes the nature of that to which it is habituated, just as firewood turns into fire. As for the example of gold, it is the gold itself that constitutes the cause for its later solidification. But since there is no further cause for the recrudescence of defilements (the sense of

"I"), it follows that they can never return, because they have been eliminated by their antidotes, like wood consumed by fire.

Finally, we must consider two special objections concerning first the cause and then the effect of the primordial wisdom of omniscience, which is the chief of yogic perceptions.

In the first place, with regard to the cause, some non-Buddhists say that omniscience is permanent and self-arisen. Aside from this, they say, there is no such thing as a primordial wisdom of omniscience that may be accomplished anew. For there is no cause for it.

On the contrary, the skillful methods of concentration, compassion, and so on, together with the wisdom of emptiness (acting together as main cause and cooperative conditions) do produce the two kinds of omniscience. The skillful means of great compassion, which is clearly manifest in primordial wisdom, forms the main cause of the primordial wisdom that knows phenomena in all their multiplicity, while the wisdom of emptiness is the cooperative condition for it. Conversely, the primordial wisdom of emptiness (the knowing subject) is the main cause of the primordial wisdom that sees the nature of phenomena, whereas the skillful means of great compassion is its cooperative condition. We are prevented from seeing the nature of phenomena as it is by cognitive obscurations, the nature of which is ignorance. These same cognitive obscurations are nullified by the wisdom of realizing the absence of self, and it is on this that we must rely.

The foregoing examination shows that the primordial wisdom of omniscience does indeed arise from causes. And since the Buddha our Teacher is unmistaken with regard to causes and effects, it stands to reason that the Buddha is a "trustworthy being."[407] As it is said:

> To you who are suffused with valid knowledge,
> To you who are intent on aiding beings,
> To you, the Teacher, Guardian, Sugata, I bow.

In the second place, there is an objection concerning the effect of the primordial wisdom of omniscience, namely, omniscience itself. The knowledge of all things is said to be impossible because there is no limit to objects of knowledge. If the unlimited is known, it becomes limited by that very fact; and that which knows it is thus a mistaken cognition. But the mind cannot know something unlimited, just as one cannot encompass the extent of space by measuring it.[408]

Omniscience, however, does not know the infinite by taking its measure and asserting its extent. Just as "all-pervading space" can encompass even the infinite, it is thus that omniscience knows all phenomena effortlessly and in a single taste. But this kind of cognition exceeds the limits of conventional perception. The way to gain certainty of how omniscience operates in a manner free from thoughts, and how it knows the three times, is explained in other texts. In the present context, if we were to establish what an omniscient being is, simply on the conventional level, we might say that such a being is one who teaches, without error, all that is of paramount importance for living beings. This concerns all that is to be undertaken, and all that is to be avoided, in respect of the path of the Four Truths. And someone who knows all this may be said to know "all things," in the same way that one speaks of the aggregate of all medicines or of all men.[409] The knowledge of other things (such as the number of all the insects that there are, and so on) is not at all indispensable for those who are intent on liberation. And though the Buddha knew them, there was little point in his setting them forth for beings to be trained. Indeed, had he done so, there would have been no one capable of assimilating such information.

We say therefore that the one who sets forth the path, established by reasoning based on the evidence of things, is the Teacher, the Buddha, who knows everything that is of relevance to beings. And from this we may infer that he does indeed know all other objects of knowledge. One who can know fully the ultimate truth, which is subtle and profound, can doubtless know also all that is not subtle. For eyes that can see a speck of dust at a distance can surely see the jar that is close by. This brief excursus on the way of establishing the paths of liberation and of omniscience, and their result, is a summary taken from the learned masters of the past who followed Dharmakirti, the lord of reasoning.

It may be observed that, in general, such refutations of non-Buddhist positions are not directed against actual adversaries and are not pursued just for the sake of arguing. For we must recognize that we too entertain erroneous thoughts and that these resemble the positions of the non-Buddhists. And by means of immaculate reasoning based on both affirmation and negation, we must uproot them, together with their associated tendencies. If we manage to do this, then it is as stanza 97 declares: "Those rich in wisdom who perceive" and so forth. An invincible trust in the path and the Teacher will grow. All of this is a most important subject for reflection.

In short, that which enables us to sever the root of samsaric existence

and to accomplish liberation and omniscience is the stainless wisdom that
scrutinizes the two truths. Such wisdom cannot simply arise, however, independently without training. It does not simply fall from the sky or grow
out of the earth. People who are pursuing the path and are endowed with
the attitude of bodhichitta will at first investigate all outer and inner phenomena by means of the argument of neither one nor many. And by means
of valid inference, they will be convinced that all things are definitely without inherent existence. Such certitude is as contrary to the misapprehension of things as light is from dark. It eradicates all the misconceptions (*sgro
'dogs*) that are to be discarded. To meditate without this kind of certitude is
to be like someone blind from birth trying to evaluate a shape. One will fail
to hit the mark. Therefore, with my palms joined in supplication, I declare
to all who dwell in every direction: Your meditation must never stir from
certain knowledge (*nges shes*)! Achieve this certainty, I pray. Free yourselves
from doubt!

Without this certainty, it is difficult to realize the ultimate truth. If reasoning lacks validity, certain knowledge will not come. This is a pith instruction that should be taken to heart by all who follow the path. The
removal of doubt is the result of learning and reflection. Confident assur-
ance (*gdings*) is the fruit of meditation. All exposition and practice that fail
to give these two results are no more than a pale reflection of the real thing.

We might, incidentally, give some slight consideration, in accordance
with the writings of holy beings, to the question of true and certain knowledge and misconception. It could be objected that if the certitude that a
concrete object like a pot is not a really existing thing and the misconception that it is a really existing thing do not have the same object of reference,
they cannot be (respectively) the agent and the object of elimination—just
as the light outside a container cannot dispel the darkness inside.

But if the object of reference is the same, is this object established or
not? If it is established, it follows that the misconception is not erroneous,
for the object in question is true. In that case, the misconception resembles
a valid cognition. On the other hand, if the object is not established, the cer-
titude-conferring cognition (*nges byed*) is invalid, for the object of assessment does not exist. In that case, the "true and certain knowledge"
resembles a misconception. Moreover, if the object of reference (of both
certain knowledge and misconception) is one and the same, some may ask
whether this object is true or false and say that if it is true, the misconception is true; if it is false, the valid cognition is false.

The answer to this conundrum is that the object of assessment is the mere vase, apprehended by means of mental other-elimination—a process that does not differentiate between things that exist (*dngos*) and things that do not exist (*dngos med*).[410] Since (in both cases) the conceived object (*zhen yul*) is one and the same, the fault is not incurred that the certain knowledge (of the object's lack of true existence) and the misconception (of thinking that it truly exists) are inadmissible as agent and object of elimination. But since the two ways of conceiving the vase (as being either truly existent or not) are different, it is possible to say that they are valid or invalid cognitions as the case may be. Certainty and misconception are respectively qualified as true or false because their *way of conceiving* the vase corresponds or does not correspond with the object itself. It is not that they apprehend an objectively "true" or an objectively "false" thing. The ear consciousness of two men may both perceive the one sound made by a conch. One may believe that it is a permanent sound, the other that it is impermanent. Their respective apprehensions come about through the blending together of the object (the sound of the conch) and their own subjective mode of apprehension, whereby they conceive the sound to be either permanent or impermanent. That is, they mix together the perceived phenomenon and their idea about it (*snang btags*). Consequently, the fault of designating the object of the valid and invalid cognitions as being either the same or different does not occur. An accurate understanding of this question will clarify numerous key points of pramana.

There is yet another objection. Are true and certain knowledge and misconception the same in the sense of being both the mind, or not? If they are one and the same, it is impossible that the one should be the object, and the other the agent, of elimination—just as it is impossible for a sword to cut itself. On the other hand, if they are distinct, it is once again impossible for them to be object and agent of elimination—just as it is impossible for the primordial wisdom of a Buddha to dispel the ignorance in the minds of beings. Our answer to this is that since, simply in terms of the mind's continuity, the two are one and the same, they are not like two distinct mind streams. On the other hand, their aspects are different.[411] The case therefore is not that of something acting upon itself.

Once again it may be asked, do these two states (of true and certain knowledge and of misconception) occur at the same time or not? They cannot be simultaneous, for this would involve the false consequence that the two thoughts (the one to be abandoned and the correct, remedial thought) coincide in the same moment. On the other hand, if they are not simultaneous, it cannot be said that they are the object and agent of elimination—just like the light of the sun and the darkness of night.[412]

We reply that since certain knowledge and misconception do not occur simultaneously, they cannot actually be in contact. However, the misconception, which has arisen first in the mind stream, is followed by true certainty, with the result that the former can no longer arise, and this is what happens when one says "the misconception has been dispelled." Indeed, all defilements and their antidotes (all of which are mental states) follow the same procedure. The past event has gone and the present is already here: No kind of injury can be inflicted on them. Neither can injury be inflicted on the future event, for this has not yet arisen. In fact, something that is momentary cannot be established as the object or agent of elimination. Nevertheless, since correct and certain knowledge acts as a preventive to the continued arising of subsequent misconception, one speaks in terms of an object and agent of elimination.[413]

Some say that defilements and their antidotes keep company with each other for many countless kalpas, because the primordial wisdom of the noble Bodhisattvas and their defiled propensities coexist for a long time.[414] This, however, is only a manner of speaking, for if defilements and their antidotes actually coexisted, the former could never be dispelled. Consequently, defilements and their remedies do not in fact coexist in the minds of the noble Bodhisattvas. Indeed, the subtle habitual tendencies related with the dualistic illusion of subject and object are not dispelled by the primordial wisdom of the noble beings who are on the path of learning. They are removed only by the vajralike concentration.[415]

The examination of true and certain knowledge and misconception, in terms of their object, nature, and time, provides an occasion for raising very pertinent questions. I have therefore discussed them here as part of a detailed examination of the words of stanza 75, "Those who sound the nature of phenomena with reasoning."

8. A reply to the third objection (since the three conditions of correct evidence cannot be established in the case of phenomena that are without inherent existence, it is impossible to speak in terms of predicate and reason)
9. The reply

76
Leave aside the subjects specially defined
In philosophic texts.
For it is to the things known commonly to all—
From scholars down to women and their children—

77a
That all these predicates and reasons
Are perfectly applied.

Now, it might be objected that in claiming that phenomena are without inherent existence, the Madhyamikas are saying that they do not exist at all. In that case, the subject with its predicate, and the evidential sign, and indeed the entire probative argument itself are meaningless—for the simple reason that the logical subject is nonexistent. The Madhyamikas may think that they formulate no probative argument, but the fact is that a thesis is not proved merely by stating it. On the other hand, if the Madhyamikas formulate an argument, that argument exists. Therefore, not everything is without inherent existence, and consequently the Madhyamaka position is contradictory.

This is a trashy argument. One should leave aside the subjects specially defined in the texts of tenets. These are not at all the subject of the proposition in question. The subject of the proposition comprises all experienced phenomena that commonly appear to, and form the consensus of, everyone, learned and unlearned alike, down to simple women and children.[416] To phenomena in this sense, predicates and evidential signs may, as verbal designations,[417] be unproblematically applied. On the other hand, if an item drawn from some assertion in scripture (that does not accord with common perception) were to be made the topic for debate, there would be no logical subject commonly appearing to the opposing parties. Consequently, all arguments formulated on such a basis would, in the absence of a common subject, be pointless. Indeed, examples cannot be given for either the predicated property or the evidence, for all evidential signs will be devoid of meaning. On the other hand, if a subject specially elaborated in the tenet literature is accepted by both parties, there is no purpose in discussing it further. Indeed to do so would imply a disregard for one's own position and suggest that one were calling it into question.

9. Any position other than the one just stated is untenable

> 77b
> How could we counter otherwise
> Such charges as "The subject is unreal"?

As explained, the subject of the proposition is mere phenomena, simply as they appear, unqualified by the discordant opinions as to whether they are "existent" or "nonexistent." If one were to do otherwise, what reply could one give to the objection that the subject, or locus of the argument, and the examples adduced are not established and are unreal? One could return no answer. For instance, Buddhists may formulate arguments to non-Buddhists such as: "The subject, sound, is impermanent because it is a (causally efficient) thing" or "The subject, the mountain pass, is fire-possessing because it is smoke-possessing." If the non-Buddhist debaters consider each of these subjects in the sense propounded in their own non-Buddhist scriptures, they will think in terms of a mountain pass as a part-possessing whole, or of a sound defined as the property of space. But since the pass and sound as perceived cannot actually be a part-possessing whole or a property of space, these subjects are not established. And since they are not established, neither can there be signs or reasons based on them—any more than one can have points on a rabbit's antlers. Neither, for such an argument, would it be possible to adduce examples applicable to the logical subject.[418] And finally, the subject to be inferred as this or that (such as a pass being "fire-possessing") and the evidential sign (smoke), on the basis of which the inference is made, would likewise be unestablished.

Therefore, if, when establishing a conventional phenomenon (carefully separating the mere thing as commonly perceived from the way in which it may be intellectually apprehended), one proceeds according to the manner in which certain knowledge and misconception were considered above, one will achieve a sound grasp of this question.

6. Dealing with the objections about the relative truth
7. It is generally acceptable to speak of proof and predicate to be proved

> 78
> Things as they appear
> I do not negate.

And therefore, unconfused,
I may set forth both predicate and evidence.

In this stanza, Shantarakshita affirms that he does not refute mere dependently arising things as they appear to the sense organs of sight, hearing, and so forth, in the common perception of all, from the learned to
infants. Nevertheless, if appearances are examined with reasoning on the
one hand, or the primordial wisdom of the Aryas on the other, they are
found to be without the slightest existent core, just like banana trees. Therefore, no claim is made that they exist on the ultimate level. Since appearances are not negated, however, the probative arguments, which remove
misconceptions with regard to such phenomena, and which establish or assess them correctly (as well as the predicated property to be inferred by
such arguments), are all set forth without the slightest fault liable to result
in confusion or lack of clarity. This being the case, the fact that phenomena
are without inherent existence is established.

Since the root verse refers by implication to the opponent's position, it
is not necessary to formulate it explicitly. The opponent is assuming that
the denial of the inherent existence of phenomena involves the negation
of their appearance. The opponent concludes therefore that the proof and
the predicate to be proved are both inadmissible. But when, at this point
and in Madhyamaka generally, it is said that appearances are not negated,
one should not jump to the conclusion that appearances have an existence
separate from emptiness and are not themselves empty by nature. Take for
example the moon reflected in water. The moon appears while being
empty; and there is nothing that is empty apart from its appearance. Phenomena are empty in the same way, and this does not necessitate the exclusion of their mere appearance. If there is no appearance, there is no
emptiness, for emptiness and appearance depend upon each other. The absence of one entails the absence of the other; the presence of one entails
the presence of the other. It is not that appearance and emptiness exist separately, like a white and a black thread twisted together. Neither are they
alternate in the sense that when one goes, the other comes. Emptiness entails appearance; appearance entails emptiness. The two can never be separate. If you gain a conviction that this is indeed the way things are—a
conviction that is irreversible though a thousand Buddhas should deny it—
you have, by learning and study, penetrated to the deepest point of the
Madhyamaka scriptures. You can then pursue in earnest the paths of the
sutras and the tantras, for you have found their vital root.

Now, if one understands that the only reason appearances are not negated is to allow one to posit commonly perceived phenomena as the subject of debate, the question still remains why appearances in themselves are not negated. But the phenomena of the common consensus are not asserted just for the sake of debate. It is important to grasp with clear conviction that the nonnegation of appearances does not contradict the Madhyamaka view in any way. If this is understood, assertions made on the conventional level are unproblematic. For since one is not basing oneself on the opaque fixations of different tenets, valid reasoning, which is acceptable to all parties, will operate unhindered. As it is said:

> Without reliance on opaque fixation,
> Conventionalities are perfectly established.
> And if one knows conventionalities,
> One will not be confused about the shastras' meaning.

Let us now consider how those who gradually enter the state of no-thought ascertain this most important point of Madhyamaka. When beginners examine phenomena with the help of arguments like that of neither one nor many, and reflect on the fact that no pot, for example, is found, they may conclude that if the pot is left unexamined, it exists, and that it ceases to exist when it is investigated—this nonexistence being the ultimate status of the pot. For such people, the aspect of emptiness that arises for them is an emptiness that alternates with appearance. Reflecting subsequently that the pot's nonexistence is also without establishment—in other words, that although it is primordially empty, the pot appears—they will be certain that though appearing, the pot is empty, and though empty, it appears, just like the reflection of the moon in water. This is said to be an understanding that the absence of inherent existence and the interdependent production of phenomena are not contradictory but that they coincide. And one will be convinced that though appearance and emptiness are distinguished verbally, they are, on the level of their nature, inseparable, there being not the slightest divergence between them. When the thought that brings together appearing phenomena (the ground of negation) with the nonimplicative negation that denies their true existence dissolves by itself, there arises an aspect of freedom from conceptual construction—an ability to leave things as they are, without refuting or affirming, denying or asserting them. Through training in this freedom from conceptual constructs, all partial and one-sided mental objects to which the mind may refer (such as different ultimate natures in relation to different phenomena) will be cleared away and an extraordinary certainty in the equality of all phenomena will be attained. Certainty in the four steps of Madhyamaka realization (emptiness, union, freedom from conceptual constructs, and equality) will occur in succession, each in dependence on the training in the foregoing stage. These key points of the essential instructions are of the utmost importance.

7. A specific explanation of how the causal interdependence of past and future lives is acceptable
8. A brief presentation of the proposition

> 79
> It should be inferred therefore
> That seeds that by their kind accord with what appears,
> And likewise with all thoughts of things and of nonthings,
> Are lodged within the mind from time without
>   beginning.

As it has been said above, it is impossible that things enjoy the slightest inherent existence. Nevertheless, the various phenomena of the world appear clearly and unceasingly. It can be reasonably inferred therefore that within our mind streams from time without beginning, there are seeds that by their kind accord with our conceptions of things and nonthings, of ourselves and others, and so forth. We may restate the root verse more easily as follows: It may be reasonably inferred that the causes of the things that appear to us, and of our conceptions—things like pillars and pots and nonthings like space—are the seeds or propensities of thought that accord with them in kind. These seeds are lodged in the mind from beginningless time.

Although, ultimately speaking, phenomena are beyond the constructs of the conceptual mind, nevertheless, the various perceptions of phenomena, and the conceptions entertained of things and nonthings, infect and spoil the minds of those whose understanding is darkened. These endless appearances cannot be causeless; they must have a cause. And reasoning can assign no other causes for them than those that are of like kind and concordant with them. It is thus shown that the causes of phenomenal appearances are causes that are of like kind.

8. A detailed presentation using rational argument
9. A refutation of the incorrect position

> 80
> And these do not occur by power of outer things,
> For outer things do not exist.
> Indeed the inherent existence of such things
> Has been extensively refuted.

> 81a
> They appear successively and therefore are not random;
> And not occurring all the time, they are not permanent.

Why is it that variegated appearances do not have causes other than seeds of concordant kind? The reason is this: If phenomena such as pots *did* have an independent existence, we could admit that specific thoughts do indeed arise in relation to them. However, the thought or appearance of a pot is no more than a mere appearance occurring in the mind. It does not arise by the power of a separate, extramental entity, for such things do not exist. It may be argued that there is no evidence for such a contention. But as it has been explained above, reasoning *has* refuted, very extensively, the inherent existence of all knowable things. How then can it be claimed that the evidence is not established? It is indeed established. Therefore, since phenomena merely appear to one's perception, and aside from this have no independent existence, there cannot be a perception of them on the ultimate level, just as one cannot have a seal when there is no corresponding stamp.

It may then be thought that, in view of the above, although things do not exist, they appear nevertheless, either without a cause or through causes other than themselves. This is not so, however. Given that appearances arise gradually, it is impossible for them to arise just like that, randomly, without the intervention of some cause. For if they were uncaused they could not arise gradually or only sometimes. They would have to be either permanently existent or permanently nonexistent, as has already been explained.

Again, it may be thought that, in that case, there is no contradiction in saying that the appearance of specific objects is produced through the agency of an extraneous cause like a creator, or that it is produced by something permanent like atman or purusha. But there *is* a contradiction. Thoughts and appearances are produced and cease at every moment. They are not occurring at all times, unceasing and changeless. Therefore, they do not arise from a permanent cause. All variegated thoughts and phenomena, which merely appear and cannot be denied, cannot arise uncaused. They are indeed caused. And since they arise neither by the power of external things nor from causes different from the things in question, it is clearly established by reasoning that they manifest from the complete ripening of habitual tendencies present in the mind.

9. A valid proof of past and future lives

81b
Therefore, in the manner of habituation,
    consciousness's first arising
Issues from a moment of concordant kind.

For the reasons just explained, different outer and inner appearances manifest by virtue of powerful habitual propensities, just as when one has a strong habit of desire or fear. It is thus that past and future existences are established. Correct reasoning proves that the first instant of consciousness produced manifests on the basis of an earlier instant of consciousness that is concordant in kind.[419] And by the same token, it is shown that there is a future existence for those whose minds are in the grip of attachment. All this can be illustrated by the experience of the present life. In previous existences one may have had the pleasant experience of touching a youthful person of the opposite sex, and this has left an inclination for this experience upon one's mind stream. Thus, again in the present existence, the mind is conditioned by the same interest.[420] And in the present existence, the mind's experience of the pleasure arising from intercourse makes way for the mind to experience the same desire later on as well. In such a way, in accordance with one's strength of habit and whatever it is one has become used to, the same will manifest more or less clearly in the future. It is like learning to read. When a man who has desire thinks again and again about some beautiful woman, or when a fearful person thinks repeatedly about the danger of snakes, by the power of their habit, they will come to the point where they actually see them as clearly[421] as if they were in front of them. The same thing occurs through concentration and meditation on the repulsive character of the bodies of those who are the object of one's sexual desire and indeed with all other kinds of mental conditioning.

Thus the first instant of consciousness (in the womb) does not manifest through the power of extraneous (nonmental) things; it does not occur through the operation of a permanent cause, and it does not occur uncaused.[422] It arises from the previous moment concordant in kind—of a consciousness that conceives of entities in terms of true existence and so on. For the present moment of consciousness does likewise.

There are many arguments concerning this matter in the *Pramanasiddhi*. But since to expound them here would require a long excursus, they have been omitted. Essentially, the principal cause of the clear, knowing consciousness is awareness itself. It cannot be an inanimate thing. And since consciousness is not dependent on anything other than the mind, it is established that the mind is beginningless. This argument gives us certainty with regard to a most crucial topic as expounded in this text. Just as the mind is shown to be beginningless, likewise it is endless. The mind of a dying person, which is not freed from attachment to "I" and "mine," will, on account of this mistaken clinging, have the potential to provoke the arising of a further moment of consciousness. And if all the causes are present and unhindered, there is no doubt that the next birth will follow. Just as the preceding moment of consciousness produces the subsequent moment, the moment of consciousness at the time of death—endowed with all the causes complete (the root of which is ego-clinging and the karma and defilements produced on this basis) and devoid of the realization of no-self (which would arrest them)—will make a link with the next existence. For as long as there is no realization that there is no self, existences cannot be halted. However, since the mind, in the sense of pure luminosity, does not itself depend on ego-clinging and is produced from the previous moment of concordant kind, it follows that even when the two kinds of no-self are realized, the causes of this luminous mind remain complete and are not obstructed, with the result that this same mind will not be halted. Such is the teaching of all the great masters of reasoning. And thus, according to conventional valid reasoning, even though the impure mind is arrested, the uninterrupted continuity of primordial wisdom is necessarily established.

But here we have digressed from the main subject. Nevertheless, it is thus that we can see that the interest of this description of the conventional level according to the view that knowledge-objects are inner mental events does not lie simply in the fact that it is generally tenable. Since it is established by reasoning based on the evidence of things, it provides a means to refute utterly every rejection of the karmic principle of cause and effect, a denial that is at variance with the abiding mode of dependently arising things. It will therefore enable one to achieve a deep-rooted conviction with regard to the law of cause and effect, a conviction superior to that gained from other paths. The Vaibhashikas and others, swayed by their aversion to the ultimate, say that to consider that phenomena are without intrinsic reality strongly undermines, among other things, the law of cause and effect. Indeed, they call it an "empowerment into nihilism." And they quote the following text:

> Denying thus the causal law,
> They harm all virtue with their evil view,
> Which is like hailstones for the crops of sacred teaching.
> Let those who yearn for goodness
> Cast away these flowers that grow in air.

Those who repeat such things have failed to understand that if phenomena existed intrinsically, the law of cause and effect would itself be illogical. On the contrary, it is because phenomena are without inherent reality that the causal law is entirely tenable. All such false assertions are refuted by Shantarakshita's system.

7. A concluding eulogy of this teaching, which avoids the views of eternalism and nihilism

82
Thus the views of permanence and nothingness
Are far from the teaching of this text.
When causes cease, effects will follow,
As plants derive from shoots and shoots from seeds.

Where there is no cause, there is no effect. When all the causes are complete, the effect is irreversible. This is the ineluctable interdependence of cause and effect. For this reason, it should be understood that to consider phenomena as permanent and not momentary, or to believe that they are causally unconnected (which is the view of nihilism), is very far from the present Madhyamaka text, which sets forth the twin approaches of the Middle Way and of the Mind Only together. Such false views are like darkness that cannot withstand the presence of light. The views of permanent existence or nihilism arise in dependence on the belief in the reality of things. But if on the ultimate level, things do not exist, how can one view them either as permanent or as nothing at all? Neither is it possible to relate such views to the relative level. For in every instant, foregoing causes cease and subsequent effects follow their respective causes. When all causal circumstances are complete, it is definite that the effects will follow. And the causal sequence is uninterrupted: From seeds come shoots, from shoots the tiny plants. As it is said in the *Ratnamegha:*

> How are Bodhisattvas learned in the Mahayana? Bodhisattvas train in all precepts, but they "observe" neither their training, nor the path on which they train, nor indeed the agent of such training. Yet, due to the presence of causes, conditions, and basis or person, they do not fall into the nihilistic view.

And the same sutra also says:

> Child of my lineage! With the aid of perfect wisdom, Bodhisattvas examine form. They examine feelings, perceptions, conditioning factors, and consciousness. When they examine form, they do not find form as something produced; they do not find its origin. They do not find the production of feelings, or perceptions, or conditioning factors, or consciousness. They do not find their origin or cessation. All this is in the light of wisdom that examines and finds that there is no production on the ultimate level. It does not refer to the relative.

The gross, simplistic view of permanence consists in considering that phenomena are not momentary. The simplistic view of nihilism is the belief that although phenomena are caused, they themselves do not generate their own effects—in the sense that the present aggregates will not give rise to future aggregates or that actions will not give rise to (karmic) results. These false, non-Buddhist views are like a yawning abyss. The way to refute them is to hold, on the one hand, that phenomena cease at every moment and, on the other, that if causes are present, effects will surely manifest. To believe that the former instant of the cause has ceased is not the extreme view of nihilism; it is the antidote that rids one of the view of permanent entities. To hold that subsequent moments of things are produced from foregoing causes is not the extreme of permanence; it is the antidote for nihilism. These two notions are in agreement with the nature of phenomena on the conventional level. However, they alone are unable to produce the correct view that transcends the world, and it is consequently necessary to recognize that all phenomena are lacking in inherent existence. And in respect of *this* recognition, the view of permanence is to hold that phenomena exist truly, whereas the view of nihilism is to hold that things have no existence whatever, even on the conventional level. As to their antidotes, conventional existence is the remedy that dispels the extreme view of nonexistence (a remedy, however, that does not imply the extreme of existence or eternalism). On the other hand, the lack of inherent existence is the antidote to the extreme of existence (without implying the extreme of nonexistence or nihilism). Nevertheless, to apprehend things in this way—holding to conventional appearance on the one hand and the lack of inherent existence on the other—is no more than a dualistic concept held in terms of subject and object. It is still necessary to cultivate the nonconceptual primordial wisdom of meditative equipoise. The thought-free state, devoid of conceptual construction, transcends the notions of existence and nonexistence. When all mental fixations with regard to this state and also with regard to the equality of all phenomena subside, one is free from the two extremes of considering that phenomena are without inherent existence and yet exist conventionally. Since at that point all views fixing on extreme positions subside, one is certainly emancipated from all views. When this freedom from conceptual extremes is reached— that is, after the simplistic, refined, and utterly refined views that hold to extreme positions are progressively eliminated (in the sense that the lower view serves as the basis for the removal of the higher view)—no further progress is possible. For this is the view that accords with the ultimate nature of things. It is consequently said that existence and nonexistence are two extreme positions, and it is important to know how to apply the nondual wisdom of meditative equipoise and the discerning wisdom of the postmeditative state to these refined and unrefined conceptual extremes that are to be eliminated.

4. The benefits of understanding the two truths correctly
5. The benefits of understanding the absence of inherent existence on the ultimate level

83
The wise who know that in phenomena there is no self
Become accustomed to this absence of intrinsic nature.

And thus they effortlessly spurn
Defilement that arises from mistaken thought.

The wise who with perfect reasoning establish the absence of self in all knowable things, both the person and phenomena, and who gain certainty in this beyond all doubt, become accustomed to this absence. It is thus that they effortlessly spurn all the defilements that manifest owing to thoughts that misapprehend the ultimate reality of things and conceive the two kinds of self, thereby obscuring the mind and fettering it. Such defilements are eliminated without deliberate effort, just as darkness vanishes in the presence of the sun.

In the case of those who are beginners in the practice, the habit to regard phenomena as real is very strong. For they have not, in the past, accustomed themselves to the methods that rectify this habit. And even if they expend great effort in the direct attempt to eliminate it, they will not succeed. On the other hand, if they grow used to such methods, then without any intentional effort on their part, the antidote will naturally occur and defilements will come to a halt. In the end, every defilement will be completely worn away and the nature of all knowledge-objects will be perceived clearly—with the same clarity that one can see the inside and outside of a myrobalan fruit placed in the palm of one's hand. All this stands to reason. For at that time, primordial wisdom, which is free from even the subtlest defilements that might hide the nature of phenomena, will be unobstructed and all the causes of omniscience will be complete. It is also proved by reasoning that the five paths are antidotes to the defilements. As Nagarjuna has said:

> Wherever there's belief that things are
>   real,
> Desire and hatred spring unendingly;
> Unwholesome views are entertained
> From which all disputes come.

> Indeed this is the source of every view;
> Without it no defilement can occur.
> Thus when this is completely understood,
> All views and all afflictions vanish utterly.

> But how may this be known?

'Tis said that when one sees that all things are dependently
   produced,
One sees that all such things are free from birth;
This the supreme Knower of the Truth has taught.

And in the *Chandrapradipa-sutra* it is said: "On the ultimate level, one
sees neither attachment, nor anything to be attached to, nor anyone who
harbors such attachment."

Neither will it be possible for defilements to block or resist the antidotes.
As it is said in the *Pramanavarttika:*

Even if one were to try
To misconstrue the nature of nonviolence
And of the ultimate, one can but fail.
For by the nature of such things the mind abides.

The general structure of the grounds and paths should be studied in
other texts. In the present context, we will speak only briefly of the way
in which defilements are eliminated. As concerns the manner in which
primordial wisdom, which realizes the two kinds of no-self, removes
defilements, there is no conflict between the views of the great charioteers of the Mahayana (Nagarjuna and Asanga). In short, we may say generally that the primordial wisdom experienced on the ten grounds of
realization is inconceivable and also that the illusory display of defilements to be discarded (relating to these grounds) is also limitless. The sutras explain that there are many defilements to be discarded and many
ways of doing so, but, broadly categorized, reasoning shows with certainty that all defilements are either emotional or cognitive. These two
kinds of defilement are posited from the point of view of what it is that
hinders the two supreme objectives of beings (namely, liberation and omniscience). It is useless therefore to speak of any other kind of defilement.
As it is said in the *Madhyantavibhanga:*

Emotional and cognitive—
Thus defilement is explained.
In these all obscurations are included.
Freedom, it is said, occurs when these have been exhausted.

All the sutras and shastras are in agreement on this point, and they do not set forth any other kind of defilement apart from these two. Even the extremely subtle obscurations that derive from habitual tendencies and prevent the nature of knowledge-objects from being evident to us belong to the category of cognitive obscuration.

What is it that veils liberation? Emotional defilements such as clinging to "I" and "mine." What is it that veils omniscience? It is the ignorance on account of which the nature of phenomena is not manifest. Although, depending on the various texts, there are numerous ways of differentiating the emotional and cognitive obscurations (in terms of their cause, nature, and function), in fact they are not different. Condensing the import of the sutras, one can say that the principal cause of wandering in samsara is afflictive emotion such as craving. And it is said that the root, without which this could not arise, is the innate sense of "I" (the so-called view of the transitory composite). All this is proved by reasoning. The afflictions that have as their cause or root the apprehension of, and clinging to, the personal self are the emotional obscurations. On the other hand, the failure to know phenomena both in their nature and in their multiplicity constitutes the ignorance of not knowing the nature of phenomena. All ignorance, both gross and subtle, the root of which is the apprehension of, and clinging to, the self of phenomena, constitutes the cognitive obscurations.

Once they have been thoroughly understood, the two kinds of obscurations may be correlated with the various stages of the path of practice. If one suffers from avarice and other afflictions arising from ego-clinging, and which are the factors that, respectively, run counter to the six paramitas, one is unable to engage actively in the paramitas concerned. Such afflictions are the emotional obscurations. On the other hand, if one engages in the practice of the paramitas without realizing that phenomena are devoid of self—that is, within the conception of the reality of the three spheres of object, subject, and action, which is rooted in the belief in the phenomenal self—all this is cognitive obscuration. As it is said in the *Uttaratantra-shastra:*

> *Conceptions of a subject, object, action*
> *Are said to be the cognitive defilements.*
> *The thoughts of avarice and so forth*
> *Are said to be emotional defilements.*

It stands to reason that if one realizes the absence of the personal self, all emotional afflictions, which have ego-clinging as their root, will be arrested. For it is certain that when it is perceived that there is no personal self, attachment, hatred, pride, and so forth—all of which arise therefrom—cannot occur, whereas when there is ego-clinging, they do. As it is said in the *Ratnavali:*

> As long as there is clinging to the aggregates,[423]
> So long will there be clinging to a self.
> And through such clinging to a self, all karmic action
>   manifests;
> From karmic action, birth results.

It is said in the *Pramanavarttika:*

> When there's self, you recognize an "other."
> From "self and other" attachment and aversion come;
> And from the interaction of these two
> All faults occur.

and:

> As long as there is a grasping to the self,
> To that extent you circle in samsara.

And as it is said in the *Madhyamakavatara:*

> Perceiving that all faults and all afflictions
> Flow from the idea of the transitory composite. . . .[424]

Ego-clinging is eliminated by its antidote: the wisdom that realizes that there is no self to cling to. On the path of seeing, the ultimate truth is directly seen and all artificial imputations of the two kinds of obscurations, which run counter to the ultimate truth, are eliminated. Subsequently, on the path of meditation, innate thought patterns are eliminated. As for what artificial imputations and innate thought patterns are, this must be found elsewhere.[425]

The Shravakas and Pratyekabuddhas meditate only on the absence of the personal self, the antidote to the emotional obscurations. They are able, as a result, to eliminate all emotional afflictions. And like a fire going out for want of firewood, they harbor no further cause for samsara and can never return to it. But because they do not complete their meditation on the phenomenal no-self, they are unable to remove the cognitive obscurations. In a general sense, all kinds of ignorance that hide the nature of knowledge-objects may be referred to as "emotional affliction." But when a distinction is made between the emotional and cognitive obscurations, ignorance is not counted as an emotional affliction, and this is an important distinction.[426]

Starting at the path of seeing, the noble beings of the Mahayana eliminate both emotional and cognitive obscurations simultaneously. On the eighth ground, ultimate reality is effortlessly broached, so that even the subtle movements of ego-clinging are worn away. Thus it is that all the seeds of afflictive emotion disappear. On the three pure grounds, such Bodhisattvas remove only the habitual tendencies of dual appearance (gnyis snang), that is, the cognitive obscurations. It is only on the level of buddhahood, however, that there remains not the slightest obscuration to veil the dharmadhatu. This is impossible while one is still on the path of learning. As it is said in the Madhyamakavatara:

> Because, without desire, their minds are henceforth free from
> faults,
> Upon the eighth, impurities are stilled, together with their
> roots.
> But though defilements are no more, and nothing in the triple
> world surpasses them,
> The boundless, spacelike wealth of buddhahood lies still be-
> yond their powers.[427]

This manner of considering the emotional and cognitive obscurations is not the exclusive preserve of the Prasangika Madhyamaka system. It is a feature of the great Mahayana sutras and is the view of all the great chari-oteers of the Doctrine.

There is indeed a tradition here in Tibet[428] that asserts that only the emotional obscurations are discarded on the seven impure grounds of re-alization. But since the antidote, the primordial wisdom that realizes the ab-sence of the two selves, is present, how is it possible that the cognitive obscurations are not discarded also? As the Madhyantavibhanga says:

> Ignorance of dharmadhatu
> Is not accounted an emotional affliction.

To the ten veils that counter the ten grounds
These grounds themselves are antidotes.

The teachings, both Buddha-word and commentary, identify cognitive obscurations as what is abandoned on the ten grounds. And this is how it should be understood. The tradition referred to above asserts that cognitive obscurations are eliminated from the eighth ground onward and that the Arhats among the Shravakas and Pratyekabuddhas completely realize the phenomenal no-self and eliminate all the emotional obscurations. Other scholars[429] contest such a position. For in such a case, it would follow that when, after becoming Arhats, the Shravakas and Pratyekabuddhas enter the Mahayana and realize the primordial wisdom, there would be nothing, on the seven impure grounds, for the antidote (the same primordial wisdom) to eliminate. What, in that case, would be remedying the "path free from obstacles"? What would the "path of freedom" be giving freedom from?[430] It would be impossible to speak of them. Furthermore, there are defilements remaining to be eliminated, in the course of two immeasurable kalpas, by meditation on no-self on the part of a Bodhisattva possessed of unlimited methods of great compassion. On the other hand, the Shravakas and Pratyekabuddhas (who have no such methods) would be able to eliminate the same defilements by meditation practiced for only three lifetimes and so forth. In that case, the Hinayana would be a swifter path to enlightenment than the Mahayana. There are many learned disquisitions of this kind. The scholars of both old and new schools have sharp, analytical faculties. With a free, unbiased mind, one has only to stand back and watch the amazing spectacle of their competition in the illusory power of reasoning!

Thus, the emotional and cognitive veils are not widely different. And it is not the case that their antidotes, the two kinds of no-self, cannot be merged. The glorious Rongdzom said that an examination may be made to see whether the defilements to be abandoned—those related to the truth of suffering and those related to the truth of origin[431]—are the same or different. In that case, one may think as follows. If they are one and the same, it follows that the subsequent antidote (namely, the one remedying the defilements related to the truth of origin) is pointless. On the other hand, if they are different, it is necessary to discard all the various afflictions belonging to the three worlds, of beings and phenomena—which is impossible.

This nevertheless is the teaching. Grounded in the notion of self, defilements arise in relation to objects apprehended as truly existent and endowed with attributes. As long as phenomena are so observed, defilements will occur in equal number to the things observed. When the notion of "I" collapses and the magician of the ego is no more, the afflictions, which are its illusory display, will no more appear. Defilements related to the truth of suffering, and those related to the truth of origin, are therefore neither the same nor different. As a means of benefiting the Shravakas, who cling to the specific and general characteristics of phenomena, the Buddha distinguished four truths, encompassing all the various instances relating to the cause and effect of samsara and of nirvana. And it is only with reference to these specific cases, as expounded by the Buddha, that primordial wisdom and also the defilements are differentiated into different categories. In fact, all primordial wisdom is one and the same; it is the wisdom that perfectly understands the phenomenal no-self. Likewise, all defilements are one and the same; they are the misconception of believing in the self. For this reason, it is not wisdom focused on the person that removes defilements. It is wisdom focused on phenomena that eliminates them by eradicating all false conceptual constructs. For defilements cannot be uprooted by anyone who considers phenomena to be really existent.

One might at this point wonder how the Shravakas—who, on the level of the partless particle of matter and the indivisible instant of consciousness, believe in the reality of things—free themselves from defilement and attain enlightenment. The teaching is as follows. According to their own tenets, they dispel afflictions and attain the uncompounded (that is, cessation). According to the Mahayana, however, those who rid themselves of actual afflictions, though not of their latent seeds, and who possess a body (the ripened result of their karma), and who remove all the fetters that bind them to the three worlds are referred to as "beings who have arrested karmic life."[432] In the *Vairochanamayajala-tantra*, in answer to the question:

> How do those within the lower vehicle,
> Who have no skillful means and wisdom
> And strongly cling to the existence of external things,
> Attain to unsurpassed enlightenment?

it is said that:

> *Two enlightenments have been explained,*
> *One that has remainder, one that is without.*
> *"Remainder" indicates the aggregates that still persist*
> *When all afflictions have been wholly burned away.*
>
> *Enlightenment "without remainder" is the absence of*
>   *propensity,*
> *And it is pure of stain like space itself.*
> *The Buddhas have with skill set forth*
> *This twofold aspect of enlightenment.*

And this is how we should understand the matter.

The following question should be addressed. It is said that enlightenment consists in the knowledge that defilements are exhausted and that one will not be reborn.[433] But it is also said that a noble being, an Arya, is identified in terms of the uncompounded. Consequently, with regard to what has been described as the three kinds of enlightenment, what does this knowledge of the exhaustion of defilement, and of no further birth, refer to?

It has been said in this regard: "When all afflictions that bind one to the three worlds are eliminated, one becomes an Arhat. When the phenomena belonging to the truth of origin are recogized as belonging to the truth of cessation,[434] this is the realization of a Pratyekabuddha. And when all afflictions, together with the associated habitual tendencies, are eliminated, this is perfect and unsurpassable enlightenment. This is the Doctrine."

All this is the teaching of Rongdzom Pandita, the protector Nagarjuna, and the venerable Chandrakirti; and others have said the same. The final root of defilement is simply ignorance or confusion. And the subtlest aspect of this is abandoned only in the vajralike concentration occurring at the end of the tenth ground. Suchness, the ultimate reality of all phenomena, can be the object only of a Buddha's primordial wisdom. And there can be only one primordial wisdom that sees the nature of phenomena as it is. It is omniscience. Accordingly, one can thus understand the profound teaching of the Vajrayana that the only difference between Buddhas and sentient beings is in their recognition, or otherwise, of the ultimate nature of things. Consequently, the perception of ultimate reality by Shravakas, Pratyekabuddhas, and Bodhisattvas is progressively pure and devoid of obscurations. The Bodhisattvas are also increasingly sublime according to the difference of the grounds on which they reside,[435] until finally ultimate reality as it is becomes manifest and the qualities of elimination and realization are all perfected in the state of buddhahood. Ultimate reality is realized by primordial wisdom. It should be understood, however, that, owing to a variation in the elimination of defilements that obscure ultimate reality, there is a difference in the purity with which primordial wisdom beholds its object, the dharmadhatu.

This shows that, in the final analysis, there is a single vehicle. All the sutras and shastras repeatedly teach this, and the same point is concisely stated by Chandrakirti:

> To dissipate the veils of ignorance, no other means is there
> than knowing suchness.
> Suchness of phenomena admits no fraction or division.
> The subject, mind, that knows it so is likewise undivided.
> And thus the Buddha taught us with a single, matchless
> vehicle.[436]

Reasoning is the only way to establish that in the end there is only one vehicle. There is no other means.

All those who follow the Mahayana say that the Shravaka Arhats do not attain an enlightenment in which all the qualities of elimination and realization are complete. Final liberation beyond all suffering is buddhahood alone. As it is said in the *Uttaratantra-shastra:*

> Without obtaining buddhahood,
> One cannot gain the state beyond all suffering.
> Likewise, you will never see the sun
> If light and sunbeams are not present.

The Shravakas and Pratyekabuddhas eliminate afflictive emotion. And since this is removed by supreme primordial wisdom on the noble grounds of realization, it will never return and these beings will not take birth in samsara as a result of karma and affliction. Their karmic life has been arrested. And this is not all. A person who has reached the level of "acceptance"[437] is unable to fall into the lower realms, even though the seeds of defilements have not been eliminated. This, once again, is established by reasoning.

When, on the first ground, the noble beings of the Mahayana behold the ultimate truth directly, it is no longer possible for them to entertain any further misconceptions [concerning the self]. And even though the subtle and innate defilements to be dealt with on the path of meditation have not yet been eliminated, it is impossible for them to be helplessly reborn as a result of karma and the afflictions. The image often used to describe this situation is that of a snake that has been cut in two. It cannot rise up and strike. As it is said:

> Those linked with the noble path,
> Who crush the essence of the view of self,
> Reveal that the afflictions, which primordial wisdom shuns
> Upon the path of meditation, are like old and tattered rags.[438]

Consequently, once Bodhisattvas have gained the noble ground of realization, they are no longer obliged to take birth in this impure world on account of karma and affliction. Nevertheless, because of their compassion, they appear in a manner consonant with the ways of the ordinary inhabitants of the world, taking birth in this impure state through one of the four ways in order to help beings. As it has been said:

> Although they have transcended birth,
> These masters of compassion show
> Birth and sickness, age and death.

As for the causes of such rebirth, it may be said that Bodhisattvas dwelling on the seven impure grounds take birth mainly by the power of their skillful means, their compassion and prayers of aspiration. Those who are residing on the three pure grounds display their incarnation and so on by the power of primordial wisdom, which is endowed with mastery over birth.[439]

To the question whether, when Bodhisattvas display their birth for the sake of beings, they experience feelings of physical and mental suffering like ordinary beings, the answer is no, they do not. As it is said in the *Sutralankara*:

> They understand that all things are illusionlike.
> Like strolling in a pleasant park is birth for them.
> And whether there be wealth or poverty,
> They have no fear of sorrow or defilement.

They joyfully deploy their qualities for others' good
And knowingly take birth, displaying miracles:
This is their joy, rejoicing in a place of wealth and
*   entertainment.*
It is the sole preserve of those who have compassion.

These great compassionate ones who labor for the sake of
*   beings,*
Who even when in Torment Unsurpassed abide
*   in joy,*
How could such as these take fright at pain
That comes to them while staying in this world?

But even if one accepts that the defilements to be eliminated on the grounds of realization are as we have described, it may still be asked whether, in the context of primordial wisdom as the antidote, the Arhats among the Shravakas and Pratyekabuddhas achieve the realization of the phenomenal no-self.

The King of Dharma, Longchenpa Drimé Özer, taught:

The learned masters of the past have debated whether the Shravakas and Pratyekabuddhas realize the no-self of phenomena. In our tradition, we find many opinions expressed on this matter— just as even among the Shravaka schools of old there were those that accepted and those that denied the existence of the personal self. Now, there can certainly be no success in the achievement of arhat- ship without the realization of the no-self of the aggregates. Yet, ac- cording to the teaching of the sutras, their realization of the phenomenal no-self is incomplete and of small account, like the hole gnawed by an insect in a mustard seed.

No one else in the Land of Snow has explained this so well.

To continue this matter a little further, when with Madhyamaka rea- soning one delves more deeply into the question of these two selves, one finds that, aside from a mere distinction at the level of the subject or basis of emptiness (whether the phenomenon or the person), there is no differ- ence whatever between them in the manner in which they are empty. Therefore, if the conceived object of innate ego-clinging—the thought "I," imputed on the apprehension of the aggregates—is not eradicated, and only the "permanent self" is refuted, it is impossible to remove the emotional afflictions. This is logically demonstrable. Consequently, when one sees that the mere "I"—that is, a particular instance of phenomenal reality—is empty, this seeing may be designated as the realization of the phenomenal no-self.

Just as when one drinks a mouthful of seawater one may be said to be "drinking the sea," in the same way, the Shravakas and Pratyekabuddhas are said to realize the phenomenal no-self. If the Shravakas and Pratyekabuddhas (who fear emptiness and concentrate on the personal no-self) were to reject emptiness altogether, they would be unable to achieve the result of their own path. It was therefore taught that the three kinds of enlightenment derive from the realization of emptiness. Nevertheless, the Arhats of the Shravaka and Pratyekabuddha vehicles do not completely realize the no-self of all knowable things. One may drink a mouthful of seawater, but the vast ocean is not consumed; similarly, a very modest achievement is described as no achievement.[440] By the same token, it is said that the Shravakas and Pratyekabuddhas do not realize the phenomenal no-self. This is said in all the sutras and shastras. To what actually does the perfect realization of the phenomenal no-self correspond? The Tibetan word *chos* (*dharma* in Sanskrit and here translated as "phenomenon") has ten different meanings.[441] In the present context, the word refers to objects of knowledge, which in turn applies to both things and nonthings, compounded and uncompounded, and so on. To know all these as empty is to know the phenomenal no-self completely. It is said in the *Madhyamakavatara*:

> And when he taught elaborately at length,
> He spoke of sixteen kinds of emptiness.
> When speaking briefly, he expounded four,
> And all of them the Mahayana teaches.[442]

But, it may be asked, if the Shravakas and Pratyekabuddhas recognize the emptiness of one phenomenon, how is it that they fail to recognize the emptiness of all phenomena? This is a poor objection. For although the nature of phenomena is emptiness from the very beginning, the fact that one recognizes one phenomenon to be empty does not automatically mean that one has seen all phenomena in the same way. Since the Shravakas and

Pratyekabuddhas are powerfully concentrated on no more than the personal no-self—the phenomenal no-self being of no great interest to them—and since they are lacking in the necessary conditions (compassion, a teacher, the Bodhisattva activity, and the perfect dedication of their merit), a complete realization of the phenomenal no-self is slow in coming. And likewise for the followers of the scriptures and reasonings of the Mahayana, it is in accordance with the degree of their strength of mind that the latter succeed or fail in establishing the phenomenal no-self in its entirety. In the same way, when they meditate, some are able, and some are unable, to meditate on the state of authentic freedom from conceptual constructs. The statement that when one sees the suchness of one thing, one sees the suchness of all things is true for someone of the highest acumen, who is able to see that all phenomena share an equal nature. It is therefore a question of spiritual insight. Moreover, if it were the case that the recognition of the emptiness of one phenomenon leads automatically to the realization that all phenomena are empty, it would follow that the mind that understands the emptiness of the infinitesimal particle in nonmental objects should come to the conclusion that all phenomena are empty. This being so, the detailed reasoning of the Mahayana would be devoid of meaning. Consequently, if the noble beings of the Mahayana, who strive for the realization that phenomena are without real existence, who have the guidance of a teacher, and who are possessed of great compassion—if even they are unable to gain a direct realization of this truth for the entire duration of a measureless kalpa, there is no need to mention the Shravakas and Pratyekabuddhas, who are without such conditions. If the realization of the emptiness of one phenomenon necessarily involves the realization that all phenomena are empty, all four schools of tenets would automatically become Madhyamaka and then all our problems would be solved! On the other hand, there will indeed come the point when the Arhats among the Shravakas and Pratyekabuddhas *will* realize this view. After a period of ten thousand kalpas, they will be summoned by the power of the Buddhas from the expanse of cessation and they will enter the Mahayana.

When one speaks of the no-self of phenomena, this implies the understanding that *all* phenomena are without inherent existence. By contrast, the understanding that only certain phenomena are without self does not imply a complete realization of the phenomenal no-self. Consequently, since both things and nonthings—the real and the imaginary—are all phenomena in the sense of being fitting objects of the mind, it follows that in realizing that they are all without inherent existence, one gains a complete realization of the sixteen kinds of emptiness. The subject that perfectly realizes the sixteen kinds of emptiness is the primordial wisdom of meditative equipoise, which is found in noble beings and is free from all conceptual extremes. Its object is referred to as the phenomenal no-self. This is an emptiness that utterly transcends both things and nonthings; it is freedom from conceptual constructs, the equality of all phenomena. Now, this emptiness is not simply an exclusion: a mere emptiness that is the object of the negating thought (a thought that, by negating the true existence of something, makes an object-universal of the "not truly existent thing," without being able to go beyond it). Consequently, although the Shravakas do indeed realize the emptiness of the personal self, if a comparison is drawn between their limited knowledge and the primordial wisdom of meditative equipoise, which is a feature of the Mahayana and is free from all extremes, the difference between them is said to be like the water contained in a cow's footprint and that which is contained in the ocean itself, or like the cavity gnawed by an insect inside a mustard seed as compared with the immensity of space. And since there is a difference in the primordial wisdom,[443] there is likewise a difference in the paths, which accordingly are high or low. For if there is no difference in realization, there can be no difference in the defilements to be discarded. If, moreover, the realization and the defilements are not concomitant with each other in terms of their interaction, it is impossible to establish validly the incompatibility between the defilements to be discarded and the wisdom that is their antidote. As a result, it is impossible for correct reasoning to establish the different paths and their results. And since this actually entails a denial of what is the case, it is not to be accepted. For it is illogical to say that defilements still remain to be discarded and then to say that no-self has been realized (thereby implying that the defilements are no longer present) or to say that there are no defilements and then to say that no-self has not been realized (thereby suggesting that the defilements are still there). It is as absurd as saying that the sun rises still shrouded in darkness or that when the sun is shining, objects remain invisible. Such things are unfitting for those who claim to speak rationally.

It may be wondered why Chandrakirti gives us to understand from the statement in the sutras to the effect that the Bodhisattvas on the first ground do not surpass the Shravakas and Pratyekabuddhas by their wisdom that the latter have realized emptiness.

If the Shravakas and Pratyekabuddhas do not realize that things[444] are
simply a conditioned appearance, it follows that, like the non-Buddhists,
they are unable even to become Aryas. And in that case, it would be reasonable to say that they are surpassed. On the other hand, the noble Bodhisattvas below the sixth ground, who have realized the emptiness of the self,
are not different from the Shravakas and Pratyekabuddhas, in that it is only
with concentrated effort that they enter the expanse in which all movement
of the mind and mental factors is arrested. It is on the seventh ground alone
that the Bodhisattvas enter perfect cessation without the slightest effort.
And it is said that, at that point, they surpass the Arhats also by their wisdom.
Rendawa and others explain that "to surpass in wisdom" marks the criterion
between the capacity or otherwise for entering and arising from the expanse
of cessation in an instant. On the other hand, the learned Gorampa Sonam
Senge and others have used reasoning to demonstrate the untenability of
this position, saying that "to surpass in wisdom" refers to the fact that on the
seventh ground, the mind no longer apprehends the conceptual characteristics of things. For my part, I think that the truth is to be found in the *Lankavatara-sutra:* "Mahamati! On the sixth ground, the Bodhisattva Mahasattvas
enter the absorption of cessation in the manner of the Shravakas and
Pratyekabuddhas. On the seventh ground, however, the Bodhisattva Mahasattvas at every instant enter the absorption in which there is no apprehension of phenomenal characteristics. This is not so for the Shravakas and
Pratyekabuddhas. For when the Shravakas and Pratyekabuddhas enter the
absorption of cessation, they do so with an effort proper to their dualistic
apprehension." When I came upon this explanation given by the Buddha
himself, I was released from every doubt. It is said, however, in this context
that all Arhat Shravakas and Pratyekabuddhas enter cessation, whereas the
Bodhisattvas do so from the sixth ground onward. This is just a brief exposition of a subject that in fact requires a great deal of explanation.

In short, the no-self of the person is included in the wider category of
the no-self of phenomena. But although the person is but a part of phenomena, nevertheless it is clinging to the personal self that constitutes the
principal cause of samsaric birth. If this clinging is halted, birth in samsara
due to karma and the afflictions ceases. And as to the path that brings this
about, it is precisely the realization of the emptiness of the personal self.
How then is this to be effected? The mere "I" is an imputation based on
the apprehension of the aggregates, or on the aggregates of an observed
object.[445] This object of innate ego-clinging is thus dependently imputed

or dependently arisen. It is, in other words, no more than a conditioned appearance. On its own, it has no existence whatever. When this is understood, ego-clinging is brought to a standstill, just as when one sees that there is no snake but only a rope. The multiplicity of the infinitesimal particles and instants of consciousness directly counteracts all clinging to a self, the conceived object of one's innate apprehension and clinging. It is by the recognition of, and the habituation to, the fact that there is no self in the particles or instants of consciousness that ego-clinging is uprooted, thanks to which affliction ends. Having seen that this alone is sufficient to release them from samsara, the practitioners of the Hinayana take no further interest in, and thus do not meditate upon, the phenomenal no-self, and therefore they fail to realize it. Consequently, they do not remove their cognitive obscurations. One imputes the "I" and clings to it for as long as one fails to analyze and dismantle the continuum and gathering of one's aggregates. As long as this is not done, there is no way to realize the personal no-self, for it is precisely the observation of, and reference to, the aggregates that gives rise to the imputation of a self. The *Ratnavali* furnishes arguments to show that since the aggregates are but the grouping together of many factors, they have no final existence even for the Shravakas. As it is said in a sutra that was taught to the Shravakas, "Forms are like bursting bubbles." In accordance with this and other statements, the understanding that the aggregates are themselves mere ascriptions imputed to the gathering of many elements corresponds to the complete realization of the personal no-self.

Referring to the verse in the *Madhyamakavatara*,[446] "The twofold view, the no-self of phenomena and persons was set forth to lead all wanderers to freedom," Chandrakirti remarks in the autocommentary:

The personal no-self was set forth in order to bring beings to liberation. The two kinds of no-self were taught so that Bodhisattvas might attain omniscience. The Shravakas and Pratyekabuddhas do indeed realize the mere conditioned appearance of interdependent phenomena. They do not, however, meditate on the phenomenal no-self in its entirety. They have the means only of discarding the emotional afflictions occurring in the three worlds. They are said to meditate on the personal no-self in its entirety.

On the basis of this text, therefore, we may be sure that the Shravakas and the Pratyekabuddhas do not have a complete realization of the phenomenal no-self. And since, when this is lacking, it is impossible to discard the afflictions in their entirety, how can the Shravakas (who do not meditate on the phenomenal no-self) be in a position to do so? For the realization of no-self and the discarding of afflictions are of a piece. The reasoning that pertains to the manner in which afflictions are eliminated through the elimination of the personal no-self is indeed very far-reaching, as is evident from the *Pramanavarttika* and Nagarjuna's texts on reasoning. The sevenfold chariot reasoning and similar arguments establish that the Shravakas realize the no-self of the person but do not have a complete realization of the no-self of phenomena. The same kinds of argument show also that a clear perception of this is to be acquired through training.

If the causes (the boundless accumulations and so forth) of extraordinary methods are not complete, it is certain that extraordinary realizations cannot occur. On the other hand, it should be understood that when the causes are complete, realization of the primordial wisdom of the first ground and so on will dawn. On its appearance, the corresponding share of defilement will cease to be. And when defilements are no more, the associated qualities will be complete. For indeed it is definite that these three factors (realization, elimination of defilement, and spiritual qualities) always occur together. Were it otherwise, all manner of permutations would be possible, and one could say, for instance, that all defilements are discarded but not all qualities are realized. But this is contrary to reason. It is thus refuted and cannot be correctly asserted in such a manner.

In short, the assertion that the Shravakas and Pratyekabuddhas enjoy a complete realization of the phenomenal no-self is difficult to defend, given what the Buddha himself said, as recorded in the scriptures and their commentaries, together with a host of logical arguments. In view of the fact that the disparity between the qualities of the Hinayana and Mahayana paths (of seeing and so on) and their results is as great as the difference between a firefly and the light of the sun, it should be understood that the same divergence exists also on the level of the realization of primordial wisdom, which is based on such paths. For intelligent people, it is enough simply to review these crucial points of reasoning concerning the manner in which defilements are removed. On the other hand, it is difficult for reason to correct the errors of those who cling to their position out of prejudice.

Generally speaking, these arguments, which concern progress on the paths of the three vehicles, are of great importance. And they are highly disturbing for people committed to maintaining that the two great systems of thought (of Nagarjuna and of Asanga) are at variance. In truth, however, there is no contradiction on any point (whether of the relative or ultimate level) between the views of the great charioteers. They are like the three sweet substances that may be added to rice. All are comfortably digested together. For one who has both learning and reflection, it is the greatest gain to rest contented and at ease just where one is, neither eager for the opportunity to put other people right nor yearning for what is explained elsewhere. As the saying goes, "One rests content though others be not so."

Ah, followers of abbot Shantarakshita, master Padmasambhava, and Trisongdetsen the pious king, who rejoice in the ancient translations of the Buddha's spotless words and the writings of the six ornaments of India and their disciples! To study and reflect on these is indeed enough; why should you take pleasure in repeating the opinions of others? Keep always to the light of the teacher, the yidam deity, and the sacred scriptures!

5. The benefits of holding that the relative corresponds to what appears as causally effective

84
Since entities of cause and fruit
Within the relative are not denied,
All the principles of both samsara and nirvana
Are posited without confusion.

People who hold to the true existence of things say that if phenomena were without inherent existence, it would be impossible to define the various objects of knowledge clearly, such as samsara and nirvana, virtue and nonvirtue, karmic cause and effect, the forward or reverse order of dependent arising, things to be evaluated and the reasoning that evaluates them, or productive causes and produced effects such as the states of consciousness in possession of evidence and the evidence from which they arise. The present stanza dispels all such wrong-headed thoughts and censures, and shows that the principle of cause and effect is tenable. The unceasing appearances of causally efficient productive causes and their produced effects do indeed exist on the merely relative level and they are

not denied. They are assessed and posited according to conventional reasoning. Consequently, the specific characteristics of the principles regarding the presence or absence of concomitant causes and effects with respect
to both samsara and nirvana pose no problems. And though it is said that
phenomena are without inherent existence, definitions concerning them
on the relative level are posited without confusion. The proponents of
true existence may object that if (notwithstanding) we are able to discuss
the defining characteristics of phenomena without invalidating them, it
follows that our assertions are in fact no different from theirs. But since
they believe that phenomena exist ultimately, just as they appear, it is incumbent upon them to prove that within the range of things, from the infinitesimal particle up to consciousness, either there is one truly existent
entity or there are many such entities. They must be able to supply answers to all that we have said above. If they succeed in establishing—by
means of rational argument—their truly existent entity, we shall give them
our assent and affirm with them that such entities are true and undeceiving even on the ultimate level. If the reverse is true, they ought to follow
the arguments set forth and say that though things appear, they are not
truly existent. It is incumbent upon them to accept our position. Otherwise, they cannot claim that we are speaking about the same things. If one
is genuinely convinced of the empty nature of phenomena, an irreversible
certainty in the principle of cause and effect will be gained. If, on the other
hand, one considers the principle of cause and effect to be untenable, this
is incompatible with the path of emptiness as explained in the Madhyamaka. It should be recognized that this is the path of nihilism masquerad-
ing as the view of emptiness and should be completely rejected. As the
master Nagarjuna has said:

> Engaging only in an academic study
> Without true recognition of this emptiness,
> Inferior beings fail to gather merit
> And they come to grief.

> The Buddhas say that actions are productive
>   of results,
> That beings wander in samsara.
> But, understanding perfectly the nature of
>   these things,
> They have described them as "unborn."

And yet, in harmony with worldly speech,
They speak of "I" and "mine" and likewise of
The aggregates, the sense-fields, and the elements,
Teaching thus according to their wisdom's skill.

Nagarjuna spoke at length of the extreme profundity of the doctrine of emptiness, which is difficult to understand. And he warned that if those of little wisdom mistake its meaning, they will come to destruction.

5. The benefits of habituation to the union of the relative and the ultimate
6. A brief explanation of how pure accumulations will occur

85
Since phenomena of cause and fruit
Are in this manner posited,
The pure accumulations also
Are acceptable within this scriptural tradition.

Since, within this text and scriptural tradition, the phenomena of cause and effect are said to be without inherent existence, it follows that the perfect path of the accumulation of merit such as generosity, joined with the accumulation of primordial wisdom unstained by any trace of ignorance, is tenable. But it is not tenable (that is, it cannot be rationally sustained) by those who believe that phenomena exist truly.

When one understands that although ultimately phenomena have no inherent existence, they nevertheless occur undeniably as dependently arising appearances on the relative level, one's training on the path becomes correct and is not marred by states of mind that are at variance with the ultimate nature of things.

People who believe in true existence say:

All acts of giving thus performed
As offerings or assistance to another
Will give rise to clear and joyful states of mind.
When nothing is observed, this is not so.

And is this nonobserving due to nonexistence of the field of
  generosity?

Or is it that the given thing does not exist?
But if they are unreal, all merits are reduced to naught,
And every hardship suffered will be meaningless.

But since the triple sphere the Buddha has himself perceived,
It cannot be that acts are objectless.
And there is also knowledge
Of one's mind and mental functions.

Thus, as it is said, when acts of generosity are performed out of the wish to do good to others or else as an offering, a clear and joyful state of mind is produced to the extent that one perceives the field of one's giving, the one to whom one gives. If, on the other hand, no field is observed, this is not the case. If it is not observed, through being nonexistent, it is pointless for Bodhisattvas to endure hardships for the sake of other beings. For there are no beings. But, so the objection continues, it is not the case that objects are nonexistent. For the Tathagata himself perceived the three spheres of donor, donation, and receiver. And how could the objects be nonexistent when the child offered, the donors, and the receiver were all aware of their own minds and mental factors?[447]

But objections of this kind are completely groundless. We do not deny cause and effect dependently produced on the relative level. We do not negate their existence. And it is on the *relative* level that the Tathagata perceives the giver, gift, and receiver and that one speaks of awareness of minds and mental contents. But on the ultimate level, since there is neither one nor are there many truly existent entities, where ultimately are the giver, gift, and receiver?

6. A detailed explanation
7. A general example showing that in the event of a cause, an effect will follow, whereas there will be no effect when there is no cause

86
When a cause is pure,
Pure is the result that comes from it.
And modes of discipline are pure
That issue from a proper view.

87
Likewise from an impure cause
Impure results will also spring—
Just as it is that from false views
Sexual misdemeanors and the rest arise.

Every effect derives from and is in accordance with its cause—or else it does not arise, its cause being absent. Therefore, the effects of causes that are pure or impure will be pure or impure accordingly. A perfectly pure cause will give rise to a perfectly pure effect. For example, the correct worldly view, namely, that good and evil actions will have corresponding karmic consequences, will give rise to correct ethical practice (the avoidance of killing, for example) and likewise to carefulness in this regard (which is a mode or aspect of such ethics). And all such results (in this case, modes of discipline) are pure because they are the results of a pure view that is their cause. The reverse is also true. An impure cause will give rise to an impure effect. For example, the wrong view that denies the reality of karmic cause and effect will result in sexual misdeeds and other nonvirtues.

7. A specific explanation of the principle of cause and effect within the context of pure and impure views

88
Since real existence is disproved by valid reasoning,
To think that things exist in truth
Is to have false understanding—
As when one trusts to things seen in a mirage.

89
And therefore on account of this,
All practice of transcendent virtues—
Like every action that arises from belief
In "I" and "mine"—will have but little strength.

90
But from the view that things have no such real
existence
Great results proliferate.

For they arise from fertile causes,
Like the shoots that spring from healthy seeds.

Having generally demonstrated in the above how an effect is pure or impure in dependence upon its cause, the text moves on to show how generosity and the rest, when performed with reference to things considered to exist truly, does not result in a perfect accumulation of merit, whereas the paramitas performed in the absence of such a belief result in a merit that is perfectly pure. How is it that merit is not pure when phenomena are considered to be truly existent? When this question is examined in the light of correct reasoning, it is found that, because they are disproved by valid cognition, phenomena are without true existence. Those who believe that phenomena exist inherently when this is not the case are hampered by misconceptions. They mistake the nature of things, just like people who take for real the water that they see in a mirage, or think that there is a circle of fire in the air when all they see in fact is a whirling firebrand. Since the apprehension of the true existence of things constitutes a mistaken cognition, it follows that the practice of generosity and the other paramitas based thereon is impaired by a mistaken thought process, owing to which the true nature of things is obscured. For example, non-Buddhists abide in the view of the transitory composite and incorrectly assume the existence of "I" and "mine." On this basis, they practice various forms of asceticism that are out of tune with the right path to perfect enlightenment. Similarly, the Buddhist path, when practiced while one still clings to the true existence of phenomena as a result of a mistaken understanding, is of little strength. By contrast, the practice of the paramitas such as generosity, arising from the view that phenomena are without true existence, will ultimately result in buddhahood. For this arises from causes that are pure and fertile and that develop into mature fruit, because they are accompanied by primordial wisdom, which is unmistaken with regard to the nature of things. It is just as with a perfect, healthy seed, which will produce both shoot and ear.

It is possible that virtue performed while one strives for perfect enlightenment (but when there is still a clinging to the self) can become a cause for omniscience. But this can only be in a roundabout way and is not directly so. As long as one is not truly free from the notion of the self, the genuine path to liberation cannot occur. And the decisive factor that prevents its arising is the fact that the mind is contaminated with a false view. Shantarakshita says in the autocommentary: "When it is said that such virtues are not in an immediate sense the factors that bring about perfect enlightenment, the expression 'not in an immediate sense' indicates that something else is necessary. Therefore, the practice of giving—whether as offering or in order to help someone—when performed within the purity of the three spheres is a cause of rejoicing for the wise. For it is a virtuous act performed without ignorance, an act in which one knows the nature of things and correctly engages in it."

Furthermore, in the *Dharmasangiti-sutra* it is said: "O Bhagavan, when all phenomena are not seen, one sees them perfectly." And in the *Vajracchedika-sutra*, we find the following exchange. "'What do you think, Subhuti?' the Buddha said. 'Is it easy to measure the space in the eastern direction?' Subhuti replied, 'Lord, it is not easy. . . .' 'Likewise, O Subhuti, it is not easy to measure the stock of merit created by the generosity practiced by a Bodhisattva who does not dwell, who really does not dwell (in the view of real existence).'"

And in the same sutra it is also said: "'So it is, Subhuti. A Bodhisattva who practices generosity while falling into the view of the true existence of things is like a man with healthy eyes who has come into a dark place and can see nothing. So it is, Subhuti. A Bodhisattva who practices generosity without falling into the view that things exist truly is like a well-sighted man, who sees different forms at the rising of the sun at dawn.'"

3. The conclusion: a eulogy of this approach to the two truths
4. An outline of the tradition in which the Chittamatra and Madhyamaka approaches are combined
5. An outline of the abiding mode of the conventional truth

> 91
> All causes and effects
> Are consciousness alone.
> And all that this establishes
> Abides in consciousness.

The question may be asked whether phenomena, which are causes and effects arising interdependently, are the mind and its mental factors alone or whether they are entities external to the mind. The master Bhavaviveka, among others, believed that they are outer entities. He said that the statements in the sutra about everything being the mind alone were intended simply to refute the notions of a divine creator or the "experiencer" (that is, purusha). The *Madhyamakalankara*, on the other hand, declares that anything that is a cause or an effect is but consciousness alone, and apart from this, there are no external objects existing separately. And whatever is established through the clear experience of this same consciousness itself abides as consciousness.[448] The situation cannot be otherwise. Indeed, whatever appears and is cognized is none other than an experience of (or rather by) consciousness. And in the absence of such a clear experience by the self-illuminating mind, it would never be possible for other (nonmental) things to be known. If it were possible, this would necessarily mean that things are perceived in the absence of clarity and cognition; but without clarity and cognition, there is no consciousness. This being so, if there is no consciousness there can be no appearance of things. Thus whatever is experienced is established as consciousness itself; it is like a form seen in a dream, or a hallucination and so forth. Even if one believes that such a form exists as an outer object separate from consciousness, this same object cannot be established by perception, since there is no link connecting object and consciousness—whether they are simultaneous or not[449] (as in the case of visual consciousness and a form and so on). Therefore, the experience of the color blue is an experience of something that is not different from consciousness; it is like the experience of a form seen in a dream.

It may be objected that, even granted that the experience of a mental aspect is necessarily consciousness, it can be inferred nevertheless that there must be an extramental object that is casting its aspect on the mind. But because the subtle particles and so on do not exist (even though they have been inferred), this is untenable. Even in those systems where the particle is considered to exist, the latter is not established by perception. It is hidden and that it exists is no more than an inference. Now, the fact that the nonexistent outer object is (only) inferred, whereas one *experiences* things clearly (in the mind) lends considerable force to the argument that phenomena are merely established by the mind itself. Indeed, this position cannot be invalidated by any other view. Such a conclusion is in harmony with the *Ghanavyuha, Sandhinirmochana, Lankavatara,* and other sutras. Thus, when analyzing experience in the postmeditation state, Madhyamikas either assert the existence of external objects on the conventional level or not. There is no third alternative.

5. An outline of the path that combines the two approaches

92
On the basis of the Mind Alone,
We should know that outer things do not exist.
On the basis of the method set forth here,
We should know that mind is utterly devoid of self.

On the basis of the knowledge that all appearing objects are but consciousness and do not exist as outer objects, one should understand that extramental objects have no real existence. Subsequently, on the basis of the
method set forth here, namely, the argument of neither one nor many, one
should understand in the Madhyamaka way that the mind also is utterly devoid of self and lies beyond all ontological extremes and conceptual constructs. As it is said in the *'jig rten las 'das pa'i le'u:* "Ah! The offspring of the
Conqueror have realized that the three worlds are the mind alone! They
have realized also that the three times are but the mind. And they have profoundly understood that the mind is without center or extremity." This text
explains the sense of the present stanza very clearly. Knowing that whatever
appears on all sides and at all times is the mind, and knowing that this mind
is beyond the extremes of arising and ceasing, as well as the intervening position defined as remaining in the present, the offspring of the Conqueror
understand that it is beyond all extremes. In the *Dharmasangiti-sutra* it is
said: "Lord, all phenomena are essentially reifications. Since they are but
the mind alone, they are insubstantial; they are rootless, like illusions."
Likewise the *Prajnaparamita-sutra* says:

> This mind therefore indeed is not a "mind";
> The nature of this mind is lucent clarity.

4. In praise of this path
5. A brief presentation

93
Those who ride the chariot of the two approaches,
Who grasp the reins of reasoned thought,
Will thus be adepts of the Mahayana
According to the sense and meaning of the word.

Those who ride the great chariot along the path that unites the two approaches, that is, the Chittamatra approach with regard to the conventional level and the Madhyamaka approach with regard to the ultimate level, have in their hands, without letting them go, the reins of reasoning and stainless wisdom, the valid reasoning that investigates the two truths. By adhering to this excellent system of thought, they acquire the title of adepts of the Mahayana according to the sense and meaning of the word. The great vehicle of the Buddha has two aspects: the profound and the vast. Similarly, the scriptures that set it forth are of two kinds: on the one hand, the words of the Buddha that expound the Madhyamaka teachings, and on the other hand, the Chittamatra teachings. Moreover, the traditions of the great charioteers Nagarjuna and Asanga, who comment upon the meaning of these two kinds of teaching, are immaculately pure. Their paths moreover are not biased in the sense of emphasizing only their respective point of view. They simply elucidate the profound and vast aspects of the Buddha's teaching. Their views complement each other. All the final teachings bestowed by the Buddha concerning the postulates of the relative truth (all phenomena encompassed by samsara and nirvana) depend on an understanding of the Chittamatra teaching. But the definitive conclusion with regard to the entire range of phenomena (from form up to omniscience) as being beyond conceptual construction is set forth by the Madhyamaka tradition. It is by means of the approach thus set forth here that one enters into the Mahayana, where the profound and vast aspects are undivided. This merging of the two approaches, whereby spacelike profundity and oceanlike vastness are not sundered, was rare even in India, let alone Tibet. For it was in India, at a time when the systems of the great charioteers Nagarjuna and Asanga were kept separate, that the master Shantarakshita united the two approaches into a single scriptural tradition greater than any other—for indeed the profound and vast aspects are equally indispensable to the Mahayana. Therefore, to uphold this perfect exposition of the two approaches is like riding in an excellent chariot. How so? Generally speaking, a vehicle is a conveyance wherein one attains a desired objective. The Mahayana has been described (in the *Sutralankara*):

> *This spacelike vehicle is like a vast pavilion;*
> *This supreme vehicle will bring one to achievement of true joy*
>   *and perfect bliss.*
> *All beings who embark on it will pass beyond all sorrow.*

As the teachings say, the Mahayana is profound like space (referring to the twenty kinds of emptiness); and it is vast like an immense pavilion (referring to its beauty). To embark therefore on this vehicle of the *Madhyamakalankara* is the best of all things. Since it befits beings of great scope, since it is not arduous and is possessed of extraordinary advantages, it is like traveling in a carriage. Since it surpasses every partial and one-sided position, it is appropriate for those who have a great mental aptitude for both the profound and the vast aspects of the teachings. Since it unites the two truths, it presents no difficulties for the accomplishing of buddhahood. And since it is endowed with infinite facets of valid reasoning, both on the conventional and ultimate levels, it is replete with riches. For all these reasons, this teaching is like a chariot.[450]

Even when one adheres to this scriptural tradition, however, it is essential to experience its meaning for oneself by means of valid reasoning. As Shantarakshita says in the autocommentary: "A scriptural teaching unsupported by valid reasoning based on evidence, that is accepted only on faith, is never wholly satisfactory." There is no need to mention those who are not even drawn by faith to this scripture—even those who adopt it out of devotion rather than through reasoning will not be fully satisfied because they lack the certainty that comes from a personal experience of its meaning. And in that case, the situation is like that of a man who is attached to certain kinds of food or precious objects but is unable to use and enjoy them. And just as one controls the horse that is pulling the chariot by means of the reins, if one holds the right and left reins of conventional and ultimate reasoning, one will be able to pursue the path with a conviction deriving from reasoning grounded in the evidence of things. It will be a path from which it is impossible to deviate. If one enters the profound and vast doctrines with a certainty deriving from the two kinds of valid knowledge, one will, with truth, be called a practitioner or adept of the Mahayana. For the Mahayana is indeed twofold; it is profound and vast. Those who not only have faith in it but are endowed with a conviction resulting from the two kinds of valid knowledge indeed possess, so to speak, the Mahayana and are therefore to be called Mahayana practitioners. If one remains attached to an incorrect system of thought, or if one argues against the correct (Buddhist) tradition, this means that one has failed to appreciate fully the Buddha's doctrine. Consequently, wise Bodhisattvas, who enter the teachings by virtue of their stainless reasoning based on the evidence of things, should examine these same teachings with integrity, in accordance with how they are set forth.

As it is said in the *Madhyamakavatara:*

The arguments contained within our treatises were not
   contrived through love of disputation.
They set forth suchness only for the sake of freedom.
They are not to be blamed if, while expounding emptiness,
They show the falseness of discordant doctrines.[451]

And it is thus that the Dharma is best protected and upheld.

5. A detailed explanation of the praise of the path, which unites the two approaches
6. The extraordinary qualities of the path

> 94
> Vishnu, Ishvara, and others do not taste
> The cause of the abiding in the measureless.
> And also those who are the crowns of all
>   the world
> Are thoroughly without a taste of it.

> 95
> This perfect state, this pure ambrosia,
> Alone enjoyed by Buddhas, those Thus Gone,
> Who are themselves results of pure compassion,
> None but they can taste of it.

The path of these two approaches is not common to other traditions. Even those who are mighty in the world, who are equipped with the clearest intellects, Vishnu, Ishvara, Brahma, Kapila, and others have not even a partial experience of it. Furthermore, even the noble Arhats and Pratyekabuddhas, who have attained the transmundane path and who are worthy of the veneration of all beings, have no experience of the path described here, which is the source of immeasurable spiritual qualities. This ultimate mode of being, divested of all error, the utterly pure ambrosia of the two truths, is enjoyed by the Tathagatas alone, who are themselves the product of great loving compassion for all beings and of a complete purification of the two obscuring veils. It may be thought that since Brahma (or Namdor), Vishnu (or Basudevaputra), and Virupaksha (or Shiva) and others also teach these two ways, there is a similarity of teaching. But this is not so, for the latter set forth a lesser kind of emptiness. Thus in the text *bdud rtsi'i thigs pa bsang ba,* Brahma speaks in terms of consciousness alone:

> *Consciousness alone is ever pure.*
> *It is a constant freedom, the awakened state.*[452]
> *"Naught to gain and nothing to reject"—be sure of this.*
> *Remain in Brahma beyond all sorrow.*

The meaning of this is that the goal to be attained is Brahma, a state beyond suffering, which has the nature of pure consciousness or freedom. As for the path, this too is the ever-pure consciousness alone, the awakened state, which is free from the sleep of ignorance (unconsciousness), from the fetters of craving, and so on. And this refers to the ultimate truth, because ignorance and attachment are adventitious. It is therefore said that aside from this there is nothing to accept and nothing to reject. This should be understood and meditated upon.

Furthermore, Kapila writes in the same vein that the supreme nature of the gunas cannot be seen. What is seen is completely hollow like an illusion. The meaning of this is that prakriti, which is the three gunas (sattva, rajas, and tamas) in equilibrium, is not something detectable by the visual and other senses. This nature, or prakriti, is absolutely real, whereas everything that is manifest, form and so forth, and which presents itself to the sight is false and illusory. Moreover, it is said that only purusha, the pure, conscious self, is the final goal.

The Vedantins believe that all phenomena, outer and inner, are the expression of consciousness, which is one and permanent. It is said in their writings:

> *When a vase or other vessel breaks,*
> *The space that is contained therein*
> *Melts into the space outside. 'Tis thus*
> *That everything dissolves in Life, the Self.*

> *We speak indeed of forms and their results.*
> *As this and that they are distinguished,*
> *But space itself has no distinctions.*
> *Thus there are no differences in Life.*

"Forms" here means "outer forms" and so on, and the individual body, which results therefrom. The entire range of outer and inner appearances is of necessity encompassed by space. And just as they are contained undifferentiatedly by space, so too are they encompassed by the life principle, or the great self. The Vedantins say that all appearances, both pure and impure, are without existence. They are illusions like the visions of a dream or as when one mistakes a rope for a snake.

> *When the self is truly known,*
> *Then all thought has disappeared,*
> *And the mind has ceased to be.*
> *Nothing is perceived, and thus there's no perceiver.*

> *Those who understand this "end of all the Vedas,"*
> *For them, just like the visions of a dream*
> *And cities of gandharvas*
> *Does the world appear.*

> *There is no ending; there is no beginning.*
> *There is no bondage; there is no achievement—*
> *There is no liberation, and no wish for it.*
> *This indeed is absolute reality.*

> *Free from craving, free from fear and hate,*
> *Those who gain the Vedas' final reach*
> *Behold the utter ending of all thoughts,*
> *The nondual stilling of conceptuality.*

But, to put the matter briefly, all these adepts fail to transcend the proposition of a permanent, conscious atman or self, the inadmissibility of which has been demonstrated above. It is only in the teachings of the Sugata, free as they are from any stain of conceptuality, that the notions of the illusory nature of phenomena and the absence of thought are tenable and fitting. When, on the other hand, the Vedanta and other systems adopt such ideas, they refute in effect their own tenets.

The "Middle Way" as set forth by Vishnu is described in the *zhag lnga:*

> *All names it utterly transcends;*
> *Of "thing" and "nonthing" it is free,*

And free indeed from all arising and cessation,
Referred to then as Basudevaputra.

Things are destitute of "thingness."
Nonthings also have no "thingness."
This absence of both "thing" and "nonthing"—
Those who know this understand the Veda.

Thus the absolute self utterly transcends all names and designations—Veda, Brahma, Basudevaputra. It is beyond such things as form, and nonthings such as the absence of form. Being beyond both origin and cessation, it is permanent. Apart from this very nature, which completely goes beyond the conventional level, things like forms are without "thingness"; they are illusory. And since things have no existence, the same is true of nonthings, which depend on things for their definition. To realize the absolute self, or atman, which is beyond both thing and nonthing, is to know the Vedas or Brahma.

The Middle Way, as taught by Virupaksha in the text *zhi ba'i mdzes pa sbyar ba'i gzhung pha dang bu'i sbyar ba,* declares:

Brahma is, my own dear son, supremely true,
Unbounded lord of knowledge.
And yet, to say that he alone exists
Is indeed described as bondage.

Addressing his disciple, whom he refers to as his own dear son, Virupaksha declares that Brahma is the only reality; everything else is false. He is the lord of knowledge, unlimited and all-pervading. This indeed is how he is said to be, and yet to believe and say that only he exists is a limitation and a fetter. To the extent that one does so, one is bound as by a rope. Freedom from extremes is also expounded in the above systems, and yet, in the final analysis, there is still a reliance on Brahma or some other mental target or reference point. This being so, how can this be the Middle Way? All possible claims that it is so have been refuted already in great detail.

The teaching of the Great Perfection is an extremely profound—indeed the ultimate—teaching. Consequently, it is difficult to realize. If one fails to rid oneself of all misunderstanding concerning ultimate reality—by receiving and reflecting on the teachings—and if one tries to meditate without the crucial and profound instructions, one's senseless meditation will be quite close to that of the systems just described. If one lacks certainty concerning primordial purity but cogitates again and again about a "ground nature that is neither existent nor nonexistent," one will get nowhere. For if one attributes an independent reality to this "ground empty of existence and nonexistence," then, whatever one may call it—the inconceivable self, Brahma, Vishnu, Ishvara, Primordial Wisdom, or whatever else—the difference will be only nominal; the meaning will be the same. But ultimate reality beyond the four conceptual extremes, the perfectly luminous Great Perfection, which is realized by self-cognizing primordial wisdom, is not at all like this. It is therefore important to rely on the authentic path and teacher. One may *say* that "phenomena are like an illusion" or talk about "the absence of true existence" and "freedom from conceptual constructs." But if one lacks the decisive certainty arising from reasoning, concerning the teaching on emptiness as set forth by the Tathagata (superior as this is to the limited emptiness spoken of in certain non-Buddhist systems), all such talk will be to no avail. But if one does have understanding, one will see that what the Buddha taught was not even remotely experienced by teachers such as Vishnu. Their Mind Only and Middle Way teachings are mere words. Thus it is that although Buddhist and non-Buddhist may seem the same as far as formulas are concerned, on the level of the profound key points of understanding, they are as different as the earth is from the sky. When Atisha visited Tibet, he said that in the India of his day, it was hard to distinguish Buddhist from non-Buddhist teachings. The same predicament has occurred in Tibet between Buddhism and Bön.

The above discussion is a brief summary of passages to be found in Kamalashila's *Commentary on Difficult Points,* which deals with various verses found in the autocommentary, and which Shantarakshita had taken from non-Buddhist treatises in order to expatiate upon the line in the root verse "Vishnu, Ishvara, and others do not taste."

As for the line "The cause of the abiding in the measureless," this refers to immeasurability in the conventional sense. How is it measureless? Even a single ray of light emanating from the Tathagatas or just one of their pores cannot be measured in terms of direction and time; it extends as far as the dharmadhatu extends. And the cause for the abiding in such a measureless reality is the abiding in, or possession of, the Middle Way, which is the union of the two truths and is in harmony with the dharmadhatu. This is similar to the statement concerning a single measureless aspect (such as time), namely, that the cause for the Tathagata's remaining for an immeasurable duration—as long as samsara lasts—is the prajnaparamita, in other words, the understanding of the equality of samsara and nirvana. In his previous existences, the Lord, the Protector, drank the elixir of immortality—perfect emptiness, which is pure like the beams of the moon and encompasses the two kinds of no-self. Consequently, his body, which is composed of the infinitesimal particles of the wisdom of emptiness and of compassion and is free from the two kinds of obscuration, will remain, supreme among all beings, for as long as samsara lasts. As it is said (in the *Abhisamayalankara*):

> *Supreme among all living beings is this mind,*
> *So too the qualities of realization and elimination.*
> *And as the self-arisen fruit*
> *Should these three great things be known.*

The ground of the propensity for ignorance, which is the most subtle of the propensities of defilement, together with karma, the aggregates, and suffering, are altogether brought to complete exhaustion. Similarly, all pure actions, the mental body, and the inconceivable passing away and transference[453] have likewise been arrested, whereupon the wisdom body, equal in all spatial dimensions and times, and beyond all extremes of arising and cessation, of permanence and impermanence, existence and nonexistence, stands revealed. This is the accomplishment of Buddhas alone.

Why is the authentic path referred to as ambrosia? It is so called because it confers a state of deathlessness forever. And since it is an elixir unspoiled by any turbid admixture, it is said to be pure. It might be thought that the sense is rendered more difficult by the positioning of the line "The cause of the abiding in the measureless" before the line "This perfect state, this pure ambrosia." But the great translators and panditas of the past were beings who took birth intentionally, and they possessed the eye of wisdom. And since there is a certain power deriving even from the mere disposition of the root verses, they translated the text thus. From the point of view of time, the Buddha remains in samsara for as long as it lasts, whereas the Shravakas and Pratyekabuddhas cannot do so. The reason for this inability is that the Shravakas and Pratyekabuddhas do not possess the wisdom that realizes the equal nature of samsara and nirvana. They therefore draw back from samsara and rejoice in the peace of nirvana. Moreover, all those who lack the capacity to acquire completely the inconceivable qualities of buddhahood are unable to comprehend the union of the two truths in the manner set forth in the Madhyamaka. It is in order to imply this and other things that the root verses are set in the present order.

Since such things are beyond the experience of even the Shravakas and Pratyekabuddhas, who are "the crowns" of the world, what need is there to speak of worldly beings like Brahma, Ishvara, and Vishnu? Here, the words "thoroughly" (shin tu) and "completely" (rab tu) do not necessarily apply to the objects praised. They serve simply to bring emphasis to the expression to which they are joined.[454] The expression "pure compassion" (thugs rje dag pa) of the root verse indicates that it is through great love for all beings that the Buddhas teach them the path as they realize it themselves. Since their wisdom is free from all impurities, their great compassion is pure. And the results of this great compassion that is utterly pure are the Tathagatas themselves. It is only they who drink of this ambrosia of the two truths. The explanations given by the learned in this regard are all founded on reasoning based on evidence. And here the verses imply that the love, on account of which the Tathagatas expound the path to others, and the stainless path that they set forth in their utterly pure wisdom, are preceded by a cause, namely, the unmistaken way in which they realize the two truths. These two authentic truths are the object of Buddhas alone, a fact that may be inferred from the evidence of the result. This and many other important points are implied by the order of the verses, but since a complete explanation would be very lengthy, I shall not mention them here.

6. This path is the source of other good qualities
7. Compassion for all beings

> 96
> Those who have the mind to follow this tradition
> Will strongly feel intense compassion
> For those who have the mind to trust
> To tenets of mistaken teachings.

Apart from the Tathagatas, no one is able to teach this path. Consequently, with regard to people who place their trust in the tenets of mistaken paths taught by teachers outside the Dharma, those who instead are inspired to follow the perfect tradition of the Tathagatas will think to them-selves: "Alas, how sad it is that people yearn for a spiritual path and yet lose their way." And they feel intense compassion.

When one examines non-Buddhist systems, one finds that they cannot hold together. It is as when strong rays of the sun fall undimmed on a lump of snow. And when one sees that the proponents of such systems are thus deceived, one's love and concern for them increases all the more. Accordingly, if one manages to establish the ultimate nature, great com-passion (unstained by the intolerance that is its contrary) arises naturally for all who are deprived of the authentic path and who, being protector-less, take birth again and again in samsara. And this compassion increases until it becomes unbounded. For as reasoning also shows, all the causes of great compassion are now present and unhindered: first, an understanding of the equality of self and others; second, the recognition that, in their ignorance, beings suffer; and, third, a freedom from the impurity of ego-clinging, which is the basis of all the harmful thoughts that are impedi-ments to such compassion. Possession of the basis, the lineage or nature of great compassion, gives rise to a sense of responsibility for all beings. When there is freedom from self-centered concerns and from the taint of clinging to the reality of things, and when there is commitment to the teaching of the Tathagata (which belongs to the lineage of compassion), a person is able to bear the burden of beings and can then be truly spoken of as one who loves perfectly.

Those who have compassion, the wish that beings be free from pain, will find that when they see that the suffering and its causes, by which beings are tormented, are increasing, their compassion will intensify, like a fire on which more and more wood is piled. On the other hand, those who dispar-age the ultimate doctrine espouse the greatest of causes for suffering. Those who kill animals such as birds and fish are—in comparison with them—great enemies neither to themselves nor to others. For even if such animals are not killed, they are in any case utterly impermanent like bub-bles on water stirred up by the wind. To slay them is but to destroy a lim-ited number of feeble animal bodies that cannot be of the slightest real benefit to the animals themselves. On the other hand, those who hate the ultimate teachings harm the body of Dharma that is linked with countless Victorious Ones, who abide while the world lasts and are beauteous with the perfected aims of self and others. This is so because those who have such hatred weaken the aspiration of others toward suchness, the seed of the dharmakaya. For this reason, it is said in the sutras that the fully ripened result of abandoning the Dharma is extremely unbearable. As master Nagarjuna has said:

> The slothful man who utterly has failed to train
> In the Dharma most profound and vast
> Becomes the foe of both himself and others,
> And in his ignorance will scorn the Mahayana.

Those who have not trained their minds in bodhichitta and in reasoning draw back in alarm from the great vehicle and denigrate it to the very extent that it is profound. The sutras say for instance that there will be many who deny it. Basing themselves on a counterfeit version that fits their understanding, they will say that the authentic Prajnaparamita, profound and hard to fathom, was never taught by the Buddha. As it is said in the *Sutralankara*:

> Small in aspiration, small in mental disposition,
> Surrounded by small-minded friends,
> It's clear that they are without interest
> In the Dharma well-explained, profound, and vast.

Those who are intolerant of the Mahayana, which because of its profundity is beyond their minds' grasp, should not be abandoned, however. We should care for them with compassion.

7. Devotion and respect for the Teacher

97
Those rich in wisdom, who perceive
To what extent all other doctrines lack essential pith,
To that extent will feel intense devotion
For the Buddha, who is their Protector.

Those who are fortunate in having wisdom, the greatest of all noble riches, understand that all other teachings, outside the Buddhadharma, are devoid of essential substance. And reflecting that the true path was set forth only by the Lord, they will be inspired with intense devotion for the

Teacher, the perfect Buddha and Protector. It is just as when one is tormented by the heat, one takes a commensurable pleasure in cool water. It may be granted that other traditions understand also the illusory nature of the extended gross objects accepted by the naïve. But here we have the perfect teachings of the Tathagata, excellent in their beginning, middle, and end. These are like gold that is smelted, cut, and polished; they can withstand threefold examination and are not faulted by perception, inference, or verbal inconsistency. For the Buddha's primordial wisdom, unmixed with the stygian darkness of samsara, sees ultimate reality without the slightest fault or taint. How could anyone, knowing where their true benefit lies, not have faith in the Lord, the Buddha, the Teacher of the world, whose lotus feet are adorned with the crowns of divine and human kings? It is indeed fitting to have faith, the heart of which is not to cling to him as being ultimately and truly real. This is essential.

Thus the authentic view gives rise to compassion for beings. This compassion is threefold: compassion that has beings for its object, compassion that has transience for its object, and compassion that is nonreferential.[455] Of these three, compassion that is devoid of reference is the one that manifests here. As for the devotion and respect for the Buddha who expounds the path, of the three kinds of faith (vivid faith, yearning faith, and confident faith), it is kinglike, confident faith that manifests, while the other two will appear as its attendant factors. As concerns irreversible faith, this is qualified as the confident faith that cannot be removed by adverse conditions. Faith and compassion are the roots of every wholesome quality. It is said that if one possesses them, the qualities of complete purity will appear. Of all the attitudes that one might have with regard to samsara and the peace of nirvana, there is nothing better than compassion, on the side of samsara, and nothing better than faith, on the side of nirvana. If one has these two, the precious attitude of bodhichitta, which is their union, will arise. Bodhichitta indeed is well known to be the unique teaching of the Buddha. In someone who has realized the authentic ultimate bodhichitta, the relative bodhichitta will always manifest. Such a person can never be without it. For when one unerringly beholds the ultimate reality of things, one is free from all self-centered thoughts and aims. It is impossible not to wish to attain enlightenment—ultimate reality made manifest—for the sake of beings who are ignorant of the ultimate. And in the tantras of the Mantrayana, it is demonstrated that on the ultimate level, relative and ultimate bodhichitta are inseparable.

When emptiness and compassion are inseparably united, one reaches the final point of the grounds and paths. One achieves the union of the two kayas: the dharmakaya for one's own sake and the rupakaya for the sake of others. For as long as space endures, one's enlightened activities will be constant and effortless, in the manner of a wish-fulfilling jewel or tree of miracles, that give to beings according to their wish, both in the immediate and in the ultimate term.

Regarding the two kayas, these are posited from the point of view of their preponderant aspect (according to whether it is oneself or others that are benefited). They are, however, indivisible and as such constitute the body of primordial wisdom. As it is said in the autocommentary:

> *Having searched for perfect knowledge in the past*
> *And ascertained with certainty the ultimate,*
> *One wholly brings compassion forth*
> *For this world wrapped in gloom of evil views.*
>
> *Heroic for the benefit of beings,*
> *Skilled in cultivating bodhichitta,*
> *Adorned with wisdom and compassion,*
> *One will practice well the Buddha's discipline.*

As it is said, the establishment of the ultimate truth will bring forth great compassion and the realization of perfect buddhahood. The autocommentary goes on to say:

> *Whoever follows out of faith*
> *Will generate a perfect bodhichitta*
> *And, practicing the Buddha's discipline,*
> *Will strive to realize perfect wisdom.*

This means that, having first cultivated bodhichitta through compassion, one establishes the ultimate, which is indispensable for those who strive for enlightenment. In any case, it is in the nature of things that the twin aspects of precious bodhichitta, the relative or appearance aspect and the ultimate or emptiness aspect, should be inseparable and should keep each other company.

2. The conclusion
3. The author's colophon

Here ends the *Madhyamakalankara-karika*, composed by the master Shantarakshita, who journeyed to the other shore of the ocean of both Buddhist and non-Buddhist tenets and placed upon his head the immaculate lotus feet of the noble Lord of Speech.

The meaning of this passage is that Shantarakshita was wise in every tenet both of the systems that are bound within the world and of those that go beyond the world. His wisdom was limitless like the ocean itself, for he was expert in every field of knowledge, without the slightest omission. And we are to understand too that he received this teaching from Manjushri in person. Finally the expression "Here ends" indicates that the text is integral and that nothing has been omitted.

3. The colophon of the translators

The *Madhyamakalankara* was translated from Sanskrit into Tibetan by the Indian scholar Surendrabodhi (*lha dbang byang chub*) and the monk translator and editor Yeshe De. The translation was later revised and checked for verbal accuracy, and its meaning established in the course of exposition.

Je Tsongkhapa says that the root text comprises both the verses and the autocommentary in prose. The commentary, being also the statement of the great master Shantarakshita himself, is extremely eminent and meaningful, and it is good to expound it at the same time as the root verses, regarding them both together as the root text.

Although there is nothing contradictory in such a proposal, and although this great being must surely have had some special purpose in explaining the matter so, the fact is that it is not usual for teachings to be expressed in such an alternating manner, sometimes in verse, sometimes in prose. The normal procedure is for the commentary to do no more than explain the root verses.

If I had used the autocommentary itself as a basis for my own explanation, the result would, on account of its extreme prolixity, have been difficult for others to assimilate. I have therefore refrained from following the autocommentary word for word. Nevertheless, since the present work covers all the important points discussed therein, it may serve as a basis for understanding all the meanings that it contains. It would, however, be good in due course to consult the autocommentary as well as Kamalashila's *Commentary on Difficult Points*.

1. The necessity for the explanation of the root verses

This treatise, which is superior to others on account of its numerous qualities, should be commented upon and expounded, for this will result in the acquisition of common and uncommon benefits, just as when one polishes a wish-fulfilling jewel.

The common benefits that accrue from it will be that once one has certainty—by means of the path of reasoning set forth in this text—in the stainless view of the Buddha's words, one may expect to reap the benefits of upholding the entire range of the Mahayana, included within the twin approaches of Chittamatra and Madhyamaka. The supreme aspect of the Dharma that may be upheld is the Dharma of realization—and to uphold it means to have brought into one's experience the teachings that one has perfectly understood. Moreover, once one has cleared away all misconceptions related to the utterly pure dharmadhatu, one will be able to explain it to others in accordance with one's own understanding. The benefits of this will be as it is said in the *Samadhiraja-sutra:*

> *For those who set this concentration forth,*
> *There is no doubt of their enlightenment.*
>
> *Possessing supreme stores of merit*
> *And boundless wisdom inconceivable,*
> *The Buddhas are alone the guides and teachers of the world.*
> *For they are great compassion self-arisen.*
>
> *No living being is their equal*
> *In stores of merit and of wisdom*
> *Inconceivable and peerless.*
> *None is there in all the universe to equal them.*

With regard to the uncommon benefits of this commentary, this great master Shantarakshita is indistinguishable from the venerable Manjughosha. It was through his compassion and by virtue of his prayers of aspiration that our land of Tibet, so hard to tame, came to be filled with the light of the Buddha's teaching and that we Tibetans received such great blessings. In particular, a text like this, concise in its expression yet so penetrating in its reasoning, is comprehensive to a degree that is rare even among the texts of India. What need is there for lengthy explanation? This is indeed evident for those who are familiar with the vast and profound teachings; it is as obvious as the radiant sheen of gold or the sweetness of treacle. And one of the many reasons for expounding the root text is the fact that it is swift to open the gate of wisdom and also that it is necessary to commemorate and repay the kindness of this master. As the glorious Sakya Pandita has observed:

> *Glorious Shantarakshita, the sacred holder of the vows,*
> *Padmasambhava, the master of both yoga and accomplishment,*
> *Losel Wangpo*[456] *and Kamalashila:*
> *These are second Buddhas in this age of decadence.*

And as Je Tsongkhapa has said:

> *He was accepted by Manjushri as disciple*
> *And reached the other shore of our and others' tenets.*
> *He is the sovereign of the teachings so profound.*
> *To glorious Shantarakshita I bow.*

> *When first he brought the Buddha's doctrine*
> *To this Snowy Land, so well did this protector lay conditions*
> *That Nagarjuna's teaching should be spread among us*
> *That even now there is a constant stream of those*
> *Aspiring for profound Madhyamaka.*
> *To spread therefore without impairment*
> *The teaching of this mighty scholar—*
> *Than this there is no better way to thank him for his kindness.*
> *Brought forth by reasoning unbounded as the sky itself*
> *And through the strength of love beyond all reference,*
> *This text that ornaments the Middle Way is great indeed.*
> *By tasting of the feast of reasoning contained therein,*
> *One will become a crown and summit of the many learned*
>   *ones*
> *Who, on the path of reasoning for many lives,*
> *Through many hardships came to mastery in proof and*
>   *refutation,*
> *Uprooting every falsehood.*
> *Even in the noble land this master's like was rarely found.*
> *Ah, such was the great fortune of the people of Tibet,*
> *He was invited by their king and sovereign!*

And as I think of it my mind
Is helplessly transported with a wondrous joy.

To recognize in this way the qualities of such a high object of praise is itself a sign that the one who so expresses himself has attained liberation. The worth of a jewel indeed is only truly appreciated by one who has a knowledge of gems.

Moreover, in the ancient spiritual instructions of Padmasambhava and others it is said that as long as there is faith in the great abbot and as long as his tradition is upheld, so long will the light of the teachings endure in the Land of Snow. And in the terma of Chogyur Lingpa, the great abbot Bodhisattva himself, the very embodiment of wisdom, compassion, and power, gave the following advice:

This precious teaching of the Buddha
In this Snowy Land I have revealed.
And you whom I accept as my disciples
Hold this Buddhadharma as supreme.
This teaching which the lord, King Trisongdetsen,
Which master Padmasambhava
And I, the Bodhisattva abbot, have set forth
Practice it, O you who are so fortunate!
When the Buddha's teaching has declined,
And when its fortunate adherents are oppressed by hardships,
Call upon, invoke the Teacher's love,
And pray to me repeatedly.
Outwardly, observe monastic discipline,
Inwardly, refine your bodhichitta,
Secretly, accomplish Secret Mantra.
And in the buddhafield of Willow Trees
Inseparable from the Lord of Secrets you will gain
     accomplishment.
Your emanations will protect the teachings in Tibet.
If you practice thus, my blessings you will certainly receive.
Supports of Buddha's Body, Speech, and Mind
Construct and venerate.
Make images of me and propagate my teachings.
Cultivate the bodhichitta. Invoking me in front of you,

Pay homage and make offerings and praise,
Pray to me—and pure will be your discipline!
Meditate on me within the center of your heart;
Thus you will perfect your bodhichitta.
Know that you and I are never separate.
Thus you will gain siddhi, and a sangha you will gather.

Consequently, as the text says, there are many reasons for expounding this text. For, among other things, it will be an aid to the Buddhadharma in this final age.

3. Colophon of Mipham Rinpoche

In the vast palace of the supreme vehicle, the lovely lady of the mind profound and vast, adorned with gems of many treatises, casts sidelong glances of the superior attitude of bodhichitta. With fingers of analysis, she plucks the lute strings of reasoning concerning the two truths and sings a melodious air of perfect exposition so pleasing to Manjushri the Gentle Protector.

Alas! Tibetan treatises are verbose and their message is slight, attended by many difficulties. However much one may study them, doubts abound and one lacks the acuity to surmount them. Why do those who have endeavored so long in their study not seize upon this scripture with eager devotion? For it grants the supreme level of wisdom and cuts through every hesitation, a text that is as sharp as Manjushri's sword. I am downcast to think of what has become of the fortune of those who do not uphold it with respect.

Unmoved by any thought of gain or reputation, but with a desire to conform to the injunction of my guru, with good intentions of helping others and a devotion for the most sublime teachings, I have commented by reasoned argument upon the supreme path of reasoning. The Dharma of the Conqueror is as vast as the sky itself, and since it is hard to fathom even for noble beings who abide upon the path of learning, what can be said of a person like me, whose mind is like that of a child? I therefore confess at once any mistakes that may have occurred in my work. Assisted by the radiance of the precious and perfect teaching, my eyes of reasoning have been opened wide and clear, and having seen the perfection of this tradition, I have composed this commentary. May its merit, spotless like the autumn moon, enable those who follow me to understand this profound

and excellent text of reasoning, a gateway to the four perfect knowledges.[457] May they in turn teach it to others, thereby accomplishing the
fearless activity of Manjushri, Lion of Speech.

May the light of Manjushri's blessing suffuse the hearts of all who teach,
study, or read this text, and may the tradition of the great abbot, king of
Dharma, be preserved from all decline. May it spread always and everywhere.

This path of reasoning, which distills the secret points of every tenet, reveals unveiled the profound and subtle meaning. Anyone able to assimilate
it is indeed the Lion of Speech himself.

When one surveys this excellent treatise, supreme jeweled ornament
that it is, all the other texts that are so celebrated and renowned become as
mere trinkets, the pride only of childish persons. Abandon any notion of
their excellence!

May the many-splendored countenance of the great abbot, who from
Manjushri is never separate, appear within the blossoming lotus of our
hearts, scattering all the darkness of our ignorance. Through his compassion, may the victory drum of the profound teachings, which are of skylike
purity, resound throughout the earth. Now in this time when the world
sinks unendingly into decline like the shadows that thicken at the setting of
the sun, may the enlightened mind of the Buddhas and Bodhisattvas shine
with the brilliance of a thousand moons in a pure and perfect sky. May the
explanation and practice of the Buddha's stainless teaching and the commentaries on the same increase and propagate the Dharma, bringing happiness to beings.

Seeing that there are many reasons for expounding the *Madhyamakalankara,* Jamyang Khyentse Wangpo, our incomparable guide, unbounded in his kindness, whose very name I hardly dare to pronounce, who
is the very personification of the compassion of the abbot Bodhisattva, of
the master Padmasambhava, and of King Trisongdetsen, who is the sovereign among the learned and accomplished, who is supreme Manjushri appearing in the form of a monk in saffron robes, and whose renown fills the
world, gave to me the Indian and Tibetan commentaries on the *Madhyamakalankara,* asking me to study them well and to compose a commentary.
And as his diamondlike injunction came down upon my head, I earnestly
gave myself to the task. And though I am a poor and lowly being, destitute
of all capacity to compose a commentary on this most subtle of treatises, it
was through the blessings of my revered Teacher that, merely by dint of fa-
miliarizing myself with the material, I acquired some slight ability.

It was then also that the great upholder of the tradition of the Old Translations, who is known as Padma, earnestly requested me to compose, with the result that I was spurred on to diligence. I began the work at the age of thirty-one, on the third day of the black month of the year of the fire mouse, continuing my labors every day in the early morning session until I completed the text on the twenty-fourth day of the same month. And since the crown of my head has touched the dust from the feet of the peerless Jamyang Khyentse Wangpo, my intelligence developed a little. Moreover, I was nurtured by the kindness of many holy beings, such as the vajradhara of the ultimate teachings, Wangchen Gyerab Dorje; the pandita of the five sciences, Karma Ngawang Yönten Gyamtso; and the leader of all learned Bodhisattvas, Jigme Chökyi Wangpo.[458] I therefore acquired a little light of faith in the Buddha's teaching. Thus it was that I, whose name, received in the course of my studies in poetry, is Jampel Gyepa'i Rangdang Tsojung Shepa'i Gesar, composed this text. Later on, I received from the Lord Guru profound instructions belonging to the short lineage transmission of the pure vision teachings of Shantarakshita, and immediately afterward, while I was instructing an auspiciously numbered assembly of twenty-one monks and upholders of the Tripitaka, I revised the text a little.

By this means, may the lion's roar of the perfect reasoning of the tradition of the Buddha, scion of the solar race, resound forever through every dimension of the universe. May it utterly vanquish the hostile strength of evil forces, those outside the teachings, and wild barbarous hordes. May it be a cause for the precious Doctrine of the Buddha to reign supreme and to spread always and everywhere.

Mangalam.

Notes

1. See, e.g., Peter della Santina, *Madhyamaka Schools in India* (Delhi: Motilal Banarsidass, 1995); T. R. V. Murti, *The Central Philosophy of Buddhism* (London: George Allen & Unwin, 1968); C. W. Huntington Jr., *The Emptiness of Emptiness* (Delhi: Motilal Banarsidass, 1992); Jeffrey Hopkins, *Meditation on Emptiness* (Boston: Wisdom Publications, 1996); Chandrakirti and Jamgön Mipham, *Introduction to the Middle Way,* translated by the Padmakara Translation Group (Boston: Shambhala Publications, 2002).

2. See Dominique A. Messent, "'The Yogachara-Svatantrika-Madhyamaka School of Buddhism and Its Influence on rnying-ma Doctrine with Special Reference to Shantarakshita's Madhyamakalamkara." (doctoral thesis, University of Bristol, England, 2003), p. 13.

3. See Messent, "Yogachara-Svatantrika-Madhyamaka," p. 16.

4. See Georges B. J. Dreyfus, *Recognizing Reality: Dharmakirti's Philosophy and Its Tibetan Interpretations* (Albany: State University of New York Press, 1997), pp. 33–41; Sara McClintock and Georges Dreyfus, eds., *The Svatantrika-Prasangika Distinction: What Difference Does a Difference Make?* (Somerville, Mass.: Wisdom Publications, 2003), p. 320.

5. See E. Gene Smith, *Among Tibetan Texts: History and Literature of the Himalayan Plateau* (Somerville, Mass.: Wisdom Publications, 2001), pp. 227–72.

6. See John W. Pettit, *Mipham's Beacon of Certainty* (Somerville, Mass.: Wisdom Publications, 1999), p. 26.

7. *Prajnapradipa-mulamadhyamaka-vrtti* and *Prajnapradipa-tika.* Both these texts were translated by Jnanagarbha and Chokro Lui Gyaltsen (*cog ro klu'i rgyal mtshan*).

8. See also the *lta ba'i brjed byang* of Rongdzom Pandita (a relevant passage is translated in Pettit, *Mipham's Beacon of Certainty,* p. 26).

9. See page 86. Some scholars, however, identify Chapa as a Vaibhashika in his epistemological theory. See Dreyfus, *Recognizing Reality,* p. 115.

10. In fact, Bhavya never mentions Buddhapalita by name. The latter is identified, however, by Avalokitavrata in his subcommentary to Bhavya's work. The commentary of Buddhapalita was rendered into Tibetan by the same scholars who translated the texts of Bhavya and Avalokitavrata.

11. See William L. Ames, "Bhavaviveka's Own View of His Differences with Buddhapalita," in *The Svatantrika-Prasangika Distinction* (see note 4).

12. This is an adumbration of a quite complex situation. Bhavya holds that the consequential arguments of Buddhapalita are not on the same footing as those of Nagarjuna. In both cases, the consequences imply negations that could theoretically be formulated as positive (syllogistic) arguments. The difference between them is that, given what is known to be Nagarjuna's intention (the negation of all four positions of the tetralemma), his negations are to be understood as nonimplicative. But such a concession is not to be granted to the commentator, whose task is to render explicit to the fullest extent the obscurities of the commented text. If the commentator uses consequences (unaccompanied by any positive and clarificatory statement), the resulting negations cannot automatically be regarded as nonimplicative. On the contrary, they are implicative and therefore undesirable in the Madhyamaka context. See *The Svatantrika-Prasangika Distinction* (see note 4), p. 54. It is worth noting that it is in Bhavya that the important distinction between implicative and nonimplicative negations first appears.

13. The *Tarkajvala,* or *Blaze of Reasoning,* is Bhavya's autocommentary to his independent work on Madhyamaka called the *Madhyamakahrdaya-karika.* Both these works were translated into Tibetan by Dipamkarasrijnana (Atisha) and Tsultrim Gyalwa (*tshul khrims rgyal ba*) at the beginning of the New Translation period.

14. The text in question is the *Madhyamakarthasamgraha,* the authorship of which is not certain. See D. S. Ruegg, "On the Authorship of Some Works Ascribed to Bhavaviveka/Bhavya," in *Earliest Buddhism: Madhyamaka (Panels of the Seventh World Sanskrit Conference, Volume 2),* edited by D. S. Ruegg and L. Schmithausen (Leiden: E. J. Brill, 1997). See Ames, "Bhavaviveka's Own View," p. 60, n. 32.

15. See also Mervyn Sprung, *Lucid Exposition of the Middle Way.* Translation of essential chapters of Chandrakirti's *Prasannapada.* (London: Routledge & Kegan Paul, 1979), pp. 25.7–26.2.

16. See Dreyfus, *Recognizing Reality,* pp. 451–54.

17. Chandrakirti used this argument in the *Prasannapada.* See Ames, "Bhavaviveka's Own View," p. 65, n. 87. Of course, to this objection Bhavya could perhaps have replied that autocommentary and commentary are not on the same

footing. Composed by the same author at more or less the same time, root text and autocommentary (the latter often being the indispensable accompaniment to the pithy expressions of the former) could be taken together as a single statement. Obviously, the situation is different for a commentary composed by someone else. This may appear at a much later stage and in a quite different cultural setting and may therefore be intended to address quite different needs.

18. See Dreyfus, *Recognizing Reality*, pp. 21–22.

19. This story is recorded in Shakya Chokden. See della Santina, *Madhyamaka Schools in India*, p. 85.

20. For example, Gorampa listed sixteen points of difference. See Georges Dreyfus, "Would the True Prasangika Please Stand?" in *The Svatantrika-Prasangika Distinction* (see note 4), p. 325.

21. See Dreyfus, *Recognizing Reality*, pp. 38 and 472, n. 88.

22. See Dreyfus, "Would the True Prasangika Please Stand?" p. 325.

23. See page 133.

24. See the colophon to the *Madhyamakavatara* in Chandrakirti and Mipham, *Introduction to the Middle Way*, p. 114.

25. See page 113.

26. See page 118.

27. See page 114.

28. See Chandrakirti and Mipham, *Introduction to the Middle Way*, p. 225.

29. See Dreyfus, *Recognizing Reality*, pp. 451–55.

30. The following paragraphs are a summary of Dreyfus's brief but illuminating account. See Georges B. J. Dreyfus, *The Sound of Two Hands Clapping: The Education of a Buddhist Monk* (Berkeley: University of California Press, 2003), pp. 282ff.

31. Translated by Jeffrey Hopkins. See *Meditation on Emptiness*, p. 539.

32. Hopkins, *Meditation on Emptiness*, p. 284.

33. See Hopkins, *Meditation on Emptiness*, pp. 550–59.

34. Dreyfus, *The Sound of Two Hands Clapping*, p. 284.

35. Dreyfus, *The Sound of Two Hands Clapping*, p. 285.

36. Dreyfus describes two methods. The first is meditative introspection where an attempt is made to identify the object of negation through imaginative experience rather than discursive argument. This technique uses investigative reflection to generate a strong sense of "I" on the understanding that this fabricated experience—which is nevertheless very real—corresponds to the object of negation: the falsely assumed truly existent "I," which is not real, as distinct from the "mere I," which is. As Dreyfus recalls, some Gelugpas are skeptical of this approach and doubt that the object of negation can be so identified before emptiness is realized. Another method, favored by Dreyfus's own teacher,

seems in effect to be a prolongation of Nagarjuna's own technique of decon-struction. The student is steered "along the Middle Way" in such a way as to avoid the extremes of eternalism and nihilism. Thus prevented from "locking itself into any one stance," the mind "is pushed into a new dimension of open-ness." To the outsider, it sounds as if the aim of Gen Nyima's method was to in-troduce, or at least approximate by dialectical means, the state of freedom from conceptual elaboration. If so, a return to the source of Madhyamaka re-sulted in a situation where the approach characteristic of Tsongkhapa seems to have been circumvented, if not abandoned. On the other hand, it was perhaps by such a means that Gen Nyima captured the real essence of Je Tsongkhapa's intentions. See Dreyfus, *The Sound of Two Hands Clapping*, pp. 285ff.

37. See page 301.

38. See pages 304 and 329.

39. See page 297.

40. See Janice Dean Willis, *On Knowing Reality: The Tattvartha Chapter of Asanga's "Bodhisattvabhumi"* (Delhi: Motilal Banarsidass, 1982); and Richard King, "Early Yogacara and Its Relation to the Madhyamaka School," *Philosophy East and West* 44, no. 4 (October 1994): 659–83; Dan Lusthaus, *Buddhist Phenome-nology: A Philosophical Investigation of Yogacara Buddhism and the Ch'eng Wei-shih Lun.* (London: RoutledgeCurzon, 2002). See also Messent, "Yogachara-Svatantrika-Madhyamaka," pp. 47–52.

41. See page 112.

42. See page 112.

43. See Dreyfus, *Recognizing Reality*, p. 464, n. 1 and 2.

44. See Dreyfus, *Recognizing Reality*, chap. 13 and passim.

45. See Dreyfus, *Recognizing Reality*, p. 339.

46. See Dreyfus, *Recognizing Reality*, p. 337.

47. See page 123.

48. See Dreyfus, *Recognizing Reality*, p. 104.

49. See Dreyfus, *The Sound of Two Hands Clapping*, p. 210, and *Recognizing Reality*, p. 201.

50. See Atisha's *Prajnapradipa, Lamp for the Path of Enlightenment and Its Explanation (byang chub lam gyi sgron me dang de'i dka' 'grel).* (Dharamsala: Council of Reli-gious Affairs, 1969), pp. 193.7–12. Quoted by Dreyfus, *Recognizing Reality*, p. 21.

51. See page 288.

52. See Kangyur Rinpoche, Longchen Yeshe Dorje, *Treasury of Precious Qualities*, translated by the Padmakara Translation Group (Boston: Shambhala Publica-tions, 2001) pp. 334–38.

53. See Kangyur Rinpoche, *Treasury of Precious Qualities*, p. 334. Yönten Gyamtso groups the last two arguments together as the "great argument that investi-

gates the nature of phenomena." The Gelugpa scholars Changkya (*lcang skya*) and Jamyang Zhepa (*'jam dbyangs bzhad pa*) group the argument of "neither one nor many" with the refutation of production from the four alternatives and add two other arguments: fivefold reasoning (*rnam lnga'i rigs pa*) and the sevenfold reasoning (*rnam bdun gyi rigs pa*) "associated with the chariot." See Messent, "Yogachara-Svatantrika-Madhyamaka," p. 71.

54. Aryadeva's text reads: *dngos po gang gang yongs btags pa / de dang de la gcig nyid med / gang gis gcig kyang yod min pa / des na du ma dag kyang med*. Compare with Shantarakshita: *dngos po gang gang rnam dpyad pa / de dang de la gcig nyid med / gang la gcig nyid yod min la / de la du ma nyid kyang med*. See Messent, "Yogachara-Svatantrika-Madhyamaka," p. 72.

55. See Sextus Empiricus, *Against the Schoolmasters*, Book VII (London: Loeb Classical Library, 1949), 73–74.

56. That is, true existence in the Buddhist sense. Entities are considered truly existent if they are independent, unchanging, indivisible, and so on. When things are understood as ephemeral events, individuated linguistically as a matter of conventional usage, it is of course acceptable for Buddhists to talk about them as being either singular or plural.

57. One source of confusion is no doubt the word *rang bzhin*, which appears twice in the first stanza. This term has different meanings according to the context in which it is used. Here, in a specifically Madhyamaka context, it is always explained as introducing the notion of inherent existence. We conclude that the best way to render *gcig pa dang du ma'i rang bzhin* is by a verbal paraphrase: "since they exist inherently in neither singular nor plural." The rendering "since they are without the nature (*rang bzhin*) of neither one nor many" leads to the mistaken interpretation just described.

58. *gcig pa zhes bya ba ni cha med pa nyid do*.

59. *du ma nyid de tha dad pa nyid ces bya ba'i tha tshig go*.

60. See Bimal K. Matilal, *The Character of Logic in India* (Albany: State University of New York Press, 1998), p. 14.

61. This oddity is undoubtedly the reason for interpreting "one and many" as uncompounded and compoundedness, since the latter case is a clear dichotomy where the law of the excluded middle *does* operate.

62. This is not the case, for example, with the *Madhyamakavatara*, which expounds the Prasangika approach exclusively, aiming at the actual ultimate truth in itself. The *Madhyamakalankara*, by contrast, in addition to mentioning the ultimate truth, deals extensively with the relative.

63. In Tibet Shantarakshita is also frequently referred to as Khenpo Bodhisattva.

64. See page 106ff (Mipham's general introduction).

65. A period of degeneration is marked by the presence of only the residues of the five ancient perfections. In other words, life span is reduced, negative emotions

are on the increase, beings are difficult to help, times are troubled by war and famine, and false beliefs are propagated.

66. Strictly speaking, pramana (*tshad ma*) means "valid cognition." In practice, it refers to the tradition, principally associated with Dignaga and Dharmakirti, of logic (*rtags rigs*) and epistemology (*blo rigs*).

67. This is an allusion to the story of the building of the Great Stupa at Bodhnath, near Kathmandu, by a poultrywoman and her three sons. As a result of the wishes they made at that time, her sons were reborn as the master Padmasambhava, the king Trisongdetsen, and the abbot Shantarakshita, who together firmly established the Dharma in Tibet.

68. *dngos po stobs zhugs kyi rigs pa,* all conventional reasoning (based on perception and inference) together with the reasoning used in arguments dealing with ultimate nature. See also page 288.

69. Just as the minutiae of monastic observance are possible thanks to the teaching of the Buddha, the subsequent achievements of generations of Dharma teachers in Tibet were made possible thanks to the compassion of Shantarakshita.

70. The six ornaments (*rgyan drug*) are the Indian masters Nagarjuna, Aryadeva, Asanga, Vasubandhu, Dignaga, and Dharmakirti.

71. Glorious "Moon" is a reference to Chandrakirti, and "Dharma's Fame" is a reference to Dharmakirti.

72. This is an allusion to the fact that Shantarakshita is considered to be an emanation of the Bodhisattva Vajrapani, who collected together the tantra teachings of the Buddhas.

73. Perfection (*rdzogs*) means to bring to perfection one's aspirations; maturing activity (*smin*) refers to the ability to bring one's disciples to realization; purification (*sbyangs*) consists in the ability to perceive the purity of everything (the impure world as a buddhafield). [Khenchen Pema Sherab]

74. This refers to *bka'i sems tsam,* the Chittamatra view as taught in the sutras of the third turning of the Dharma wheel and commented upon by Asanga. This is different from the Chittamatra tenet (*grub mtha'i sems tsam*) that teaches that the self-knowing mind, empty of subject-object duality (*gnyis stong gi shes pa*), is an ultimately existent reality. Only the tenet system is a fit object of refutation, not the Buddha's word, which is in full agreement with the Madhyamaka view. The Buddha never taught that pure consciousness empty of duality is ultimately existent. [KPS]

75. In this context, one should understand that the Madhyamaka refers to the *Prajnaparamita-sutras,* and the Chittamatra refers to the *Lankavatara-sutra,* etc.

76. The Tibetan *snang ba* refers to the cognitive event in which a phenomenon occurs to consciousness. It may be translated either as "appearance," thus focus-

ing on the phenomenon itself, or as "perception" if the notion of the perceiving mind is uppermost.

77. *snang med.* Such a yogi knows that phenomena are empty even though they appear. [KPS]

78. In this context, "primordial wisdom" in fact refers to enlightened activities (*phrin las*). [KPS]

79. The texts of scripture referred to here are those that have just been mentioned: the *Lankavatara* and the *Samadhiraja-sutra*, also known as *Chandrapradipa-sutra*.

80. This refers to the *gtan tshigs gcig du bral,* the argument of neither one nor many.

81. *shes bya,* defined generally as "that which can arise as an object of the mind."

82. See Chandrakirti and Mipham, *Introduction to the Middle Way,* commentary to chap. 6, vv. 23, 28, and 29; pp. 192–201.

83. Given that phenomena are streams of point instants, they are more nonexistent than existent. Compared with the period of existence that has elapsed and the future moments of the thing's continued existence, the present moment, in which the phenomenon is experienced, is practically a nullity.

84. Desire and fear are bound up with instinctive responses to things and situations built up by repeated action over a long period. An ingrained dread of snakes, for example, makes one naturally inclined to jump with fright at the sight of a coil of rope in a dimly lit place.

85. I.e., the imputed reality.

86. When subjected to analysis, phenomenal experience will be found to be a matter of mental projection or manifestation.

87. It is felicitous in being immune to attack. In denying the reality of external phenomena, it escapes the difficulties of the atomic theory.

88. I.e., the conventional and the ultimate valid reasoning, as well as their respective fields. The reference is to certain Tibetan Prasangikas.

89. Such as the Svatantrikas formula "on the ultimate level" (*yang dag par*).

90. The Prasangikas refute all the four extremes at once. And since their position is from the standpoint of the realization of the inseparability of the two truths in meditative equipoise, they do not separate the two truths (as the Svatantrikas do). [KPS]

91. In other words, if one fails to make a distinction between language about the ultimate and language about the relative, and understands according to the ultimate when the relative is intended, it follows that any statement about anything would imply a belief in the real existence of that thing. Thus, the mere fact of speaking about the practice and of someone realizing emptiness, for instance, would be understood to imply the inherent existence of such things—which is absurd.

92. I.e., according to the views of Sautrantika-Svatantrika and Yogachara-Svatantrika respectively.

93. Just as Chandrakirti does in the *Madhyamakavatara*.

94. Gorampa criticizes Tsongkhapa for claiming to be a Prasangika while asserting validly established phenomena (*tshad grub*), thereby slipping willy-nilly into a Svatantrika view.

95. This is a reference to the view of "exclusive *gzhan stong.*"

96. The first way of positing the two truths is in accordance with the teachings of the second turning of the Dharma wheel, while the second way follows the teachings of the third turning. [KPS]

97. See page 82.

98. I.e., appearance and emptiness.

99. When the name of an object appears in the mind, all the characteristics related to this object will appear too. [KPS]

100. I.e., the lack of inherent existence in the person and other phenomena.

101. See Kangyur Rinpoche, *Treasury of Precious Qualities,* p. 390. The first is unchanging, completely existent nature (*'gyur med yongs grub*) and the second is unmistaken, completely existent nature (*phyin ci ma log pa'i yongs grub*).

102. I.e., the two truths, appearance and emptiness, and also the Chittamatra and Madhyamaka approaches.

103. Skill in meditation is not enough; one must be in possession of the correct view.

104. In the chapter entitled *Ratnagunasanchayagatha (The Digest of Precious Qualities).*

105. A reference to the demon Rahu, who, by swallowing the sun, causes eclipses.

106. I.e., the sugatagarbha.

107. *Madhyamakavatara,* chap. 6, v. 89. See Chandrakirti and Mipham, *Introduction to the Middle Way,* p. 256.

108. See Shantideva, *The Way of the Bodhisattva,* translated by the Padmakara Translation Group (Boston: Shambhala Publications, 1997), chap. 9, v. 3; p. 137.

109. I.e., the difference between the occasions when assertions are or are not made; in other words, the difference between the field of discerning wisdom in postmeditation and the field of nonconceptual primordial wisdom experienced in meditative equipoise.

110. Namely, the extraordinary way of the Prasangikas.

111. I.e., Tsongkhapa and others.

112. Reflexive self-awareness is the luminous, self-presencing condition of the mind operative in all cognitions. Following Bimal K. Matilal, *Perception* (Oxford: Clarendon Press, 1986), pp. 148–53; and Dreyfus, *Recognizing Reality,* e.g., pp. 338–41, we use "reflexive" to refer to this nonthematic self-awareness: the

fact that in being conscious and knowing objects, the mind knows itself in the sense simply of being self-revealing. This is in contrast to "reflective" self-awareness, which involves a separate subject-object duality.

113. In general, *rang snang* and *sems kyi snang ba* are synonymous. [KPS]

114. These seven features are to be found in the *Sutralankara* (*mdo sde rgyan*) of Asanga.

115. The three knowledge sources (*dpyad pa gsum*) are: perception (*mngon sum*) for manifest phenomena (*mngon 'gyur*), inference (*rjes dpag*) for hidden phenomena (*lkog pa*), and scriptural authority (*lung gi tshad ma*) for extremely hidden things (*shin tu lkog pa*). [KPS]

116. I.e., the ultimate reality that dwells in neither extreme of existence or non-existence.

117. *gzhal bya* (*prameya*, object of assessment), defined as that which may arise as the object of valid cognition. Compare with *shes bya* (object of knowledge), defined generally as that which can arise as an object of the mind. According to this distinction, *shes bya* includes even imaginary objects such as a rabbit's horns. [KPS]

118. I.e., an object-free mind (*shes pa yul med*), a reflexive state of awareness. See note 112.

119. Conventional reasoning ascertains production; ultimate reasoning ascertains the absence of production.

120. Like fire, which burns, sheds light, etc.

121. They cannot be perceived by nonconceptual consciousness.

122. *gzhan sel* (*anyapoha*). See note 230 and also Dreyfus, *Recognizing Reality*, chap. 11.

123. In contrast with a functioning, impermanent thing.

124. Appearance (*snang ba*) refers to nonconceptual perception of something in terms of its shape, color, and so forth. Elimination (*sel ba*) refers to the conceptual process of designation or imputation, which occurs through the process of "other-elimination."

125. *lkog na mo;* i.e., concealed behind the veil of mental representation. According to Sautrantika, the mind does not have direct access to extramental objects but only to mental aspects or representations of them. Nevertheless, the Sautrantika does assert the objective reality of nonmental things.

126. In other words, something that *in its nature* is simultaneously and reflectively (not reflexively) self-cognizant.

127. I.e., a subject that is made the object of its own self-regarding. Note that the critique of this notion is to be found in the ninth chapter of Shantideva's *Bodhicharyavatara*.

128. According to Gyalwa Longchenpa, the Chittamatra conventional truth has two modes: the appearing mode (*snang tshul*), referring to all apparently ex-

tramental things, both animate and inanimate (*bems shes gnyis*), and the mode of abiding (*gnas tshul*), or true status, which simply means that these same appearances *have the nature of the mind* (*snang ba sems kyi bdag nyid*). It should be understood that the "mode of being" referred to here is *a part of the conventional* and does not refer to the ultimate level. The *bka'i sems tsam* (the Chittamatra doctrine as found in the Buddha's actual teaching) affirms that on the ultimate level the mind does not exist. By contrast, the *grub mtha'i sems tsam* (Chittamatra formulated philosophically as a tenet system) declares that the mind is ultimately real. [KPS]

129. As the Chittamatra tenet system (*grub mtha'i sems tsam*) would have us believe.

130. That is, the mind's projection or appearance.

131. *rtogs pas bzhag pa tsam*, the outcome of long-term mental habituation. See Chandrakirti and Mipham, *Introduction to the Middle Way*, p. 241.

132. See note 158.

133. The root of the Dharma refers to the purification of defilements and the elimination of suffering.

134. Shantideva, *The Way of the Bodhisattva*, chap. 9, vv. 32–34; p. 141.

135. *yid la mi byed yang dag 'das / nye bar zhi dang ngo bo'i don/ mngon rtags 'dzin pa rnam pa lnga / spong ba'i rang gi mtshan nyid do*. This citation has been translated according to the explanation given in the *Norbu Ketaka*, Mipham's commentary on the ninth chapter of the *Bodhicharyavatara*. Freedom from discursive thought can only be described apophatically, by denying all its possible qualifications. The first of these (the absence of mentation) refers to the state that is wholly free from the mental process of identification of objects with names (*sgra don 'dres dzin gyi rtog pa*) experienced for instance by a very young baby. "Pure transcendence" refers to the state without analytical thought, gross or subtle, characteristic of the form-realm samadhis. "Pure subsiding" is the disappearance of thought as when one falls into a faint or is in a state of deep sleep. "Insentience of matter" refers to the total absence of consciousness characteristic of material and wholly nonmental objects. "Willed fixation" is a state in which all perception and conception is forcibly excluded. Freedom from discursive thought is a state of nonconceptual primordial wisdom from which the five states just described are absent. See Mipham Rinpoche, *Norbu Ketaka* (Chengdu: Sichuan edition, 1993), p. 406.

136. For example, the term "unborn" (*skye med*) simply refers to the absence of origin, that is, emptiness.

137. The Charvakas accept only perception as valid cognition. Intrinsic to their materialist position is the denial of pre- and post-existence. But they necessarily arrive at this conclusion by means of an inference. In other words, their position is self-defeating.

138. Where there is no object, there is no subject.
139. Mipham Rinpoche expresses his views on "true existence" at great length in his commentary on the *Madhyamakavatara*. See Chandrakirti and Mipham, *Introduction to the Middle Way*.
140. See Chandrakirti and Mipham, *Introduction to the Middle Way*, commentary on verses 34, 35, and 36, chap. 6, pp. 204–221. The three undesirable consequences are as follows: The meditative equipoise of the Aryas would bring about the destruction of phenomena (*'phags pa'i mnyam bzhag dngos po ni 'jig gyur thal ba*); production could not be disproved on the ultimate level (*don dam par skye ba mi khegs pa'i thal ba*); conventional truth would resist analysis (*tha snyad bden pa rigs pa'i dpyad bzod du thal ba*). See also page 297.
141. See Chandrakirti and Mipham, *Introduction to the Middle Way*, pp. 314–22.
142. See Tsongkhapa's eight special features of the Prasangika and flaws of other philosophies.
143. This is a reference to Chandrakirti's refutation of Bhavaviveka in the Prasannapada.
144. This is a reference to the valid establishment (*tshad grub*) of the Gelugpas.
145. *Mulamadhyamaka-karika*, chap. 13, v. 7.
146. This can be said of Tsongkhapa and the Sakya master Rongtön, who attach great importance to the nonimplicative negative (*med dgag*).
147. Namely, the fact that the Madhyamaka teachings were first propagated in Tibet in their Svatantrika form.
148. The Charvakas believe that the four elements are truly existent, whereas the phenomena composed of them are unstable.
149. I.e., behave like a sadhu. Their view, in other words, resembles that of the Hindu schools.
150. This moment corresponds to the path of seeing.
151. *rtogs pa bzhi'i gtan tshigs*. This is a way, according to the Mahayoga tantra, of establishing that the phenomena of samsara and nirvana, the spontaneous display of the ordinary mind and of primordial wisdom, manifest within the indivisibility of the two truths.
152. For example, Tsongkhapa at one end of the spectrum and Dolpopa at the other.
153. Four reliances, *rton pa bzhi*. These are: (1) reliance not on the person of the teacher but on the teaching; (2) reliance not on the mere words of the teaching but on its intended meaning; (3) reliance not on the expedient but on the ultimate meaning; and (4) reliance not on intellectual understanding but on nonconceptual wisdom that sees the ultimate truth directly.
154. I.e., that of an exclusive assertion of the nonimplicative negative (*med dgag*) or an exclusive assertion of extrinsic emptiness (*gzhan stong*).

155. Since, in their eulogies, such sectarian persons ascribe their own narrowness and intolerance to their own teachers, they are in fact denigrating them.

156. *gzhung lugs;* i.e., whether of sutra or of tantra.

157. The argument of dependent arising belongs to the investigation into the nature of phenomena and constitutes an implicative negative (*ma yin dgag*), while the argument of neither one nor many (which pertains also to the investigation of the nature of phenomena) constitutes a nonimplicative negative (*med dgag*). See Kangyur Rinpoche, *Treasury of Precious Qualities,* app. 9.

158. See Chandrakirti and Mipham, *Introduction to the Middle Way,* p. 325. Generally speaking, acceptance (*bzod pa*) is the name given to the mental state that has the capacity to see the ultimate truth. The acceptance on the path of joining is in concordance with it. The middle kind of acceptance is reached on the path of seeing when the profound ultimate truth is seen directly. The great kind of acceptance is said to be reached on the eighth ground, because here the gross mental activity connected with dual appearance (*gnyis snang*) subsides.

159. According to this classification, the Ground Madhyamaka refers to the union of the two truths (*bden gnyis zung 'jug*); the Path Madhyamaka refers to the union of the two accumulations (*tshogs gnyis zung 'jug*); and the Fruit Madhyamaka refers to the union of the two kayas (*sku gnyis zung 'jug*). [KPS]

160. The *Sutralankara* says that an ornament has three functions: (1) it adorns, (2) it illumines and makes visible, and (3) it brings joy to the observer. As Mipham shows, the present text displays all three functions. [KPS]

161. They are cognized with the two kinds of reasoning, conventional and ultimate. [KPS]

162. Chandrakirti and Mipham, *Introduction to the Middle Way,* chap. 6, v. 80.

163. The term "unmistaken relative" (*yang dag pa'i kun rdzob*) refers to the approximate ultimate (*rnam grangs pa'i don dam*) which, in being a reflection of the ultimate in conceptual terms, is, as Mipham Rinpoche has just explained, an aspect of the conventional.

164. This may denote Zhang Yeshe De. It could, however, refer to Vairotsana, who adopted this name when translating sutra texts (he used the name Vairotsana when translating the tantras, and Indra Vairo when translating Bön teachings). [KPS]

165. The Abhidharma teachings comprise two subsections. The first deals with conventional phenomena, whereas the section on ultimate teachings deals with the two truths, emptiness, and so on.

166. Enlightened activities have three features: They are constant (*rtag*), all-pervading (*khyab*), and effortlessly spontaneous (*lhun grub*).

167. See note 56.

168. In translating *sbyor ba* (*prayoga*), we have generally avoided the term "syllogism." Given the latitude with which Aristotle uses this term as meaning any kind of validly constructed demonstration, it could be argued that there is no prima facie reason for not using it in the context of Indian logic. In practice, however, the word has come to be almost exclusively associated with the traditional tripartite deductive formula. There is an area of overlap between Indian and Aristotelian practices, but the use of "syllogism" tends to obscure the fact that the prayoga contains nondeductive elements, which differentiates it in important ways from the Aristotelian syllogistic. In order to avoid confusion, we translate *sbyor ba* as "probative argument" or simply "argument." See Matilal, *The Character of Logic in India*, p. 15, and Robin Smith, *Logic*, p. 30 in *The Cambridge Companion to Aristotle*, ed. Jonathan Barnes (Cambridge, UK: Cambridge University Press, 1995). Consider also Dreyfus's statement that "an Indian argument is not an axiomatic demonstration but a dialectical tool used conversationally." See Dreyfus, *The Sound of Two Hands Clapping*, p. 208.

169. *chos can* (*dharmin*). This term, which is often translated as "subject," literally means "property possessor." It refers to an entity (which can be a place or a time, a concrete or an abstract object) related with which a predicate will be proved in terms of other predicates that the subject is known to possess. For instance, it is demonstrated that there is fire on the hill because it is observed that there is smoke there. To the English reader it may seem at first odd that within such a sentence the logical subject is not the fire or smoke but the hill. This is made clear when one considers the Sanskrit formulation, which is closely followed in Tibetan: "The subject, the hill, is fire-possessing because it is smoke-possessing." In practice, whenever a substantive expression is followed by *chos can* ("the subject"), one knows that the statement is being formulated according to the rules of logic.

170. The creation of a systematic theory of inference is in large measure attributed to Dignaga, according to whom the validity of an inference is ensured by three conditions: the predicate's being the property of the subject, and the two kinds of pervasion (See Matilal, *The Character of Logic in India*, p. 88). Any property in a given subject can be the evidential sign for the presence of a second property, provided that (1) it has been observed with the second property at least once (the forward pervasion) and (2) no example of the contrary possibility has been observed or cited (the reverse pervasion). It is the evidential sign that ensures certainty and removes all possibility of error. According to Dharmakirti (see Matilal, *The Character of Logic in India*, p. 108), three kinds of evidential sign render arguments conclusive: (1) the evidence of the result (*'bras rtags*), (2) the evidence of the thing's nature (*rang bzhin gyi rtags*), and (3) the contradictory sign or sign of a nonperception (*'gal ba'i rtags*). The first two

are known as probative signs; the third is a sign that consists in something being "not observed" (*ma dmigs pa'i rtags* or *khyab byed ma dmigs*). As an example of the third sign, it may be said that "juniper" is an instance of "tree." Being a juniper entails being a tree, or, to put it more traditionally, "juniper" is pervaded by "tree." In the same way, "being a truly existent thing" is pervaded by "being either singular or plural." If it is proved that there are no trees on a rock, we know for certain that there are no junipers there, for "tree" is the wider category in which all junipers are included. The proof that there are no junipers on the rock is provided by the "contradictory sign," the "nonobserved evidence," or "evidence consisting in a nonperception" namely, that there are no trees there. In the same way, when it is shown that there are no inherently singular or plural things, it is shown with certainty that there are no inherently existent things.

171. In other words, there are no truly existent entities whatsoever.

172. The five aggregates are the basis of labeling for the personal self, whereas the characteristics exhibited by outer things are the basis for the labeling of the phenomenal self.

173. The divine creator, purusha, prakriti, and so on.

174. I.e., personal and phenomenal.

175. The first kind of argument is called *don sgrub kyi gtan tshigs* or *don sgrub kyi rtags*. It is used to communicate with someone who is familiar with a term but does not know what it refers to, and it constitutes a correct argument in which the sign is not a mere definition of the predicated property. For example, in the proposition "Sound is impermanent because it is fabricated," fabricatedness is not the definition of impermanence but gives the reason sound is impermanent. The second kind of argument is called *tha snyad sgrub kyi gtan tshigs*. Here one is familiar with the factual nature of the predicated property but is unfamiliar with the terms that should properly be used. In this argument, the sign and predicated property are related in the manner of definition and term to be defined. "Sound is impermanent because it is momentary." The predicated property, namely, the term, is demonstrated by the sign—which in this case is simply a definition of the property.

176. Dignaga said that a correct evidential sign must fulfill three conditions or must possess three characteristics (*tshul gsum*): (1) It should be present in the logical subject (i.e., the case or location under consideration) in which the characteristic property of the subject is also present (*phyogs chos*); (2) it should be present in all cases similar to the predicated property (*rjes khyab*); and (3) it should be absent from all dissimilar cases to the predicated property (*ldog khyab*). See Matilal, *The Character of Logic in India*, pp. 6–7, 90ff. The second and third characteristics show that the sign or reason is inseparably connected with the pred-

icated property. This inseparable connection between them is called pervasion or concomitance (*khyab pa*). See also note 197.

177. I.e., the Madhyamikas do not accept their existence.

178. This refers to the first condition (*phyogs chos*) that the evidential sign must fulfill.

179. "It follows that the subject, all the entities asserted by the opponent, are either truly singular or truly plural, because they are truly existent." (*Phyi rol gyi dngos po thams cad chos can bden pa'i gcig dang bden pa'i du ma thal / bden par grub pa'i phyir*) [KPS]

180. Permanence necessarily implies oneness.

181. For example, the truly existent nondual consciousness propounded by the Mind Only school.

182. *gzhan sel,* an isolation that separates out the concept of Ishvara from all that is not Ishvara.

183. I.e., the older school, following Chapa, upheld by the Gelugpas, and the new school, following Sapan, upheld on the whole by non-Gelugpas.

184. In other words, the three conditions of the sign are once again incomplete, and therefore the argument cannot establish what the property predicated refers to (*don sgrub*). [KPS]

185. This is a reference to the view of Tsongkhapa as expressed in his *Notes on the Madhyamakalankara* (*dbu ma rgyan gyi zin bris*). See Donald S. Lopez Jr., *A Study of Svatantrika* (Ithaca, N.Y.: Snow Lion Publications, 1987), p. 191. To ascribe A to B suggests that B exists and that A is its property. In such cases, the subject and the predicate are different from each other, and when the ascription is refuted, the thing as the basis of the designation continues. The refutation, in other words, constitutes an implicative negative. (In most situations, this is not problematic; it becomes so, however, when the attribute in question is itself the object's existence.)

186. We can habitually say things like "Mama is big," verbally separating the subject from its predicate. But in actual fact, we only ever come across "Big Mama." The subject and predicate are never divided—Mama on one side and her bigness on the other. The separation is no more than a mental construction.

187. I.e., the arguments establish the fact itself or the term denoting it. Such problems arise only for those who believe in true existence (*bden grub*). [KPS]

188. According to Dharmakirti, there are two kinds of relation. The first is a relation of single nature (*bdag gcig 'brel* or *ngo bo gcig 'brel*). The second is a relation of provenance or causality (*de las de byung*).

189. See note 124.

190. And the previous questions arise.

191. And there arises a truly existent form of the face.

192. *gzhon nu ma len* (*The Taker of Girls*). This is the Tibetan name of "the teacher of the Vaishnavas." See Jeffrey Hopkins, *Maps of the Profound* (Ithaca, N.Y.: Snow Lion Publications, 2003), p. 134. The doctrines associated with this teacher seem to coincide with those advocated by the Mimamsaka master Kumarila. We have been unable, however, to establish definitively whether the names Zhönumalen and Kumarila refer to the same person.

193. The Sakaravadins, *rnam bcas pa*, are represented on the non-Buddhist side by the Samkhya and Vedanta, on the Buddhist side by the Sautrantikas and the True Aspectarian Chittamatrins.

194. *rnam med pa*, i.e., those who reject the theory of aspects, saying that apprehension is direct and unmediated. According to, for example, the Vaibhashikas, it is the visual organ that directly apprehends its object (a material thing apprehends another material thing), and the visual consciousness is just accompanying this process. Conceptual consciousness then identifies the perceived form. But since the three factors (object, sense organ, and consciousness) are simultaneous, there can be no causal relation between them. [KPS]

195. The term used by Mipham here is *bsgrub bya*, which is usually means proposition or thesis. However, in the ancient texts, it is used in the sense of *bsgrub bya'i chos*, property or predicate to be proven. [KPS]

196. I.e., the property must be absent from the contrary case. In other words, if there are truly existent things, they must be *either* one *or* many.

197. Pervasion or concomitance is an inference-warranting relation between the reason and the predicated conclusion.

198. It must be partless, aspectless, omnipresent, and eternal or outside time, without any kind of temporal duration.

199. If there existed a single, absolutely partless entity, it would be untouched by spatial or temporal distinctions. And there could be no other things apart from such an entity, for it would be impossible for anything to come before it or after it or to be related to it in terms of spatial location. In other words, if such a thing exists, nothing else does.

200. *rtag dngos*. This refers either to the creator or universal cause of the Hindu schools, or to the partless particle advocated by Buddhists. In Madhyamaka, *dngos po* always denotes a truly existing thing.

201. Actual pervasiveness (*khyab pa mtshan nyid pa*) is to be distinguished from seeming pervasiveness (*khyab pa ltar snang*). The first is as when feeling pervades the body or oil the mustard seed. The second is the pervasion by a universal of its particular instances.

202. This is a reference to the logical axiom that when a cause is complete, there being no obstructing power, its effects must be precipitated immediately.

203. I.e., it could not have successive effects.

204. I.e., due to the presence or absence of contributory conditions.

205. *rdzas yod,* lit. substantial or real existent thing. It can be defined as that which is causally effective.

206. For the Vaibhashikas, this analytical cessation has real existence because, when it is achieved, it constitutes a really existent obstacle to the subsequent arising of further defilements. [KPS]

207. In the case of perception, the Vaibhashika theory resembles commonsense understanding. When one sees a flower, for example, one does not think that it is the flower that has set consciousness in motion. The feeling is rather that the visual organ has simply apprehended the flower, to which the visual consciousness independently adverts. See note 194. Beginning with the Sautrantika school, it is considered that objects trigger consciousnesses; there is no such thing as consciousness without an object of consciousness.

208. A reference to the proponents of an exclusive extrinsic emptiness (*gzhan stong*).

209. I.e., the cognitive content at a given moment, for example, a consciousness apprehending a vase or a consciousness apprehending a pillar. If the content of two cognitive moments is exactly identical, there is no way whereby these two moments may be distinguished.

210. This instant should be understood as the time required for the completion of an action (*bya ba rdzogs pa'i skad cig*). [KPS]

211. This is inconsistent with the Vaibhashikas' own position, namely, that object and subject are simultaneous.

212. The cognitive event would be no more than a thought (without an external referent).

213. *ltos med gtan tshigs,* i.e., the argument that disintegration is not dependent on extraneous factors but is intrinsic to things.

214. *dmigs rkyen.* One of the four conditions mentioned by Vasubandhu to explain the causal process implicit in an act of cognition: (1) the causal condition (*rgyu'i rkyen*), (2) the dominant condition (*bdag po'i rkyen*), (3) the object-condition (*dmigs rkyen*), and (4) the immediately preceding condition (*de ma thag pa'i rkyen*).

215. In other words, the object has a known aspect and an unknown aspect, in which case it is not unchanging—a fact that contradicts its supposed oneness (*gcig*).

216. There would be the *thing in itself* and the *thing as known* (by the subject).

217. I.e., the infinite display of phenomena. [KPS]

218. The uncompounded has no intrinsic existence; it is a concept arrived at through a process of *gzhan sel* (*anyapoha,* or elimination of other). As such it is

permanent, in contrast with *dngos po,* a functioning thing, which is impermanent by definition, as Dharmakirti said. Whatever is truly existent, single, and
independent of causes and conditions cannot act or be acted upon. Neither
can it be cognized by something external to it. Otherwise it has different aspects, etc., and many contradictions ensue.

219. Whatever may be urged or thought to be proved about such entities, the functioning of the phenomenal world is left wholly unaffected thereby.

220. The Buddhist position is not an apologetic, defined dogmatically in opposition
to the beliefs of theists or proponents of the self, etc. It is grounded in a profound but verifiable understanding of the nature of phenomena, and it is in relation to this alone that it engages in the refutation of opposing views.

221. I.e., respectively, the self or atman, and the partless particle and instant of consciousness.

222. Only individual, functioning things exist "in the concrete." Universal ideas, or
"nonthings," as they are called here, are abstractions defined intellectually in
relation to things. They are mere ideas, pseudoentities, and apart from their
existence as notions, there is nothing left to be refuted or denied. Buddhism
rejects the philosophical realism of Nyaya.

223. In this Buddhist context, it should be understood that the term "person" (*gang
zag*) is applied not merely to humans but to all the beings of the six realms.

224. Namely, the gathering of the five aggregates.

225. The founder of the Vatsiputriya school is said to have been a Jain who con-
verted to Buddhism and eventually attained arhatship. His controversial definition of the self has been attributed to the powerful habitual tendency
created by his former beliefs. He could not bring himself to deny the self completely. Since the view of the personal self propounded by the Vatsiputriyas is
not in agreement with the "four seals," which are the hallmark of authentic
Buddhist teaching, some scholars say that although the Vatsiputriyas are Buddhist by virtue of refuge, they are not Buddhists according to tenet. See Geshe
Lhundup Sopa, *Lectures on Tibetan Religious Culture* (Dharamsala: Library of
Tibetan Works and Archives, 1983), p. 107.

226. Feelings, perceptions, conditioning factors, and consciousness.

227. Paradoxical as this may seem, emptiness, as Nagarjuna says, does not undermine the apparent changes of relative existence (as the substantialists would
claim). On the contrary, it is precisely emptiness that makes such changes, including spiritual development, possible. When reflecting on the karmic
process, it is worth bearing in mind that it is not that there is some continuing
entity linking the perpetrator of actions with the experience of the results, but
there is a continuous imputation of individual selfhood. This delusion of the
mere "I" perishes and is renewed moment by moment, passing from birth to

death and from life to life, through an endless stream of moments of consciousness and oblivion.

228. I.e., in the sense of the *kun gzhi* as propounded by the Chittamatrins.

229. E.g., time, atomic particles, the atman.

230. As we go about our daily business, we encounter "things." These are the so-
called middle-range objects that make up the world, which our senses are capable of detecting and with which we are more or less familiar. We
unthinkingly interact with such things as houses, cars, roads, tables, and
chairs. We assume their objective existence and, as a rule, do not have time to
wonder about the process whereby we become aware of them as specific
items. It is only on reflection that we discover how complicated this process is.
Dignaga and Dharmakirti make a sharp distinction between perception, the
process whereby the material presence of external objects is detected
(through the operation of the physical senses), and conception, the process
whereby these objects are recognized and apprehended. Consciousness in itself cannot literally lay hold of external objects but relies on the bridge provided by the sense powers. The five senses, being nonconceptual, do not in
fact detect the composite, extended phenomena with which we are familiar.
They do not recognize them as this or that. What they detect, according to
their nature, are characteristics, such as shape and color, sounds, and textures.
The task of recognizing and deciding what it is we are up against belongs to
conception. For example, we may encounter a large brown four-legged shape
equipped with horns, hooves, udders, and the capacity to emit a loud mooing
noise. We conclude that we are in the presence of a cow. But how do we do
this? Looking around, we may see that there are other similar objects and
think, "This is a cow, that is a cow," and so on. Following our manner of thinking and speaking, we might assume that all these creatures share a single property, namely, "cowness," and we might even assume that this property exists
separately on its own account, distinct from the individual cows themselves.
After all, "this animal" is a perfect case of "cow," but "cow" does not cease
when this individual dies. According to Dharmakirti, this way of thinking is
mistaken and overshoots the mark. When we recognize something as a cow,
it is not that we have come across an example of cowness but rather that, on
the basis of past experience, we recognize that the object in question shares
certain similarities with other objects. And by isolating these same characteristics, which are shared by the class of things in question and which mark those
things off from whatever does not belong to that class, the mind arrives at a
general idea that is then associated with a name. This is how we recognize and
identify things as this or that. And in the explanation of this process, it is not
necessary to assume (as certain realist philosophies do) the existence of uni-

versals as real, thus leading to a useless proliferation of entities. For instance, in meeting the large brown grass-eating object, we may say that this is an animal; this is a cow; this is a French cow, this is Farmer Giles's cow, and so on—and in so doing we do not have to assume that the predicates in these various sentences correspond to actual objective realities. The individual items are recognized according to general concepts, constructed negatively by the mind through a process of isolating shared, and excluding alien, features. Dharmakirti makes a distinction between the individual, *specifically characterized* thing (*rang mtshan*) that alone is the object of sense perception, which is functional and can be said to be part of the real world, and the *generally characterized* thing (*spyi mtshan*), the mental construct that the mind uses in the process of recognition just described. And in terms of the tenet system of Sautrantika-following-reasoning, which Dharmakirti generally adopts, it will be remembered that it is on the basis of this distinction that he distinguishes the two truths. The specifically characterized, being real, corresponds to the ultimate, while the generally characterized, being no more than a mental construct, corresponds to the relative. When we say, "This is a cow," the real element in this experience is contained exclusively in the term "this." "Cow," on the other hand, is a construct arrived at negatively through exclusion or isolation.

231. If, as the Samkhyas say, the universal were substantially one with its particulars, the destruction of a single particular would involve the destruction of the universal itself (and of all other particulars as well). If, on the other hand, the universal and particular were substantially different, the former could survive the destruction of the latter.

232. A primary distinguisher or isolate is, for example, the term "pot," which distinguishes a bulbous water-carrying object from all that is non-pot. A secondary distinguisher might be "golden pot," which isolates a golden pot from other kinds of pot.

233. See Dreyfus, *Recognizing Reality,* pp. 58–59. These are the arguments used by Dharmakirti in his refutation of the Nyaya school.

234. *'dus bas 'brel ba.* The general position of the Nyaya is that language and conceptuality form an accurate image of the extramental world. Therefore, since we have a strong feeling of the unitary nature of extended objects, distinct from the parts that constitute them, this intuition must correspond to a real entity. The table, for example, is not reducible to its parts but is a synthetic whole that comes into being when the parts are assembled. It exists in these parts but is different from them. Wholes and parts are different things that nevertheless coincide in the same place. They are not perceived as different, the Nyaya says, because they are welded together in a relation of "inherence" (*samavaya*). The Nyaya goes as far as to say that, since it is a new entity, a cloth

is actually heavier than the threads of which it is woven. The difference in weight is, however, too small to be detected. See Dreyfus, *Recognizing Reality*, p. 57 and index.

235. In this context, the expression "endowed with form" does not refer merely to "shape and color" (the object only of the visual sense power) but to materiality as a whole. These ten dhatus are considered material as distinct from mind.

236. The term *gzugs* derives from the verb *'dzugs pa*, which means "to pierce or penetrate."

237. According to the Vaibhashikas, there are three kinds of imperceptible form (*rig byed ma yin pa'i gzugs*): the vow, nonvow, and intermediate vow. These are "grounded" in the four elements of the body and are broken or maintained through the activity of the body, and they cease when the body is destroyed. See Kangyur Rinpoche, *Treasury of Precious Qualities*, app. 4, p. 287, for a definition of nonvow and intermediate vow.

238. Terms may either be just conventional designations (*sgra 'jug*) or they themselves embody descriptions of what they refer to (*sgra bshad*), or they are both (*sgra bshad 'jug*). See page 318.

239. In this case the term is an applied conventional designation (*sgra 'jug*) only.

240. The "rabbit particle" is so called because it is of a size to fit on the tip of a fine rabbit hair; similarly for sheep, etc., the fur of which is progressively more coarse, thus indicating larger and larger particles.

241. These are particles of the four elements (earth, air, fire, and water, without space) together with particles of form (shape), smell, taste, and touch. In other words, given that matter, being detectable to the senses, has shape, color, taste, and tactility, the smallest fragment available to the senses must consist of at least one particle of each of the elements together with one particle for each of the sense powers. It should noted that the five sense faculties included in the ayatanas are material substances, not consciousnesses.

242. Given the belief in extramental material substances, some kind of atomic theory seems logically inevitable. And the indivisible partless particle is posited in order to avoid an infinite regress that would leave unexplained the experiential fact of extended objects.

243. Partlessness rules out different directions. Thus the partless particle is no more than a mathematical abstraction. In terms of the actual construction of extended entities, it is unintelligible.

244. This assertion follows if the central particle is partless.

245. I.e., appearing momentarily in the continuum of a given object.

246. The problem of extension, previously discussed in spatial terms, is now considered from the point of view of time. According to the doctrine of subtle

impermanence, phenomena are constantly replaced moment by moment. In other words, at a given moment every particle of a given mass is in fact part of a continuum that extends through time. To explain the relatedness of each individual particle to those that precede and follow in any given continuum, it is necessary to posit, within each particle, an earlier or a later part. If this is really so, the particle in question cannot be partless. If, on the other hand, the particle *is* partless, this means that the later part and earlier part coincide, with the result that chronological extension is impossible.

247. *kun 'gro lnga.* The five omnipresent factors. These are so called because they are present in every mental process and are necessary for every act of cognition. See Kangyur Rinpoche, *Treasury of Precious Qualities,* p. 288.

248. *ldan min 'du byed,* conditioning mental factors that are neither mind nor matter, such as acquisition and duration. See Kangyur Rinpoche, *Treasury of Precious Qualities,* p. 295.

249. The eighteen dhatus (*khams bco brgyad*) are the six sense organs, their six objects, and the six kinds of consciousness.

250. The Vaibhashikas refer to the subtle sense powers in two ways, depending on whether they are functioning in relation to their proper objects. The "sense power supplied with its support" (*rten bcas dbang po*) corresponds, for example, to the open eye; the "sense power deprived of its support" (*rten tshum dbang po*) corresponds to the eye when it is closed. It should be remembered that the sense powers are material but subtle entities located in the physical organs that serve as their supports. [KPS]

251. See notes 194 and 207.

252. Strictly speaking, transparency is ruled by the terms of their theory. Only the glass should be visible. Since that which sees is a material object, an eye, it should be obstructed by another material object, in this case, the glass. [KPS]

253. In other words, it does not mean that appearing aspects, cognized by nonconceptual consciousness, arise uncaused by external objects.

254. In terms of shape and color.

255. When, for example, a crystal is placed on a colored surface, it takes on the same color and appears to be filled with it. As in the case of the reflection of an object in a mirror, the color appears to be present in the crystal, but it is not.

256. E.g., Gorampa.

257. For more details on the Gelugpa understanding of the mental aspect, see Dreyfus, *Recognizing Reality,* pp. 408ff. N.B., the Gelugpas are realists in their explanation of perception and reject the representationalism of the Sakyapas.

258. "Perceptual imparity" is correct here because the different perceptions are identical in the mind in that they have the same nature of clarity and knowledge. [KPS]

259. *zla'i stobs kyis.* Apprehending aspects and apprehended aspects relate to each other as subject and object.
260. The following paragraphs are an answer to the possible objection that in the case of perceptual parity several cognitions of the same kind occur simultaneously.
261. I.e., as being true on the ultimate level (Shantarakshita accepts this theory on the conventional level).
262. See the commentary to stanza 49.
263. For example, self and no-self, love and hate. In other words, the Buddha was not, on that occasion, discussing perception.
264. See commentary to stanzas 25 (page 210) and 46 (page 240).
265. Compare Sapan's comment on the theories of Tibetan realists: "They confuse the functions of perception and conception—and that's all! *de dag gis ni mngon sum dang / rtog pa'i byed pa 'dres par zad* (Sakya Pandita, *tshad ma rigs gter,* 16.a. 4–5, cited in Dreyfus, *Recognizing Reality,* p. 394).
266. *rigs gcig.* I.e., as parts belonging to the imputed pot.
267. The cognition of the pot's mouth, etc., is a nonconceptual perception; the conceptual recognition of the pot as "pot" involves the general idea arrived at by means of "other-elimination."
268. There can be no identification of an object as this or that without an appeal to the universal.
269. If we can say that a single nonconceptual consciousness (perception) apprehends the different parts of the pot (its top and bottom, for example), we can also say that the apprehension of the pot and of the water contained in the pot also constitutes a single nonconceptual consciousness. This remark is probably directed at the "early logic" tradition (Chapa and his Gelugpa followers), who assert that a single consciousness perceives all aspects of an object together and at once.
270. I.e., Dignaga and Dharmakirti.
271. In the first moment, the different aspects are apprehended by different cognizing aspects, and in the second moment, the conceptual consciousness synthesizes them into one.
272. *lcugs sgra.* Lit. the "twig word argument." In Sanskrit the word *lata* means "twig"; the word *tala* is the name of a tree. If the word *lata* is repeated quickly, the separation between each word becomes difficult to discern and one might just as well be repeating the word *tala.* In other words, quick succession entails imprecision. Applying this argument to the butterfly's wing, it is contended that the rapid sequential perception of all the colors would lead not to a clear apprehension of all the colors but to a blurred confusion.
273. Since, in that case, several apprehended aspects have as their counterpart only one apprehending aspect, the consciousness cannot be valid. [KPS]

274. If only one consciousness apprehends a multicolored object, there can be only one apprehended aspect of that object, and the different colors could not be distinguished.

275. This is an answer to the possible objection (not stated in the root text) that there would be two consciousnesses of a same kind.

276. They are both consciousness. [KPS]

277. The sword cannot cut itself, etc.

278. Consciousness is autocognizant by virtue of the fact that, in knowing other things, it reveals itself. It is not self-knowing according to the mechanism of a subject-object duality.

279. Consciousness implies awareness of consciousness. On the other hand, Mipham is saying (following Sapan) that consciousness does not know itself in the same way that it knows things other than itself, i.e., as a separate object of cognition. It is like a lamp, which reveals itself while shedding light and illuminating the objects around it. In the same way, in knowing other things, consciousness does not know itself as a separate entity. It simply declares itself in the act of knowing. It is thus said, in the present case, that consciousness is "reflexive," meaning that its self-cognition does not extend beyond the boundaries of an exclusively subjective experience. It is not "reflective" in the sense that it turns back on itself and makes itself its own object. Self-awareness in the reflexive sense is refuted only on the ultimate level.

280. In other words, existent or nonexistent.

281. A nonexistent cause is by definition powerless to produce effects.

282. *smyong ba*. The experience of pleasure and pain is known, identified as one's own, without the presence of another conscious knower.

283. By contrast, the *apprehended* aspect (*gzung rnam*) of other-consciousness (e.g., visual consciousness) is not self-cognizing.

284. They are but clear and knowing consciousness.

285. Consciousness experiences all objects, itself included.

286. In other words, non-Buddhist schools, as well as the Vaibhashikas and others.

287. As it is for the Samkhyas.

288. This will be treated at length in the commentary to stanza 56.

289. The Sakaravada—that is, representationalism—is only an apparent solution to the problem of perception since it leaves unexplained the relation between the extramental object and the mental aspect. The Sautrantika system in fact provides no solution to this problem. See Translators' Introduction, page 33.

290. I.e., Sautrantika and Chittamatra.

291. According to this view, discussed later, the object (however complex) casts only one aspect, which is cognized by a single mental consciousness. This is the split-eggist theory, *sgo nga phyed tshal*.

292. This is the theory of perceptual imparity, *sna tshogs gnyis med*.

293. This is the theory of perceptual parity, *gzung 'dzin grangs mnyam.*
294. See Dreyfus, *Recognizing Reality,* p. 409. According to the Gelugpas, who advocate the theory of perceptual imparity, every cognition has two sides. There is an external factor (*kha phyir lta'i cha*), an object aspect whereby the external object is perceived, and an internal factor (*kha snang lta'i cha*), which is the subjective aspect that perceives the objective aspect. The cognitive relation between these two factors is not apperceptive in the sense of a reflexive self-awareness. It is reflective; the subjective factor knows the objective factor as an object. Logically, this should lead to a regress, and in order to avoid this, the Gelugpas (refusing to adopt the theory of reflexive apperception propounded by Sapan) say that "the cognition qua external perception and the cognition qua internal perception are two aspects of the same mental state, which can be distinguished only on the basis of their functions. Since these functions are exclusive of each other, external and internal cognitions are distinct, although they do not exist separately."
295. The split-eggist system (*sgo nga phyed tshal*) is a compromise between the other two systems. Having opted for the single apprehending consciousness, they try to render their view consistent by insisting on a single, synthetic, apprehended aspect.
296. Mipham Rinpoche specifically mentions "clear" appearance, which is a property only of nonconceptual perception. Conceptual consciousness, being approximate, lacks this clarity. [KPS]
297. The split-eggists claim that the instantaneous impression of a composite thing as a single whole is an illusion created by the continuous, rapid, alternating observation by the subject consciousness of the different aspects of the object in question. This procedure is so swift that the different elements seem to be existing side by side in perfect simultaneity. This is easy to understand in the case of physical objects that we can see. But what is true of sights must also be true of sounds. In order to cognize a word like *lata* as a single, self-contained item, consciousness must observe its two constituent syllables successively at high speed. But here there is a problem. Whereas on the visual level, according to the split-eggists, quick succession is expected to produce a clear synthetic impression (the quicker the succession, the clearer the impression), the same does not apply for sound. The rapid review of the two syllables that make up the word *lata* in fact brings about the dissolution of the word as a clearly defined entity. As Mipham goes on to show, there is literally no way of telling whether the word in question is *lata* or *tala.*
298. This belongs to the Sautrantika theory of perception. In the first moment, the object, sense organ, and consciousness act as the cause; in the second moment, the mental aspect of the object is produced, i.e., the result. [KPS]
299. If there is no link, the possibility of gradual, sequential cognition is excluded.

The split-eggists propound a single consciousness that gradually and quickly does the rounds of all the various aspects of an object. But they also say that consciousness is instantaneous, and this is a contradiction.

300. Such as being impermanent or fabricated. [KPS]

301. This is a vexed question, and there is no consensus as to whether the consciousness in question is conceptual or nonconceptual. The *Pramanavarttika* simply says "consciousness." It is difficult to believe that the subject of the perception is a nonconceptual mental consciousness. For it could suggest that it is the visual consciousness that sees the impermanence and fabricatedness of the object. [KPS]

302. Clarity and knowing.

303. See commentary to stanza 16, pages 197–200.

304. Namely, to nonconceptual perception and conceptual inference.

305. Generally speaking, the main mind (*gtso sems*) is the consciousness that apprehends the basic presence of the object, while the mental factors (*sems byung*) apprehend and react to particular aspects or qualities of the object.

306. In the present context, nihilism is understood in a metaphysical sense and is the rejection of the belief that mind is distinct (i.e., arising from different causes) from matter and thus able to preexist a given incarnate existence and survive its destruction. Such a view may entail the kind of moral nihilism familiar from the history of Western thought, but it is not identical with it. Eternalism is the belief in the existence of real, unchanging entities.

307. See note 238 and page 318.

308. *gzhan 'phrul dbang byed,* "Mastery over the Magical Emanations of Others," the highest of the six heavens of the desire realm.

309. Thus expressed, this idea seems very odd, but it does in fact reflect our inner intuitions. In saying that the self is unconscious, the Vaisheshikas mean that it is distinct from the mind and is the object, rather than the subject, of awareness. This view, which in some respects resembles certain theories about the soul in Western thought, does of course correspond to what we feel when we think about "our selves" and consider, for instance, whether we have succeeded in making ourselves comfortable. For the Samkhyas, by contrast, purusha or the self is the conscious principle par excellence. But it is immobile. Thus pleasure, pain, and so forth, are not part of purusha; indeed, they are what consciousness enjoys, or "consumes."

310. E.g., not speaking.

311. As in the story of Angulimala. See Patrul Rinpoche, *The Words of My Perfect Teacher* (Walnut Creek, Calif.: Altamira, 1998; Boston: Shambhala Publications, 1999), p. 389, note 174.

312. Namely, that many different items form one thing.

313. The denial of past and future lives destroys the hope and fear of reward and punishment for present action in the hereafter, and by the same token affirms present happiness as the only reality and goal. With their scruples thus disposed of, the gods could cheerfully embark upon the slaughter of their enemies.

314. Given the preceding tenet, the religious practices of the Charvakas presumably did not include belief in the existence of the gods. Perhaps they acted like the skeptics of ancient Greece and regarded acquiescence in the external rituals of religion as socially expedient.

315. "Your death is your nirvana."

316. But it is not itself a material substance.

317. E.g., one predominating over the others.

318. See S. Radhakrishnan, *Indian Philosophy* (Delhi: Oxford University Press, 1923), p. 430.

319. See M. Hiriyanna, *The Essentials of Indian Philosophy* (Delhi: Motilal Banarsidass, 1955), p. 21.

320. Hiriyanna, *The Essentials of Indian Philosophy*, p. 24.

321. It should be noted that Shantarakshita (like Bhavaviveka) was conversant with the writings of Gaudapada, whose work the *Mandukya Karikas* (also known as the *Agama Shastra*) he quotes. Gaudapada is representative of Vedanta in its pre-Shankara phase. See Murti, *The Central Philosophy of Buddhism*, pp. 114–15.

322. See Hiriyanna, *The Essentials of Indian Philosophy*, p. 173. "The Upanishads themselves declare that when a person has seen this truth for himself, he outgrows the need for the scriptures. 'There a father becomes no father; a mother, no mother; the world no world; the gods, no gods; the Vedas, no Vedas.' Thus we finally get beyond both reason and revelation, and rest on direct experience (*anubhava*)."

323. This is a reference to the doctrine of exclusive *gzhan stong*. The fact that this doctrine seems to attribute permanent and real existence to the Buddha-nature (a doctrine that Mipham Rinpoche rejects) is not a reason to dismiss their view as a form of Hinduism. Whatever defects exclusive *gzhan stong* may display, those who propound it are nevertheless within the Dharma.

324. See Gyalwa Changchub and Namkhai Nyingpo, *Lady of the Lotus-Born*, translated by the Padmakara Translation Group (Boston: Shambhala Publications, 1999), pp. 110ff. for a description of this event.

325. A distinction is being made between "things" and "nonthings," the objects of perception and conception respectively. The former are individual concrete objects that we encounter by means of our physical senses, thanks to which we discover *that* they exist. Once an object is encountered, we may go on to

discern *what* it is, by identification and naming. This is done by the process of exclusion, whereby the object in question is isolated from all that it is not and is consequently classified with other things that resemble it by sharing more or less the same isolating characteristics. In the process of identification, naming plays an essential role in the sense that a name—at least a generic name—enables us to locate a thing within a wider category of similar objects. The name, however, is adventitious to the object itself. It is only an attached label applied to the thing as a matter of convention and language. In the case of individual, "concrete" phenomena, we could say that the thing comes first and the name follows. It should be noted, moreover, that in the case of specific things, it is always possible, at least provisionally, for our experience of them to remain at the level of perception alone, as when we come across something completely new and unrecognized that we do not know how to name.

The situation with so-called nonthings is very different. When we conceive of mythical objects, general ideas, and so on, for which there is no actual correlate available to sense perception in the extramental world, we are able to grasp these ideas only through the process of exclusion and the fixating effect of the name. We could perhaps say that, in conception, the name fulfills the same synthesizing and anchoring role that is performed by the concrete, physical object in the process of perception. Certainly, without using a name it would be very difficult to isolate and render stable the corresponding concept. How, for instance, can we conceive of "humanity" without invoking, if only silently, the actual word? The difference between a cow's horn and a rabbit's horn is precisely that, in the absence of the known name, we can always go and grab hold of the former, whereas we cannot do so with the latter. And in the case of a "rabbit's horn" it is only the name that acts as the enduring, purely linguistic referent for such a figment. It is therefore clear that language plays an essential role in the conceptual process. According to such thinkers as Dharmakirti and Shantarakshita, the same is true of space, which is not a positive entity. It too is a nonthing in being just a privation, the absence of solid contact. It is defined only in relation to solid objects. And the fact that, in the case of an empty but demarcated area, space appears to have a shape is not an argument for claiming that it is a real thing that we can directly perceive.

326. The Tibetan word *nam mkha'* means both "space" and "sky." The southern face of Mount Meru is composed of sapphire. This accounts for the blue color of the sky above Jambudvipa, the part of the cosmos that we inhabit.

327. When one presses one's eyes, one sees double. One sees two moons, for instance, but this impression is not concordant with the outer object.

328. If they were different substances, they could only be linked in a relation of cause and effect, but the latter is ruled out, given the simultaneity of the consciousness and its supposed stimulus.

329. In being general, it is distinguished from the necessarily partial sense consciousnesses that it underlies.

330. It should be noted that the Nyingmapas consider that Shantarakshita subscribes to the theory of perceptual parity on the conventional level. Tsongkhapa believed the opposite: that Shantarakshita propounded the theory of perceptual imparity. See page 197ff.

331. See the commentary to stanza 16, page 198ff.

332. The Chittamatrins are guilty of special pleading. Having refuted extramental phenomena by showing that the supposedly indivisible particle has parts, they cannot now claim that consciousness is partless. Particles of matter and consciousness are on a level, for both can be broken down into smaller constituent elements.

333. Compare the commentary to stanza 12.

334. This is the format preferred by Dharmakirti (see Dreyfus, *The Sound of Two Hands Clapping*, p. 207). The first sentence consists of a statement of universal concomitance between the reason and predicate (the forward pervasion, *rjes khyab*) and the example. The second sentence is a statement of the presence of the sign in the subject (*phyogs chos*).

335. The True Aspectarians say, in the Chittamatra manner, that there is no external world and that the perception of the supposed outer objects is nothing but the mind experiencing itself and is therefore, in a sense, true. By contrast, the False Aspectarians say that the aspects (and this amounts to external things) are not mind but pure illusions, in other words, nothing at all. As an interpretation of Chittamatra, the position of the False Aspectarians can be shown to be incoherent and is thus regarded as incorrect. It could perhaps be said that, given the interdependence between subject and object, it is a step toward the destruction of the central Chittamatra tenet that the mind is an ultimate existent and in this the view of the False Aspectarians approximates that of the Madhyamikas. Gorampa said that the False Aspectarians are the best of the Mind Only school. See Dreyfus, *Recognizing Reality*, p. 557, n. 14.

336. This mention of unmediated cognition probably does not refer simply to the Vaibhashikas, since their theory has been refuted. It is perhaps a reference to the Gelug approach, a form of direct realism that nevertheless uses an aspect. The Vaibhashika school "proposes a direct contact between perceptual consciousness and its object. Its view, however, is also phenomenalist, for it holds that the object of perception is not a commonsense thing, but *sensibilia*. Among Tibetan traditions, the Ge-luk theory of perception also belongs to this category, but differs from the Vaibhashika view in that it holds that perception directly apprehends commonsense objects. It also differs from the Nyaya position in its insistence on a strict causal theory to account for the

relation between perception and its object." (Dreyfus, *Recognizing Reality*, p. 331; see also pp. 410ff.)

337. The False Aspectarians say that consciousness exists but that what it experiences (in the way of aspects) is wholly illusory. But in the present (Chittamatra) context, to discount consciousness as the object renders consciousness as the subject also untenable.

338. This is the "causal" principle whereby things are called into existence by the power of their interrelation. It is because of breadth (the cause) that there is narrowness (the result). A defining characteristic of an efficient thing is the cause of giving it a certain name.

339. Both factors are momentary, being produced and disintegrating at every instant. Thus in the first instant, they meet without the possibility of harming each other. In the second instant only, the stronger undermines the weaker, and in the third instant, the continuity of the weaker element is interrupted. [KPS]

340. They would happen in successive moments, which means—given the doctrine of momentariness—that they are unrelated.

341. This is in the case of a Buddha.

342. Since they are completely unconnected.

343. I.e., of a Buddha.

344. See Kangyur Rinpoche, *Treasury of Precious Qualities*, p. 390.

345. I.e., a dissimilar location where the likes of the inferred property will never be present.

346. I.e., given the argument, the predicate is self-evident. In other words, having established the argument of neither one nor many, one comes to the conclusion that nonexistent things are nonexistent. Thus, so the objection runs, the argument and conclusion are trivial. Finally, no more than two of the three elements of the probative argument are present, with the result that the argument is inconclusive. [KPS]

347. In other words, the argument is not redundant as the opponents have complained.

348. Here the real (*yang dag pa*) is to be understood as "truly existent." [KPS]

349. I.e., *kun rdzob pa nyid*, "the relative itself," meaning "the relative alone."

350. I.e., identification, whereby contrary features are excluded.

351. Exclusion and detection are the two procedures whereby the mind comes to grips with objects of knowledge: objects that either do or do not exist on the conventional level. These knowledge-objects (defined as whatever may arise within the ken of the mind) are either nonthings (*dngos med*), like space or a rabbit's horns, or things (*dngos po*) such as material objects, sound, etc. All nonthings are qualified by being conceptually excluded or isolated from all

that they are not—isolated in the sense that they are distinguished through the elimination of an "object of negation" (i.e., all that they are not). The situation with sense objects is more straightforward, since they cast their aspects on the mind and in the process eliminate all that they are not. [KPS] In this case, the cognitive procedure is called *yongs gcod,* which we have translated as "detection."

352. *dbyu gu,* a period of twenty-four minutes.

353. The cause of production is the cause of destruction.

354. *rnam byang,* i.e., nirvana.

355. *gcig bsgrub pa na de rten dang / gzhan btang snyoms lta bu dang.*

356. For it produces the cognition in that aspect. [KPS]

357. Mistaken (*log*), the thing in question does not function according to the way it appears; unmistaken (*yang dag*), the thing in question does function according to the way it appears.

358. Names appear in the clear and knowing consciousness and are of the same nature as it. From this point of view, they are causally efficient things, and the fault of their not being included in the two truths does not occur. [KPS]

359. This is how sense perception (which is nonconceptual) works. When one encounters an object in the world, this same object, located in a specific place and point in time, presents itself to the visual consciousness to the exclusion of all else. The impression gained is that the object impinges on us and we perceive it passively. To know a table in this way constitutes a detection (*yongs gcod*). When cognizing an abstraction, on the other hand, for which there is no material correlate available to perception, the mind proceeds actively, by exclusion of all that is not the idea in question (*rnam bcad*), and arrives at a general concept or term (corresponding more or less to the universal of Western philosophy). When one cognizes a concrete object through the medium of the senses, the presence of this object naturally eliminates all that is not that object.

360. Establishment through detection refers to implicative negations and things; establishment through exclusion refers to nonimplicative negations and nonthings. It is helpful to see that *rnam bcad* and *yongs gcod* proceed in opposite directions. In the case of *rnam bcad* the isolation of the concept is the result and goal of the process of exclusion; in the case of *yongs gcod,* exclusion follows from the perception of the thing. The distinction between these two procedures is a kind of mirror image of the distinction between implicative and nonimplicative negations, which is why the two sets of definitions are juxtaposed in the text. The nonimplicative negation says, "This thing does not exist"; its reverse, "This exists (I can see it before me)," corresponds to *yongs gcod.* The implicative negation says, "This is not a *vase*"; its reverse, "This is a *vase*," is *rnam*

bcad. Another way of looking at it is to say that *rnam bcad* is used in the process of identification and implies the use of a universal idea. By contrast, *yongs gcod* occurs in the process of detection and makes use of the nonconceptual functioning of the sense consciousnesses. When in everyday life one comes across an object and says, "Oh, this is a vase"—that is, one notices that something exists and one recognizes what it is—both *yongs gcod* and *rnam bcad* are working together. The first establishes *that* a thing is; the second identifies *what* a thing is. It is worth remembering that for Dharmakirti, universals have only a nominal, imputed existence. When one says, "This is a vase," one is, according to Dharmakirti, referring to only one entity, the object corresponding to the word "this." There is no separate entity corresponding to the word "vase." In Dharmakirti's system, there is no such thing as disembodied "vaseness." Thus *rnam bcad* implies *dngos med; yongs gcod* implies *dngos po.*

361. The "verbal or word exclusion" (*sgra'i rnam bcad*) is an exclusion that occurs by expressing a term or name that eliminates all the other terms. When one says "vase," all other terms are eliminated. The meaning-exclusion (*don gyi rnam bcad*) is an exclusion in which the meaning of the word arises in the mind by excluding all the other meanings than the one conveyed by the word.

362. First one is confronted by the existent thing (*yongs gcod*), which then calls for identification (*rnam bcad*).

363. If I say "the rabbit's horns" and "my chair," the two expressions are on a level in both being composed of words. But whereas "my chair" refers to something real (i.e., something in the world), "the rabbit's horns" does not. Both terms, however, are expressive of meaning, and the question is, by what process do they do so? Since "the rabbit's horns" corresponds to nothing real but only to something imaginary, the expression derives its meaning from the words alone, the meaning of which is established through an exclusion (*rnam bcad*) of all that the words do not mean. "My chair," on the other hand, is not imaginary. It corresponds to a (conventionally) real object that impinges on my experience. I know *that* it is and *what* it is through *yongs gcod* and *rnam bcad* respectively.

364. In respect of an object such as a vase, its definition is "a narrow-necked, bulbous, liquid-carrying object." Its name (*mtshon bya*) is "vase." *Mtshon bya* is sometimes translated as "definiendum," but this is misleading since the Latin word would normally refer to the thing defined and not the name, which is what is intended here. The definition (*mtshan nyid*) is understood as that which defines the name (*mtshon bya*), not the named object. And the basis, or locus, of definition is the specific instance or object, e.g., a particular gold vase.

365. A reference to the Vatsiputriyas.

366. I.e., the long-term outcome of mental habit. See Chandrakirti and Mipham, *Introduction to the Middle Way,* p. 241.

367. Whatever is proved adequately by the lower tenets does not need to be further demonstrated by the higher tenets.

368. Compare with stanza 8 of the root text.

369. Even a Svatantrika does not always use the expression "on the ultimate level," and, conversely, a Prasangika may occasionally use it. [KPS]

370. Namely, that the definition pervades both the term and the object. This means that the definition is connected with the term it defines, by a relation of same nature, within the given object.

371. *tha snyad sgrub pa'i gtan tshigs.*

372. In other words, in order to construct a universal idea (or general term), one must start from the particular objects encountered in experience. All such things are specifically located in time and space. Thus one uses one's experience of the pillar at the eastern end of the house as the basis for the general idea "pillar," which can then be extended and used in the identification of other similar objects.

373. I.e., a divine creator, etc.

374. In this expression, the "fourfold name" refers to the four psychic aggregates (feelings, perceptions, conditioning factors, and consciousness); "form" refers to the body or form aggregate.

375. In Tibetan, these four kinds of reasoning are respectively called *bya ba byed pa'i rigs pa, ltos pa'i rigs pa, chos nyid kyi rigs pa,* and *'thad pa sgrub pa'i rigs pa.*

376. Investigation by direct perception for manifest objects, by inference for hidden objects, and by trustworthy scriptures for very hidden objects.

377. Conventional reasoning ascertains the nature of things on the relative level (e.g., fire is hot), while the ultimate reasoning ascertains their emptiness.

378. As in the case of karma, where an action may result in an effect only a long time afterward.

379. *thob pa* and *chud mi za ba'i rdzes.* The first is the belief of the Vaibhashikas, the second of the Sautrantikas.

380. They would be simultaneous.

381. I.e., in the sense of barley seeds producing rice.

382. E.g., compoundedness or impermanence.

383. For example, the seed in a given location or at a specific time.

384. Rice could produce barley, and everything would be in chaos.

385. And so on ad infinitum. The process would obviously lead to a regress, and Gorampa comments that the whole of space would be filled with disintegrated entities. [KPS]

386. I.e., indivisible particles, moments of consciousness, or nondual consciousness. The critique is being applied to Buddhist realism.

387. These consequences do not invalidate the Svatantrikas' position of *rnam grangs pa'i don dam.* They would apply only if the Svatantrikas asserted

phenomenal existence according to characteristics when establishing the authentic ultimate in itself (*rnam grangs min pa'i don dam*), which of course they do not do. [KPS]

388. See page 148. These verses show that the *Madhyamakalankara* is the ornament not only for the Svatantrikas but also for the Prasangikas.

389. I.e., in distinction from the great emptiness, which is never separate from appearance.

390. See Shantideva, *The Way of the Bodhisattva*, chap. 6, vv. 139, 140.

391. See Shantideva, *The Way of the Bodhisattva*, chap. 6, v. 110.

392. I.e., in a nondual manner, not in terms of a subject-object experience.

393. *bsal bzhag med pa*, that is, without the removal of defects (*bsal ba*) or the addition (*bzhag*) of qualities.

394. *Madhyamakavatara*, chap. 11, v. 13. See Chandrakirti and Mipham, *Introduction to the Middle Way*, p. 106.

395. Some say that the ultimate truth must be observed, otherwise it would be a mere nothingness. But here it is important to distinguish. It may be said that from the standpoint of *rnam bcad*, the ultimate *is* established as an object of knowledge—but only as the opposite of something that cannot be known at all—i.e., in terms of conceptual definition. It cannot, however, be an object of knowledge from the point of view of *yong gcod*, for this would entail that it exists, in which case it would be existent for the senses (like any other object lying around in the world). [KPS]

396. Form, for instance, in the case of the visual consciousness.

397. Including existence or nonexistence.

398. It is therefore said that this is not union but only juxtaposition, as when a black thread and a white thread are twisted together. [KPS]

399. And the possibility of knowing nonconceptually, i.e., in the manner in which the Buddhas and Aryas know.

400. Given the correct functioning of the organs in question, perception is always accurate; it is only in the process of conceptual assessment that mistakes occur. One may think that the rope is a snake, but the eyes only ever perceive the thing that is actually there, namely, the rope. Therefore, when one perceives phenomena, one only ever perceives phenomena that are empty and unreal (for emptiness is their nature)—however much one may mistakenly believe that they are truly existent.

401. The Nyaya-Vaisheshika school advocates a realistic theory of universals similar to, though perhaps not as extreme as, the Platonic theory of forms. For the Nyaya-Vaisheshikas, universals are real entities distinct from the multiple phenomena that instantiate them. In being unitary and indivisible, timeless and indestructible, these universals are obviously much more real than their

evanescent instances and would continue to exist even if the latter were all destroyed and were to vanish from the world. See Matilal, *Perception*, pp. 382–86, and Dreyfus, *Recognizing Reality*, pp. 52–59.

402. *yul gyi longs spyod*, i.e., the ultimate nature of things. [KPS]

403. The Pratyekabuddhas are classified according to whether they appear alone (in which case they are metaphorically referred to as "rhinoceros-like") or in a group (in which case they are referred to as "parrot-like"). In the present text, the first group is presumably understood as standing for all.

404. In other words, the mind is unmistaken.

405. Sensory perception is always nonconceptual, as also is the first moment of mental perception.

406. Where there is a seed, a plant will sprout; when a naga is present, water will occur; where there is grass, the land is green; and fruit may be gathered when a fruit tree grows.

407. *tshad ma'i skyes bu*. The primary meaning of this term is not that the Buddha is a source of valid knowledge (although he is) but that his mind is constantly in a state of valid knowledge.

408. When something is known, it is, by that very fact, circumscribed. Therefore, the idea that the boundless can be known seems contradictory. For one can only know quantities, and something unlimited is not a quantity.

409. In other words, omniscience may be interpreted in the present context as the knowledge of all useful or relevant things. In other words, "all things" here is taken to be a circumscribed quantity, such as "all men" or "all medicines."

410. The conceived object (*zhen yul*) remains the same irrespective of the existence or otherwise of the thing in question. Mental other-elimination only identifies and names things. In itself, it does not establish their existence—only experience does this.

411. In the sense that they apprehend phenomena either rightly or wrongly.

412. The sunlight must, as it were, meet the darkness for the latter to be dispelled.

413. To describe true knowledge as a corrective to the false one is no more than a manner of speaking. The one cannot act on the other, for they never occur at the same time. Correct and certain knowledge simply supplants the misconception in the ongoing continuum of the mind.

414. In the case of Bodhisattvas on the grounds of realization, the primordial wisdom is present, for it has been realized on the path of seeing and is actualized in meditative absorption throughout the stages of the path of meditation. On the other hand, the cognitive obscurations continue, though they are gradually being purified, on account of which the Bodhisattvas have the dualistic experience of phenomenal appearance in the postmeditation state.

415. The vajralike concentration (*rdo rje lta bu'i ting nge 'dzin*) occurs at the end of the tenth ground.

416. For argument to get under way, there must be a subject on which the two opponents agree. As will become clearer as the commentary proceeds, since the argument is precisely about the existential status of phenomena—*all* phenomena—the Buddhist and the non-Buddhist are diametrically opposed, since they hold radically different views. But to hold that phenomena do or do not enjoy true existence is a matter of philosophy, of tenet systems. These produce ideas about things which those who subscribe to them naturally assume when they interact with or speak about phenomena. Consequently, for a debate on this matter to be possible between Buddhists and non-Buddhists, it is necessary to take that part of phenomena that is common to all parties, namely, their simple appearance, shorn of whatever philosophical theories have been superadded to them.

417. Things that are names and descriptions (*tha snyad kyi dngos po*) are contrasted with things that are actual objects (*don gyi dngos po*). [KPS]

418. I.e., such as to command the assent of the opposing party.

419. The first moment of consciousness produced refers here to the first moment of consciousness in the womb. This manifests on the basis of an earlier conscious moment that is concordant in kind, i.e., that is by nature mere clarity and knowing (*gsal rig gi ngo bo*).

420. Sexual desire is not something that has to be learned.

421. In their imagination or dreams.

422. Extraneous causes here means that the mind does not manifest from matter (as materialism would have us believe), nor does it occur through the power of a creator.

423. Note the difference in the way the old and new schools interpret this verse. The majority of the new schools understand that the "clinging to the aggregates" refers to the clinging to the inherent existence of the aggregates such as form or consciousness. In other words, they believe that the Arhats must realize the lack of inherent existence of the five aggregates (at the level of the partless particle and instant of consciousness) in order to get rid of ego-clinging. This means that they realize the phenomenal no-self. According to the old school as represented by Mipham, clinging to the five aggregates means the clinging to them as a single, discrete whole. If one is able to deconstruct this idea, one will be able to get rid of ego-clinging. In other words, the Arhats do not realize the phenomenal no-self. They simply realize the personal no-self. [KPS]

424. Chandrakirti and Mipham, *Introduction to the Middle Way*, chap. 6, v. 120.

425. See Kangyur Rinpoche, *Treasury of Precious Qualities*, nn. 69 and 70, pp. 361–62.

426. See Chandrakirti and Mipham, *Introduction to the Middle Way*, pp. 281–82.

427. See Chandrakirti and Mipham, *Introduction to the Middle Way*, chap. 8, v. 2.

428. That of Tsongkhapa.

429. E.g., Gorampa and Mipham himself.

430. The "path free from obstacles" *(bar chad med pa'i lam)* is the name of the antidote that directly eliminates the obscurations related to a given ground of realization. It is so called because it eliminates hindrances to the attainment of the primordial wisdom of the ground in question. The "path of freedom" *(rnam grol ba'i lam)* is the actual wisdom that is subsequently attained. It is so called from the standpoint of the actual freedom from obscurations. See Longchen Rabjam, *grub mtha' mdzod*, p. 216.

431. See Kangyur Rinpoche, *Treasury of Precious Qualities*, pp. 129ff.

432. In other words, they will not be reborn in samsara.

433. This constitutes the last of the six preternatural knowledges and is one of the qualities of buddhahood. See Kangyur Rinpoche, *Treasury of Precious Qualities*, p. 299.

434. Pratyekabuddhas realize the personal no-self and the no-self of the form aggregate. They do not realize that the mental aggregates lack inherent existence. This lack of inherent existence of the person and of the form aggregate is the truth of cessation.

435. With regard to the emptiness aspect, Bodhisattvas on the first ground have the same realization as a Buddha. Nevertheless, they experience an evolution of the clarity aspect as they progress upon the grounds of realization.

436. *Madhyamakavatara*, chap. 11, v. 45. See Chandrakirti and Mipham, *Introduction to the Middle Way*, p. 111.

437. One of the stages of the path of joining.

438. I.e., they fall apart naturally by themselves.

439. This refers to one of the ten powers of a Buddha (which are shared by the Bodhisattvas on the pure grounds), by virtue of which a Buddha or Bodhisattva may choose to be born in any of the six realms.

440. It is also reasonable to say that one does not drink the ocean, even though one may in fact drink a tiny part of it.

441. See Kangyur Rinpoche, *Treasury of Precious Qualities*, n. 82.

442. See Chandrakirti and Mipham, *Introduction to the Middle Way*, chap. 6, v. 180.

443. I.e., realization of primordial wisdom.

444. The Tibetan here reads *bdag rkyen nyid 'di pa tsam*, where *bdag* was explained as meaning "things."

445. Namely, a person.

446. See Chandrakirti and Mipham, *Introduction to the Middle Way*, chap. 6, v. 179.

447. As for instance in the account of two parents offering their son to the Buddha, thus allowing him to become a member of the Sangha.

448. This is a reference to the argument called *snang ba thams cad gsal rig gi ngo bor skyes pa'i rtags*. [KPS]

449. If the sense consciousness and its object are simultaneous, they cannot be linked in a relationship of the same nature, since their simultaneity must mean that they are different kinds of entities. If the object and consciousness are not simultaneous, they cannot be linked in a relation of provenance (i.e., cause and effect), because the object has already ceased to exist when the consciousness comes into being.

450. According to Mipham, Shantarakshita is the third "great charioteer," on a par with Nagarjuna and Asanga.

451. See Chandrakirti and Mipham, *Introduction to the Middle Way*, chap. 6, v. 118.

452. The word used in the Tibetan translation of this citation is *sangs rgyas*, which in other contexts is translated as "buddhahood."

453. These are the specific attributes of the Arhats and Pratyekabuddhas.

454. The words "thoroughly without a taste of it" simply mean that the Shravakas and Pratyekabuddhas do not experience the union of the two truths.

455. See Chandrakirti and Mipham, *Introduction to the Middle Way*, p. 146.

456. I.e., Vairotsana. [KPS]

457. Four perfect knowledges (*so so yang dag par rig pa bzhi*) of all the ways of helping beings. See Kangyur Rinpoche, *Treasury of Precious Qualities*, p. 299.

458. I.e., respectively, a Gelugpa master Wangchen Gyerab Dorje, Jamgön Kongtrul Lodrö Thayé, and Patrul Rinpoche.

Works Cited

Abhisamayalankara by Maitreya/Asanga, The Ornament for Clear Realization, *mngon rtogs rgyan*

Akshayamatinirdesha-sutra, The Sutra Taught by Akshayamati, *'phags pa blo gros mi zad pas bstan pa' mdo*

Avatamsaka-sutra, The Great Assembly Sutra, *mdo phal po che*

Bodhicharyavatara by Shantideva, The Way of the Bodhisattva, *spyod 'jug*

Chandrapradipa-paripriccha-sutra, The Sutra Requested by Chandrapradipa, *zla ba sgron mes zhus pa'i mdo* (another name for *Samadhiraja-sutra*)

Dharmadharmatavibhanga by Maitreya/Asanga, Discerning Phenomena and Their Nature, *chos dang chos nyid rnam 'byed*

Dharmasangiti-sutra, The Sutra That Resumes Perfectly the Dharma, *chos yang dag par sdud pa*

Ghanavyuha-sutra, The Sutra of the Dense Array of Ornaments, *rgyan stug po bkod pa*

Hastikakshya-sutra, The Sutra of the Elephant's Power, *glang po'i rtsal gyi mdo*

Jnanalokalankara-sutra, The Sutra of the Light of Wisdom, *ye shes snang ba rgyan*

Lalitavishtara-sutra, The Sutra of Great Display, *rgya cher rol pa'i mdo*

Lankavatara-sutra, The Visit to the Lanka Sutra, *lang kar gshegs pa'i mdo*

Madhyamakahridaya by Bhavaviveka, The Heart of the Madhyamaka, *dbu ma snying po*

Madhyamakalankara-panjika by Kamalashila, Commentary on Difficult Points of the Madhyamakalankara, *dbu ma rgyan gyi dka' 'grel*

Madhyamakalankara-vritti by Shantarakshita, The autocommentary on the Madhyamakalankara, *dbu ma rgyan gyi 'grel pa*

Madhyamakaloka by Kamalashila, The Light of the Middle Way, *dbu ma snang ba*

Madhyamakavatara by Chandrakirti, Introduction to the Middle Way, *dbu ma la 'jug pa*

Madhyamakavataraprajna by Chandrakirti, Introduction to the Wisdom of the Madhyamaka, *dbu ma shes rab la 'jug pa*

Madhyantavibhanga by Maitreya/Asanga, Discerning the Center from the Extremes, *dbus mtha' rnam 'byed*

Mahakarunavatara-sutra, The Sutra of Entering into Great Compassion, *snying rje chen po la 'jug pa'i mdo*

Mahaparinirvana-sutra, The Sutra of Mahaparinirvana, *mya ngan las 'das pa'i mdo*

Mahayanasamgraha by Asanga, The Compendium of the Mahayana, *theg pa chen po bsdus pa*

Manjushrimulatantra, The Root Tantra of Manjushri, *'jam dpal rtsa rgyud*

Mulamadhyamaka-karika by Nagarjuna, The Treatise of the Middle Way Called Wisdom, *dbu ma rtsa ba shes rab*

Panchakrama by Nagarjuna, The Five Stages, *rim lnga*

Pitaputrasamagama-sutra, The Sutra of the Meeting of the Father with the Son, *yab sras mjal ba'i mdo*

Prajnaparamita-sutra, The Perfection of Wisdom Sutra, the Mother of the Conquerors, *rgyal ba'i yum*

Pramanasiddhi by Dharmakirti, The Valid Establishment (a chapter from the *Pramanavarttika*), *tshad ma grub pa*

Pramanavarttika by Dharmakirti, A Commentary on the Compendium of Valid Cognition, *tshad ma rnam 'grel*

Prasannapada by Chandrakirti, The Clearworded, *tshig gsal*

Ratnagunasanchayagatha, The Digest of Precious Qualities, *yon tan rin po che'i sdud pa*

Ratnakara-sutra, The Sutra of the Source of the Three Jewels, *dkon mchog 'byung gnas kyi mdo*

Ratnakuta-sutra, The Jewel Mound Sutra, *dkon mchog brtsegs pa'i mdo*

Ratnamegha-sutra, The Cloud of Jewels Sutra, *dkon mchog sprin mdo*

Ratnavali by Nagarjuna, The Jewel Garland, *rin chen 'phreng ba*

Sagaramatinirdesha-sutra, The Sutra Taught by Sagaramati, *blo gros rgya mtshos bstan pa'i mdo*

Sagaranagaraja-paripriccha-sutra, The Sutra Requested by the Naga King Sagara, *klu'i rgyal po rgya mtshos zhus pa'i mdo*

Samadhiraja-sutra, The King of Concentrations Sutra (requested by Chandrapradipa), *ting 'dzin rgyal po'i mdo*

Samadhyagrottama-sutra, The Sutra of Supreme Concentration, *ting 'dzin dam pa'i mdo*

Sanchayagathaprajnaparamita-sutra, Condensed Prajnaparamita-sutra, *mdo sdus pa*

Sandhinirmochana-sutra, The Sutra Decisively Revealing the Wisdom Intention, *dgongs pa nges 'grel gyi mdo*

Separating from the Four Clingings by Dragpa Gyaltsen, *zhen pa bzhi bral gyi man ngag*

Sutralankara by Maitreya/Asanga, The Ornament of the Sutras, *mdo sde rgyan*

The Sutra Taught to the Shravakas, nyan thos la bstan pa'i mdo

Treasure of Wish-Fulfilling Jewels by Longchen Rabjam, *yid bzhin rin po che'i mdzod*

Udanavarga, The Intentionally Spoken Discourse, *ched du brjod pa'i tshoms*

Uttaratantra-shastra by Maitreya/Asanga, The Sublime Continuum, *rgyud bla ma*

Vairochanamayajala-tantra, The Tantra of the Phantasmagorical Net of Vairochana, *rnam snang sgyu 'phrul drwa ba*

Vajracchedika-sutra (Trishatikaprajnaparamita-sutra), The Diamond Cutter, *rgyal ba'i yum sum brgya pa*

Vyavaharasiddhi by Nagarjuna, The Establishment of the Conventional, *tha snyad grub pa*

Yuktishashtika by Nagarjuna, The Sixty Reasonings, *rigs pa drug cu pa*

Bibliography

Tibetan Sources

Kamalashila. *Madhyamakalamkara-panjika. (dbu ma rgyan gyi dka' 'grel).* Derge edition, Tengyur 3886.

Longchen Rabjam *(klong chen rab 'byams).* The Treasury of Tenets *(grub mtha' mdzod).* Varanasi.

Mipham *('jam mgon 'ju mi pham rgya mtsho).* An explanation of the meaning of the ninth chapter, called Norbu Ketaka *(shes rab kyi leu tshig don go sla bar rnam par bshad pa nor bu ke ta ka).* Chengdu: Sichuan edition, 1993.

_____. An explanation of [Shantarakshita's] Ornament of the Middle Way entitled A Teaching to Delight My Master Manjughosha. *(dbu ma rgyan gyi rnam bshad 'jam dbyangs bla ma dgyes pa'i zhal lung).* Varanasi: Central Tibetan Institute of Higher Tibetan Studies, 1999; Chengdu: Sichuan edition, 1999; Bylakuppe: Thegchog Namdröl Shedrub Dargyeling Monastery, 1998.

Nagarjuna *(klu grub). Mulamadhyamaka-karika (dbu ma rtsa ba shes rab).* Varanasi: Pleasure of Elegant Sayings Press, 1974.

Western Sources

Ames, William L. "Bhavaviveka's Own View of His Differences with Buddhapalita." In *The Svatantrika-Prasangika Distinction: What Difference Does a Difference Make?* Edited by Sara McClintock and Georges Dreyfus. Somerville, Mass.: Wisdom Publications, 2003.

Barlingay, S. S. *A Modern Introduction to Indian Logic.* Delhi: National Publishing House, 1965, 1975.

Chandrakirti and Jamgön Mipham. *Introduction to the Middle Way (Madhyamakavatara).* Translated by the Padmakara Translation Group. Boston: Shambhala Publications, 2002.

Changchub, Gyalwa, and Namkhai Nyingpo. *Lady of the Lotus-Born*. Translated by the Padmakara Translation Group. Boston: Shambhala Publications, 1999.

Della Santina, Peter. *Madhyamaka Schools in India*. Delhi: Motilal Banarsidass, 1995.

Dreyfus, Georges B. J. *Recognizing Reality: Dharmakirti's Philosophy and Its Tibetan Interpretations*. Albany: State University of New York Press, 1997.

_____. *The Sound of Two Hands Clapping: The Education of a Buddhist Monk*. Berkeley: University of California Press, 2003.

_____. "Universals in Tibetan Tradition." In *Tibetan Studies*. Narita, Japan: Naritasan Shinshoji, 1992, 29–46.

_____. "The Yogacara Philosophy of Dignaga and Dharmakirti." In collaboration with C. Lindtner. *Studies in Central and East Asian Religions* 2 (1989): 27–52.

Hiriyanna, M. *The Essentials of Indian Philosophy*. Delhi: Motilal Banarsidass, 1995.

Hopkins, Jeffrey. *Maps of the Profound*. Ithaca, N.Y.: Snow Lion Publications, 2003.

_____. *Meditation on Emptiness*. Somerville, Mass.: Wisdom Publications, 1983.

Huntington, C. W. Jr. *The Emptiness of Emptiness*. Delhi: Motilal Banarsidass, 1992.

Kangyur Rinpoche, Longchen Yeshe Dorje. *Treasury of Precious Qualities*. Translated by the Padmakara Translation Group. Boston: Shambhala Publications, 2001.

King, Richard. "Early Yogacara and Its Relation to the Madhyamaka School." *Philosophy East and West* 44, no. 4 (October 1994): 659–83.

Lopez, Donald S. Jr. *A Study of Svatantrika*. Ithaca, N.Y.: Snow Lion Publications, 1987.

Lusthaus, Dan. *Buddhist Phenomenology. A philosophical investigation of Yogacara Buddhism and the Ch'Eng Wei-Shih Lun*. London: Routledge Curzon, 2002.

Matilal, Bimal K. *Perception*. Oxford: Clarendon Press, 1986.

_____. *The Character of Logic in India*. Albany: State University of New York Press, 1998.

McClintock, Sara, and Georges Dreyfus, eds. *The Svatantrika-Prasangika Distinction: What Difference Does a Difference Make?* Somerville, Mass.: Wisdom Publications, 2003.

Messent, Dominique A. "'The Yogachara-Svatantrika-Madhyamaka School of Buddhism and Its Influence on rnying-ma Doctrine with Special Reference to Shantarakshita's Madhyamakalamkara." Thesis, University of Bristol, England, 2003.

Murti, T. R. V. *The Central Philosophy of Buddhism*. London: George Allen & Unwin, 1968.

Pettit, John W. *Mipham's Beacon of Certainty*. Somerville, Mass.: Wisdom Publications, 1999.

Radhakrishnan, S. *Indian Philosophy*. Delhi: Oxford University Press, 1923.

Ruegg, D. S., and L. Schmithausen, eds. *Earliest Buddhism: Madhyamaka (Panels of the Seventh World Sanskrit Conference, Volume 2)*. Leiden: E. J. Brill, 1997.

Sextus Empiricus. *Against the Schoolmasters*, vol. 2, book vii. London: Loeb Classical Library, 1949, 73–74.

Shantideva. *The Way of the Bodhisattva (Bodhicharyavatara)*. Translated by the Padmakara Translation Group. Boston: Shambhala Publications, 1997.

Smith, E. Gene. *Among Tibetan Texts: History and Literature of the Himalayan Plateau*. Somerville, Mass.: Wisdom Publications, 2001.

Smith, Robin. "Logic." In *The Cambridge Companion to Aristotle*. Edited by Jonathan Barnes. Cambridge, UK: Cambridge University Press, 1995.

Sopa, Geshe Lhundup. *Lectures on Tibetan Religious Culture*. Dharamsala: Library of Tibetan Works and Archives, 1983.

Sprung, Mervyn. *Lucid Exposition of the Middle Way*. Translation of essential chapters of Chandrakirti's *Prasannapada*. London: Routledge & Kegan Paul, 1979.

Vidyabhusana, S. C. *A History of the Mediaeval School of Indian Logic*. Delhi: Motilal Banarsidass, 1970, 1978.

Willis, Janice Dean. *On Knowing Reality: The Tattvartha Chapter of Asanga's "Bodhisattvabhumi."* Delhi: Motilal Banarsidass, 1982.

Index

Padmakara Translations
into English

Chandrakirti and Mipham Rinpoche. *Introduction to the Middle Way.* Shambhala Publications, 2002.

The Dalai Lama. *A Flash of Lightning in the Dark of Night.* Shambhala Publications, 1993.

Dilgo Khyentse Rinpoche. Editions Padmakara. 1990.

Dilgo Khyentse. *Enlightened Courage.* Editions Padmakara, 1992; Snow Lion Publications, 1994.

Dilgo Khyentse. *The Excellent Path of Enlightenment.* Editions Padmakara, 1987; Snow Lion Publications, 1996.

Dilgo Khyentse and Patrul Rinpoche. *The Heart Treasure of the Enlightened Ones.* Shambhala Publications, 1992.

Dilgo Khyentse. *The Wish-Fulfilling Jewel.* Shambhala Publications, 1988.

Dudjom Rinpoche. *Counsels from my Heart.* Shambhala Publications, 2001.

Gyalwa Changchub and Namkhai Nyingpo. *Lady of the Lotus-Born.* Shambhala Publications, 1999.

Khenchen Kunzang Pelden and Minyak Kunzang Sönam. *Wisdom: Two Buddhist Commentaries.* Editions Padmakara, 1993, 1999.

Khenpo Ngawang Pelzang. *A Guide to The Words of My Perfect Teacher.* Translated with Dipamkara. Shambhala Publications, 2004.

The Life of Shabkar: Autobiography of a Tibetan Yogi. SUNY Press, 1994.

Longchen Yeshe Dorje, Kangyur Rinpoche. *Treasury of Precious Qualities.* Shambhala Publications, 2001.

Patrul Rinpoche. *The Words of My Perfect Teacher.* International Sacred Literature Trust—HarperCollins, 1994; 2d edition, Sage AltaMira, 1998; Shambhala Publications, 1999.

Ricard, Matthieu. *Journey to Enlightenment.* Aperture, 1996.

Shabkar Tsokdruk Rangdrol. *Food of Bodhisattvas.* Shambhala Publications, 2004.

Shantideva. *The Way of the Bodhisattva (Bodhicharyavatara).* Shambhala Publications, 1997.